# Globalism, Nationalism, Tribalism

# Globalism, Nationalism, Tribalism

## Bringing Theory Back In

*Towards a Theory of Abstract Community, Volume 2*

Paul James

SAGE Publications
London • Thousand Oaks • New Delhi

© Paul James 2006

First published 2006

Apart from any fair dealing for the purposes of research or
private study, or criticism or review, as permitted under
the Copyright, Designs and Patents Act, 1988, this publication
may be reproduced, stored or transmitted in any form, or
by any means, only with the prior permission in writing of
the publishers, or in the case of reprographic reproduction,
in accordance with the terms of licenses issued by the
Copyright Licensing Agency. Inquiries concerning
reproduction outside those terms should be sent to
the publishers.

SAGE Publications Ltd
1 Oliver's Yard
55 City Road
London EC1Y 1SP

SAGE Publications Inc
2455 Teller Road
Thousand Oaks, California 91320

SAGE Publications India Pvt Ltd
B-42 Panchsheel Enclave
Post Box 4109
New Delhi 110 017

**British Library Cataloguing in Publication data**

A catalogue record for this book is available
from the British Library

ISBN-10 7619 5513 5 ✓   ISBN-13 978 0 7619 5513 9
ISBN-10 7619 5514 3    ISBN-13 978 0 7619 5514 6

**Library of Congress control number available**

Typeset by C&M Digitals (P) Ltd., Chennai, India
Printed on paper from sustainable resources
Printed and bound in Great Britain by Athenaeum Press, Gateshead

*For Stephanie*

| | |
|---|---|
| BRADFORD COLLEGE GROVE LIBRARY | w |
| DATE 11/06 | LOC. GB |
| ORDER No. 06001056 | |
| CLASS No. 305 JAM | |
| BARCODE No. 11752696 | |

# Contents

| | | |
|---|---|---|
| *Acknowledgements* | | xi |
| 1 | Introduction: Global Savage | 1 |
| **PART I** | **Returning to a Theory of Social Formation** | **11** |
| 2 | Social Relations in Tension | 13 |
| | *Globalism and localism* | 14 |
| | *Relating polity and community* | 17 |
| | *Defining globalism, nationalism and tribalism* | 20 |
| | *From Rwanda to Kosovo and Iraq* | 33 |
| | *Notes* | 38 |
| 3 | Contending Approaches in Outline | 43 |
| | *Problems of understanding* | 46 |
| | *Epochs of order: Ernest Gellner* | 48 |
| | *Tracks of social power: Michael Mann* | 50 |
| | *Patterns of practice: Pierre Bourdieu* | 54 |
| | *Structures of agency: Anthony Giddens* | 58 |
| | *Unstable patterns of meaning: Michel Foucault* | 61 |
| | *Notes* | 62 |
| 4 | Theory in the Shadow of Terror | 65 |
| | *Figures of abstraction, tableaux of life* | 69 |
| | *Mapping an alternative method* | 73 |
| | *Levels of analytical abstraction* | 80 |
| | *Levels of integration* | 83 |
| | *Conclusion* | 95 |
| | *Notes* | 96 |

## PART II  Rethinking Formations of Practice and Being — 101

**5  Constituting Customary Community** — 103
- *Reciprocity as a dominant mode of exchange* — 105
- *Analogy as a dominant mode of enquiry* — 120
- *Genealogical placement as a dominant mode of organization* — 126
- *Notes* — 129

**6  Communication and Exchange, Money and Writing** — 133
- *Forms of value: means of exchange* — 137
- *Forms of interchange: means of communication* — 149
- *Consequences for tribalism, nationalism and globalism* — 153
- *Notes* — 156

**7  Time and Space, Calendars and Maps** — 158
- *The abstraction of time* — 161
- *The abstraction of space* — 172
- *Notes* — 176

**8  Bodies and Symbols, Blood and Milk** — 179
- *From natural symbols to techno-machines* — 181
- *Tribal bodies, traditional bodies, modern bodies* — 189
- *To the body as an individualized postmodern project* — 197
- *Conclusion* — 201
- *Notes* — 202

## PART III  Rewriting the History of the Present — 205

**9  State Formation: From Kingdoms and Empires to Nation-States** — 207
- *Bringing the state back in – as social form* — 209
- *Empires, kingdoms and monarchical states* — 216
- *Nation-states* — 221
- *Notes* — 229

**10  Nation Formation: From the Medieval to the Postmodern** — 231
- *Across the traditional–modern divide* — 233
- *In the context of empire* — 243
- *The (dis)continuities of tribalism in a postcolonial nation-state* — 247

|    | *From traditionalism to postmodernism in a modern nation* | 249 |
|----|---|---|
|    | *Conclusion* | 258 |
|    | *Notes* | 259 |
| 11 | Global Formation: From the *Oecumene* to Planet Exploitation | 262 |
|    | *Arguing about globalization* | 266 |
|    | *Structures of globalization* | 269 |
|    | *Globalism, empire and the politics of structured subjection* | 276 |
|    | *Conclusion* | 286 |
|    | *Notes* | 288 |
| 12 | Conclusion: Principles for a Postnational World | 292 |
|    | *Liberation movements and the politics of modern nationalism* | 294 |
|    | *The misplaced faith in postnationalism and cosmopolitanism* | 297 |
|    | *An alternative approach to solidarity and community* | 304 |
|    | *Elaborating ethical complications* | 309 |

| *Glossary* | 318 |
|---|---|
| *Select Bibliography* | 327 |
| *Index* | 340 |

# Acknowledgements

Writing can be no more than a craft of reflexive passion – and perhaps ideally should be no less. The disposition of the work here is inspired by the classical social theorists: Emile Durkheim, Marcel Mauss, Max Weber, and most importantly Karl Marx, for whom all questions about the human condition are always ethical-political. It is not the specificity of their approaches that animates the present work, but the fact that they were insightful theorists writing with a generalizing and critical force at a time when the nature of disciplinary boundaries still encouraged productive boundary-crossing. The material in the book is also utterly dependent upon the wealth of brilliant research currently being conducted over the past few decades within the fields of sociology, political theory, anthropology and history. When it comes down to it, the present theoretical essay is no more than a speculative and critical synthesis of some of the research insights first elucidated by writers such as Benedict Anderson, the late Pierre Bourdieu, Maurice Godelier, Jack Goody, Tom Nairn, Richard Sennett and Geoff Sharp – to name but a handful of the extraordinary scholars working across the turn of the twenty-first century.

The book was first drafted in Edinburgh, although the gestation and framing began more than a decade earlier. Tom Nairn deserves special thanks. Apart from being an inimitable social critic whose writing brings politics to life, he sponsored my stay at the University of Edinburgh. Sheila Thomas at the Institute of Social Sciences was wonderfully supportive during that time, and I wish her all the best after the Institute closes under the weight of economic rationalism. I bear the ignomy of being its last Fellow. At Edinburgh, Russell Keat prompted new lines of understanding on old problems, and, together with other members of the 'Social Theory Group', critically interrogated some of my newly drafted writing in their fortnightly discussion group. I particularly want to thank Jukka Siikala for invitations to the University of Helsinki supported by the Departments of

Anthropology and Ethnography. I learned more about anthropological method from Jukka and his colleagues Karen Armstrong, Clifford Sather and Timo Kaartinen in those all-too-short periods than I could have in years of silent reading. Alan Chun of Academica Sinica in Taiwan facilitated the first writing of Chapter 12 and generously provided the setting for its first public presentation. Chen I-chung and Chen Kuang-hsing, at the 'Postnationalism and Violence' conference, critically discussed the paper at length, and James Goodman provided the venue for a second round of criticism at the University of Technology, Sydney. The details of recent and long-ago remembered conversations, suggestions, and extended notes of criticism from Ben Anderson, Sigrid Baringhorst, Jerry Bentley, Joe Camilleri, Jonathan Carter, Peter Christoff, Bill Cope, Phillip Darby, Robyn Eckersley, Jonathan Friedman, Bernard Giesen, Gerry Gill, Barry Gills, David Goldsworthy, James Goodman, Richard Higgot, John Hutchinson, Micheline Ishay, Graeme James, Bruce Kapferer, Roni Kaufman, Bruno Latour, Tim Luke, David Lyon, David McCrone, Peter Mandaville, Walter Mignolo, Sergiu Miscoui, Joel Robbins, Alan Roberts, Jan Aart Scholte, Gyorgy Scrinis, Geoff Sharp, Manfred Steger, Alison Tate, Stephanie Trigg and Oren Yiftachel, sent me off on many sessions of after-hours writing and rewriting.

I want to express deep gratitude to my friends and colleagues with whom I once worked at Monash University: Peter Lawler (now at Manchester), Andy Linklater (now at Aberystwyth), Robyn Eckersley (now at Melbourne University), Michael Janover, Andy Butfoy, Gloria Davies, Peter Lentini, and Chris Reus-Smit (now at the Australian National University), for providing the environment that sustained my enthusiasm for teaching and research. From reading scribbled critical pages of notes by Michael to struggling with the theoretical architecture of Chris's *The Moral Purpose of the State*, academic life was always rewarding and the chapters of the book were developed over a decade-long period of teaching a subject called 'Abstract Communities'. Graduate students such as Chris Scanlon and Leanne Reinke provided excellent research support on questions of money and communications. Tsaelan Lee Dow inspired my thinking across a broad range of areas from notions of the body politic to the nature of the face-to-face. She and Freya Carkeek, Bianca Lowe, Andrew Phillips, Matthew Ryan, Michele Willson, and many others expressed everything from deep criticism to gentle bemusement in ways that influenced the slow gestation of the material. Chapter 8, for example, began during that time as an essay first written with Freya and was originally published in *Arena*. I have used that essay as a palimpsest for writing the present chapter. Although the current version has taken on quite a new life, the conjointly researched manuscript lies buried beneath the chapter's rewritten surface. I thank David Holmes for suggestions for rewriting that essay.

At RMIT University where I now feel very much at home, I thank in particular Mary Kalantzis and Michael Singh for their foresight in initiating the 'globalization and cultural diversity' project, and my extraordinary colleagues in the Globalism Institute for making it happen: Kate Cregan, Damian Grenfell, Hariz Halilovich, Martin Mulligan, Yaso Nadarajah, Tom Nairn, Peter Phipps, Leanne Reinke, Chris Scanlon, Manfred Steger and Chris Ziguras. I could not ask for a more stimulating group of people, or for a more productive environment. Kate and Damian, in particular, have been insightful interlocutors, always struggling to clarify my flights of theoretical abstraction. Hariz compiled the bibliography. Anne Trembath painstakingly constructed the index. *Globalism, Nationalism, Tribalism* is one small expression of two interconnected collaborative projects on 'Sources of Insecurity' and 'Community Sustainability' that we are developing in the Globalism Institute with scholars around the world including Tonathan Friedman, Roni Kaufman, Vasilia Kourtis-Kazoullis, Ashis Nandy, Paul van Seeters, Ram Rattan Sharma, Imre Szeman, John Tulloch, and Oren Yiftachel.

The Australian Research Council provided extensive research-funding support, as did RMIT itself, with Neil Furlong and the Research and Innovation group showing the continuing faith in the Globalism Institute that saw it grow exponentially. I would like to thank the librarians at RMIT, Monash University, the University of Edinburgh, and the London School of Economics, as well as Sarah Millard at the Bank of England archives and the staff in the British Museum's money and time collections.

Sage Publications is another institution to which I owe a great deal. Robert Rojek, David Mainwaring and Lucy Robinson at Sage have become much more than correspondents over the pragmatics of publications. In this instance, I thank Chris Rojek and Mila Steele for their support and patience, despite a delay of a couple of years after the original contracted date for delivery of the manuscript.

Perhaps most importantly, the political context for *Globalism, Nationalism Tribalism* is the Melbourne-based journal *Arena*. I particularly thank Alison Caddick, Simon Cooper, John Hinkson, Guy Rundle, Matthew Ryan, Chris Scanlon, Geoff Sharp, and Nonie Sharp. I have been writing this book in my head ever since I first read an internationally little-known but seminal article of Geoff's called 'Constitutive Abstraction and Social Practice' published in *Arena* in 1983. As late as I am in responding to that article, *Globalism, Nationalism, Tribalism* is my way of coming to terms with his ground-breaking writings. In a way this book is a long methodological footnote to his work. He will disagree with parts of the present essay, particularly with its systematizing quality, but he will understand that it is written in a common political project.

## ACKNOWLEDGEMENTS

After many years of talking about, and teaching across, its themes, I drafted the text in an intense period of writing, followed by a series of late-night rewritings spaced over a number of years. From contradictory states of passionate hibernation and haphazard crafting, I no longer have any idea if the argument makes sense to the general reader. If it does not, I have only my dear friends to blame for humouring me too much in their reading, and Joel Trigg for sustaining my optimism. Robyn Eckersley and Peter Christoff gave their imprimatur to a couple of chapters at a vital moment, despite suggestions that inevitably led to further rewriting. For what it is worth, the argument makes complete sense to me. It is only in moments of face-to-face candour that I will admit to its many weaknesses. Any remaining gaps I still blame on that anonymous person who once on a hot summer's night in Melbourne left me frozen in ragged pain. It was the night I left my computer unattended in the study at the front of the house, with much of the first draft on its hard drive. I went to watch television. The front door was left open to allow a gentle breeze to enter. When I returned, the computer was gone: in the words of the state, I was the victim of an 'Agg. Burg. Incident'. To make matters worse, the Microsoft backup system failed, and despite the best efforts of friendly experts, including our brilliant neighbour, Alan Roberts, no one could reinstall the compressed files without the source codes that Microsoft held close to its commercial-in-confidence heart. In a chance meeting of embodied localism and commercial globalism, the failed electronic manuscript threw me back to rewriting much of the project.

Finally, I thank Stephanie Trigg for her fabulousness. I dedicate the book to her in love, enduring appreciation, and with the hope that the world in which we live will begin to step back from its current madness.

# ONE Introduction: Global Savage

A suit-wearing European man sits in the dark talking with three tribal men around a campfire. The night sky behind them is deep purple, and into the colour of the sky is written the words, 'Talk anyone's language: Windows 2000'. Advertising images such as this provide windows onto contemporary worlds. They provide us with heavily researched and creatively engineered reflections of our times. They are reflections that perversely re-present the surface reality of contemporary social relations, and which nevertheless take us into the intensities of its promises, fears and dreams. Ironically, this advertising image reflects the tensions and contradictions that *Globalism, Nationalism, Tribalism* is trying to understand. What is happening to the world under present conditions of intensifying contradiction, and how did we get here? What does it mean, for example, when a Vodafone advertisement depicts a satellite picture of the globe with clouds swirling over Africa, shrouding a Europe that is flattened by the parallax of perspective? The inscription on that advertisement reads, 'Vodafone spoken here'. Like the Microsoft advertisement, Vodafone projects the globalism as transcending difference. However, at the same time, its very accentuation of a 'possible world' of open communication makes us aware that place and identity still intensely matter. It gives the impression that globalization is wonderfully inclusive. However, at the same time, we are implicitly reminded that the present world can be characterized as 'global savage' in a second sense – that is, globalization as a savagely distancing and mediating; globalization that cares little for those who cannot keep up, and fears those who are its 'others'.

Microsoft's Noble Savages are postmodern motifs for everything primitive *and* modern: their spears speak of many remembered images. Like other postcolonial lads, as I grew up I watched the 1964 film *Zulu* and read Rider Haggard and Doris Lessing. Now, in the contemporary representations of popular culture it seems that 'the tribes' are coming again – and either they are becoming us, or, alternatively, for example in the case of the ethnic nationalists of Eastern Europe, the supposedly more primordial of us have always been them. Look closer into the Microsoft advertisement and you can see that the warriors are wearing tartan, just like the clans in Mel Gibson's *Braveheart* (1995). It is ye olde clothe of the medieval 'Scot', William Wallace, as he patriotically ran into battle against Edward I of Hollywood's England. In shops in Scotland, years after *Braveheart* swept through the land, you can still find depictions of the American-born Australian-claimed actor, Mel Gibson, his nose and cheeks smeared blue with Celtic woad. The Scottish artists who lovingly paint Gibson's face did not care that the director of a film about this nation's 'birth' was an Australian-in-Hollywood rather than a son of the Highland soil. Nor did the stone mason who set out to capture the spirit of William Wallace through Mel Gibson's body. The statue is located at the entrance to the National Wallace Monument in Stirling, a spear's throw from Stirling Bridge where the 1297 battle against the 'English' took place. Gibson as an outsider, like the Irish actor Liam Neeson in *Rob Roy* (1994), is non-English enough to depict a Scot.

Elaborating upon this illustration of the connections between tribalism, neo-traditionalism, and globalism, Gibson's *Braveheart* provides significant inspiration for the League of the South, a group that began in 1994. On 4 March 2000 they signed their Declaration of Southern Independence. 'We, as citizens of the sovereign states of the South, proclaim before Almighty God and before all the nations of the earth, that we are a separate and distinct people, with an honourable heritage and culture worthy of protection and preservation.' Their Southland is the land of the losers in the American Civil War, currently part of the United States of America. At their annual honouring of Jefferson Davis, last president of the Confederate States of America, a kilted piper plays *Scotland the Brave*. The League has its own confederate tartan approved by the Scottish tartan authority, as incidentally do the expatriate Scots in Australia, with both tartans commercially available over the internet. The globalizing world is thus an amazing and contradictory place of local allusions and national recursions. It is not simply an open series of invented traditions, advertising slogans and postmodern film narratives, but nor is it a place of simple primordial depth or straightforward continuities from the past.

As I write the first draft of this chapter, sitting in an office built above the medieval city wall of old Edinburgh, the writing is both abstractly connected to everywhere *and* thoroughly bound in time and place. A 'moment' ago, I used Netscape, one of Microsoft's rivals, to find out the year when *Zulu* was made. I found myself in a place that I had never been, reading a person I will probably never meet. On the University of Wales, Swansea Student Union website, I was reading Louise Burridge's response to a posting that said '*Zulu* is quite possibly one of the best films of all time'. Two years after writing that last sentence – note how temporally confusing the abstraction of print can be – I find myself in Leeds (June 2002), reading a brochure for an exhibition called 'The Mighty Zulu Nation' at the Royal Armouries Museum. The vice-president of the Anglo-Historical Zulu Society, pictured on the African savannah in safari garb, is advertised as giving a lecture, accompanied by a screening of *Zulu* and by 'artefacts from his own collection for visitors to handle'. Six months later again, at a granite monument in Pretoria, two men put their lips to ram's horns to mark the most sacred moment of the year for the Afrikaners. At precisely noon, a ray of sun shines through a hole in the roof of an empty tomb symbolizing the death of the 470 pioneers who 164 years earlier, with guns and God on their side, defeated 10,000 Zulu warriors in the Battle of Blood River. Later still, on a plane returning from Chicago (September 2004), I read that airlines communicate globally in a single world-standard idiom called 'Zulu'.

Abstracted language-protocols? Artefacts to handle? An empty tomb symbolizing glorious embodied death in the name of the nation? The globalization of film culture? This world, like all the others before it, is a place of a myriad messy interconnections, immediate and abstracted, embodied and disembodied. *Globalism, Nationalism, Tribalism* attempts to make some sense of these connections, all the while keeping in mind their messy unevenness and the way that they are caught up in vast permutations of power. It ranges from questions of apparently irrelevant detail such as 'Who is Gillian Stone, the narrator in the Nescafé advertisements?' and 'What is the relationship between things of stone, wood and flesh in Maubisse, East Timor?' to those of more obvious importance and generality. 'Is it actually resurgent tribalism that is the basis of accentuated global violence today?', 'What is the significance of the war on terror?' and 'How can we understand the formations of nationalism in an era of globalism?' The title of the book and of this introduction attempt to express the ambiguities of the present and its normative confusions. On the one hand, globalization has, with the Good War on Terror, become increasingly savage about how 'others' are treated. The world is seething in a modern abstract barbarianism that allows the four horsemen of the apocalypse to continue to ride this planet, this time in metal machines – sometimes under the banners of humanitarian intervention, military, economic and political. On the other hand, relations of tribalism and traditionalism that were once derided for their backward primordial 'savagery' have not disappeared as proclaimed by the many soothsayers – from the Social Darwinists to the End-of-History ideologues. The chapter title 'Global Savage' is thus intended to be at once critical and ironical, discouraged and empathetic to the way that all social relations on this planet are increasingly forced to come to terms with globalization.

Rather than treating 'globalism', 'nationalism' and 'tribalism' as discrete formations – with globalization replacing all that has gone before – the present study takes them as recurrent formations with rough-knotted intertwined histories. It helps to explain how they can be concurrent realities in the present. With the tropes of 'tribalism' now increasingly revisited by social theorists with gay abandon,[1] and globalism studies becoming all the rage, nationalism is the one formation of the three that is usually projected as having a dubious future. This is ironic given that for nearly a century the nation-state had been taken for granted as the dominant setting for the intersection of community (as nation) and polity (as state). A revolution in theories of the nation began in the 1980s as the processes of what might be called 'disembodied globalization' were taking substantial hold and the intersection of nation and state had begun to come apart. However, almost as soon as the theories gained a readership, the historical future of the nation-state was called into question. A series of debates began and still continues today. They continue to ask whether or not the nation-state is in crisis, and whether old-style community is still possible.

What tends to be missing from these debates is an appreciation of questions of comparative social form, the question at the heart of this study. In one way this is not surprising – investigating such questions tends to give way to an understandable emphasis upon immediate issues and social exigencies, the very issues brought to the fore by the galloping transformations in social form. In another way, however, it is alarming how the debates fail to take cognisance of the substantial and highly-relevant research that has been going on in a number of quite disparate disciplines. Social theorists are exploring the impact of different modes of communication or technology upon social relations.[2] Critical geographers are doing path-breaking work on the nature and forms of spatial extension lived by different types of communities.[3] Anthropologists are writing challenging works on the changing forms of identity in national and postnational settings.[4] This study is intended to draw synthetically upon these disciplines and others – particularly history and sociology, political theory and international relations – to provide an alternative framework for understanding the current tensions between polity and community, nationalism and globalism. Underlying the entire approach is the presumption that an adequate theory of tribalism, nation formation or globalization requires a generalizing theory of changing social formations. In other words, a phenomenon such as globalization or nationalism cannot be understood in terms of itself.

If the central focus is on changing forms of social relations, it is always with the view to relating the practices of the past to present trajectories. This is the sense in which the research can be described as a history of the present. It involves comparing tribal reciprocity, past and present – oral cultures involved in gift exchange and production by the hand – to the formations of empire, kingdom and sodality characterized by the development of script/print, paper money and new techniques of production. This is in turn related to the developments in communication, exchange and production that lie behind the emergence of the modern nation-state. It involves comparing face-to-face community with the structures and subjectivities of globalism. We trace the reconstitution of the nation-state as it has undergone unprecedented change – change based in part upon the development of mass communications, fiduciary exchange systems and computer-based production. Throughout, the aim is to draw conclusions about the contemporary underpinnings of polity and community in a globalized world.

The volume would at first glance appear to have the same massive historical scope as Ernest Gellner's *Plough, Sword and Book*.[5] However, except for its generalizing methodological pretensions, *Globalism, Nationalism, Tribalism* is intended to be much more modest. Rather than sweeping across history, it uses anthropology, comparative historical sociology and political studies in order to understand the structures of the present. Gellner's book is a history of ideas, rarely talking about ploughs, swords and books. *Globalism, Nationalism, Tribalism*, by contrast, is intended as a genealogy of the underpinning processes of *contemporary* tribal, national and global practices and institutions. The equivalent motifs to Gellner's 'plough, sword and book' are stone and wood, money and clock, book and computer. This is not to imply that we simply move historically from 'things of stone and wood',[6] to things of book and screen. In contemporary tribal life we find the assimilation of these themes into changing but continuous cosmologies. For example, Elizabeth Traube describes the integrative culture of the Mambai of East Timor as incorporating the layers of the invasion of that country – the Portuguese and the Catholic Church – into the passing on of authority structures. The stone and the book come together in their difference:

> Then Father Heaven, the great divider distributes a patrimony between his sons. To the eldest, Ki Sa, he gives the sacred rock and tree, tokens of the original ban and signs of original authority over a

silent cosmos. Upon the youngest, Loer Sa, he bestows the book and the pen, which the Mambai regard as emblems of European identity.[7]

As important as the continuities and assimilations within and across communities are, the differences between communities still have to be theorized. In addressing this issue, the discussion will move across different dominant *levels* of the analysis.[8] At one level – that is, at the level of analysing conjunctural relations – the focus will be on the following *modes of practice*: first, the changing forms of communication and information storage from print to electronic communication; second, the changing forms of exchange from gift exchange and barter to abstract money; third, the changing forms of production from manual production to robotics; fourth, the changing forms of enquiry, particularly the rise of techno-science; and fifth, the changing forms of organization, with the increasing predominance in the contemporary period of bureaucratic rationality. At a more abstract level of analysing categories of social ontology the focus will be on the changing way in which we live the categories of time, space, the body and ways of knowing.[9] Moving across these levels of analysis, the task will be to examine how the changing modes of practice – disembodied communication, abstracted exchange, post-industrial production, techno-science and technical rationality – bear upon the subjectivities and practices of political community in the age of disembodied globalism. The writing will explore the ways in which more abstract forms overlay (rather than replace) earlier modes of practice. In doing so, the book will attempt to draw political conclusions about alternative possibilities for polity and community as they play themselves out in the realms of tribe, nation and globe.

The present study thus enters into debates in social and political theory. One of the dominant avant-garde approaches in social theory continues to be post-structuralism, while the dominant mainstream emphasis in the academic disciplines is on empirically-grounded studies or rational-choice style approaches. Across these diverse, and I think unsatisfactory, ways of approaching social explanation, there is a common tendency to criticize the possibility of generalized analyses and to dismiss approaches which attempt to understand the 'social whole'. In some circles it is an anathema to talk of structures of social practice or to make broad characterizations about a social formation. There are good reasons for the post-structuralist critique of generalizing approaches, but the methodological problems they point to are not insurmountable. On the contrary, there is a pressing urgency to bring together and rethink the respective strengths of old and new ways of theorizing. Moreover, unless we develop a more synthesizing overview of the trajectories of the present and its historical antecedents, we will be left with only vague renditions of contemporary life as a postmodern condition dissolving into difference, or as a fragmented world of self-interested rational choice. As a contribution to this political-methodological problem, the project is intended as an analytical interpretative history of some of the central institutions of the present, taking the intersection of polity and community as one of its key framing themes. It is an attempt to find a pathway between and beyond the modern confidence in grand theory and the postmodern rejection of other than piece-meal explanations for this and that discursive practice. It does so, not by setting up a grand theory, but by setting up a sensitizing and generalizing 'grand method' to explore the structures and subjectivities of social formations that traverse history as we know it.

Carrying through the concurrent themes of globalism, nationalism and tribalism, the book is divided into three parts. The first part is concerned with critically introducing existing theories of social formation, and setting up an alternative approach. Choosing which theorists to discuss was guided by three antithetical desires: the first was to keep the discussion as introductory as possible. The second desire was to give an adequate sense of both the complexity of individual theorists and the incredible range of theoretical traditions and approaches. The third was to choose generalist writers who would be most acutely useful for developing an alternative approach to understanding the abstractions and contradictions of social formation in the present. With these principles in mind, the following writers were selected: Ernest Gellner, Michael Mann, Pierre Bourdieu, Anthony Giddens, and Michel Foucault. Even as I am critical of their approaches, they provide us with a wealth of provocative writing. Chapter 3 elaborates their methods of analysis, and later chapters expand upon the details of their research and theoretical direction in the context of trying to develop an alternative position that can carry forward their strengths. These theorists, as if in a novel, thus become central characters, along with lots of other figures of occasional reference, throughout the rest of the book.

The second part, 'Rethinking Formations of Practice and Being', begins with the question of how customary or tribal community is constituted through relations of reciprocity, kinship and analogy as the dominant modes of exchange, organization and enquiry (Chapter 5). The chapter serves as a comparative base for later chapters on the changing dominant formations of traditional, modern and postmodern society. Chapter 6 continues the themes of communication and exchange, tracing the development of writing and money as they fundamentally change from conditions of social reciprocity. It is an incomplete story. The study does not really cover the full diverse implications of the overall method. It concentrates on the modes of communication and exchange, but these are intended as indicative rather than *the* primary modes of practice. Similarly, when we come to Chapters 7 and 8 on the nature of time, space and bodies, the analysis is indicative rather than comprehensive. The basic argument through these chapters is that when dominant patterns of social change are drawn out from the incredible complexity of social life, we can trace an increasing abstraction of temporality, spatiality and embodiment across human history, layers of abstraction that overlie and reframe prior ways of being.

This analysis is intended to provide a schematic framework for understanding the changing forms of polity from traditional to nation-states, and the stretching forms of community from the local to the global. State as polity and nation as community are thus the focus of Chapters 9 and 10 respectively. These two chapters begin Part III of the book, 'Rewriting the History of the Present', with a third, Chapter 11, focussing upon questions of globalization. The book ends with Chapter 12 turning to what should be integral to any social theory – an account of its ethical assumptions and implications.

If the overall theoretical argument of the work is that the dominant constitutive level of contemporary society is becoming increasingly abstract,[10] the overall political-ethical argument is that we have to forge a counter-practice that revivifies the social importance of more embodied and continuing relations of mutuality and co-operation. We have to reflexively reconfigure social life in such a way as to qualify the runaway excesses of the abstract globalizing society, without treating the processes of social abstraction as bad in themselves. This position will be caricatured as anti-globalist and backward-looking by a dominant neo-liberal position. It is not. What it intends, first, is a counter-position to the dominant and utterly-blinkered faith in modern globalizing progress. This belief is characterized by displacement-projections about the putative sources of evil in the world today. In the words of one apparently-congenial and very powerful global administrator: 'Extreme nationalism, protectionism and tribalism are the curses of our species and inevitably lead to the restriction of liberties, blocking the advance of human rights and lifting of living standards and conditions.'[11] By contrast, I argue that nationalism and tribalism are ways of life – again, neither intrinsically good nor bad – but important to what it has meant to be historically human. What this book intends, moreover, is the development of a counter-position that allows us to make decisions about political-ethical directions on the basis of an understanding about the complexities of different forms of community and polity, rather than on the basis of ideologically-driven prejudice about the essential virtues of savage globalization.

## Notes

1 Albeit, loosely: they are never delineated in what I suggest needs to be distinguished as traditional, modern and postmodern forms. On what will later be defined as postmodern tribalism see, for example, Michel Maffesoli, *The Time of the Tribes: The Decline of Individualism in Mass Society*, London, Sage, 1996. For reasons that I cannot understand, he posits the unsustainable thesis that the new tribalism signals the end of individualism. See Michael Walzer ('The New Tribalism: Notes on a Difficult Problem', in Ronald Beiner (ed.), *Theorising Nationalism*, State University of New York Press, Albany, 1999) for an example of tribalism used as a loose rhetorical device. Ironically, this expanded currency of the term is occurring at the very time anthropologists are becoming increasingly wary of it as applied to traditional reciprocal communities.

2 Two prominent examples, both of which I think are provocative but methodologically flawed, are Mark Poster, *The Mode of Information*, Polity, Cambridge, 1990; and Gianni Vattimo, *The Transparent Society*, Polity, Cambridge, 1992.

3 The literature here is burgeoning. Early seminal texts include the following: Derek Gregory and John Urry (eds), *Social Relations and Spatial Structures*, London, Macmillan, 1985; and Henri Lefebvre, *The Production of Space*, Blackwell, Oxford, 1991.

4 See, for example, Tone Bringa, *Being Muslim the Bosnian Way: Identity and Community in a Central Bosnian Village*, Princeton University Press, Princeton, NJ, 1995, and Birgit Meyer and Peter Geschiere (eds), *Globalization and Identity: Dialectics of Flow and Closure*, Blackwell Publishers, Oxford, 1999.

5 Ernest Gellner, *Plough, Sword and Book: The Structure of Human History*, London, Collins Harvill, 1988.

6 The name of an Australian rock-music band in the 1990s, part of the revival of interest in tribalism.

7 Elizabeth G. Traube, *Cosmology and Social Life: Ritual Exchange among the Mambai of East Timor*, University of Chicago Press, Chicago, 1986, p. 55.

8 See Chapter 4 for a full discussion of 'levels' of theoretical abstraction. For examples of other recent books which have been part of developing the same methodology and drawing upon the 'constitutive abstraction' or 'levels' method associated with *Arena Journal*, see Simon Cooper, *Technoculture and Critical Theory: In the Service of the Machine*, Routledge, London, 2002; and Christopher Ziguras, *Self-Care: Embodiment, Personal Autonomy and the Shaping of Health Consciousness*, Routledge, London, 2004.

9 Talking at this level of abstraction I should really say 'categories of temporality, spatiality, embodiment and epistemology', but the technical distinction is not important for the moment.

10 The lineages of this social abstraction involve variously a number of processes that have been much discussed in the literature on social change: (1) rationalization; (2) commodification; (3) codification; (4) mediation; (5) objectification; and (6) extension. For example, Marx takes commodification as the driving social force of modern capitalism, while Weber emphasizes the processes of rationalization including bureaucratization of management and the secularization of religious life. The argument that I draw upon comes from writers associated with the *Arena Journal* such as Geoff Sharp who conceives of abstraction as a socially-constitutive and material process.

11 Mike Moore, *A World Without Walls: Freedom, Development, Free Trade and Global Governance*, Cambridge University Press, Cambridge, 2003, p. 9. Mike Moore is Director General of the World Trade Organization.

# Part I

## Returning to a Theory of Social Formation

# TWO Social Relations in Tension

We live in confusing times. One of the dominant trends in the present period is the deepening of a set of social contradictions that have only been generalized for a few decades. On the one hand, globalization, a process with long historical roots, has been developing at an unprecedented pace through the end of the twentieth century and into the new millennium. A rough, uneven blanketing of capital and commercialized culture crosses and connects the world in unprecedented ways. On the other hand, there is an intense fragmenting and reconfiguring of social relations at the level of community and locality. Systemic processes of rationalizing homogenization integrate the globe at one level, while ideologies and practices of difference and radical autonomy frame the popular imaginary at another.[1] These are material and lived contradictions rather than simply inexplicable paradoxes.

It is not that we fail to recognize the surface expressions of these contradictions. In their immediate expression we see them quite dramatically. At the turn of the century it has become commonplace for soothsayers to say that the key trends in the coming period will be globalism and tribalism. While the naming of those interlocking but contrary formations is helpful in its starkness, the projections of their prominence are often confusingly presented as a paradox of conflicting epochs. Social life is presented as if we are simultaneously going forward into the technologically-driven world of open globalism, e-commerce and Planet Hollywood, and back into the ambivalent, anachronistic gloom of neo-national tribalisms. Places such as Rwanda, Bosnia, Kosovo and Chechnya supposedly stand for the past. They are located in mystical times when social life was ruled by warlords, blood ties and village feuds. They are found in backward settings from where primordial and atavistic sentiments come to seep through the curtain of rational modernity. Through this confusion of times, 'contemporary' social relations are supposedly held together by well-networked individuals winging their way into the future, carrying with them – as light rather than cumbersome baggage – the residual comfort of earlier forms of personal and community connections. It is a confusion of times expressed in recent futuristic films and novels. In the West, we are either portrayed in bleak romanticism as going back to the future in films such as *Pleasantville* and *The Truman Show*,[2] or more blackly shown in cybernetic novels such as *Snow Crash* and *Virtual Light*[3] as going forward to a world of mega-corporations acting as neo-imperial states, with cyborg outsiders living on the edge in neo-medieval burbclaves. Concepts like the 'global village' appear to transcend the tension of past and future but only by leaving the traditional sense of village behind. In the same way that Disney World's Tomorrow Land has been recast as an historical artefact, the concept of 'global village' is now the romantic version of the newer cyberspace term, 'virtual village'.

## Globalism and localism

The related tension between globalism and localism is everywhere. In the north London borough of Islington, the global corporation Microsoft randomly chooses a street to create what company executives and Blair government ministers proclaim to be the first computer community in Britain. Not to be outdone, IBM announces a trial project, the first Wireless Virtual Village, based on their new 'WebSphere Everyplace' software and covering a one-kilometre radius and the homes of 5,000 Helsinki residents. In Malaysia, the universalistic Muslim organization Mendaki expresses concerns about the dying of Malay community spirit, *gotong-royong*. In Singapore, Lee Kuan Yew gives a speech to the Tanjong Pagar Development Council about vision Singapore 21, a state-run program aimed at drawing the counter-identities of what he calls the 'cosmopolitans' and 'heartlanders' into a new cohesive knowledge-based economy. In Mauritius, a cyber-city of call-centres and back-office operations is being built with a completion date of 2005, now passed. It is projected as somehow overcoming the tendency towards locals working in jobs of low skill and long hours.

Across the world, signs of this tension between the local and the global have seeped into the popular imagination. As an indication of the new sensitivity, advertising campaigns in the mid-1990s began to explain how transnational corporations transcend the divide between different senses of locale in the global village. In Australia and New Zealand, the worldwide franchiser of hamburger outlets, McDonald's, began an advertising campaign explaining how each of its franchisees will organize local community notice-boards.[4] In Cambodia, the 'Japanese' car manufacturer Toyota ran a campaign under the banner headline 'This is Our Town'. To the backdrop of a photograph of planet earth spinning in space, the patronizing copy speaks with postcolonial sophistication of the mutuality of the global project, all the while slipping between different meanings of the 'local' and different meanings of the 'we':

> It's the global village. We live here. You do, too. We're neighbours. And since we're neighbours, we should be friends. It seems that we are all of us - everywhere - slowly coming to this realization. But how do we do it? In a practical sense what steps do we take? We can't speak for others, but for ourselves we can say this: we will do our part to bring the world together by building up the global auto industry ... For the first half of the century we thought of ourselves as a Japanese company ... Now we think of ourselves as a world company. Our responsibility is to everyone.[5]

Despite this self-conscious commercial-political emphasis on the intersecting trends of globalism and community, and despite its embeddedness in everyday life, we still have a poor understanding of the structures, systems and institutions that in the age of disembodied globalism both integrate polity and community and simultaneously threaten to break them apart. Social theorists over the past decade have made globalization a constant point of reference. However, in turning to ugly concepts such as 'glocalization', defined as the simultaneous globalizing and localizing of social relations, they have named the processes that need to be worked through rather than given us the tools with which to do so. Roland Robertson notes that the concept of 'glocalization' comes from the Japanese word *dochakuka*, originally *dochaku*, which means 'living on one's own land'.[6] However, dragged into the context of global micro-marketing campaigns such as 'This is Our Town', the term came to be instrumentalized as the act of adapting locally to meet global circumstances. This in itself should have given pause for thought, but nevertheless the term quickly became part of the social theory lexicon as an easy shorthand concept for an extraordinarily complicated phenomenon. It is not so different from the way in which the Finnish concept *kännykkä*, 'extension of the hand', used as a Nokia trademark for their mobile telephone, subsequently passed into the generic parlance of Finnish teenagers as the word for phone.[7] More than that, the embedded and grounded meaning of the terms themselves – living on one's own land, extension of the hand – carry us further into the contradictions of our time. The expressions of the abstraction of our relationship to others are often carried in the relatively concrete language of the body and of grounded place.

*Globalism, Nationalism, Tribalism* attempts to understand these contradictory processes of globalism-localism, universalism-particularism, homogenization-fragmentation, and abstraction-embeddedness, though neither simply by posing them as dualistic opposites, nor by coming at them directly. The globalism-localism debate has become a bit like the burning bush during Moses' exodus from the desert: best not looked upon too directly for a source of enlightenment. The present discussion approaches the problem through a discussion of the changing nature of modes of practice – in particular, production, exchange, communication, organization and enquiry – placing these practices in historical context while relating them to lived categories of time, space, embodiment and knowing. The book is directed towards understanding the dominant forms of polity and community in the present, but this entails making some broad comparisons to other forms of exchange, communication, production, organization and enquiry, and to ontologically different ways of living in time, place and corporeality. This is to take up the relatively unfashionable subject of what Scott Lash, in his search for a second modernity, calls 'forms of social life':

> This ground – which alternatively takes the form of community, history, tradition, the symbolic, place, the material, language, life-world, the gift, *Sittlichkeit*, the political, the religious, forms of life, memory, nature, the monument, the path, fecundity, the tale, habitus, the body ... has been too much forgotten by cultural theory and reflexive sociology.[8]

The trouble with this evocative list is that it lists an extraordinary range of incommensurably-named phenomena. They are things that, variably defined, are part of all social formations, not just Lash's underside to 'rational modernity'. Still, such lists are instructive. Theorizing the ground of contemporary life has to be able to keep this messiness to the fore while, at the same time and seemingly in contradiction with acknowledging that messiness, finding ways of providing an account that allows us to explore its structural patterns. Lash's list has some of the same qualities as the taxonomy from Jorge Borges's apocryphal Chinese calendar, the one that Michel Foucault famously quotes as his inspiration for *The Order of Things*. This list, linked as an Arabic alphabetical series, and devoted to different kinds of animals, begins with (a) belonging to the Emperor, and serially goes through those animals that are embalmed, tame, sucking pigs, sirens, fabulous, stray dogs, included in the present classification, and frenzied. It finishes with (n), those that from a long way off look like flies.[9] Foucault, writing in the period of his intellectual history before he was taken over by the enthral of post-structuralism, responds by saying that there may be a 'mute ground upon which it is possible for entities to be juxtaposed',[10] a ground made invisible by

Borges's intentionally comic device of alphabetical ordering. This 'ground' for Foucault is not the essentialized ground of being, but an unconscious level of knowledge broken up into epistemological fields or what he calls 'epistemes' that can be discerned by archaeological excavation (discussed in Chapter 3). Although sympathetic to the notion of 'an archaeology of knowledge', *Globalism, Nationalism, Tribalism* is an attempt to find a methodological pathway between and against the ideas that social life can be understood either in terms of an essentialized ground or a series of discursive formations. There is a *missing middle* of structural-subjective patterning that this study wishes to address, and to do so will entail moving between the headiness of abstract theory and the glorious grubbiness of life's particulars to set up a method of structures of connection.

## Relating polity and community

The relationship between polity and community is historically one of the most discussed themes in contemporary social theory – at least as an implicit theme – and yet one of the most under-theorized areas of social relations. One of the reasons in the past for this lack of direct attention was a curious theoretical stumbling point that afflicted writers well into the twentieth century. Let me take one illustration. In 1915, in the cataloguing spirit of high modernism, the now-unknown Basil Hammond published a magisterial world history that took the political forms of community as its direct subject. For all this attention, he was unable to overcome one of the common issues of his time: the difficulty of treating an abstract community and associated bodies politic as ongoing forms of social relations. In other words, how does a thing called a 'community', abstracted from the living bodies of its constituent members, live on even though members of that community will die? The question is a real one, and not to be dismissed too quickly from our comfortable contemporary vantage point. Hammond wrote:

> A community or a body politic retains its personal identity complete only from the death of one of its members to the death of the next; and as soon as all its members are dead its existence as a body consisting of certain definite persons is entirely ended. But through the space of thirty years, for which a generation remains in its prime and is not superseded by its sons, the persons gathered in a group for common purposes remain for the most part the same. Thus the lifetime of a community or body politic is about thirty years.[11]

The telling phrase here is 'personal identity'. By contrast, even at a time when the state was still being theorized in embodied terms as having a personality,[12] Hammond, like others, found it somewhat easier to deal with the abstraction of the state than the abstraction across time and embodiment of polity-communities. He did this through invoking the legal doctrine initiated, he said, in the seventeenth-century age of treaty-making states. The doctrine suggested that the word 'state' can be 'adopted as a technical name for any succession of bodies politic which transmit rights and obligations from generation to generation'. For states, Hammond confidently concluded, 'bear no relation to concrete things'.[13] Thus, his approach becomes thoroughly confused. The state is wrongly conceived as immaterial because it is hard to form in the mind as a 'complete image' and the body politic is wrongly conceived as its opposite and reduced to a perceptible body of bodies:

> A body politic, on the other hand, may be a perfectly concrete thing. All the members of a German tribe, or of a Greek city, or of the modern republics of Andorra or San Martino could, or can, be seen at a glance; the German tribesmen could all be heard at once if they murmured disapproval, or the citizens of Athens if they shouted or groaned ... And beyond that every body politic ... is like a concrete thing in its capacity for acting as if it were a single person.[14]

This persistent theoretical stumbling point, only misleadingly 'resolved' in Ferdinand Tönnies' distinction between *Gemeinschaft* (community) and *Gesellschaft* (society), was one reason for the lack of direct attention to the relationship between community and polity. A second reason became the very obviousness of the modern interrelation between community and polity. The nation-state embodied the intersection of state as polity and nation as community, and by the middle of the twentieth century even in the discipline of international relations the nation-state came to be taken for granted as the unified and framing category of analysis. Mirroring the limits of Max Weber's methodological individualism, this was the development of 'methodological nationalism'. The nation was the society and the society was the nation. It was not until the 1980s – ironically as the predominance of the nation-state began to be questioned and processes of globalization became more obvious – that theories of the nation-state took a leap in sophistication. The outstanding book of this renaissance was Benedict Anderson's awe-inspiring work *Imagined Communities*.[15] However, in the rush to theorize the nation-state, there was an overriding interpretative trend to over-accentuate the invented and modernist nature of the nation.[16] This became a third reason for the lack of direct attention. Whether or not the authors of such studies intended it, the emphasis upon contingency and cultural invention became part of a broader postmodern trend to criticize any engagement in Grand Theory and any attempts to draw out broad (contingent) structural patterns in contemporary life.

At the same time, with a number of notable exceptions to be discussed in a moment, the boundaries between disciplines such as political science, anthropology, cultural studies and economics became firmer. Into the 1990s, questions of polity and community continued either to be subordinated or separated out into distinct realms. The window of opportunity that had been opened as writers no longer took the intersection of polity and community for granted was half-closed as the (post-structuralist) aversion to generalizing theory combined with the emphasis in the mainstream disciplines on particularizing studies. For example, thinking about the changing nature of the polity remains largely the preserve of political science, and then all too often with a narrow emphasis on the state as an institution of public administration.[17] Philosophers embrace questions concerning the ethics of community,[18] sociologists and anthropologists conduct case studies of particular communities, and geographers tend to limit themselves to the spatiality of community.

Throughout this period, some important social theorists continued to write against the trend carried within both mainstream and avant-garde theories that reject generalizing approaches to the social. Theorists who stand out in this respect include Jürgen Habermas, Pierre Bourdieu, Anthony Giddens, Maurice Godelier, Michael Mann, and Ernest Gellner.[19] They each in their various ways attempt to understand the structures of our society and to research the relation between structure and culture.[20] I intend to draw synthetically upon the work of these theorists in a way that they perhaps would not appreciate. For all that their research is extraordinarily enlightening, there is much in their approaches of which to be critical. The very breadth of their respective projects blinds them to methodological issues raised by their academic 'competitors'. Though they work in kindred realms, they barely acknowledge the influence of the others upon their thinking.

The present study draws critically upon these writers, using their writings to explore the relationship of polity and community, generalizing the approach that I earlier outlined in *Nation Formation*.[21] To narrow down the terms of the project, the background themes of polity and community are focussed upon two constellations of reference points: first, the social relations of the computer, money and print; and second, the social relations of time, space and embodiment. The reference point of 'print', for example, allows us to talk about the modes of communication relevant to both the constitution of different forms of polity and the integration of different forms of community. The most exciting research in this area is by Jack Goody. His numerous books include *The Interface between the Written and the Oral*.[22] Other researchers in this field include Walter Ong, Elizabeth Eisenstein and Florian Coulmas.[23] The extraordinary thing about Goody's work, and also Ong's, is the demonstrated connections made between a technology and technique of communication and forms of human subjectivity and social organization. This kind of analysis cries out to be connected into an understanding of the history of contemporary forms of community-polity.

## Defining globalism, nationalism and tribalism

The heightened reflexivity about social relations explains why apparently simple concepts such as 'tribe', 'race', 'nation', and 'ethnicity' are now so hard to define. It is why, across various disciplines, scholars are increasingly shying away from using these concepts. In fact, what theorists tend to do is problematize the terms so that they no longer work, and then use the very same terms anyway. This has made it increasingly difficult to write anything about the social without careful definitions of every inherited concept and the inventing of a thousand new concepts to deal with the perceived problems of the old. For example, some writers even want to give up on the rich and complex term 'culture' with one theorist writing that the concept was now too baggage-laden to be still useful. It should be replaced, he said, following Michel Foucault, with the concept of 'powerful discursive formations, globally and strategically deployed'.[24] Apart from making for very long sentences, here the theoretical assumptions of the writer are blatantly evident – maybe that is a good thing, allowing us to criticize his instrumentalist assumptions – and those assumptions are developed in a way that limits rather than extends our understanding of the rich complexity of lived cultures. What I intend to do here is use old words rather than neologisms, but to define a few key concepts in relation to each other as part of an interconnected method of understanding. Each new definition will appear to 'stand alone', as much as it is possible for the meaning of any concept to stand alone. Beyond that, a deeper understanding of the revisited old terms does depend upon understanding how they fit into the weaving of the overall theoretical approach. From this it should be possible to work out the definitions of the thousand other concepts that have been left implicitly rather than rigorously defined.

One concept that does need explicit attention is social formation. It had its origins in the neo-Marxist attempt to get away from what was earlier referred to as 'methodological nationalism'. Rather than treating society and nation as coextensive, conceiving of a social formation was to write in a more abstract register. In this sense, a social formation was a community-polity in all its historical specificity, but with its cultural-political boundaries crossed by broader social forces. Those forces were framed in theory by the dominant mode of production in articulation with other modes of production. I want to use the term in a more generalized way than the 'mode of production' approach. It will be used as the generic term for patterned formations of social practice and discourse (notice here that the word 'formations' acts simultaneously as a noun of outcome and of process). These formations can be described at various levels of analytical abstraction. At the level of empirical analysis, a nation or global community, or even a kinship group, can be called a social formation, always keeping in mind that such a formation is never unitary, homogenous or self-constituting. At the much more abstract level of categorical analysis, for example, it is possible to distinguish social formations by the way in which practices and subjectivities of temporality, spatiality, embodiment and epistemology are framed: that is, in terms of social formations as ontological formations – tribalism, traditionalism, modernism and postmodernism.

In contrast to the concept of 'social formation', the terms associated with 'globalism'[25] appear to be the easiest set of concepts in the world to define: in one way, globalization is simply the spatial extension of social relations across the globe. It is literally evoked in the picture that we have become accustomed to seeing in satellite photographs. However, that definition leaves us concentrating on the past few decades.

### Globalism and historicalism

A working definition of the cluster of terms around 'globalism' begins from the method that I have begun to outline, relating the various intersecting modes of practice to the extension of social relations across world-space. Across human history, as those practices have at one level become more materially abstract, they have tended to maintain or increase their intensity while becoming more extensive and generalized. 'Globalization' is thus most simply the name given to the extending matrix of those practices and subjectivities as they connect people across world-space.[26] Exemplary contemporary systems of materially-powerful but disembodied extension include the stamping presses of finance capital, electronic warfare, or electronic broadcast culture. There are, however, earlier or more concrete forms of globalization that need to be incorporated into any definition. There are lines of *traditional* global connection carried by agents of the early expansionist imperial states, by traders on the silk routes, and by crusading war-makers going off to smash the infidels 'because they were there' living in the same world.[27] In the contemporary period there are continuing movements of people as refugees, migrants and travellers that have an obviously continuing embodied character.

Given this long-term history and its changing nature, globalization is defined not as the annihilation of space, or as an end-state that we will finally reach when the local is subsumed by the global. Rather, it is the extension of matrices of social practice and meaning across *world-space* where the notion of 'world-space' is itself defined in the historically-variable terms that it has been practised and understood phenomenally through changing *world-time*. Globalization is thus a layered and uneven process, changing in its form, rather than able to be defined as a specific condition. It is a matrix of ongoing practices and associated ideas and sensibilities that may become more totalizing but can never be complete – at least while we remain human and bound to some extent by our bodies and immediate relations. Here I am very sensitive to the critical excursions of Justin Rosenberg in his raunchy polemic, *The Follies of Globalisation Theory*.[28] As he argues, changes in the nature of time and space have been elevated by some writers into a grand architecture of explanation that has the potential to dehistoricize the processes of global extension. Nevertheless, notwithstanding Rosenberg's telling methodological injunction that if globalization involves spatial extension, it cannot be explained by invoking the claim that space is now global – the explanation and the thing-being-explained, he rightly says, are thus reduced into self-confirming circle – it is still legitimate to treat globalization as a *descriptive* category referring to a process of extension across a historically constituted world-space. With a few refinements that is all that I am doing here. An explanation as to why the dominant modes of practice contribute to the genie of globalization is not contained inside the definition, even if a method for beginning such an enquiry is inferred.

The associated concept of 'globalism', at least in its more specific use, is defined as the dominant ideology and subjectivity associated with different historically-dominant formations of global extension. The definition thus implies that there were pre-modern or *traditional* forms of globalism and globalization long before the driving force of capitalism sought to colonize every corner of the globe, for example, going back to the Roman Empire in the second century CE, and perhaps to the Greeks of the fifth-century BCE.[29] In the case of the Greeks, globalism was conceived as a contested field mostly confined to the mode of enquiry, one with little impact on other modes of practice. Later, the Roman Empire drew lines of organizational connection across vast expanses of the known world, though this was still very restricted by comparison to what might be called *modern* globalization. Claudius Ptolemaeus (*c*.90–*c*.150) revived the Hellenic belief in the Pythagorean theory of a spherical globe. He wrote systematically about a world-space stretching from Caledonia and Anglia to what became known as Java Minor. Ovid's *Metamorphoses* begins with 'the god, whichever of the gods it was' taking care to shape the earth into a great ball, so that it might be the same in all directions.'[30]

Alongside the secular Roman Empire, the Roman Catholic Church, as its name suggests – *katholikos* universal, *kata* in respect of, *holos* the whole – had globalizing pretensions. This does not mean that global*ism* was the dominant or even a generalized understanding of the world. Sacred universalism, for example, was and is not necessarily the same as globalization. By contrast to the European clerics of globalization,[31] the Chinese form of universalism tended to be inwardly turned. For example, although the Celestial Kingdom had produced printed atlases that date long before the European Ortelius's supposedly first historical atlas, early maps of China show the world as fading off beyond the 'natural extent' of territory.[32] While evidence suggests that the Chinese may have travelled the world as far as the Persian Gulf and the coast of East Africa, this does not mean that they acted through a subjectivity of globalism. In other words, the Chinese centred their empire, symbolized by the decision in 1436 to prohibit the construction of seagoing ships.[33] On the other hand, we have to take seriously the evidence that the Romans actively extended theirs across the *known* globe. If the Roman Peutinger Table is any indication, the Roman world-view travelled in geometric lines that stretched as far as the travelling eyes of the agents of Empire could see.[34] Beyond military integration, as Jerry Bentley has convincingly argued, commercial trade, micro-biological integration and cross-cultural interaction began to connect societies across the globe long before the onset of the modern.[35]

The definition thus is also sensitive to Roland Robertson's argument that globalism is a deep historical and variable process. However, by including the Roman Empire as having both globalizing sensibilities and practices, it extends Robertson's chronicle of the 'germinal stage' back long before the beginning of *modern* forms of globalism in the fifteenth century with the *revival* of a spherical view of the world.[36] The earlier form of globalism is what I have been calling *traditional* globalism – with all the attendant issues of social form that the concept of 'traditionalism' entails. This means that the present approach fundamentally questions modernists like Anthony Giddens who suggest that globalism is a consequence of modernity, and utterly rejects theorists such as Martin Albrow who, in a fit of theoretical exuberance, claims that globality is now replacing modernity.[37] Giddens, in this view, does not have more than a single-layered sense of history, and Albrow makes a stunning category mistake. Albrow overlooks the issue that 'modernism' and 'globalism' come to us from two categorically different levels of analysis: 'globalism' is a descriptive term, an empirical generalization made about various practices, processes and subjectivities of spatial extension; whereas 'modernism' is a categorical term that can only be understood in terms of positing either a kind of subjectivity/aesthetic or a general ontological formation. Processes of globalization developed long before modernity (always understood provisionally in epochal terms only as a dominant not totalizing formation), and they will probably continue long after its heyday. However, this does not mean that globality is replacing modernity. It means, as writers such as Jan Aart Scholte and Manfred Steger have recognized[38] that the dominant form of globalization and globalism is changing, as is the once-assumed dominance of modernism.

In the early forms of *traditional* globalism, from perhaps the Roman Empire, through to the *modern* mercantile globalism of the seventeenth and eighteenth centuries, the connections were carried as lines through a landscape. New ethnographic interpretation suggests first, that rather than passively accepting of change, indigenous peoples responded actively to imperial extensions, and, second, that ongoing interaction preceded formal empire. Beyond the intensely concentrated lines of movement emanating out from the imperial centres, it can still be argued that social life largely carried on regardless in all its localized tribal complexity, however, new archaeological evidence suggests that the lines of the Roman Empire need to be understood as intensifications of interactions that had been going on for generations.[39] New forms of *traditional tribalism*, including new social hierarchies of leadership, came to overlay *customary tribalism*. Nevertheless, the limited extent of this layering effect still makes it fundamentally different from modern globalism. However brutal traditional colonization may have been, the intention of traditional imperialists was to 'civilize' or to dominate traditional and tribal forms of life rather than completely remove them from the face of the planet. By contrast, modern globalization became much more than lines of interconnection. It came to be carried as a plane of connections.

Like earlier forms of globalization, this layer does not completely transform all before it, but, unlike the past, it blankets various social forms of community and polity with the effects and imperatives of disembodied modes of practice: commodity and financial exchange, computerized production, electronic communication, techno-science, and so on. This blanketing can no longer be passively ignored with the hope that it will go away, if it ever could. And even as modern forms of globalism and imperialism continue, they are overlaid with postmodern forms: from the globalization of capital as it commodifies future-time through speculative hedging, to the globalization of cinematic culture with its postmodern sensibility signalled, for example, in the title of a new magazine of Hollywood gloss – *Empire*.[40] Abstracted from history through a process of modern and postmodern *historicalism*, the title carries only residual irony.

If *globalism* refers to the ideologies and subjectivities of generalizing connection across space, it can be inferred that, despite the process being largely ignored in the literature, there is a parallel temporal subjectivity for the generalizing connection across *world-time* – namely, *historicalism*. The concept refers here to the developing subjective consciousness of history as linking past, present and future in itself rather than as a teleologically or messianically connected frame. 'Historicalism' is related to the more familiar term 'historicism' but is quite different. The latter was employed by writers such as Karl Popper as a term of abuse to refer to a particular theoretical method for analysing history, whereas 'historicalism' is intended here to refer to an increasing distance of people before the activities of humans as agents in history – epistemological abstraction as linking time either from a more reflexive subjectivity or as an objective and material process. Just as globalism has a long history, historicalism has an equally deep history. In this case it is related to the practical possibility of abstraction across time rather than across space, particularly through the changing modes of communication and enquiry. It is a process, for example, made possible by the storage of memory in the form of written texts. Until the early-modern period, historicalism was subordinated by the subjectivity of messianic time and translated into sacred knowledge. Although its symbolic high-point arrives relatively late with the development in the nineteenth century of the formal discipline of History, it is extraordinary that the concept of 'historicalism', however it is named, remains a hidden presence, while the concept of 'globalism' rolls breathlessly off the tongues of politicians, business persons and commentators. We can see images of globalism everywhere in the form of spherical cloud-covered icons of planet earth, thus collapsing near and far, but we are unable to envisage the meaning of the concurrent collapsing of past and present. This is despite new sensitivities to questions of time and history.

## Nationalism and the nation

Part of the problem of defining terms such as *nation*, and related concepts of affinity such as *ethnicity* and *race*, derives from our increasing self-consciousness that the boundaries of these terms of relationship get more and more blurred as we turn our analytical microscopes on the specificities that were once said to define the boundaries of actually existing communities. It used to be, and often still is the case, that without thinking much about it, commentators took the particularities of embodied difference as the essentialized markers of the edge of an ethnic or racial grouping. They then made ethnicity one of the central factors – alongside other commonalities such as those of language, history and territory – through which members of one nation can be distinguished from another. Along these lines, *race* is seen unproblematically as a genetic category, *ethnicity* is seen as an extension of kinship and inhering in the body of the person as born ethnic, and the *nation* is seen as an extension of ethnicity as the most important variable factor of cultural commonality. Thus nation-states are understood to be formed in the tension between the unchosen identity of kinship-ethnicity and the daily plebiscite (Ernest Renan) of chosen civic identity. This is not entirely a caricature. Parts of that picture can, I suggest, be retrieved. However, to do so we have also to challenge its challengers. The dominant theoretical approach has now moved quickly, too quickly, to the opposite conclusion. From this position, rather than being natural, ethnicity is no more than a discursive fiction. Researchers found examples of where ethnicity, usually understood as ascribed identity, could be achieved by taking on another cultural regime or marrying into an existing ethnic grouping. Even when ethnicity was given, it became obvious that ascribed ethnic status could over a single generation be made, remade, and changed from above on political-religious grounds, and could come to be lived and naturalized. The theoretical challenge now is to take this evidence seriously while not dissolving social life into a play of signifiers.

In a similar over-hasty move, some social theorists came to argue that the nation was an invented formation. Again, once the mystique of the natural is lifted, it is objectively easy to find evidence of instances of cultural invention. However, to conclude that the 'nation' is no more than a social fiction is to miss the point. As used here, the 'nation' is defined in a way that takes seriously its contradictory objective–subjective form. A nation is at once an objectively abstract *society* of strangers, usually connected by a state, and a subjectively embodied *community* whose members experience themselves as an integrated group of compatriots – hence my use of the oxymoron, 'abstract community'. Even in these late-modern or postmodern times, the continuing phenomenal experience of the embodied community as made up of kindred souls is brought home, so to speak, at times of crisis. Pictures of fire officers emerging out of the flame and dust of the disintegrating World Trade towers on September 11 served to 'unite' a society that in important respects continually seems to be on the verge of socially disintegrating. One week after the terrorist attack, in a remarkable act of national solidarity, actors and singers from Hollywood and MTV mourned the tragic loss of life that occurred in attacks on the World Trade Center and the Pentagon. The program, a telethon fundraiser entitled *America: A Tribute to Heroes*, was broadcast to 210 countries. Tom Hanks, all-American boy-next-door and star of Steven Spielberg's blockbuster war movie, *Saving Private Ryan*, opened the evening in a low-key manner. He named the brave souls who reacted to the hijacking of Flight 93 and intoned their last words, 'We're going to have to do something'. Celine Dion sang 'God Bless America'. Clint Eastwood, affecting the same expression that he wore in his film *In the Line of Fire* (1993), spoke with gravel-voiced intensity about 'ultimate triumph':

> It was the twenty-first century's day of infamy. It was a day that will live in the annals of courage and patriotism. Tonight we pay tribute to those who were lost and those who survived the fire and the fate that rained down upon them, and the heroes at ground zero who had life and death wear an indelible badge of honor. We celebrate not only them, but all our fellow Americans, for the intended victims of this attack were not just on the planes, and at the Pentagon, the World Trade Center. They were wherever else they roam the sky. The targets were not just the symbols of America but they were the spirit of America. And the intended victims were all three-hundred million of us. The terrorists foresaw a nation fearful, doubtful, ready to retreat. Oh, they left us wounded, but renewed in strength. And we'll stand and will not yield. The terrorists who wanted three-hundred million victims, instead are going to get three-hundred million heroes, three-hundred million Americans with broken hearts, unbreakable hopes for our country and our future. In the conflict that's come upon us, we're determined as our parents and our grandparents were before us to win through the ultimate triumph – so help us God.

It is easy to be cynical about what each of these public figures was doing. They were making the nation. However, the question remains – how is it subjectively possible for the magical trope of 'three-hundred million' to stand in for the community of America? Why didn't Clint Eastwood have to ring up the Bureau of Statistics and find out exactly how many people were living in that society that night? How can these inconsequential Hollywood actors speak on behalf of all Americans? It is because the community of the nation subjectively and objectively remakes *itself* every day. The evening ended with the now iconic video-image of the US flag flying silently over the debris of the collapsed towers. No commentary. No introductions. No credits. Everybody who mattered was supposed to naturally know what the image meant. By a generalizing shift, expressed first in the words of politicians in the United States, the attack on the World Trade Center thus became an attack on 'us all' – and we could choose to step into the interpellated space of 'us all', either as national or global citizens ... or we could choose to be disloyal.

This continual return from the abstract to the embodied sense of palpable – from the chosen to the unchosen connection – helps to explain the usual definition of a nation as a community of people who name themselves as such on the basis of perceived commonalities. It is important to note that these, however, are not just any commonalities. The deepest and (interestingly) most prevalent of the categories of perceived commonality relate to what I argue are basic and largely unchosen categories of sociality: shared history (temporality), common territoriality (spatiality), and genealogy-ethnicity (embodiment). The other themes of commonality – such as language and address (communication), economic interest (production), institutional heritage and civic culture (organization) – work more at the level of chosen commonalities that we can strive to improve.

## Tribalism

In parallel with the problematizing of the areas of ethnicity and nationalism studies, anthropological research found that kinship relations – one of the defining conditions of tribalism – could be formed of real or fictive blood-ties. This led to an overturning of many of the taken-for-granted assumptions about what constituted a tribe. It led to much confusion, ranging from inappropriately applying *tribalism* in all situations of seeming primordial intensity such as the Balkans, to pronouncements that the word is too politically charged to use at all. Writing at the time when the concept of 'tribe' first began to be challenged, Lloyd Fallers cautiously suggests that

> The word 'tribe', in its classical sense, properly applies to only *some* precolonial African societies, as it does to some pre-Roman European ones. 'Tribalism' today usually means ethnic 'divisiveness'. I shall avoid these words because of *their* divisiveness, but the problem to which they draw attention cannot properly be dodged. African states *do* contain diverse primordial loyalties, as do most other societies, and these solidarities, in Africa as elsewhere, sometimes rise insistently to self-consciousness and become divisive, occasionally threatening the integrity of states. Fostering the illusion that these phenomena do not exist or may be made to disappear rapidly by ignoring them is both dishonest and unhelpful.[41]

Unfortunately such a response gives us no place to stand. Are tribes, then, a modern invention? Answering 'no' brings us much closer to the complex truth than saying 'yes'. The concept of 'tribe', derived from the traditional Latin term *tribus*, names real, self-reproducing and changing communities framed by the social dominance of face-to-face integration and living in the world today. Making the issue more complicated, it is possible to have tribalism beyond traditional tribes. The problems of definition are now more than lexical. The common application of the generalized concept of 'tribalism' has become almost tautological. Used to denote how those face-to-face communities we once unproblematically called 'tribes' are different from modern abstracted communities such as the nation, the concept of 'tribalism' begins to turn on a convention of self-naming. This has opened up the possibility of a postmodern relativism that says that you are part of a tribe if you name yourself as such. The question of self-naming is only one of the dimensions of community.

As a way out of the problem, tribalism is treated here as an ontological formation, in the same way as traditionalism, modernism or postmodernism were used earlier in the chapter. *Customary tribalism* is defined, most generally, as the framing condition of a certain kind of community in which persons are bound beyond immediate family ties by the dominance of modalities of face-to-face and object integration, including genealogical placement, embodied reciprocity and mythological enquiry. (These concepts are themselves defined and developed in Chapter 5.) Historically, the most sustained of these modalities has proved to be *genealogical placement* – that is, extended kinship relations, either blood-related or constituted around others ways of placement – but this on its own, at least in its thin versions, does not make a tribe. Furthermore, as tribal communities have fundamentally changed across modern history we have to treat tribalism as an ontological formation that is most often now framed in intersection with other formations.

A few examples will give a sense of the diversity of possibilities. The Tutsi, once the royal genealogy of a precolonial kingdom that formed on the flat grasslands of Rwanda's Lake Mohasi, are now a *modern* tribe-caste intent on nation-building. The Jews, once the twelve tribes of Israel, are now spread across the globe as variously a diaspora nation, an ethnicity and a religious creed; but no longer a tribe. And the Campbells, once the tribal clan bound to Glenorchy, are now simultaneously actual families, a globally-disconnected national family name spread by the waves of emigration, and the sign of abstract kilted nostalgia. Perhaps the most unexpected example comes to life in Riccardo Orizio's work on what calls the 'lost white tribes', small groups of European colonists such as the Dutch Burghers in Ceylon and the Blancs Matignon in Guadeloupe, left behind with the end of formal empire and sustained by strict inter-marriage and memories of the past.⁴² Such examples give a sense of the kinds of complexities that have to be taken into account. As a way of handling this, it is proposed that definitional distinctions should be drawn between different kinds of tribalism: pre-traditional or *customary* tribalism, *traditional* tribalism, *modern* tribalism or *postmodern* tribalism. According to this definition the contemporary Jews and the Campbells of Scotland can no longer be considered *tribes*, even though they sometimes embrace the subjectivities of *tribalism* in a process of ideological legitimization,⁴³ and the 'lost white tribes' tend to be outcast face-to-face groups rather than modern tribes. This approach thus treats tribal community as fundamentally different from an ethnic group or the abstracted community of the nation, even if the nation sometimes draws on some of the same ideologies of kinship and blood ties. It criticizes the loose, ideologically-charged use of the concept of 'tribalism' to describe the internal break-up of the postmodern nation-state or to distance civic nationalism from the primordial intensity of situations of violent national conflict. Carolyn Marvin's messy use of the metaphor of tribalism to explain the blood sacrifices of the American nation-state, for example, leaves us understanding less about the contemporary United States than about how contemporary intellectuals often completely misunderstand the complexities of actual tribalism.⁴⁴

*Traditional* tribalism (as distinct from *customary* tribalism) denotes a variety of formations. They range from groupings based on complex extended genealogies of proximate kinship to groupings still bound by genealogical placement but so stretched across place as to resemble the kinds of traditional kingdoms (as polity though not as community) that we associate with Europe and Northern Africa. *Modern* tribalism is, world-historically, a phenomenon related to modern processes of nation formation and globalization. Gathering momentum from the end of the eighteenth century, practices and ideologies coming from outside of existing tribalism including the imperialism of globalizing capitalism to the proselytizing of rationalized Christianity, over-determined the reconstitution of many settings of *traditional* tribalism. This is not to say that modern tribes were simply invented in this process. People, both 'on the ground' and at a distance, made them. When one reads the substance – as opposed to the preambles and glosses – of the various books that took versions of the notions of 'invention of tribes' into their titles, the (usually careful) documentation in those books does not show invention *per se*. Rather, they evidence colonial cultural management, administrative codification, bureaucratic schematizing, imperial romanticism, literary distortion, scholarly overgeneralization, ideological framing, *and,* as is too often overlooked, various forms of indigenous self-authentication.

In the writing of these books, the concept of *invention* quickly becomes 'invention' in inverted commas. It becomes the metaphor that does not really mean what it says. In its banal sense it comes to signify, quite rightly, that social life is socially constituted, and representations of it are just that – *re*presentations. Adam Kuper's *The Invention of Primitive Society*[45] does not show that anthropologists invented tribes, but rather that anthropologists over-generalized their descriptions around ethnocentrically driven evolutionary schemas. Daphna Golan's *Inventing Shaka*[46] does not show that the nineteenth-century Zulu chief was an invention of the Inkatha tribe, but rather that tribal history, as representation, is a contested terrain based on traditional oral narratives that have a different purpose from modern written histories. Ali Jimale Ahmed's *The Invention of Somalia*[47] does not show that Somalia was invented, but rather that the mythologies of traditional tribes and clans are used and contested, synthesized and refabricated in populist representations of modern nation formation.

Customary tribes now tend to live at the intersection of different formations. An example of the over-laying of customary tribalism with modern and postmodern layers can be seen in a case reported in the British *Daily Telegraph* in 2004 of Africa's last 'absolutist monarch', King Mswati of Swaziland selecting his thirteenth bride during a dance of '20,000 bare-breasted virgins' – after the traditional reed dance the unnamed bride was taken away for an AIDS test. From the other side of the supposed Great Divide, modernists 'look back' to tribal formations as the grounding condition of their own positions. For example, Israeli Prime Minister Ariel Sharon, having been complicit in reworking the tradition of the 'tribe of Israel' into a new ascendant culture of the Jewish warrior, talks comfortably of Israel having survived a long historical war of attrition still relevant today.

> When I say travel in, let's say, the mountains of the tribe Binyamin, say the area of Ramallah or west of Ramallah, I used to close my eyes a little bit, so you don't see the electrical grids and all these things ... In my imagination, I always felt that I see those warriors of the tribe of Binyamin, you know with spears, running there on the terraces.

He then makes the link of modern Zionism to a refabrication of history that lives in the present: 'And you know, those terraces that you see there – terraces were not built by the Arabs. Those terraces are old Jewish terraces.'[48]

The intersection of tribal, traditional and modern formations is not always so politically vexatious. At its most crass, it is evidenced in the way that in the West we are told that we can go tribal, or at least become Robinson Crusoe, just by eating a chocolate bar called 'Bounty' – experience the exotic. As a deeper subjectivity it can be seen in the changing body fashions of the West, particular among the young and disenfranchised. Body piercing, so normalized in the 1980s and 1990s that Princess Anne's daughter Zara, part of the British Royal Family, is allowed to have her tongue pierced, has in the new millennium joined in the search for the truly tribally 'authentic'. This kind of *postmodern* tribalism is an emergent formation in late-modern capitalist societies. Tribal branding and tattooing, scarification, metal implanting and earlobe stretching has spread across Europe, Australia and the United States with chains of body-art studios opening with names such as Tribe, Tribal Tattoo, Tribal Art and Primal Piercing. Across the West, New Age mysticism meets deep and re-energized desires to reconnect *'the tribal'*. Starbucks Coffee joins with Womad to bring out a CD of world music including the drummers of Burundi. In Leeds, a shop offering crystals from around the world calls itself 'Global Tribe'.

This whole discussion is open to easy misinterpretation. That a person or a group is enamoured with the trappings of postmodern tribalism does not mean that they are part of a tribe. When Ethan Watters appears on *Good Morning America* to proclaim the new phenomenon of urban tribes[49] – groups of American singles caught in quixotic webs of friendship, rivalry and shared pizzas – he is talking about the formation of relatively ephemeral close-knit networks, not tribes. He is riding the wave of *Seinfeld, Survivor* and *Friends* as yet another ideological expression of this postmodern reclamation of more concrete relations without any of the structures of embodied interrelation that define a tribe as such.

The ideological and subjective power of postmodern tribalism does, however, point to the new formation of lived postmodern tribes within the spaces of capitalism. One complicated example comes to us from Jonathan Friedman's work on the *sapeurs* of the Congo.[50] In this instance, a community of people who have been lifted out of existing tribal relations by the disruptions of global capitalism have taken on a layer of postmodern aesthetics by using haute couture fashion-garments from Paris as a means of asserting their social status. The dominant framing of this process is hypermodern, including the institution which gives the group its name – Société des Ambianceurs et Personnes Elégantes – but to the extent that this consumerism becomes a life-and-death struggle and draws upon customary approaches to knowledge and meaning, we have a continuing form of tribalism.

Other examples in the West have different trajectories. They tend to be more short-lived in duration and one-dimensional in generational terms than communities under conditions of traditional and modern tribalism. However, it may be that those ongoing face-to-face gangs and subcultural groupings in places as diverse as Kuala Lumpur, Berlin and London can be considered neo-tribal. I am not referring to ephemeral gangs of football hooligans attending the World Cup or to punk subcultures of people who meet only on the dance floor, but to face-to-face communities of outsiders who bind themselves together in embodied communion-unto-death. Insofar as these communities understand their dominant identities and interrelations through subjectivities of genealogical placement *and* they enact that relationship through more than the empty rhetoric of pseudo-kinship – the talk of 'brotherhood' and 'sisterhood' – then a new kind of community is developing. While I remain quite unconvinced by Maffesoli's claim that this is the time of the tribes, Gerd Baumann's research in the postcolonial British suburb of Southall is suggestive of new developments that need to be addressed.[51] In many cases, the short-lived nature of the groups calls into question the usefulness of considering these groups to be tribes as such; however, they certainly take on the trappings of postmodern tribalism (treating the adjective 'postmodern' in the strong sociological sense of the word).

## From Rwanda to Kosovo and Iraq

In order to introduce some of the problems of explanation that haunt the present study, it is instructive to take a couple of examples of community-polities in flux. In some ways, the two examples chosen could not be more different, but there is much in them that overlaps including the themes of globalism, nation-building and changing forms of identity. One example is the *modern* tribalism of Rwanda caught between traditionalism and modernism as it descended into a postcolonial hell of genocide against the Tutsi. In 1994, about 800,000 people were killed in one of the most horrific periods of concentrated slaughter in recent history.[52] Nearly two million people fled as refugees. It was a period with some parallels to the Nazi Holocaust and the attempted genocide of the Jews. The other example is the nationalist violence in the Former Yugoslavia as the postnational war-machines of the United States of America and the United Kingdom attempted to extricate themselves from a war that was never declared. What I hope to open up in these examples is a twofold complication. The first complication is that, in contemporary society, different ontological formations – tribalism, traditionalism, modernism, postmodernism – overlay each other in ways that always disturb, and in some cases completely fracture, the kinds of ontological security sustained through their very different forms of social identification and political organization. The second complication is that this violent fracturing of felt-security is bound up with the contradictions generated between embodied ways of experiencing the self and the layers of more materially abstracted processes of social formation. I am not suggesting that the intensification of these contradictions always, or even mostly, leads to breakdown and violence. It should be said, at the other extreme, that the intensification of contradiction can, under certain conditions, sustain a rationalized indifference to difference.[53] However, *indifference*, either passive or cold-blooded, was certainly not the outcome in Rwanda. The point of dwelling upon an episode such as the 1990s' genocide is that we can see the process of intensifying contradictions most starkly when people's sense of ontological security is so broken apart.

### Violence in Rwanda: from nation-building and modern tribalism to genocide

On 6 April 1994, an aeroplane carrying the Rwandan and Burundi presidents was shot down over Kigali. The incident became the apparent trigger for a state of genocide that would see approximately one-tenth of the population murdered over the period of a few intense weeks. Eighty per cent of the victims of the Rwandan genocide, most of them Tutsi, were killed by the third week of May. Apart from a few AK-47 rifles and grenades held by the elite, the predominant killing instruments were those of the hand – machetes or slashing knives, common agricultural tools called *panga*. The use of these instruments entailed that the executioners faced their victims directly, saw the blood run from their wounds, watched them die ... and then slashed at another living body, again and again and again.

The immediate question is, why did it happen? How did we get to the point where the intended genocide of the Tutsi population of Rwanda became both thinkable and attempted? A thousand questions follow, some that bear also upon an understanding of the other case to be discussed: the break-up of Yugoslavia and the NATO air-war over Kosovo. One question that permeates this book concerns the abstracted communities of identity – the 'nation' as a community of strangers, and even the *modern* 'tribe' as analogously abstracted when it too has become a post-kin-related community. How could such abstracted associations generate such powerful embodied personal and social identities as nationalism and tribalism? How do those often-positive identifications intensify to the point that a person is willing to kill a known 'other' for that identification? How, if at all, is globalism relevant to that intensification? More specifically in the cases of Rwanda or Bosnia and Kosovo, what impels people to kill other persons with whom, at the level of face-to-face *interaction* they have been living in an erstwhile fragile and ritualized amity? In the language of the present argument, they are questions about the relationship between the embodied level of face-to-face relations as such relations are overlaid by more abstract forms of social life, and extended across time and space by institutional and disembodied means. These issues will be taken up again when we return in later chapters to elaborate the Rwandan example. At this point, it is important to note that in the pre-colonial period there is no evidence of *systematic* violence between the Hutu and Tutsi as such. Genocide, I suggest, is a modern phenomenon. When the Western media described the genocide as 'tribalism gone mad', they missed out on the complexity of the event. Before moving to the next example, I would like to go back over the same event from a different perspective.

The genocide was clearly underway by the evening of 7 April with the Presidential Guards beginning to work through the death lists of priority targets in the capital, and it quickly spread through the bureaucracy of the (French-trained) *Interahamwe* and *Impuzamugambi* militias and out to the countryside. The cold language of 'priority targets', 'bureaucracy' and 'work', is intentionally used here, for there is strong circumstantial evidence that the killing began that way – as a modern, institutionalized and premeditated operation of intentional genocide against the Tutsi and their sympathizers. The killing-machine, the *Interahamwe*, meaning 'those who work together', may have been haphazard but it was also a state-run volunteer service linked to involvement in a series of earlier massacres. While the carefully targeted killings quickly broadened into mayhem, a layer of institutional efficiency (and 'indifference' to the emotional consequences) remained behind the scenes. Gérard Prunier records that garbage trucks were used in Kigali to help dispose of the dead. To prevent epidemics, some 60,000 bodies were removed from the capital for burial. In short, the genocide was both a modern incident requiring instrumental planning and a neo-traditional fugue grounded in embedded differences. It was both an orchestrated single event conducted at a 'distance' by institutionally-framed action and, once the slaughter had been initiated, a sporadic series of events spurred on by embodied face-to-face confrontation.

**War over Bosnia and Kosovo: from modern nationalism to disembodied violence**

Just as in pre-colonial Rwanda there is no evidence of systematic violence between the Hutu and Tutsi as such, in pre-war Bosnia, peoples of different *narod* (nation) and religion lived side by side in relative peace.

At least at the level of village life, Catholic Croats, Orthodox Serbs and Bosnian Muslims, later named as the three markers of ethnic cleavage in the Bosnian war, lived together in carefully-negotiated, criss-crossing civic identity. As Tone Bringa describes the situation, the social and moral geography of the village provided points of interaction, and even social integration for the different groups, despite kinship networks and rituals of intimacy and religion remaining separate – as did the architecture and culture of the household.[54] The war changed all of this 'from above', although some patterns of interchange continued. For example, large numbers of Serbs worked underground to support those who were singled out for ethnic cleansing.

In Kosovo, the situation was similar with the driving force for systematic violence coming from the political leaders and institutionalized military responses as they incited local concerns.[55] Though fuelled by a decade of tension, the first overt grassroots moves towards violence came as late as the mid-1990s. Just before Christmas 1997 in village of Llaushe, armed members of the newly-formed Kosovo Liberation Army appeared for the first time to confront Albanians at a funeral. It closed a circle of determinations. The thousands of Albanians had gathered to mourn the death of a schoolteacher killed by Serb police. Without wanting to suggest that face-to-face community is free of violence, it is galling to read the opposite – namely that it was the subjectivities of face-to-face community and its primordial memories of past grievances that underlay the war. The depictions in newspapers such as *The New York Times* were bad enough, but there were also academic writings attributing the causes of war to tribal divisions – primordial cleavages supposedly restrained by Tito's Yugoslavia, now bursting forth as ethnic nationalism. Tron Gilbert, for example, writes that 'the beginning of nationalism in the Balkans was, in reality, a form of tribalism'.[56] His writing is different only in tone and detail from newspaper articles such as, 'Old Tribal Rivalries in Eastern Europe Pose Threat of Infection'.[57] His argument combines all the worst problems of such attributions, though nicely synthesized in an apparently subtle scholarly analysis. The argument is based on the usual ethnocentric claim about the differences between Western and Eastern nationalism, the first, civic and accepting of diversity, the second, ethnic, culturally homogenizing and bad. 'Cultural nations', he says wrongly, 'lend themselves to tribalism, whereas political nations do not'.[58]

From there we follow the well-trodden path to the necessity of Western intervention: 'Tribes in possession of modern weaponry and destructive techniques can only be constrained by counterforce'.[59] This pronouncement tells us more about the dominant political culture of the

West during the Bosnian-Kosovan and Afghani interventions than it does about the complexities of life on the ground in the Balkans or Afghanistan. It is to this side of the story – the dominant political culture of the United Kingdom and the United States – that I want to direct the focus of this study, trying to open up the problems of understanding rather than developing any conclusions at this stage. The analysis will be further elaborated in Chapter 12 below.

What was the cultural-political context that normalized the necessity of NATO's massive interventions in Iraq, Kosovo and Afghanistan? What does it tell us about the changing nature of nationalism that when Bill Clinton and Tony Blair talked about the necessity of the 'humanitarian bombing' of Kosovo or the 'anti-terrorist bombing' of Afghanistan when it was done in the name of globalism rather than national interest? What does it mean that these political leaders were so concerned that the war in Kosovo should remain undeclared and strategically mediated by technological military means? What is the basis of the relatively new political obsession about not putting mass troops on the ground (the Second Gulf War notwithstanding), and having no body bags return home to mark the tragedy of the conflict?

The simple answer to these questions is that NATO did not want to be there in Kosovo. They were forced to be so by a series of their own contingent blunders and misunderstandings, including a politics of ultimatum against Milošević that was never going to work without either carpet bombing Kosovo and Serbia or putting massive numbers of troops into the region. Against the backdrop of inaction during the 1994 Rwandan massacre and the 1992–95 episodes of Bosnian Muslims being ethnically cleansed – both of which gradually became media-broadcast sources of Western guilt – Clinton and Blair and others, even including George W. Bush, had to find a Third Way. This sensibility and the structure of international considerations from outside Yugoslavia, together with a modern revival of neo-traditionalism from inside that federation, ended in a postmodern air-war of vast destruction from above and a ghastly modern ground-war of ethnic cleansing from below. As that last unwieldy sentence attests, the simple answer is not wrong, but as with the Rwandan situation an answer in terms of the content of international relations is far too thin. It takes far too much for granted.

The Second War in Iraq is continuous with the War in Afghanistan, but it has taken us a step further into what could be called a condition of meta-war, part of the new totalizing layer of globalization. We are in new and changing territory: a combination of strategic abstract strikes and embodied incursions that are effectively projected by a single hegemon at a widening series of fronts.

No pretence was made – as it had been in previous postmodern-dominated wars, the First Gulf War, Kosovo and Afghanistan – that military violence would be clean, surgical and precise. Long before it came to power, the members of the current war-cabinet exhorted the path of pre-emptive strike, including with weapons of mass destruction if necessary, to 'deter any challenger from ever dreaming of challenging us on the world stage'. 'I made up my mind at that moment that we were going to war', said George W. Bush a decade on, just after being told that the second plane had hit the World Trade Center.[60] (Although, at that time, in true postmodern fashion, he had no idea on whom he was declaring war.) Overall, however, the uniqueness of the Second Gulf War is one of a convergence of developing trends rather than a simple break with the past. It is important to remember some of the longer-term structural conditions that lay behind the present condition. The Second Gulf War is the culmination of a historical shift in the dominant nature of war that goes back at least to one driving campaign in World War II, culminating in the dropping of a nuclear bomb on the civilian population of Hiroshima. It is part of a more general shift in the dominant structures that have been intensifying across the course of the late-twentieth century and into the present.[61]

Understanding the nature of these changes (and continuities) helps us to understand the broader seriousness of the current situation. It will take us masses of background work in order to get back to developing the methodological framework for a more satisfactory account.

## Notes

1 Here the concept of 'imaginary' is used with a double reference: first, with an unwritten capital 'I', the framing of what is commonsensical, right and good. This is a socially-constituted version of the Lacanian use of the term. It describes the framing of sensibilities, subjectivities not always available to conscious reflection. 'Autonomy' in this sense is one of the key subjectivities of our age. Second, it refers to the imaginary with a lower-case 'i'. In this sense, autonomy is an ideology, in different ways for different people part of our conscious image (small 'i') of ourselves as free and choosing persons.

2 *Back to the Future*, 1985, directed by Robert Zemeckis; *Pleasantville*, 1998, directed by Gary Ross; and *The Truman Show*, 1998, directed by Peter Weir. *Back to the Future* is one of the twenty highest grossing films of all time. It spawned two sequels, an animated television series, and become the stock-in-trade title for dozens of books, some with dubious claim to using it. One example is an instructively entitled attempt to bring 'dry documents' back to life for a people who have never seen them as dead: *Back to the Future: Reclaiming America's Constitutional Heritage*, 1998.

3 Neal Stephenson, *Snow Crash*, Penguin, Harmondsworth, 1992; William Gibson, *Virtual Light*, Bantam Books, New York, 1993. Richard Rorty (*Achieving Our Country: Leftist Thought in Twentieth-Century America*, Harvard University Press, Cambridge, MA, 1998) uses *Snowcrash* as paradigmatic of a 'rueful acquiescence' about the end of good old-fashioned national pride.

4 *Woman's Day*, 27 November 1995. The continuing tension here with McDonald's still seen to be a pre-eminently global corporation is exemplified by the violent targeting of one of their outlets in Davos at the 2000 World Economic Forum. Going back further, in 1985, London Greenpeace organized an International Day of Action against McDonald's. Leaflets were distributed, which over the next few years became the basis for a libel trial that was to take two-and-a-half years, concluding in June 1997. The action taken against two community activists in London became known as the McLibel Trial. This theme is discussed below in Chapter 11.

5 *The Cambodia Daily*, 13 July 1994.

6 In the early 1990s, Roland Robertson (*Globalization: Social Theory and Global Culture*, Sage, London, 1992, pp. 173-4) used the concept advisedly. However, by the middle of the decade it unreservedly took a centre-place in his writings ('Glocalization: Time-Space and Homogeneity-Heterogeneity', in Mike Featherstone, Scott Lash and Roland Robertson (eds), *Global Modernities*, Sage, London, 1995).

7 Steve Silberman, 'Just Say Nokia', *Wired Magazine*, vol. 7, no. 9, 1999, downloaded from www.wired.com/wired/archive. In 1998, of the 165 million mobile phones sold in the world – that is, more mobile telephones than cars and computers combined – Nokia manufactured 41 million units.

8 Scott Lash, *Another Modernity: A Different Rationality*, Blackwell Publishers, Oxford, 1999, p. 1. While I am sympathetic to his notion of a 'groundless ground', the approach taken here however differs considerably from that taken by Lash. It neither searches for a second grounded modernity nor affirms the 'neo-world of technological culture' (p. 14).

9 Michel Foucault, *The Order of Things: An Archaeology of the Human Sciences*, Routledge, London, (1966), 1991, p. xv.

10 *Ibid.*, p. xvii.

11 Basil Edward Hammond, *Bodies Politic and their Governments*, Cambridge University Press, Cambridge, 1915, pp. 1-2.

12 See, for example, Otto von Gierke, *Political Theories of the Middle Age*, Cambridge University Press, Cambridge, 1900.

13 Hammond, *Bodies Politic*, pp. 3 and 4.

14 *Ibid.*, p. 4.

15 Benedict Anderson, *Imagined Communities: Reflections on the Origins and Spread of Nationalism*, Verso, London, 2nd edition, 1991.

16 The most widely read book of this kind was Eric Hobsbawm and Terence Ranger (eds), *The Invention of Tradition*, Cambridge University Press, Cambridge, 1983. Anthony Smith was the only effective voice against this modernist trend. See his *The Ethnic Origins of Nations*, Blackwell, London, 1986.

17 For a good general survey of the most theoretical of these approaches, see Clyde Barrow, *Critical Theories of the State*, University of Wisconsin Press, Madison, WI, 1993.

18 See, for example, Jean-Luc Nancy, *The Inoperative Community*, University of Minnesota Press, Minneapolis, 1991; and Elizabeth Frazer and Nicola Lacey, *The Politics of Community*, Harvester Wheatsheaf, New York, 1993.

19 Of their voluminous writings, see, for example, Anthony Giddens, *The Consequences of Modernity*, Polity Press, Cambridge, 1990; Michael Mann, *The Sources of Social Power*, vol. 2, Cambridge University Press, Cambridge, 1993; and Ernest Gellner, *Culture, Identity and Politics*, Cambridge University Press, Cambridge, 1987.

20 It is worth noting that three of the five theorists that I mentioned are included as central in Dennis Smith's study *The Rise of Historical Sociology*, Polity Press, Cambridge, 1991. Of the others, Bourdieu is a cultural anthropologist and Habermas is philosopher-social theorist.

21 *Nation Formation: Towards a Theory of Abstract Community*, Sage, London, 1996. The present book thus carries the related subtitle, *Towards a Theory of Abstract Community*, Vol. 2.

22 Jack Goody, *The Interface Between the Written and the Oral*, Cambridge University Press, Cambridge, 1987.

23 Walter Ong, *Orality and Literacy: The Technologizing of the Word*, Methuen, London, 1982; Elizabeth Eisenstein, *The Printing Revolution in Early Modern Europe*, Cambridge University Press, Cambridge, 1983; Florian Coulmas, *The Writing Systems of the World*, Blackwell, Oxford, 1989.

24 James Clifford, cited in Marshall Sahlins, 'Two or Three Things that I Know About Culture', *Journal of the Royal Anthropological Institute*, vol. 5, no. 3, 1999, p. 410.

25 'Globalism' is at this point is being used as the inclusive category for associated terms such as 'globalization', 'globalizing' and 'global formation'. At other points it will be used to refer to the ideologies of globalization. This is similar to the way that the concept of 'nationalism' is used in the literature to stand in for the cluster of associated-but-differently-defined terms – 'nation', 'nation-state', 'national sentiment', and so on, while also used to refer to the ideology and subjectivity, the '-ism'.

26 The concept carries in its multiple meanings the contradictorily embodied/disembodied nature of abstracted social relations that the present study is attempting to describe. In its most general meaning, a matrix is a setting in which something takes form, has its origin or is enclosed. In obstetrics 'matrix' refers to the body of the womb. By contrast, in mathematics it refers to a regularized array of abstract elements. And in engineering (my personal favourite given the current expressions of globalism), it refers to a bed of perforated metal placed beneath an object in a machine press against which the stamping press operates. With thanks to Kate Cregan for discussions about the concept of 'matrix'.

27 At this stage 'smashing the infidels' meant civilizing them by means of sword and burning oil, not engaging in genocide. The term *traditional* is intended to carry the significance of the profound differences to *modern* globalization. See the section later in the chapter on genocide in Rwanda. For accounts of the history of globalization, see Robbie Robertson, *The Three Waves of Globalization: A History of a Developing Global Consciousness*, Zed Books, London, 2003; and A.G. Hopkins (ed.), *Globalization in World History*, Pimlico, London, 2002.

28 Justin Rosenberg, *The Follies of Globalisation Theory: Polemical Essays*, Verso, London, 2000.

29 William Arthur Heidel, *The Frame of the Ancient Greek Maps*, Arno Press, New York, 1976.

30 Ovid (43 BCE–17 CE), *Metamorphoses*, Penguin, Harmondsworth, 1955, p. 30.

31 See, for example, Solomon Ibn Gabirol (c. 1021–c. 1058) writing in *A Crown for a King*, Oxford University Press, Oxford, 1998, pp. 14–15, discussing God as making 'the globe of the earth'.

32 See Jeremy Black, *Maps and History: Constructing Images of the Past*, Yale University Press, New Haven, CT, 1997, pp. 2–3, on Standen's thesis about the ahistorical depiction of the Great Wall, whether or not it had been built.

33 The point being made here is only a relative one. The ban was lifted by the middle of the sixteenth century, and the period of the Ming-Qing transition is associated with significant trade in silver and sugar. The Qing ban on maritime trade in 1661 was imposed as a response to the power relations effected by objective global connections. Hans van de Ven, 'The Onrush of Modern Globalization in China', in A.G. Hopkins (ed.), *Globalization in World History*, Pimlico, London, 2002.

34 A stylized map of the Empire, about 12-feet long and rolled out like a narrow scroll; known from a thirteenth-century copy. In modern cartographical terms it is unrecognizably distorted. Made more than two thousand years earlier, a Mesopotamian clay tablet with a circular Assyroncentric map shows the Euphrates joining the Persian Gulf and surrounded by the 'Earthly Ocean'. See Norman J.W. Thrower, *Maps and Man: An Examination of Cartography in Relation to Culture and Civilization*, Prentice-Hall, Englewood Cliffs, NJ, 1972.

35 Jerry H. Bentley, 'Hemispheric Integration, 500–1,500 C.E.', *Journal of World History*, vol. 9, no. 2, pp. 237–54.

36 Robertson, *Globalization*, 1992. His historical mapping of the 'phases' of globalism is the subject of Chapter 3 in that book.

37 Giddens, *Consequences of Modernity*, 1990; Martin Albrow, *The Global Age*, Polity Press, Cambridge, 1996.

38 Jan Aart Scholte, *Globalization: A Critical Introduction*, Palgrave, Basingstoke, 2000; Manfred Steger, *Globalization: A Very Short Introduction*, Oxford University Press, Oxford, 2003.

39 Peter S. Wells, *The Barbarians Speak: How the Conquered Peoples Shaped the Roman Empire*, Princeton University Press, Princeton, NJ, 1999.

40 *Empire*, EMAP consumer magazines, first published in the UK in 1992, began publication in Australia in 2001. Website: www.empireonline.com.au.

41 Lloyd A. Fallers, *The Social Anthropology of the Nation-State*, Aldine Publishing, Chicago, 1974, p. 37.

42 Riccardo Orizio, *Lost White Tribes: Journeys among the Forgotten*, Vintage, London, 2001.

43 On the process of transformation in Scotland, for example, see Robert A. Dodgshon, *From Chiefs to Landlords: Social and Economic Change in the Western Highlands and Islands, c. 1493–1820*, Edinburgh University Press, Edinburgh, 1998. That the Campbells are no longer a tribe does not mean that tribalism is now only confined to 'residual' groups in the Third World. See, for example, the section immediately below on postmodern tribalism.

44 Carolyn Marvin and David W. Ingle, *Blood Sacrifice and the Nation: Totem Rituals and the American Flag*, Cambridge University Press, Cambridge, 1999. The methodological approach of this book will be critically examined in Chapter 10.

45 Adam Kuper, *The Invention of Primitive Society: The Transformation of an Illusion*, Routledge, London, 1988.

46 Daphna Golan, *Inventing Shaka: Using History in the Construction of Zulu Nationalism*, Lynne Reinner Publishers, Boulder, CO, 1994.

47 Ali Jimale Ahmed (ed.), *The Invention of Somalia*, Red Sea Press, Lawrenceville, 1995.

48 *The Age*, 18 September 2004.

49 Ethan Watters, *Urban Tribes: A Generation Redefines Friendship, Family and Commitment*, Bloomsbury, New York, 2003. See in particular pp. 65–9 where Watters draws on socio-biology to show how natural the process is.

50 Jonathan Friedman, *Cultural Identity and Global Process*, Sage Publications, London, 1994.

51 Michel Maffesoli, *The Time of the Tribes: The Decline of Individualism in Mass Society*, Sage Publications, London, 1996; Gerd Baumann, *Contesting Culture: Discourses of Identity in Multi-Ethnic London*, Cambridge University Press, Cambridge, 1996.

52 Among the many articles and books now written on Rwanda, I am particularly indebted to Mahmood Mamdani, 'From Conquest to Consent as the Basis of State Formation: Reflections on Rwanda', *New Left Review*, vol. 216, 1996, pp. 3–36; and Gérard Prunier, *The Rwandan Crisis: History of a Genocide*, Columbia University Press, New York, 1997. The figures are all approximations, but I have cross-checked multiple sources. For a good overview of other relevant literature see Alexander Johnston, 'Ethnic Conflict in Post Cold War Africa: Four Case Studies', in Kenneth Christie (ed.), *Ethnic Conflict, Tribal Politics: A Global Perspective*, Curzon Press, Richmond, 1998.

53 See Michael Herzfeld, *The Social Production of Indifference: Exploring the Symbolic Roots of Western Bureaucracy*, University of Chicago Press, Chicago, 1992. This 'indifference' can itself in turn become the basis of state-legitimized violence from a distance. Rationalized violence, as evidenced in the wars over Iraq and Kosovo, is, however, usually *framed* at a more abstract or technologically mediated level. In practice, of course, war is fought across the various levels of embodiment to disembodiment, but the *framing* of war has become increasingly abstract over the course of history even if the flesh-and-blood bodies of civilians increasingly bear the brunt of military action.

54 Tone Bringa, *Being Muslim the Bosnian Way: Identity and Community in a Central Bosnian Village*, Princeton University Press, Princeton, NJ, 1995.

55 See, for example, Heather Rae, *State Identities and the Homogenisation of Peoples*, Cambridge University Press, Cambridge, 2002, Chapter 5.

56 Trond Gilbert, 'Ethnic Conflict in the Balkans: Comparing Ex-Yugoslavia, Romania and Albania', in Kenneth Christie (ed.), *Ethnic Conflict, Tribal Politics: A Global Perspective*, Curzon Press, Richmond, 1998, p. 67. Michael Keating ('Minority Nationalism or Tribal Sentiments') writing in the same volume rightly distances himself from the moral assumptions of the civic-ethnic nationalism sentiments, but then falls for the parallel moral dichotomy. The new nationalisms, he writes, 'may be benevolent, democratic and progressive [i.e., good], or represent a retreat into tribalism [i.e., bad]' (p. 35).

57 *New York Times*, 13 October 1991. On representations of the war, both academic and popular, see David Campbell, *National Deconstruction: Violence, Identity and Justice in Bosnia*, University of Minnesota Press, Minneapolis, 1998, pp. 53–81.

58 *Ibid*. This claim forgets, for example, the self-proclamations of Celtic tribal roots by the southern leagues of the United States, that is, in the 'pre-eminent Western civic nation' upon this planet. See Edward H. Sebesta, 'The Confederate Memorial Tartan', *Scottish Affairs*, no. 31, 2000, pp. 55–84.

59 *Ibid.*, p. 76. While I basically disagree with the analysis, this is not to say that tribalism is not crucial to understanding Balkan history or that it is irrelevant to its present. In the present there can be said to be elements of tribalism to the extent that the organized gangs that emerged with the collapse of communism became an encompassing way of embodied life for some people. On the past and its incorporation into the traditional state and society, see M.E. Durham, *Some Tribal Origins, Laws and Customs of the Balkans*, George Allen & Unwin, London, 1928.

60 Dan Balz and Bob Woodward, 'The First Twenty-Four Hours', *Washington Post*, syndicated to *The Sunday Age*, 3 February 2002.

61 For a development of that last paragraph, see Tom Nairn and Paul James, *Global Matrix: Nationalism, Globalism and State-Terror*, Pluto Press, London, 2005.

# THREE Contending Approaches in Outline

The early twenty-first century is a good time to discuss the grand social theories. Like supernovae, they have exploded and begun to cool. This chapter briefly introduces and counter-poses a number of approaches which explore the nature of social life and social formation. In order to narrow down the many possible approaches that might be discussed the chapter focuses upon a small representative range of well-known writers.

From the Durkheimian-Weberian traditions, the chapter takes the work of Ernest Gellner and Michael Mann. From the Critical Theory responses to the neo-Marxist and historical materialist traditions, the chapter examines the contributions of Pierre Bourdieu and Anthony Giddens. And from the post-structuralist and postcolonialist traditions, it focuses on Michel Foucault. As will quickly become apparent, Gellner, Mann and Bourdieu substantially rework the traditions of classical social theory. Nevertheless, Gellner and Mann's approaches, for all their idiosyncrasies, are still what might be called neo-classical, whereas Bourdieu's approach joins the long march of those numerous writers that leave behind many of the methodological assumptions of classical historical materialism. Anthony Giddens is discussed as a seminal example of the reflexively modern synthesis of classical theory conducted in this self-conscious passage from classical to the post-classical theory. Michel Foucault is examined as exemplifying the post-structuralist rejection of generalized theories of social formation.

I should say from the outset that my own approach, developed in the next chapter, comes out of the politically-critical spirit of historical materialism, but it is marked by substantial divergences from that tradition. Overall, *Globalism, Nationalism, Tribalism* attempts to address the many methodological limitations of existing theory. I will hint at these differences throughout the chapter, but the main task here is just to describe critically a few lines through contemporary social theory. Moreover, the chapter limits its discussion to merely sketching the *analytical methods* employed by these central writers rather than the full complexity of their approaches and theories. This narrowness of focus will be broadened as the book proceeds. I will come back time-and-again to writers such as Gellner, Mann, Bourdieu, Giddens, and Foucault, as well as other representative figures such as Benedict Anderson, Maurice Godelier and Arjun Appadurai in later chapters. The overall work of these theorists, with all its splendid glories and tawdry low points, will serve as points of discussion through the entire study.

A couple of limitations should be noted. The first striking failing of this list of theorists is that it is made up only of men. Despite making path-breaking contributions in important specific areas, theorists such as Mary Douglas, Annette Weiner, Donna Haraway, Gayatri Chakravorty Spivak and Julia Kristeva, have not written works of generalizing social and political theory. A second failing of the list is that many other prominent writers such as Fredric Jameson, Jürgen Habermas, Jack Goody, Zygmunt Bauman, W.G. Runciman, Niklas Luhmann and Bryan Turner have been relegated to secondary or footnoted characters in the following narrative. Despite the prominence of those theorists, in some cases it is because their work has taken other turns than generalizing social and political theory. In some cases it is either just because of lack of space or my lack of knowledge.

It is worth beginning this chapter again. This time I want to start from the perspective of the world today. I want to begin with what we want to understand, rather than from the narrower question of who is attempting such understandings. As described in the previous chapter, the contemporary world is a contradictory and extraordinarily complex place. These are actual contradictions, not metaphysical dialectics. Our world is experiencing powerful processes of globalization that are contributing to reconstituting the local, but at the same time globalization is making people more aware of the meaning of local embeddedness. We are living through a time when grand universalisms, from the sacred universalisms of Islam, Hinduism and born-again Christianity to the secular universalisms of techno-science and neo-liberalism are being argued about and proselytized with renewed intensity. However, this is also a time of focussing back upon the particular with a general scepticism about some grand narratives. It is also at once a conjuncture of the ascendancy of revived modernism, and a period when emergent postmodern practices and sensibilities compete with revivals of tradition.

In this context, classical narratives have re-emerged wearing new clothes – grand-nation exceptionalism, for example, has recently taken on the garb of freedom and democracy in countries such as the United States and Britain. 'Freedom' was the constant refrain in George W. Bush's speeches as the 'Coalition of the Willing' invaded and steadfastly occupied Iraq. This is a time when processes of mediation and disembodiment – from missiles to the media – carry the dominant *objective* tracks of power. However, it is also a time when, *subjectively*, the world is focussed back upon particular and intense concerns for issues of the body: from fascination with the ethnically-cleansed, the Abu-Ghraib degraded, and the decapitated, to fetishisms for body shops, perfumeries and *Extreme Makeover* episodes. It is a period when inequalities are massively increasing – not this time predominantly on the back of enslaved human labourers or by ripping resources out of the Third World (though this is of course still happening), but rather by a super-charged attention to managing the abstract relation between time and value. The contradictions of the contemporary period are compounding.

These kinds of issues will be expanded upon in subsequent chapters, but they raise a key question. Given these complexities, what do we want to understand and what is the purpose of *engaged social theory*? In the argument put forward here, understanding the parts of our world entails getting closer to understanding social relations in general. An adequate approach needs to address the way in which different dominant practices and subjectivities in the present contribute to constituting life-worlds and patterns of sustainability, well-being, routine, insecurity, and wretchedness. In order to do this, it has offer ways of being clearer about both the complexity of the past *and* the complexity of other contemporary but subordinated social forms. Along the way, we cannot afford to lose sight of the important potential for learning from alternative social formations in the urgently necessary process of remaking the dominant configurations of our world – socially, politically and economically.

The matrix of contemporary contradictions that has just been described has its own conjunctural meaning, but the task in hand in understanding the present is essentially no more or less difficult than describing any intersection of formations at any time in human history. The main difference is that the evidence about the present appears to be more readily available. An adequate method should help us understand the nature and conditions of social life across a series of world-times and across different forms of sociality. In the unique setting of the present, one of the key tasks thus implied by engaged social theory is to examine the integrative forms, the structures both objective and subjective of the dominant form of polity-community. Today it is still the nation-state in a globalizing system. However, an adequate method needs to be sensitive to the many living, vibrant, but currently subordinate or emergent social forms of the organization of power and culture – tribe, village, kingdom, empire and network.¹ And such a method needs to be useful in exploring processes of social change: how we got here.

All of this already entails a massive undertaking, but the task goes further. We need to understand the nature and limitations of any understandings that we do happen to develop. This means that an adequate engaged social theory has to be epistemologically aware. It needs in particular to be reflexive first about its own limitations, including the constitutive foundations of what makes it possible to develop such a theory. Second, it needs to be aware of the horrors to which insights of social theory have been put in the past – from providing the anthropological background for controlling indigenous populations under colonial indirect rule to running concentration camps, or, more benignly, to running successful election campaigns for dangerous political leaders.

## Problems of understanding

In setting up a theory of social formation there are many dangers, problems and pitfalls. One challenge, as already intimated, is to understand different social formations without setting up a Great Divide between them or alternatively reducing different ways of living in different societies to a single plane of being – differences that do not make a difference; differences of content and style, differences as flat pluralism.² The grand distinctions between forms of sociality from Ferdinand Tönnies's distinction between *Gemeinschaft* (community) and *Gesellschaft* (society) to Benjamin Barber's 'Jihad versus McWorld' have all tended to assume a dichotomy between one way of life and another. Before long, unintended value judgements and valuations have tended to inhere on one side or other of these Divides, however they are expressed. On the other hand, pseudo-democratizing approaches which deny the profound ontological differences that exist between different kinds of communities and polities are equally unhelpful. Like the liberal ideology of equality-equals-sameness, they effectively wipe out other ways of life in the name of not differentiating between them, or discriminating for or against them. (See Chapter 12.)

A second challenge arises in attempting to understand the *patterns* of social life. As evidenced in debates around the concept of 'structure' this has to be done without treating those patterns (structures) as hard and determining in themselves. There are unfortunately a number of unhelpful tendencies in the literature. There is a tendency to over-emphasize one side or other of the subject–object divide. Some writers have treated structures either as reified things like city grids that passively compel people to move in certain directions rather than in others. Equally unhelpfully, structures have been treated as active forces 'out there' that bear back upon 'subjects' with all the ferocity of a hardened steel stamping-press. As I will touch upon later, Anthony Giddens has, in attempting to get beyond the hardening of historical materialism into classical structuralism, set up his method around the dialectic of agency and structure.[3] He talks of structures as no more and no less than rules and resources used by knowledgeable actors. However, for me this just reinstates a version of the same problem to the extent that it treats agency as a matter of choice, as against structures as constraining or enabling patterns of life beyond the person. By contrast, the present approach attempts to make it possible to talk of the structures of both objective and subjective relations. More explicitly, in contradistinction to the structure/agency dialectic, it suggests that we should be able to talk about different structures of agency. In this sense, the structural dimension of a situation is understand as no more and no less than the patterns of life that are relevant to that situation. Structures are therefore in Giddens' terms both enabling and constraining, but more importantly they are the instantiated patterns of practice and subjectivities constitutive of the nature or *social form* of those enablings and constraints, including contemporary ideologies that emphasize choosing and freedom.

A related problem arises for those approaches that counterpose structure to fragmentation, as if instances of fragmentation mean that structures are falling away. In the same way that there can be patterns (structures) of agency, there can be patterns (structures) framing processes of fragmentation. The challenge is to be able to talk of structures in terms of specified levels and places of patterning. For example, it should be quite possible to argue that in the contemporary period contingently called 'late-modernity', social life is fragmenting at the level of the face-to-face while more abstract structures of integration such as through the media are constraining and enabling people in new ways.

A fourth challenge involves the importance of moving beyond the tendency to either reduce social life to the determinations of material conditions or alternatively to give ideas a life of their own. That is known in the literature at the *materialism/idealism* dichotomy, and it would be good finally to lay that ghost to rest. A parallel methodological dichotomy, the *contingency/determination* dichotomy, is set up in the debate between those who say that everything is determined (classical structuralists) and the counter-claim that everything is deeply contingent (classical post-structuralists). To make sense of the world, it is clear that we need to explore the reasons why things happen. If you accept that claim, then it follows that an adequate method needs to take seriously the question of determination, but without being reductive about what that quest for understanding means. This might seem optimistic, but I want to argue that we need to be able to say, with any postmodern trickery, how particular practices and sensibilities are both contingent and structured at the same time. This entails being clear about the epistemological standpoints from which such apparently contradictory claims are made. Responding methodologically to those kinds of challenges is the task of the next chapter. The present chapter sets out to take some of the existing approaches to task for failing to deal adequately with such issues. We start with the neo-Weberians and end with the post-structuralists and postcolonialists.

## Epochs of order: Ernest Gellner

Ernest Gellner was Professor of Philosophy at the London School of Economics and, in turn, Professor of Anthropology at Cambridge University, and Director of the Centre for the Study of Nationalism at the Central European University in Prague. This gives some sense of his breadth of interests and the reach of his approach. His books include *Nations and Nationalism* (1983), *Plough, Sword and Book* (1988), and *Encounters with Nationalism* (1994).[4] He describes his ancestors as 'provincial Bohemian petty bourgeois' and states that his family was of Jewish-Czech background.

In this context it becomes understandable why his approach emphasizes both the epochal nature of social change and the invented ideologies associated with those changes, including the culture of nationalism. The nation-state of Czechoslovakia came into existence after World War I with the collapse of the Austro-Hungarian Empire, and the Nazis and Communists subsequently drove military forces through that area. Gellner lived through the shock waves of a series of incredible social changes,[5] and came to argue about the relative irreversibility of the steps of change in human history. He does not argue that earlier changes necessitate later ones, or that there are obligatory developmental patterns. Nevertheless, he characterizes history in terms of three basic stages: hunting-gathering, agrarian society and industrial society. Gellner is a classical modernist in this designation, but an epistemologically-sophisticated one. The schema may be simple, but it depends for its validity on its analytical usefulness rather than any assertion of essential or naturalized truth about human development. This is an insight that we will need to take forward without necessarily using his approach to grand stages of history.

Table 3.1   Ernest Gellner's approach: relating epochs to modes of practice

|  | Production | Coercion | Cognition | |
|---|---|---|---|---|
| Foragia | not discussed in any detail | not discussed in any detail | Wild, uncultivated and savage | Neolithic revolution |
| Agraria | – new techniques of food production<br>– class-divided 'division of labour' | – specialized agencies of the military<br>• state formation | – specialized agencies of clerics<br>• literacy | ↓<br>Industrial revolution |
| Industria | – systematic innovation in addressing nature<br>– a mobile division of labour | – coercion coinciding with legitimation<br>• nation-state formation | – a single, unified epistemological space<br>• generic science | ↓ |

*Source*: Developed from Gellner, *Conditions of Liberty*, p. 21.

Gellner's second analytical step is to set the three stages of history against a threefold classification of human activity: production, coercion and cognition. Other theorists have made similar moves to set up an approach to modes of practice, and whether or not this one works, the generality of the move is instructive. W.G. Runciman, for example, chooses production, persuasion and coercion as his basic categories of practice.[6] Gellner, by this step, arrives at a three-by-three matrix of forms of society in relation to forms of activity (see Table 3.1). In his understanding, production, coercion and cognition remain relatively undifferentiated in tribal society. However, with what he calls 'the Neolithic revolution' – a revolution in the production and storage of food – everything changes and opportunities develop for an increasingly complex division of labour.

In the second great revolution of *industria*, and the shift from agrarian society to industrial society, changes are similarly wrought in the basic fabric of living. In relation to the mode of cognition we see the development of what he calls 'a turn-over ontology'. The clerics of truth and redemption are replaced by 'maintenance and servicing personnel of a new and symbolically coded social structure',[7] intellectuals who trade in the turn-over of ideas. Unlike traditional processes of classification where meanings are relatively stable, in *industria* diverse conceptualizations compete with each other and are tested against experimentation and experience. Science, he argues for example, has no fixed base-line ontology. In relation to the mode of coercion, the specialized agencies of *agraria* become even more specialized in *industria*, and coercion itself becomes 'both easier and probably less necessary'.[8] In Gellner's representation the sword is supplanted by the market as the instrument of social extension.

We move towards the freedom of civil society, he says, with the egalitarianism of market-democracy.⁹ Here his politics of right-wing liberalism become very clear.

There are a number of problems with Gellner's approach that can be listed briefly. The first is the issue of epochalism – Gellner writes with such a desire for uncluttered absolutes that he only begrudgingly acknowledges basic qualifications to his dramatic world-picture, and then tends to ignore those qualifications completely in developing his approach. His naming of the epochs does not help in this process. For example, while it is clear the industrial production has *supplanted* agrarian production as the dominant mode of production, it is not so clear that 'modernism' has *replaced* 'traditionalism'. Instead of talking of relations-in-dominance, an easy way out of the problem, Gellner sets up the modern as a single epistemological space conquering all.

Second, Gellner faces the problem of determination. For example, in explaining the formation of nation-states, the three-way matrix of determinants drops away to give primacy to industrialization. Nation-states are formed in the new mobility of labour made possible by industrial production. Persons become modular agents carrying their culture with them. And what institution is of sufficient size and complexity to bind this mobile culture? There is only the state. States claim the community of the nation for themselves and the nation-state emerges as a uniquely modern development. The problem with this is not Gellner's attempt to show how such a powerful force upon our modern souls as nationalism is explicable in the context of certain social conditions. Bringing together the subjective and the objective is a central requirement of any grand social method. The problem is that it is situated in a reductive argument – the nature of the social world, including the subjectivity of nationalism, is reduced to a certain kind of division of labour: industrialism. This is the third major issue – all of Gellner's explanations about the nature of the contemporary world start with the emergence of labour roles that are divided in complex and cumulatively changing ways. It is a huge weight for the industrial division of labour to explain, especially when the first nationalist movements occurred as a response to imperial changes across the world in places where industrialization itself had not yet reached (elaborated in Chapter 10).

## Tracks of social power: Michael Mann

Michael Mann draws inspiration from Ernest Gellner's notion of an episodic history, but unlike Gellner, he has no grand schema of epochs. This rejection of epochalism is something that I want to also carry forward into the next chapter when we try to set up an alternative approach, but not necessarily in the way that Mann presents it. Mann puts the emphasis on changing and overlapping networks of social interaction, arguing that 'societies' are formed and traversed by intersecting networks of power (forms of power as ideal types). These are what he calls the 'sources of social power'. Instead of choosing Gellner's production, coercion and cognition as his basic categories of analysis, he chooses the ideological, economic, military, and political. These sources of power are treated as having 'tracklaying' primacy. During key moments, changes in one or other of these sources of social power can fundamentally shift the direction of social development. In this process one of the key factors is what he calls 'social caging', the containment of communities and polities within confining social and territorial boundaries. For example, in Mann's argument, the first 'civilizations' formed as they were trapped by both the ecology of their alluvial river-corridors and their own reactions to them, into particular social and territorial relationships that intensified overlapping power networks. This leads to two further caging tendencies: first, in the area of the economic, through the instigation of quasi-private property, and second, in the area of the political, through the formation of the state.

Michael Mann has made a major contribution in the field of historical sociology.[10] His magnum opus *Sources of Social Power* is projected into a number of volumes of densely-researched, theoretically-informed writing. His research is both deep and broad, and he has developed a laudable tendency to reflect auto-critically on the status of his own generalizations in the context of a convincing assessment of available secondary material. I want to take a little time to unpack his approach (in part because he fundamentally calls into question an analytic metaphor that will become central to the approach that I want to set up as an alternative in the next chapter – the metaphor of levels). The following discussion, as with my description of all the writers' methods, sounds a little critical, but the issues raised only partially qualify the richness of the analyses.

Mann begins in a way that recognizes the real problems of setting up more than contingent lines of determination or social boundedness. His ambivalence is clear, but in the end unfortunately it ties his approach up in theoretical knots. In a striking methodological gambit, he sums up his approach in a statement that contains a basic term he wants to problematize: *'Societies are constituted of multiple overlapping and intersecting sociospatial networks of power'* [11] The problem term is 'society'. Within a few sentences he moves from ambivalence about the term to almost sacrificing 'society' altogether, saying that he wishes that it could be struck from the sociological lexicon. It is not helpful, he says, to distinguish between internal and external determinants of the social.

In chess a gambit involves the sacrifice of a minor piece in order to make a major gain. Here it becomes a source of major confusion. The concept of 'society' continues on in his work, centrally relevant to his analysis, but without consistent force.

Michael Mann's rejection of uses of 'society' that treat it as a totality or a single unifying whole is important, as is his concern that social relations should not be reduced to any 'last instance' determination such as the mode of production or the division of labour. It is a caution that I will take forward into the rest of the book. However, he goes on to reinstate the concept of 'society' by defining it in fairly conventional terms. Along the way he contradicts his earlier dismissal of internal-external and endogenous-exogenous distinctions. It suggests that all he actually rejects is the Parsonian systems-model of society, a model now largely forgotten by most theorists anyway. By dropping the word 'system', Mann says, we can develop a better definition. The definition concludes with the following proposition: 'A society is a unit with boundaries, and it contains interaction that is relatively dense and stable; that is, it is internally patterned when compared to interaction that crosses its boundaries.'[12] Along the same lines, as we shall see, Mann rejects master categories and then quietly sets one into the centre of his analysis, effectively reducing everything else to that category. In my terms rather than his, everything is reduced to the play of the 'means of organization'. Here is his big statement:

> Conceiving of societies as multiple overlapping and intersecting power networks gives us the best available entry into the issue of what is ultimately 'primary' or 'determining' in societies. *A general account of societies, their structure, and their history can best be given in terms of the interrelations of what I will call the four sources of power: ideological, economic, military, and political (IEMP) relationships.* These are (1) *overlapping networks of social interaction*, not dimensions, levels of factors of a single totality ... (2) They are also *organizations, institutionalized means of attaining human goals.* Their primacy comes not from the strength of human desires for ideological, economic, military or political satisfaction but from the *organizational means* each possesses to attain human goals, whatever these may be.[13]

Notwithstanding an over-emphasis on power as the defining process of being human (an over-emphasis shared by Michel Foucault), this could be a workable formula, except that it falls into a mass of tensions.

To summarize, the first set of problems surrounds the sophisticated move of rejecting the idea of a primary determinant, except as part of a proximate method, then treating the 'determination' in the same way that the figure of 'society' is treated. It is at once displaced but still the basis of all the manoeuvrings in his work. In this process the *means of organization* becomes the decapitated white king, sitting in the back row alongside the ghost piece 'society' as the knights and bishops of IEMP go forth in multiple contingent determinacy. At the same time, in a well-placed concern to avoid essentializing the 'motivational drives' to power, the term 'power' is emptied of its variable ontological meaning. In other words, at this level Gellner's dual focus on organization and culture is emptied of cultural depth. The four sources of social power come down to alternate organizational means of exacting social control – a very reductive way of setting up 'a general account of societies'. This is not even a '*mode* of organization' argument to match Marx's '*mode* of production' argument where the concept of 'mode' recognizes different forms of power. Organization, in Mann's approach, is reduced to a capacity question.

'My history of power rests on measuring sociospatial capacity for organization', he says.[14] Mann has given us the impression that his method gives us multiple sources of determinacy in the form of four sources of social power, but, at a more abstract epistemological level, *organization* becomes the one-dimensional master category. He writes: 'In various times and places each has offered enhanced capacity for organization that has enabled the form of its organization *to dictate* for a time the form of societies at large'.[15] It could not be a more forceful categorical claim – the dominant available means of organization *dictates* the form of the society, and not just for those wielding the power, but also 'at large', including presumably those upon whom it is imposed.

The second set of problems stems from having the four sources of power working at different levels of abstraction, or in different categorical registers. The realms of the ideological, the economic, and the political are conventional modernist analytically-distinguishable categories, thus the first thing that Mann has properly to do is to generalize them so that they are relevant across formations other than the modern. Ideology, for example, is broadened to refer to meanings, norms and aesthetic/ ritual practices. (This becomes his cultural dimension, though as I will discuss in a moment this will cause other problems.) However, the category of the political cannot be so broadened, because otherwise, given the contemporary use of the term as pertaining to the practices and institutions of social power, he would tautologously be talking about capacities for power deriving from practices of power. Thus political power is unceremoniously reduced to state power, and therefore it is mysteriously, unlike other forms of power, always territorially centralized, if not bounded.

That this solves one problem to set up another problem should be fairly obvious. For a project that sets out as the subtitle of the *Sources of Social Power* suggests – to be a history of power from the beginning – it is a profound limitation to close down the possibility of making sense of 'political power' in pre-state or non-state settings. Another problem is that reducing political power to state-power (defined as centralized and usually territorially bounded) is in tension with his forceful claim to challenge conventional notions of the boundedness of power.

Military power is the odd category out. The concept of military power is already narrower than the other three categories and does not relate to them as they potentially relate to each other. In conventional terms, military power refers to the dedicated institutionalized capacity to exert violent force, and for Michael Mann it is not much different – hence again it is not a category of analysis that can be used effectively in pre-state or non-state settings. Tribal community-polities do not tend to have institutions of warfare. The heading for his Chapter 2 gives the game away: 'How Pre-historic Peoples Evade Power'. Here Gellner's category of coercion would have been much more useful in this respect.

A third set of problems arises in relation to the analytical status of these sources of social power. In Mann's terms, drawing upon Max Weber's metaphor of the nineteenth-century railways, they are 'switchmen' or tracklaying vehicles with intermittent effect. Sometimes the dynamic of society is laid down by the economic (for example, Iron Age Europe), or the military (the 'Ancient Near Eastern' empires), or the ideological (for example, early Christendom). What this means gets confused. At one point he says that 'they are half ideal types, half actual social specifications'.[16] This is where a problem hinted at earlier comes back in with methodological consequences. If ideology is defined very broadly as meanings, norms and aesthetics/rituals, then it is always relevant at every tracklaying moment. The decisive rise of the European pike phalanx, for example, depends, as Mann himself tells us, not just on military tracklaying, but also on a multitude of ideological dimensions such as the egalitarianism of Flemish burghers, Swiss burghers and yeoman farmers.

## Patterns of practice: Pierre Bourdieu

While Michael Mann skims across world-history like a glider-pilot surveying the peaks and ridges of the terrain from above, Pierre Bourdieu is more like an on-the-ground cartographer, at once mathematically triangulating distances between landmarks *and* pacing out those distances on foot.[17] Whereas Mann is a historical sociologist who views human history through the frame of power *per se*, Bourdieu is a social theorist-anthropologist-sociologist who is much more interested in the world of meaning and values. Power in Bourdieu's hands is only one dimension of the constitutions of persons as acting subjects, not the all-encompassing means of tracking human history in general – but then he has almost no interest in the changing nature of social formations in history at all, and this for our purposes is one of the fundamental limitations of his approach. He is only interested in particularistic histories.

Bourdieu tends to use the concept of 'power' in terms of how it is accumulated in those particular histories and how it is expressed symbolically:

> symbolic capital is nothing more than economic or cultural capital which is acknowledged and recognized, when it is acknowledged in accordance with the categories of perception that it imposes, the symbolic power relations tend to reproduce and to reinforce the power relations which constitute the structure of the social space. More concretely, the legitimatization of the social order is not the product, as certain people believe, of a deliberately biased action of propaganda or symbolic imposition; it results from the fact that agents apply to the objective structures of the social world structures of perception and appreciation that have emerged from these objective structures and tend therefore to see the world as self-evident.[18]

The concept of 'capital' used here is taken from the tradition of historical materialism, but Bourdieu wants to take the concept further to understand how its use is commonplace and comes to be understood as self-evidently necessary. What is at stake is the accumulation of particular forms of capital – economic and cultural – across different fields of activity. Such activity is framed by what he calls *habitus*: 'systems of durable, transposable dispositions, structured structures predisposed to function as structuring structures, that is as principles which generate and organize practices and representations.'[19]

Whereas historical materialism, particularly in its structuralist version, put its emphasis on persons as subject to larger structures, and social relations as framed by the dominant mode of production as the base-category of determination, Pierre Bourdieu treats persons as agents with interests, acting within overlapping and variable normative conditions or *habitus*. In this respect, Bourdieu's approach can usefully be compared to a French contemporary of his, the Marxist anthropologist, Maurice Godelier. At the core of Godelier's position is the argument that 'a set of social relations dominates when they function simultaneously as social relations of production, as the social framework and support for the materialist process of the appropriation of nature'.[20] Here, Godelier stays unhelpfully faithful to the orthodox Marxist emphasis upon the mode of production. Indeed, he has to put his position through self-recognized contortions to save his variant of the base-superstructure framework. Although he has progressively become less happy with this analytical position, from his perspective, kinship in tribal societies becomes simultaneously relations of genealogy and relations of production. 'The truth', he says, however, 'is that one cannot and probably should not attempt such a correlation, because the main function of kinship relations is to reproduce human beings socially by acting upon them, and not to produce their material conditions of existence by acting upon nature.[21] Bourdieu, by contrast, hardly worries about issues of social determination. Instead we effectively get a brilliant general theory of particularistic social framing, handled quite differently through the concept of the *habitus* as an incorporated structuration of what people do and feel.

The concept of *habitus* is one of the most important recent contributions to contemporary social theory. As a concept, it leaves space for understanding how people participate in the everyday practice of making the various fields of their worlds, and contribute to framing, structuring and therefore to reproducing those worlds. Bourdieu comes closer than many Marxists to giving space to Marx's injunction that people make history but not under conditions of their own choosing. In this, Bourdieu is a structurationist (a concept that, as discussed in a moment, Anthony Giddens takes from Bourdieu and makes his own by giving it some different emphases). That is, Bourdieu is interested in how the patterns of practice can *be seen* to be objectively outside of the particular practices of persons even as the patterns were constituted by those persons as they subjectively took hold of the possibilities of acting in and through such a *habitus*. This last point also contains Bourdieu's second important contribution to social theory. He helps us to understand how to think about the object–subject relation; about the relation between life as practised and life as conceived from the distance of objectifying study. For example, his approach sensitizes us to recognizing what theory does when it abstracts an objective pattern of practice from the improvised messiness of life-ways. To the extent that humans are regulating self-conscious beings, there are objective patterns to practice, and both social theorists and 'ordinary people' can abstract these patterns. However, for the most part, people operate by just doing things and subjectively feeling what is practically possible.

Knowing about a social phenomenon and objectifying the patterns of that phenomena allows us (trained social theorists and unschooled social interpreters alike) to see social practices in a new light. It shows us a new 'truth' about the patterns of practice. However, it also epistemologically abstracts from those life-ways and therefore subtly, or not so subtly, changes their meaning. (This crucial point is developed and qualified in the first section of the next chapter 'Figures of abstraction, tableaux of life'.) This insight allows Bourdieu to distinguish three modes of knowledge: in the first mode we know the world phenomenally by living it sensually and practically; in the second mode we can objectify patterns from the unarticulated knowledge of the first level; in the third mode, as we break from the second, the observer observes and reflects on the nature of objectifying knowledge of the second mode. This last mode is the mode of reflexive theory that he thinks allows for good theory – reflexive in the sense that it reflects on the epistemological basis of its own knowledge claims; good in the sense that it has the potential to get beyond subjectivism or objectivism.

As Derek Robbins notes, the problem with this insight is that Bourdieu overgeneralizes the availability of each of these modes of knowledge to all people across quite distinct social formations. For Bourdieu, the tribal or traditional Algerians and French peasants that he studies can move up and down those levels in much the same way as a theoretically-informed anthropologist, even if they tend not to for the purposes of day-to-day practicalities.[22] For the present analysis, the point is not whether or not such moves are possible outside of reflexively-informed social theory – of course they are – but whether or not they are meaningfully structured into the dominant *habitus* of those formations. Here the term 'dominant' is important. A dominant frame or *habitus* here refers to a frame that imposes itself by a process of naturalization. It is presented as the obvious way of doing and thinking about things. Bourdieu uses such a notion of 'dominance', akin to Antonio Gramsci's concept of 'hegemony', but he does not carry this through to describing the ontological difference between different social formations, for example, to describing the difference between the tribalism and Berber traditionalism of the Kabyle in Algeria and the modernism of the Algerian fieldworkers from the Association pour la Recherche Démographique who interviewed the Kabyle people for his research.

Despite the strengths of Bourdieu's approach, its limits for developing a generalizing method for understanding the different basic formations in the world today are therefore significant. Perhaps indicative of the secret aversion to grand method even among some of the grand theorists themselves, Bourdieu tends to treat tribal, traditional and modern ways of life as taking basically the same social form with different content. There is the rare hint that Bourdieu is willing to countenance the notion of different forms of social formation constituted in the dominance of different ontological modes, but it is done with hesitation.

> Although I am suspicious of big dualist oppositions (hot societies versus cold societies, historic societies versus societies without history), one could say that as societies become more highly differentiated and as those relatively autonomous 'worlds' that I call fields develop in them, the chances that real events (that is, encounters between independent causal series, linked to different spheres of necessity) will happen in them will continue to increase, and so, therefore, will the liberty given to complex strategies of the *habitus*, integrating necessities of different orders.[23]

Those big dualist oppositions to which he refers are indeed a problem, but there must be a better way forward than either collapsing different forms of sociality into each other or distinguishing them in terms of the level of their differentiation between social fields. This proposition that societies move from being more to less integrated is the opposite of Mann's thesis of cycles of caging, beginning with the lack of integration in pre-state-bound clans and tribes and finishing with the caging of the nation-state. It actually accords with and has some of the same problems as Gellner's return to the process of the division of labour as the prime mover of social change. Overall, then, Pierre Bourdieu's major contributions to social theory are the concept of the *habitus* (that I will take forward in the notion of 'social framing' or 'enframing', used in a broader sense than the Heideggerian inflection that defines enframing as the demand to order nature[24]) and his rethinking of the object–subject relation (that I will take forward to help us rethink what it means to set up a grand method analysis at all).

## Structures of agency: Anthony Giddens

Anthony Giddens is very aware of the importance of history. His development of what he calls structuration theory appears implicitly to take on many of the insights of Pierre Bourdieu and to avoid some of its limitations (even though Giddens rarely acknowledges Bourdieu's massive influence on sociology and anthropology). Like Bourdieu, Giddens emphasizes the *reflexivity* of social agents. His variation on Bourdieu's modes of knowledge is to treat persons as knowledgeable actors grounded in three layers of consciousness: the unconscious (from Freud), practical consciousness (from Marx and Wittgenstein), and reflexive consciousness (unattributed).[25] This has the effect of bringing Freud and Marx's work into contention. This is Giddens' great skill – synthesizing the work of

Table 3.2  Anthony Giddens' approach: structures as they relate to orders of life

| Structure(s) | Theoretical domain | Institutional order |
|---|---|---|
| Signification | Theory of coding | Symbolic orders/modes of discourse |
| Domination | Theory of resource authorization | Political institutions |
|  | Theory of resource allocation | Economic institutions |
| Legitimation | Theory of normative regulation | Legal institutions |

Source: Giddens (1984), *The Constitution of Society*.

others into his own systematic schema. Similarly, the concept of 'structure', like the concept of *habitus*, is defined in terms of rules and normative frames. However, Giddens takes this further and adds in the dimension of resources: composed of authoritative resources (from Weber), which store the power to co-ordinate and drive the activity of other people; and allocative resources (sort of from Marx), which give the power to control the world of material products.[26] Giddens puts the emphasis on agency, and his method of structuration talks of agents living within the framework of structures, both constraining and enabling.

Whereas Gellner uses production, coercion, and cognition as his three basic modes of practice, Giddens uses domination (drawing upon authoritative power and allocative or productive power), signification, and legitimation. Like Michael Mann, Giddens unnecessarily makes the organization of power the master process: Domination 'is the very condition of the existence of codes of signification'.[27] Hence we are given Table 3.2.

From this base schema, Giddens distinguishes three fundamentally different types of society: tribal society, class-divided traditional society, and class society (namely capitalism). It is a tripartite series very similar to that presented by Ernest Gellner. As both of them would say, 'global history is not a world-growth story'. There is no teleology, no end-point, and no inevitability about the way we arrived at the present. One major difference is that Giddens' approach displays none of Gellner's reductiveness in taking the division of labour as the driving force of history. On the other hand, Gellner's strength is in driving through the full implications of his method to develop an extraordinarily influential theory of the nation. His is an approach with such power that writers in the area had to attend to it despite its weaknesses. By comparison, Giddens never applied his approach in a systematic way to explaining any actual social formation. For example, his work on the nation-state is full of brilliantine but undeveloped insights. In the end, his major book *The Nation-State and Violence* gives us little more than a series of analyses of the factors that were associated with the rise of this new form of polity-community: namely, the centralization of administrative power, including the development of the surveillance state; the abstraction of law over customary sanctions; the fiscal reorganization of money including the development of tax systems; and military developments both in the area of technology and organization.[28] There is a chapter in the book on 'Capitalism, Industrialism and Social Transformation', but it does not present any substantive analysis on what this means for the formation of the phenomenon that he is trying to explain. Giddens had other areas to cover, from the rise of modernity[29] to the meaning of globalization,[30] and he did not have time to linger.

There is not the space here to give more than an inkling of Anthony Giddens' extraordinary historical range and theory-composing gymnastics. What I want to do is point to Giddens' one great contribution to the theory and method of understanding social formation. Like Bourdieu's concept of the *habitus*, it had a profound effect in opening up new ways of thinking about and naming a social process. I am referring to the concept of 'time-space distantiation'. The 'generic concern of the theory of structuration', he says, 'is with how social systems "bind" time and space'.[31] Time-space distantiation refers to the way in which different social formations are stretched across time and space beyond the immediacy of embodied presence. The whole of human history is characterized by the coexistence of different kinds of societies with different dominant frames of time-space, living alongside or overlapping each other along what he calls 'time-space edges'. Tribal formations are characterized by high-presence availability whereas modern formations extend social relations across increasing reaches of time and space by the various media of storage – for example, writing offers the possibility for storing and regulating modes of discourse in a way that human memory does not; money offers possibilities for 'bridging distances' (Simmel's phrase) in a way that direct exchange does not. There is a lot to follow up here, but there are also problems to be overcome. As Derek Gregory writes:

> Giddens treats time-space distantiation as essentially progressive, entailing the gradual widening of systems of interaction. By doing so he minimizes the volatility of these extensions. The landscapes of modern capitalism provide some of the most vivid examples. They are riven by a deep-seated tension between polarization in place and dispersal over space. On the one side, constellations of productive activity are pulled into a 'structured coherence' at local and regional scales, while on the other side these territorial complexes are dissolved away through the restructuring and resynthesis of labour processes. The balance between them – the geography of capital accumulation – is drawn through time-space distantiation as a discontinuous process of the production of space.[32]

I want to carry forward Giddens' work on time-space distantiation, but instead of getting caught in the double bind of a spatial metaphor (distance) applying also to time, I will use the insights of Geoff Sharp in reworking the concept as *time-space abstraction*, where abstraction is discussed in terms of processes of rationalization, commodification, codification, mediation, and objectification, as well as distantiation or what I will rather tend to call 'extension'.

## Unstable patterns of meaning: Michel Foucault

One writer who cannot be accused of any form of progressivism or of treating the world as a *stable* ordered pattern is Michel Foucault. Even in his book *The Order of Things*, a study of the process of ordering some schemes of Western scientific knowledge from the seventeenth century to the beginning of the nineteenth, he is careful to say that 'order' is based on an ambiguous epistemology:

> Order is, at one and the same time, that which is given in things as their inner law, the hidden network that determines the way they confront one another, and also that which has no existence except in the grid created by a glance, an examination, a language; and it is only in the blank spaces of this grid that order manifests itself in depth as though already there, waiting in silence for the moment of its expression.[33]

While that book contained very little methodological signposting, his next book *The Archaeology of Knowledge* is more explicit. As he sets up his archaeological method, Foucault makes it clear that his aim is to document adequately different fields of human practice and discourse while avoiding the imposition of any categories which presume cultural totalities whether they are ideal types or assertions of a 'spirit of the age'.[34] But having eschewed ideas of structure or totality, he is happy to argue for the discursive patterning of social life: 'whenever, between objects, types of statement, concepts, or thematic choices, one can define a regularity (an order, correlations, positions and functionings, transformations) we will say, for the sake of convenience, that we are dealing with a discursive formation'[35]

How is this different from a history of ideas? For one, Foucault recognizes the contingency of the order that he analyses as characterizing discursive formations. However, more than that he argues that layers of contradictions run deep within the dominant expressions of coherence and ordering. Third, he suggests that archaeological method avoids theorizing general forms in favour of outlining only particular configurations. Fourth, it emphasizes breaks, changes, gaps, transformations, thresholds and ruptures without fetishizing those ruptures and changes as signifying anything monumental or all-embracing. Finally, for Foucault, archaeological method sets out to achieve a reflexive distance before the material that it is examining.[36]

Of those claims it is the third that I have trouble with. To use Foucault against himself, if it is important not to simply reverse the process of concentrating on totalities by fetishizing ruptures and discontinuities – thus essentializing change rather than continuity as the basis of social life – then it should be equally important not to fetishize the study of the particular rather than the general.

Within the provisos and qualifications as set out throughout the course of this chapter, including Foucault's proviso relating to the contingency of any method for describing social formations as we move from the particular to the general and back again, the stage is set for the next chapter. Is it possible to develop a grand method that qualifies its status as a generalizing method without completely wiping itself out before it begins? Is it possible to set up a method that is useful for understanding the complexities of the world without becoming so complex itself that it loses any purchase on how we live today? Developing a response to those questions is the task of the rest of *Globalism, Nationalism, Tribalism*.

## NOTES

1 Empire is included in this list notwithstanding the large number of writings these days that are beginning to use 'empire' as a master category of the new world order. While the empire-of-capital-and-signs has been given a new life, despite its extensions of abstract power, I argue that it has overlaid rather than supplanted the nation-state.

2 The concept of 'plane of being' is taken from Geoff Sharp, 'Constitutive Abstraction and Social Practice', *Arena*, 70, 1985, pp. 48–82.

3 Anthony Giddens, *A Critique of Historical Materialism*, vol. 1, *Power, Property and the State*, Macmillan, London, 1981.

4 Ernest Gellner, *Nations and Nationalism*, Basil Blackwell, London, 1983; *Plough, Sword and Book: The Structure of Human History*, Collins Harvill, London, 1988; *Encounters with Nationalism*, Blackwell Publishers, Oxford, 1994.

5 For a discussion of Gellner's life as a 'pure visitor', see John A. Hall, 'Conditions of Our Existence: Ernest Gellner (1925–1995)', *New Left Review*, no. 215, 1995, pp. 156–60.

6 W.G. Runciman, *A Treatise on Social Theory*, vol. 2, *Substantive Social Theory*, Cambridge University Press, Cambridge, 1989.

7 Gellner, *Plough, Sword and Book*, p. 92 and Chapter 2.

8 *Ibid.*, p. 197.

9 Ernest Gellner, *Conditions of Liberty: Civil Society and its Rivals*, Penguin, Harmondsworth, 1996.

10 Michael Mann, *The Sources of Social Power*, vol. 1: *A History of Power From the Beginning to A.D. 1760*, Cambridge University Press, Cambridge, 1986; 'The Autonomous Power of the State: Its Origins, Mechanisms and Results', in John A. Hall (ed.), *States in History*, Basil Blackwell, Oxford, 1986; *States, War and Capitalism: Studies in Political Sociology*, Basil Blackwell, Oxford, 1988; *The Rise and Decline of the Nation State* (editor), Basil Blackwell, Oxford, 1990; *The Sources of Social Power*, vol. 2: *The Rise of Classes and Nation-States, 1760–1914*, Cambridge University Press, Cambridge, 1993.

11 *Ibid.*, *Sources of Social Power*, vol. 1, p. 1 (his italics).

12 *Ibid.*, p. 13. Compare this to his the statement on page 1: 'We can never find a single bounded society in geographical or social space.' In the light of his own definition we clearly can find such a society. Why did he not just say that the status of the claim to define social space as a lived society is always a contingent and relative one? Societies are always cross-cut by other societies and social formations. By this definition we can also find his dreaded 'dimensions' or 'levels'. Just like 'sources of power' (his terms of abstraction) they can be useful analytical abstractions.

13 *Ibid.*, p. 2. (his emphasis).

14 *Ibid.*, p. 3.

15 *Ibid.*, emphasis added.

16 *Ibid.*, p. 507.

17 Pierre Bourdieu's *Outline of a Theory of Practice* (Cambridge University Press, Cambridge, 1977) sets out the overall framework of his approach. Later important contributions include *Distinction: A Social Critique of the Judgement of Taste*, Cambridge University Press, Harvard, 1984; *Homo Academicus*, Polity Press, Cambridge, 1988; *The Logic of Practice*, Polity Press, Cambridge, 1990; and *Language and Symbolic Power*, Polity Press, Cambridge, 1991.

18 Pierre Bourdieu, *In Other Words: Essays Towards a Reflexive Sociology*, Polity Press, Oxford, 1990, p. 135.

19 Bourdieu, *The Logic of Practice*, p. 53.

20 Maurice Godelier, *The Mental and the Material: Thought, Economy and Society*, Verso, London, 1988, p. 20.

21 *Ibid.*, pp. 21–2. By contrast, I will argue later (Chapter 5) that, in the spirit of Godelier's concern not to reduce 'the mental' to 'the material', kinship is central to the organization form of tribal society, and in this capacity bears back on the other modes of practice, including the organization of relations of production. That is not to say, however (*pace* Godelier), that kinship is the basis of the mode of production.

22 Derek Robbins, *The Work of Pierre Bourdieu*, Open University Press, Milton Keynes, 1991, pp. 82–4.

23 Pierre Bourdieu, *In Other Words: Essays towards a Reflexive Sociology*, Polity Press, Cambridge, 1990, p. 73.

24 Martin Heidegger, *The Question Concerning Technology and Other Essays*, Harper & Row, New York (1954–5) 1977, pp. 19ff.

25 Anthony Giddens, *The Constitution of Society: Outline of the Theory of Structuration*, Polity Press, Cambridge, 1984, Chapter 2.

26 Anthony Giddens, *A Contemporary Critique of Historical Materialism*, vol. 1: *Power, Property and the State*, Macmillan, London, 1981.

27 Giddens, *The Constitution of Society*, p. 31.

28 Anthony Giddens, *The Nation-State and Violence: Volume Two of a Contemporary Critique of Historical Materialism*, Polity Press, Cambridge, 1985.

29 Anthony Giddens, *The Consequences of Modernity*, Polity Press, Cambridge, 1991.

30 Anthony Giddens, *Runaway World: How Globalization is Reshaping our Lives*, Profile Books, London, 2nd edn, 2002. By the time he reaches his study of globalization, his original method barely informs the analysis. As with *The Transformation of Intimacy*, most of the work on the structuring of society-in-dominance has been dropped. See Anthony Giddens, *The Transformation of Intimacy: Sexuality, Love and Eroticism in Modern Societies*, Polity Press, Cambridge, 1992.

31 Giddens, *Contemporary Critique*, p. 90.

32 Derek Gregory, 'Presences and Absences: Time-Space Relations and Structuration Theory', in David Held and John B. Thompson (eds), *Social Theory of Modern Societies: Anthony Giddens and his Critics*, Cambridge University Press, Cambridge, 1989, p. 207.

33 Michel Foucault, *The Order of Things: An Archaeology of the Human Sciences*, Tavistock Publications, London, 1970, p. xx.

34 Michel Foucault, *The Archaeology of Knowledge*, Routledge, London, (1969) 1989, p. 15.
35 *Ibid.*, p. 38.
36 It is this last implicit claim that leads Hubert L. Dreyfus and Paul Rabinow (*Michel Foucault: Beyond Structuralism and Hermeneutics*, University of Chicago Press, Chicago, 1982, p. 100), to suggest that '*The Archaeology of Knowledge* is followed by a self-imposed silence that is finally broken by two books in which the author, while still using archaeological techniques, no longer claims to speak from a position of phenomenological detachment.'

# FOUR Theory in the Shadow of Terror

Across the globe, we face a general and slow crisis. The generality of the crisis is peculiar because, apart from environmentalists talking about the slow degradation of the planet through processes such as global warming, generalized doom-saying had until recently tended to retreat to the margins of social discourse. The crisis is marked, paradoxically, both by fast, localized episodes and by a 'slow' generality that seems to elude social theoretical explanation. The dual metaphor of immediacy and slowness helps us, at least provisionally, to evoke the continuous momentum of transformation over the past century and, at the same time, to encapsulate the various and immediate moments of upheaval. It is a crisis about which we now tend to talk in the plural: crises of meaning, crises of structural adjustment, and crises of international organization. It is as if the multifarious and particular crises are not part of an explicable and interconnected pattern of change, a pattern that is fundamentally disrupting prior forms of social life. At best, it seems that all we can do in describing that uneven pattern is to point to the speed of change or the globalization of effect.

The general processes that underlie the various crises are rarely named explicitly. And when they are, theorists turn to reductive or unconvincing metaphors such as the rise of Empire, the clash of civilizations, or the battle between Jihad and McWorld.[1] The anti-globalization movement calls it 'globalization', but with far too much emphasis on peak institutions such as the World Trade Organization. More usually the processes of crisis are evoked in terms of countless *trouble spots* around the world: the Israeli-Palestine question, the Kosovo aftermath, or the Congolese slow genocide. The acts of one day – the day of terrorism on September 11 2001 – subjectively could have changed this sense of multiple unconnected crises, but they did not. It refocussed the concern of the mainstream on one aspect of the globalizing response. Ignoring core questions about where the world is headed, politicians and pundits explained away terrorism as irrational hatred and attributed previously unconnected activities to the networked genius of a single shadowy organization variously called 'al-Qaida', 'al-Qa'ida' or 'al-Qaeda'. When those then-unnamed terrorists attacked the World Trade Center and the Pentagon, the act was not taken as a sign of a world-in-crisis economically and militarily, politically and culturally. It was all too quickly brought under ostensible control by desperately seeking to name both the perpetrators and the international response. Hence, a 'network of networks' with a small core network was named 'al-Qaeda'[2] and a series of half-thought-through military retaliations was projected as a purposive and sustainable response and called 'the War on Terror'. The one-day crisis was over, but the 'war' would continue for years.

At an analytic or theoretical level, the inability to understand the generality and cross-cutting connections of the crises has related manifestations. One issue can be elucidated through a discussion of the way that the concept of 'crisis' no longer fits its age-old definition – at least not in the sense that the concept was taken to refer to a particular and definitive turning-point. Except for that one act, now known in the United States by its convenience-store appellation, '9-11', a crisis is no longer contained as a dangerous time when normality is suspended and the future requires an immediate response. In particular, it no longer carries the Greek root of *krisis*, turning point of a 'decision'. Our political leaders cannot admit to the fact that they need to rethink policy. In more comprehensive terms, contradictions between layers of social relations from the local to the global have become so stretched as to undermine the possibility that a single decision or even set of decisions can be assumed to make a definitive impact on a generalized problem.

Anthony Giddens gets at part of the problem when he argues that under these circumstances, although crises cannot be easily routinized, they have become a 'normal' part of life. However, when he says that 'understanding the juggernaut-like nature of modernity goes a long way towards explaining why, in conditions of high modernity, crisis becomes normalized',[3] his position becomes shaky. It certainly goes some way to providing a single-level explanation, but in the process the comment flattens out what a more adequate explanation should entail. Pointing, as Giddens rightly does, to the way that the disembedding of traditional verities leaves people feeling dependent on the security of late-modern expert systems and day-to-day routine, still misses out on the continuing and contradictory relevance of both traditional ways of life and the emerging relevance of postmodern subjectivities and possibilities. These simultaneously make this new and brave savage-world an exciting and horrifically daunting place.

It immediately raises two challenges for an adequate theoretical method. These are challenges that emerged long before September 11, but which the awful events of that day highlighted. The first is to understand the emerging 'totalization' and abstraction of social life by high-tech, information-based globalizing capitalism; the second is to take into account the simultaneous impact upon this earth of countervailing formations of social life, sensibility and practice – for example, forms of *re*-traditionalization or reconstituted tribalism. In effect, these are two sides of the same question, addressing what Louis Dumont referred to as a 'culture closed in upon itself and identifying humanity with its own specific form'.[4]

The first challenge suggests that we need to be able to theorize a new formation of social being that some writers such as Anthony Giddens refuse to acknowledge – a level of postmodern abstraction from the limits of traditional and even modern relations. In the military realm, the examples of the postmodern war-machine are chilling, particularly when the systematic effects of the new weaponry on human populations is described. This is only made more striking by the dominant tendency to categorize civilians who get killed in war by the abstracting euphemism of 'collateral damage'. The contemporary war-machine is, in part, dependent upon a way of being that allows persons to sit in hermetically sealed cockpits, so high above that world that their planes cannot be seen, and safely press buttons to release bombs called 'daisy cutters' on abstracted strangers far below. In other words, the deployment and scientific enhancement of ways of killing-at-a-distance – a drive with many lines of continuity to the classical modern war-machine – have been taken to a new level. The dropping of the atomic bomb on Hiroshima and the use of napalm in Vietnam to the flying of flechettes in the Gaza Strip, cannot be explained simply in terms of attempts to re-establish national security, at least not in the modern sense.[5] The dominant reality is obviously very different, as partly captured by Ulrich Beck's notion of the risk society.[6]

The second related methodological challenge is to place the continuing relevance of tribalism and traditionalism into the heart of the approach. Whether we are trying to understand the aftermath of September 11 and the wars in Afghanistan and Iraq, the plight of the world's 20 million AIDS sufferers in the face of mercenary pharmaceutical companies, or the techno-scientific turn to experiment on human embryo parts, social life cannot be reduced to the effects of the juggernaut of abstract globalization – as powerful as it is. Even in relation to the dominant machines of globalization, we need to be able to acknowledge the continuing if 'subordinate' importance of tribal and traditional ways of life. Here 'subordinate' is a relative term, only understood as such in terms of power, and relative to the force of contemporary hyper-modernizing and postmodernizing practices.

Massed against the Anglo-American military in Afghanistan, what did we see other than intellectually-trained (modern-influenced) clerics who had chosen a neo-traditional form of Islam, finding an alliance with tribal people who still live in communities bounded by lines of kinship and reciprocal exchange? It is important to remember that after the calling to Holy War, hundreds of Pashtun tribesmen, most of whom had never before fought for the Taliban, moved across the Pakistani border region and into towns such a' Quetta.

This relates to a third manifestation of the difficulty of talking about the contemporary crisis, and in turn to a third challenge for method. It can be seen in the way that locality, community, has become simultaneously lived as a haven and horror, as a source of nostalgic retreat and a place where evil resides just beneath the civil surface. Emphasizing one side of those sensibilities – whether it is portrayed through the small-town surface of *Blue Velvet* or the all-American neighbourhood of *Arlington Road*[7] – the commercial mainstream is happy to run with tag-lines 'fear thy neighbour, ... your paranoia is real'. They now accept that 'terrorism' can strike here deep into the heart of our personal, familial and national bodies. Emphasizing the other side, globalizing corporations paradoxically offer up local places, local heroes or local accents as sources of solace and interconnection when they address their various markets across the world. A classic Nescafé advertisement draws on the current Western nostalgia for 'old-style' face-to-face community. Backed by images of rural idyll, the narrator speaks of a world that can still exist if you make the right life-style choices:

> My name is Gillian Stone. I feel like this valley has chosen me. There's a closeness, a realness here, that many I know have lost or put away like a winter coat in spring, there but forgotten ... I envied them. Even the simple act of sharing coffee somehow melted the barriers that I was so used to putting up ... I can't ever remember being quite so together as I have been in this valley. Here when people ask 'How are you?' they are interested in the answer. It is as if I'd tumbled like some fairy-tale Alice into a different kind of place ... It's a place where friendships are easily made, as easily as sharing a cup of Nescafé and having a chat.[8]

The advertising line here is cynically *postmodern*, just as the sentiments expressed reflect a lived *modernist* nostalgia for a putatively *traditional* sense of place when face-to-face communion bound self and community together. How different is this from the layers of meaning in the title of the US office of Homeland Security. Life is now so confusing. How is social analysis to cope with the reality that such nostalgia for home and embodied connection is more than either a postmodern disembodied simulacrum or modern media-projection? How is it possible to develop a methodology that neither reasserts a modernist confidence that all can be revealed by a structural analysis of the form of mediation nor accepts the postmodern collapse of lived meaning into the play of signifiers? The task here is to recognize, both practically and methodologically, the contradictions both between the layers of ontological formation – from the tribal to the postmodern – and between the layers of social integration – from the face-to-face to the disembodied.

In short, what I am suggesting is that the slow crisis in social life is accompanied by a slow crisis of explanation in social theory. This chapter attempts to set up an alternative form of interpretative method that attempts to directly confront this problem of explanation as it hits the reality of a world constituted in contradiction. As the opening stage of that task we have to enter the labyrinthine netherworld of epistemology. That is, we have to seek a way of seeing things – whether from a distance or close to the detail – that always acknowledges where it stands as it attempts analytically to draw out meaningful patterns from the 'chaos' of human practice and meaning. This then is the fourth methodological challenge: to develop an approach that enables us to make generalizing claims about the dominant patterns of practice in the world today without overlooking the sometimes messy, contingent, often accidental confluence of happenings, feelings and face-to-face encounters that make each of our lives meaningful. In the shadow of an earlier reign of terror, given expression in the Nazi Holocaust, the Stalinist gulags and the US unleashing of the abstract war-machine upon the people of Hiroshima, significant traditions of social theory retreated. In particular, they retreated along two parallel lines into a postmodern or empiricist fear of Grand Theory. They were concerned that attempting to explain the patterns or structures of life involved, by analogy, a totalitarian imposition of generalizing abstract theory upon everyday life, akin to Stalin's Gulag. Postmodern writers came to locate the only legitimate form of analysis at the level of contingent micro-practices and settings, while empiricists were afraid to venture out beyond the safety of their gatherings of facts.

These concerns might even be half-right, but in being also half-wrong, they distort an important task of our time. They reduce the task of understanding of how we live now in such a way that, first, made it impossible to develop a sense of the social whole, and, second, made us embarrassed about projecting the possibilities of together acting differently. Meanwhile, the totalizing juggernaut rolls on with new bells and whistles, with new items for consumption, and with new techniques of killing.

## Figures of abstraction, tableaux of life

'It is not necessary to read on if methodological explanation does not thrill you.' We've read variations of that sentence many times in books written at the end of the twentieth century and the beginning of this. Have you ever wondered why, when an author is about to explain the secrets to his or her approach, they become embarrassed? In the nineteenth century and at its turn, theorists were unabashed that readers would have to do the hard work. Karl Marx confidently says that any reader 'who on the whole desires to follow me must be resolved to ascend from the particular to the general'.[9] Georg Simmel begins the first chapter of his magnum opus at the deep end with a discussion conducted under the heading of 'Reality and value as mutually independent values through which our conceptions become images of the world'.[10] Thereafter, he never comes up for air. Now, with the different demands of late-modernity it is relatively uncommon for a book of generalizing social theory to be published. However, the next part of the present chapter does traverse unfamiliar ground. For what it is worth, I can say that it is possible to read the rest of this book without knowing how the parts of the general approach are systematically interconnected. Many sentences or sections further down the way will remain mysterious; however, it is quite possible to understand the face of the argument or use the method in its parts. Perhaps like contemporary computer games that take the players to more and more hidden levels as they become more familiar with the terrain, rules and methods of the game, this book might have been better organized by hiding the methodology chapter at the end. However, I am working on the assumption that when reading theoretical material, it is useful to have the map available from the beginning.

One pathway into the problem is to introduce the mystery of maps and tables. Just as they are not the real world in *toto* but rather epistemological abstractions from and in that world, we should be under no illusion that the maps and figures presented here are much more than analytical approximations of the incredible social complexity that surrounds us.[11] These abstract representations of the narrative landscape, even with all their heaped-up qualifications, have to be taken as orienting guides rather than rigid directives. The following discussion in this chapter, and those that follow, makes extensive use of figures or tables as ordering devices. However, they are used to simplify entry into the analysis, not to make it look social scientific. They are provisional attempts to make sense of things. They are inductively put down on paper after a time of continually moving back and forth between practice and theory. Sometimes the tables will be minimal matrixes, sometimes they will be tables that run into text, but they are always intended as conditional ways of sensitizing research, rather than as fixed templates.[12] Three very different writers – Michel Foucault, Pierre Bourdieu and Geoff Sharp – have opened up instructive ways of thinking about the nature of tables and diagrams, although by the end of this discussion the present approach will have departed quite significantly from the work of Foucault and Bourdieu.

Harking back to the earlier discussion of the Chinese encyclopedia (Chapter 1), Foucault suggested that Borges gives us an entirely inappropriate connection between the elements of taxonomy when he sets the elements out in an enumerated list from 'a' to 'n'. The illustration is well known, but there is a paragraph that is usually skipped over. It carries a residual modernism that is rarely read into Foucault:

> [Borges] does away with the *site*, the mute ground upon which it is possible for entities to be juxtaposed ... What has been removed, in short, is the famous 'operating table' ... I use that word 'table' in two superimposed senses: the nickel-plated rubbery table swathed in white, glimmering beneath a glass sun devouring all shadow – the table where, for an instant, perhaps forever, the umbrella encounters the sewing machine; and also a table, a tabula, that enables thought to operate upon the entities of our world, to put them in order, to divide them into classes, to group them according to names that designate their similarities and their differences – the table upon which, since the beginning of time, language has intersected space.[13]

Ordering and abstraction are thus lived human activities, which makes the reflexive (theoretical) orderings of life a difficult but not empty task. Beyond Foucault we can confirm that umbrellas do encounter sewing machines off the *analytical* operating table. The material abstraction of money (discussed extensively in Chapter 5), for example, makes them momentarily commensurable on the lived and thus material tableaux of exchange value.

The second quote comes from Bourdieu. He is concerned to say that while the mapping is not the same as the world from which it is abstracted, setting the map out on paper is still of heuristic value:

> So care must be taken not to see anything more than a theoretical artefact in the diagram that brings together in condensed synoptic form the information accumulated by a process of collection that was initially oriented by a semi-conscious intention of combining all the productions recorded so as to construct a kind of unwritten score ... However, although they are perfectly inadequate theoretically, ... [diagrams] are useful in two ways. First, they offer an economical way of giving the reader information reduced to its pertinent features and organized in accordance with a principle that is both familiar and immediately visible. Secondly, they make it possible to show some of the difficulties that arise from the endeavour to combine and linearize the available information and to give a sense of the artificiality of the 'objectified calendar', the idea of which has been taken for granted and has oriented all collections of rites, proverbs and practices.[14]

Thus, in Bourdieu's qualified sense, tables are useful theoretical artefacts. However, probably because in this passage he is writing about predominantly oral cultures, Bourdieu exaggerates the divide between analytical tables and the tableaux of life. I want to make one more claim – that under some historical conditions tables are accorded a status approaching maps and calendars.[15] In some cases this parallel is obvious. Think of the extent to which the multiplication table and the Periodic Table of Elements have been naturalized as pictures of their respective universes. Tables, like theories, are artefacts of a kind that people in textual cultures use without necessarily being aware of it – sometimes at a loss, sometimes to distort or oversimplify and mislead, and sometimes as figures of new insight. As Geoff Sharp puts it 'the periodic table lays some sort of claim to representing abstractly the "real" building blocks of nature in a way that is scarcely available to direct perception or to commonsense'.[16] In his terms, however, because this epistemological abstraction is embedded in a broader culture of abstracted social relations the table itself is lived as 'really real'. It is the ordered 'reality' which lies beneath the messiness of the phenomenal world.

What is the Freudian figure of the levels of the conscious and unconscious, or the Marxian-Weberian topoi of the layers of class – working and ruling, higher and lower – other than lived tableaux of abstraction? In psychoanalytically-educated and self-consciously-classed societies, we use them practically and act through them all the time in everyday contexts. Why is a line of perspective or a line of weather map called a 'cold front'? Bourdieu himself put it better than I ever could. Writing in an earlier volume, he says the problem is that the theoretical calendar, just like the commonplace calendar that hangs on our walls, 'cannot be understood unless it is set down on paper'. At the same time, 'it is impossible to understand how it works unless one fully realizes that it exists only on paper'.[17]

I would change only one word of that quote: the word 'only'. It is impossible to understand how tables and calendars work unless one fully realizes that although they may come into reflexive existence 'on paper', they often have a practical existence in thought and deed. There are two qualifications implied here. First, it is quite possible to develop abstract schemas within tribal and traditional societies that do not depend upon the being abstracted on paper. For example, the Mambai of East Timor metaphorically lift knowledge out of nature and talk of keeping a treasure of 'words ... inside their stomachs'.[18] They also use the metaphor of the tree of knowledge, in parallel to biblical writings. The second qualification relates to the question of theory or literature itself. Yes, these sheets of paper are sometimes illuminated through analytical and political necessity by an artificial 'sun devouring all shadow'. However, the figures that they carry can nevertheless be drawn in ways that add layers of shading. Paradoxically, in this case, one of those layers of shading is added by drawing attention to the fact that the shading itself is only an analytical technique of abstraction. However, here the word 'only' does not take away from the immense ontological power of that process. Witness, for example, the French novelist Gustave Flaubert (1821–1880) writing about the exotic city of Cairo: 'Each detail reaches out to grip you; it pinches you; and the more that you concentrate on it the less you grasp the whole. Then all of this becomes harmonious and the pieces fall into place themselves, in accordance with the laws of perspective'.[19] In other words, at the point that the barbaric otherness of the place becomes overwhelming, Flaubert finds the solace of harmonious order in the modernist abstracting principle of perspective. In a continuity that carries us from Queen Victoria and Lawrence of Arabia to George W. Bush and Benjamin Barber, the Orient is thus brought into line – Jihad versus McWorld according to more or less taken-for-granted laws of metaphorical abstraction.

## Mapping an alternative method

Sensitive to the problems discussed here and in the previous chapter, the method comes out of the tradition of historical materialism. However, it attempts critically and selectively to subsume some of the language and insights of other traditions: from anthropological thick-description and historical sociology to structuralism and post-structuralist deconstruction. How is this possible without being reduced to contradictory eclecticism?

The method begins by presuming the importance of a first-order abstraction, here called empirical analysis. It entails drawing out and generalizing from on-the-ground detailed descriptions of history and place. This does not mean accepting 'what the natives say' (Geertz) as an adequate explanation of the determinations and framing of social life. However, it does take such descriptions seriously as expressive of the phenomenal experience of the world. All social theories, whether they acknowledge it or not, are dependent upon a process of first-order abstraction. This first level either involves generating empirical description based on observation, experience, recording or experiment – in other words, abstracting evidence from that which exists or occurs in the world – or it involves drawing upon the empirical research of others. The first level of analytical abstraction is an ordering of 'things in the world', before any kind of further analysis is applied to those 'things'. From this often taken-for-granted level, many approaches work towards a second-order abstraction,

```
1. empirical analysis
2. conjunctural analysis      increasing abstraction
3. integrational analysis
4. categorical analysis
```

Figure 4.1  Levels of analytical abstraction

a method of some kind for ordering and making sense of that empirical material.[20] At the very least, they occasionally move to an unacknowledged second level either to explain or to rationalize the first. The present approach works across four such levels of methodological abstraction. Thus, empirical generalization is one level, set within a broader theory of different levels of *analytical* abstraction. Figure 4.1 shows the different levels of analytical abstraction.[21]

There is nothing magical about having chosen four levels.[22] These levels of analysis are simply understood as four different ways of looking at social phenomena. For example, if we wanted to examine the formation of the nation-state, we could (and should) in rich comparative detail describe the extant nation-states of the world and their histories.[23] We could then draw out empirical generalizations about the historical events and processes, political pressures, ideas and practices, that in giving rise to each one of those nation-states gave rise to the social formation we call *the* 'nation-state'. The processes of globalization can be analysed in the same way. However, what are these things, 'events' and 'processes', so innocently written into the previous sentences? They are patterns of activity, categorized by concepts of abstract ordering. Already smuggled into this first-order abstraction of method – this level of empirical generalization – are even more abstract presumptions about events and processes of social life. All that I intend to do in the following discussion is take away the innocence of those abstract presumptions. Events, ideas, categories, processes, patterns, practices, and structures all lead a double life. They are at the same time, practical lived ways of being and – to rewrite Foucault's earlier comment through Geoff Sharp – materially-abstracted *tableaux* upon which, since the beginning of acculturated natural time, meaning *and* practice have intersected as ways of being in the world.

The second level of analytical abstraction, *conjunctural analysis*, draws on the strengths of neo-Marxist approaches to historical materialism while rejecting any moves to reduce social practice to the determinations of the mode of production. It similarly rejects the argument of writers such as Claude Lévi-Strauss when they posit that the basis of all life is the mode of exchange.[24] Thus the second step of the method entails examining the conjunctures of various modes of practice in any particular social formation, from production to communication. In other words, the primacy of the category *mode of production* is displaced, taking it out of its orthodox location in an economically-reductionist base–superstructure framework. This is done not by rejecting the category itself, but by extending Marx's analysis of the mode (the means and relations) of production to an understanding of other *modes of practice*, in particular, modes of exchange, communication, organization and enquiry. Thus, the emphasis of a writer such as Max Weber on modern bureaucracy can be drawn into a much broader framework and discussed in terms of the dominant modern mode of organization. In general terms, the second level of analytical abstraction involves identifying and more importantly examining *the intersection* of various modes of practice (established sociological, anthropological and political categories of analysis) or ways of framing the 'things in the world' defined in the first level.

It would be easy, and for the purpose of understanding the full complexity of social life, necessary to extend upon this list of modes of practice – for example, to add further modes of practice such as consumption or reproduction – but the present list is sufficiently comprehensive for what I want to do. *The mode of consumption* (from Jean Baudrillard and Chris Rojek) can be derived from the intersection of the modes of production and exchange. Similarly, the *mode of regulation*, discussed by the French regulationist school of Alain Lipietz and Michel Aglietta, can be derived from the intersection of the modes of exchange and organization. The *mode of reproduction*, discussed by feminist writers such as Heidi Hartman and Catherine MacKinnon, can be understood in terms of the intersection of other modes of practice, including production, organization and enquiry, when deployed in relation to the level of the embodied or face-to-face relations of integration. The *mode of domination* (Pierre Bourdieu) can be analysed by examining how power operates through all the modes of practice. The approach thus parallels, but has significant divergences from, Jürgen Habermas's move to recognize the analytical and political advantages of separating out communication and production.[25] It also overlaps with Mark Poster's discussion of the importance of what he calls the 'mode of information'. However, it rejects any implicit suggestion in his work, and that of others such as Gianni Vattimo, that in the contemporary period a new mode of information is assuming an emergent pre-eminence over the mode of production.[26] Rather, it argues that to understand the transition from industrial capitalism to globalizing information capitalism as the dominant but not exclusive *formation of practice*, we have to study each of the changing modes of practice and the uneven conjunctures between them. Our examination of the changing nature of polities and communities proceeds by the same method to explore how they have been reconstituted by changes in the modes of production, exchange, communication, organization and enquiry. This has the side-effect of facilitating a manageable approach to questions that have never been adequately addressed in the literature. What is the relationship between globalizing capitalism and the nation-state? Is the nation-state in crisis? These questions become relevant here as background to the argument that with the change in the form of capitalism (understood as a social formation structured as intersecting modes of practice), the form of the nation-state has also been changing. It allows us to say that the modern nation-state may be in slow crisis, but that does not mean that it is fragmenting across all levels of social life.

The third level of entry into discussing the complexity of social relations, *integrational analysis*, examines the intersecting modes of social integration and differentiation. These different modes of integration are expressed here in terms of different ways of relating to and distinguishing oneself from others – from the face-to-face to the disembodied. Here we see a break with the dominant emphases of classical social theory and a movement towards a post-classical sensibility. In relation to the nation-state, we can ask how it is possible to explain a phenomenon that, at least in its *modern* variant, subjectively explains itself by reference to face-to-face metaphors of blood and place[27] – ties of genealogy, kinship and ethnicity – when the objective 'reality' of all nation-states is that they are disembodied communities of abstracted strangers. How is it possible to understand the subjective power of nationally-bounded ethnicity when objectively it is a lived *and* materially-abstracted category of integration, not a genetically verifiable connection of related bodies? It becomes possible, I suggest, through analytically distinguishing different modes of integration (discussed in more depth later) and exploring the tensions and contractions brought to the fore by such a method.

When we examine the dominant modes of practice in relation to different social formations, described in terms of how they are integrated, certain patterns emerge. In Table 4.1 any one of the modes of practice can be described in infinitely more complex and nuanced ways than I have done.[28] All that I am trying to achieve here is to set up an artefact with which to think – one that does not politically or empirically simplify the world in a way that is unhelpfully distorting; one that nevertheless allows us to discern dominant patterns of social life across all of human history and across the wealth of contemporary variation and difference.

Finally, the most abstract level of analysis to be employed here is what might be called *categorical analysis*. This level of enquiry is based upon

Table 4.1  Dominant modes of practice in relation to different formations

⟶ *Increasing abstraction of the dominant modes of practice* ⟶

| | **Societies formed in the dominance of tribalism to traditionalism** | **Societies formed in the dominance of traditionalism to modernism** | **Societies formed in the dominance of modernism to postmodernism** |
|---|---|---|---|
| Dominant mode of production | From hunting-gathering to subsistence agriculture and limited fabrication either directly based on the work of the hand or a one-stage extension of *manual* power. | Mostly agricultural with extended fabrication, and in some societies the rise of limited *manu*facture, that is, machine-extended work of the hand. | From industrially organized machinofacture to computer-mediated fabrication only residually dependent on the work of the hand. |
| Dominant mode of exchange | Reciprocal exchange and barter, with culturally restricted exchange of commodity goods. | Barter with limited commodity exchange, but increasing on the basis of the use of script and coinage. | Fetishized commodity exchange based on standardized and later fiduciary electronic money. |
| Dominant mode of communication | Oral, with objects acting as literal or analogical mediations. | Writing: from script to print | From print to electronically based media. |
| Dominant mode of organization | Genealogical placement, most often as kinship but not always, with embodied connections mediated by lore and mythology. | From patrimonial to bureaucratic organization based upon law and procedures.<br>– imperial to absolutist state<br>– embodied corporation. | From abstracted bureaucracy<br>– nation-state<br>– corporation to automated organization. |
| Dominant mode of enquiry | Science of the 'concrete' to the science of magic. | From magic to 'natural' science. | Stretched between the interpretative and the techno-sciences. |

an exploration of the ontological categories such as temporality and spatiality. Here we are interested in modes of being and the dominant forms that they take in different social formations. If the previous level of analysis emphasizes the different modes through which people live their commonalities with or differences from others through such categories as blood, soil and history, at the level of categorical analysis, those same categories are examined through more abstract analytical lenses. Blood, soil, history and knowledge are thus treated as phenomenal expressions of different grounding forms of life: respectively, *embodiment*, *spatiality*, *temporality* and *epistemology*.[29] At this level, generalizations can be made about the dominant modes of categorization in a social formation or in its fields of practice and discourse. It is only at this level that it makes sense to generalize across *modes of being* and to talk of *ontological formations*, societies as formed in the uneven dominance of formations of tribalism, traditionalism, modernism or postmodernism. Put another way, it provides us with a much more systematic but less reductive way of defining different dominant ontological formations. For example, whereas Jean-François Lyotard reduces the definition of postmodernism to one of the modes of being – that is, epistemology, with postmodernism being used to describe a condition of knowledge that is incredulous about grand narratives[30] – the present approach defines postmodernism as an ontological formation formed in the systematic abstraction of all categories of being, including knowledge. Similarly, whereas Fredric Jameson defines postmodernism as the cultural logic of late capitalism – with capitalism understood as a mode of production[31] – the present approach does not reduce the definition of an ontological formation to a single determinative mode of practice from which all else follows.

Each of these formations – tribalism, traditionalism, modernism or postmodernism – might exist as dominant formations (or in Jameson's wonderful phrase as a 'cultural dominant'), but rarely if at all do they exist as exclusive characterizations of a given society. In archetypical late-modern nation-states, such as the United States of America, for example, where power increasingly resides in the intersection of postmodern exchange systems of fiduciary capital and modern extensions of electronically-mediated military and surveillance power, we find quite different formations of practice. There are continuing tribal communities arguing for customary rights (the Navaho), isolated traditional communities eschewing modern ways of life (the Amish), and emerging neo-traditional fundamentalists self-consciously enacting forms of sacred and secular counter-modernism (the World Church of the Creator). Within the iron heart of the American military establishment itself, we find that the intensifying modernizing push to make the killing machine more efficient has fallen into step with the revival, in postmodern form, of a once traditional ethic that juridical modernism had previously attempted to de-legitimize. This ethic is contained in the concept of *jus ad bellum*, or the right to make war. The point here is that we have to be able to address the contradictory intersection of ontological formations in order to challenge the new 'ethics'. Describing the development in a methodologically-consistent way helps to make sense of Hardt and Negri's concern that:

> There is something troubling in this renewed focus on the concept of *bellum justum* ... two traditional characteristics have reappeared in our postmodern world: on the one hand, war is reduced to the status of police action, and on the other, the new power that can legitimately exercise ethical functions through war is sacralized.[32]

It is an important insight politically, however, one that neither works historically nor analytically. First, rather than war-as-policing being a traditional characteristic, this development is a hyper-intensification of a *modern* conception of the routinization of security. Second, rather than the sacralizing of 'humanitarian intervention' being a further traditional characteristic, this involves a *neo-traditional* revival of calls to God made possible because the postmodern destabilizing of the sacred makes even such instrumental enterprises as a Gulf War or War on Terrorism open to being given a higher purpose.

At the level of categorical analysis, we thus open up the possibility of discussing ontological contradictions that beset the political landscape: for example, understanding the transformations of the *modern* nation-state under conditions of an emergent *postmodern* layer of global information exchange and casino capitalism.[33] To speak of 'postmodernism' here is to conduct a discussion at the level of categorical analysis; to talk of capitalism is to work at the level of conjunctural analysis, and to use the language of nation-state or globalism is to use concepts of empirical analysis. The present project thus travels in the same direction, while not going as far, as John Hinkson[34] to suggest, first, that postmodernity is an emergent layer of practices and meanings rather than an epochal shift transforming all before it. Second, it suggests that what we are calling a 'postmodern layer' is to be understood as an emerging set of more abstract structures rather than the dissolution of structure into fragments – with structures being understood simply as instantiated patterns of practice. Third, it suggests that the formations of postmodernism are in a contradictory relationship with other continuing formations (Table 4.2).

Thus, with this method it is possible, without getting caught in self-defeating methodological contradiction (rightly held to be a bad thing in the world of social theory) to argue that processes of tribalizing, traditionalizing, modernizing and postmodernizing are occurring in the contemporary world at the same time. One of the outcomes of the research is to show how these processes are in substantive, commonplace, and *actual* contradiction with each other. This move is a necessary one if we are to understand the complexities of processes that lie behind the intensification of both localization and globalization, processes that simply *are* contradictory and cannot be explained away through concepts of 'glocalization'.

Table 4.2  Categories of being in relation to different ontological formations

| Modes of categorization | Ontological formations | | |
|---|---|---|---|
| | Tribal to traditional | Traditional to modern | Modern to postmodern |
| Temporality | From the dominance of natural time to that of mythic or sacred time | From sacred to empty time | From empty to relativized time |
| Spatiality | From natural to mythic or sacred space | From sacred to empty space | From empty to relativized space |
| Embodiment | From analogical to mythic embodiment | From sacred to rationalized and increasingly self-reflexive embodiment | From rationalized to cyborg embodiment |
| Epistemology | From perceptual and analogical knowledge to analogically-extended 'wisdom', based on written re-tellings and abstracted confirmations of embodied experience | From analogically and technically-extended 'wisdom' to systematized knowledge, increasingly based on written storage of information | From technologically-extended and analytically-derived 'knowledge' to 'data capture' in the context of relativized interpretation |

Fourth, the method thus points directly to fracture lines in contemporary society that are central to exploring the crises of the present. Rather than putting the explanatory weight on the speed of complete change in late-modernity, it emphasizes the *layers in contradiction* of differently-constituted, differently-changing formations of the social. In short, then, these different ontological formations (tribal, traditional, modern, postmodern) are just ways of naming the dominant forms in which people are framed by ontological categories.

## Levels of analytical abstraction[35]

Drawing upon the foregoing discussion, let me now attempt to summarize the 'analytical abstraction' method in a more formal way. As has been suggested, the overall argument of the approach is that a comprehensive theory of social relations and subjectivities has to work across a matrix of analytical levels – levels understood through a broader theory of epistemological abstraction. Table 4.3 is set out as one possible way of conceiving such a matrix. It is a table-that-runs-into-text and is intended to simplify the method as much as possible.

Table 4.3  Levels of analytical abstraction

*1. Empirical analysis*
Analysis at this level involves in the first instance developing descriptive accounts that relate and make first-order connections from factual research to descriptions of particular institutions, fields of activity or discourses, persons or communities. Generalizing across these particular accounts and studies, it is then possible to describe comparative and long-term patterns. Analysis at this level, that emphasizes the particular and does not reach for more abstract ways of understanding, runs the risk of superficiality or empiricism, however detailed its description. Nevertheless, empirical analysis is the basic level of analysis for any approach attempting to avoid abstract theoreticism.

*2. Conjunctural analysis*
Analysis at this level of theoretical abstraction proceeds by resolution of particular modes of practice. The present approach complicates classical 'historical materialism' and its emphasis upon the mode(s) of production by analytically distinguishing the following primary modes of practice:

- production
- exchange
- communication
- organization
- enquiry.

Generalizing across analyses of particular modes of practice, the approach is then able to describe conjunctures between such modes. Generalizations can be made about the structural connections that make up dominant *conjunctural formations*, for example, capitalism or feudalism. This is the level at which Marxist and historical materialist approaches have tended to concentrate their method. In the neo-Marxist literature conjunctural formations would be called 'social formations'. However, I want to keep the concept of social formation as a much broader descriptive term, one that fully takes in the complexity of describing social life across all the levels of analysis.

*3. Integrational analysis*
Analysis at this level proceeds by resolution of modes (or levels) of social integration-differentiation.[36] While, in theory, one could distinguish any number of modes of integration, the present approach distinguishes the following such modes:

- face-to-face integration
- object-extended integration
- agency-extended integration
- disembodied integration.

Generalizing across analyses of modes of integration, generalizations can be made, first, about the intersections and contradictions between these modes set at (ontologically) different levels, and secondly about dominant *integrative formations*: community, market, polity or corporate body, and society or network. Although approaching the problem of theory in very different ways and using different conceptual tools, this is the level at which theorists as wide-ranging as Jürgen Habermas and Anthony Giddens have concentrated their work.

4. *Categorical analysis*[37]

Analysis at this level works by reflexively 'deconstructing' categories of social ontology, for example, time and space, culture and nature, gender and embodiment. The way that we measure or understand *time*, for example, can be discussed at any level of abstraction, but working at the level of *categorical analysis* produces structural genealogies of particular *modes of categorization*. This is distinct from 'classical' histories or descriptions that were discussed as being drawn out and generalized through *empirical analysis*. This is the level at which post-structuralists such as Michel Foucault, Jean Baudrillard and Jacques Derrida have tended to focus their work. In Foucault's case, he links categorical analysis (of a kind) back to the level of detailed empirical analysis (of a kind). The key criticism of these writers is that they leave out other levels of analysis that could give a more structured *and* nuanced account of social relations – it is what might be called the 'missing middle' of post-structuralist theory. At this level, analysis that is not tied into more concrete political-ethical considerations is in danger of abstracted irrelevance, utopianism without a subject, or empty spiritualism. I want to concentrate on the following ontological categories: temporality, spatiality, embodiment, and epistemology itself. Generalizing across such categories it is possible to conceive of the basis of different ontological formations:

- tribalism
- traditionalism
- modernism
- postmodernism.

As with all other concepts in the present approach, the notion of categorical analysis remains provisional. It is always tested against the criterion 'Is it useful for understanding the complexities of social life?'

Expressed in this short-hand fashion, the method that I am employing sounds technical and inaccessible. However, in the practice of writing and research, the method is intended as an orienting and organizing schema rather than a self-generating demon. Methodologically, all that is being argued is that in abstracting from the details of lived practices and ideas, social formations can be helpfully understood in the following way:

- as overlaying patterns of lived practices, ideas and values;
- as overlaying modes of practice;
- as overlaying modes of integration;
- as overlaying modes of categorization.

In a metaphorical sense, these are maps or ways of viewing the world from different vantage points. Some vantage points take us closer to the material under study, and some abstract us to a greater analytical distance from it. The different 'levels of analytical abstraction' thus described are simply different forms of theoretical analysis. They sound unfamiliar because they are elucidated in the most general of terms.

The approach also, incidentally rather than by primary intention, provides a way of thinking about the difference between various theories: from empiricism to post-structuralism. There are many other ways of thinking about theory. For example, it is possible to differentiate approaches by the content of what they study, the field from which they come, and the political stance that they take – or any number of other empirical generalizations about patterns of theory. In categorizing different theories, the constitutive abstraction approach asks, 'What is the analytical basis by which different approaches proceed to make sense of the world?'

Rather than continuing any further down the path of exploring the nature of how we know things about and beyond ourselves (epistemology), I want to now see how each of the analysis can be opened up to a broader thematic. The thematic includes ways of knowing and engaging within it, but extends right across the social nature of being human. This is the question of ontology. The following discussion begins to do this in terms of an elaboration of what was earlier called *integrational analysis*. Different levels of integration can be analytically separated out in terms of their level of abstraction from the embodied world of nature–culture. In other words, just as different ways of theorizing can be distinguished in terms of levels of analytical (epistemological) abstraction, so different modes of integration can be understood in terms of their level of ontological abstraction. For example, the relationship of national citizens as body politic is more ontologically abstract – more stretched across time, space and the particularities of each person's body – than a kinship-related bond constituted in the dominance of face-to-face relations. The next section is intended to do no more than illustrate one part of the method in its quest for sensitizing social research and political argument.

## Levels of integration

### Face-to-face integration

As developed in the earlier companion to this volume, *Nation Formation*, the first-order analytical level of integrative relations is the face-to-face, or what

Chris Scanlon equally appropriately calls 'the embodied extended'. The metaphor of 'the face-to-face' does not imply that sociality is constituted at the level of literally looking into the face of another. Nor does it refer to the importance of mediated images of faces as a way of generating subjective responses. On 7 May 1945 the face of Adolf Hitler crossed by a bloody X is used to mark Germany's defeat. On 11 September 2001 a young girl smiles for a family photograph while in the background a jet aeroplane flies into the World Trade Center. On 21 April 2003, the cover of *Time* magazine crosses Saddam Hussein's face with the same bloody X. While these are not instances of face-to-face relations, they are indicative of the fact that 'the face' is the most powerful metaphor that we have for signifying the joy and horror of human relations.[38]

The concept of face-to-face integration refers to a particular form of relation to others – a social relationship grounded in the importance of embodied presence. It is characterized by persons living that relation *as if* they are in always-continuing embodied co-presence, including potentially with those persons who are separated by spatial or temporal distance – most dramatically, for example, separated by death. It is an analytical metaphor. None of the tribes in the world today, or in known history, live only at this one constitutive level. The argument here is only that the complexity of tribal and traditional-tribal life is most adequately understood as constituted in the *dominance* of face-to-face relations – even as more abstract relations, particularly modalities of object extension such as gift exchange, overlay that level. The dominant modalities of face-to-face integration, lived across all social settings from the tribal to the postmodern, are in these terms understood as connected to questions of relatively concrete attachment as located by embodiment, temporality, spatiality and knowledge. A number of modalities can be analytically singled out – in particular, consanguinal, ritual, perceptual and convivial relations – though it is important to note that they are lived in intersection with each other.

One primary form of face-to-face integration, defined primarily in terms of embodiment is *consanguinal relations* or the social ties of 'blood' and kin that connect birth and death. This appears to be a readily understandable modality, though, as we will see, the 'blood' of consanguinal ties is always already a cultural category that only comes to social life in and through other modalities of integration. It is, for example, carried by the traditional meaning of 'friends by blood', in the sense that feudal European 'friendship' most often resided in kinship relations.[39] A second form, defined primarily in terms of temporality, involves *ritual relations* of connection, for example, as *extended* kinship rituals through marriage or adoption – the kith side of 'kith and kin'. These rituals serve initially to place and then continually to reconfirm the ongoing presence of the persons in simultaneous time across generational separation. A third form can be understood in terms of a particular way of knowing: that is, through *perceptual relations*. This is most easily evoked through the Old Testament metaphor of sexual union as 'knowing another'; or, to take a later example by linking 'knowing' to 'facing another' Robert Browning writes:

I knew you once: But in Paradise,
If we meet, I will not pass or turn my face.[40]

The thicker the relation between people, the more all of these social modalities 'condense' together (to use Freud's concept). For example, in intersection with consanguinal relations, the notion of perceptual relations allows us to understand what the anthropologists call 'fictive kinship' – consanguineous relations that are not based on actual blood ties but nevertheless involve an enacting of the perception that the blood-like ties do exist and are binding. Beyond these relations there is a fourth form defined primarily in terms of spatial connection: that of continuing and patterned convivial contiguity. This modality of *convivial relations* is potentially the most misleading because it does not refer to just being in proximity, even regularized proximity, with other people as accidental features of where one lives or works, drinks beer or shops for milk. It does not mean simply entering a situation of friendly interaction or festivity as the modern and trivializing meaning of the word would have it. Rather as used in this context, convivial relations – from the Latin *vivere*, meaning 'to live', and extended to concepts such as *convivium*, feast – refers to relations of direct, continuing and socially meaningful contiguity. Convivial forms of relationship range from tribal co-initiate groups who live for a period of their lives in the same houses to deep friendship in the modern sense.[41] I need at this point to recall a distinction that I have long found useful: that between interaction and integration. *Interaction* names the fact of an act of interchange, whereas *integration* names the instantiated social form that frames any one interaction. It is the form of integration that I am primarily interested in here. We also have to make a distinction between subjective sensibilities and objective relations. Conventionally it would be said that subjectivities of the face-to-face such as blood-ties are often drawn upon when attempting to evoke the power of national identity without there being an objective basis to those subjectivities.[42] Working through a 'levels argument' allows for a more precise argument. While the embodied subjectivities of nationality-ethnicity have little grounding at the level of the face-to-face, they are carried objectively at more abstract levels of integration through institutions such as the state.[43]

Convivial relations change in different settings. In general, it can be defined as a social situation where proximity gives rise to continuing embodied relations of care or, alternatively, of abiding embodied tension.[44] As one indication of this tension the English term 'host' and French *hoiste* simultaneously mean embodied victim and Eucharistic offering. More positively, the French word *hôte* (in old French, *hoste*) carries something of the cross-over of the modalities of consanguinal and convivial relations in its conjoint meaning as 'host' and 'guest' and 'denizen'. This is potentially the form of relationship that a localized community could enact as it meets the needs of strangers (refugees or immigrants) welcomed into the space of the host. In one of the recent indications of the power of the tribal-traditional form of this relation, Pashtun tribes in areas such as North Waziristan welcomed the fleeing Taliban as guests, despite their differences. By contrast, as the 'realities' of the globalized movement of refugees have confronted the abstract community of the nation, the fragile balance of tensions has become increasingly shifted towards legally screening uninvited guests to see if they are worthy of temporary or extended accommodation. In previously self-defined 'welcoming nation-states' such as Australia, Britain and the Netherlands, refugees have come to be seen as figures of intense ambiguity – cautiously welcomed as needy individuals in a discriminating rhetoric of care, and feared as mass usurpers of the integrity of the nation in a noisy rhetoric of securing borders. When, for example, during the 2001 Tampa crisis the Australian defence minister acted to prevent the media from taking any photographs of the asylum seekers that could 'humanize or personalize' them, he was effectively trying to play on the 'fear' side of the tension intrinsic in being a host.

Having discussed the face-to-face at some length, we need only to treat the other levels of integration in an indicative way.

## Object integration

At this level of integration the relation between persons is abstracted from the face-to-face through networks of mediation that are carried by exchangeable or symbolically placed things. The pre-eminent modern example is money, a medium that carries a systemic and material relation between people, but one that no longer requires the particularity of anybody's embodied self to stand behind the network of value (discussed at length in Chapter 6). However, not all mediating relations of object extension are so abstract in their form as currency or financial objects. Sacred objects, by comparison, are to all social intents and purposes, inalienable and not exchangeable (discussed at length in Chapter 5). Such objects nevertheless carry a more abstract relationship between people than the bonds of face-to-face relations. Like money or commodities, they do not rely upon the forging of particularistic relations between those who look upon them to sustain their integrative power. Similarly, the exchange of valuable objects in gift or reciprocal exchange allows for limited though more abstract relations than immediate and particularistic kinship ties. Basic objects, those available for exchange through mutual use, barter or as currency objects such as food can even become tribal commodities in the restricted sense of that term. Although basic usefulness is never a criterion for entering formal networks of reciprocal exchange or for being sacred, they are often mutually shared in immediate relations of reciprocity. Commercial forms of object extension, on the other hand, treat basic goods as fetishized commodities within an abstract marketplace where face-to-face forms of relations are subordinate to the dominant logic of the mode of exchange.

## Agency or institutional integration

At this level, integrative relations are carried through agents and institutions of agency – abstracted institutions such as the state, the church or the corporation, but also more embodied institutions such as guilds, leagues, brotherhoods and communes. These institutions mediate and extend social integration beyond the face-to-face. There are instances of agency extension in tribal societies. Maurice Godelier writes of the 'third party' in tribal exchange systems such as the *kitoum*,[45] and Christopher Gregory writes about the agents of mercantile kinship.[46] However, these kinds of *reciprocal agency* are limited and far from central to the integration of tribal society as a whole (see Table 4.4). They become much more important in traditional formations. One of the primary forms of agency extension is the patrimonial or the traditional-bureaucratic, characterized by the carrying of embodied ties and loyalties into new hierarchy of power. Renaissance scholars attempted to explain this kind of sovereign subjectivity, a body politic, in terms of the passing over to the subject of an extension of spirit: 'Howsoeuer the body be termed passiue, in regard of the soules working in and by his instruments, yet vnto it also the soule imparteth his power of mouing and acting, and the more noble parts thereof bee the more indued and enabled ...'.[47] In other words, the sovereign extends his soul to the passive administrative body and gives it the power to move and act. Moreover, it is in the nature of that extension as body and soul are united that an agent can only have one sovereign: no 'agent or deputie for the soule', says Forset, 'in the workes to him assingned shall intrudingly vsurpe, arrogate, and possesse the place, name and office of the soule it selfe; except wee should imagine two soules in one body, like two sunnes in one firmament'.[48]

Other kinds of relations of agency-extension include the ecclesial (traditional-universal, connected by religious calling), the martial (autocratic-hierarchical, connected by military authority), the commercial (abstracted-commodified, connected by market concerns), the institutional (abstracted-bureaucratic, connected by corporate place) and the professional (abstracted-technocratic, connected by common vocation). The common thread that analytically ties together all these forms is that they extend relations among persons through instituting mediating relations. These relations no longer depend primarily on the genealogical particularity of the embodied person, but rather on their skills, aptitudes, training or realizable capital. It's not who you know, but what you know and control.

### Disembodied integration

Disembodied integration takes social relations to a further level of abstraction. This is the level of integration at which disembodying media, technologies and techniques such as mass communications come to mediate and extend social integrations beyond that even carried by institutional arrangements and their agents. Disembodied integration describes the process by which social relations are stretched across time and space in a way that no longer (formally) depends upon the embodied relations of known or institutionally-related others. Certainly, there are means of disembodied extension available to all cultures – for example, iconic signs and images continue to carry contextualized meaning long after their original inscribers cease returning to the cave or temple wall. However, with the advent of techniques and media for abstractly encoding meaning (writing) or value (money) new possibilities for systemically connecting strangers were opened up. Coupled with new means of generalized dissemination (from print, to digital transmission), and pushed along by an ever-expanding mode of production (capitalism), the new media of disembodied integration came to be central to modern social formations through the simultaneous but separate actions of masses of people just going about their everyday lives. In the process, we increasingly came to live those more abstract possibilities as if they were naturally necessary to the proper functioning of society.[49]

Along the way, the process was embedded in the subjective imaginary through an explicable but nevertheless contradictory twist. As the dominant social form became more abstract, we became more and more obsessed by making the content more palpable, more embodied, more 'real'. For example, as the means of integration became increasingly abstract in *form* – for example, with the possibility of digitally encoding colour pixels for television broadcasting – the producers and audiences of the media carried forward the old obsessions of film-makers with giving embodied *content* to the disembodied medium. Instead of lists of news items being textually presented, we wanted a newscaster to give life to the transmitted information. Instead of treating the face-on-the-box as a mere purveyor of decontextualized transmission data, the newscaster was invested with face-to-face familiarity. Similarly, while use of the cinema tools of digital colouring and 'intermediation' has meant that the colour of many films such as *Lord of the Rings* is entirely abstracted from the natural world, cinematographers came to manipulate the palette for what they call 'emotional story-telling'. George Clooney's film *Confessions of a Dangerous Mind* uses a different palette for each life-phase of the self-described CIA assassin. In other words, contemporary late-modern society is integrated across all the levels that I have been elaborating. Under the ontological dominance of relations of disembodied integration, people continue to draw heavily upon and yearn for the embodied. This is where the organizing level of social power resides. That is, even if many of the ideologies of our time are grounded in the continuing resonance of the face-to-face – such as in 'My name is Gillian Stone. I feel like this valley has chosen me' – extended power now comes through attempting to control processes of systematic abstraction: the mass media, the war-machine, the financial markets, and the techno-sciences. It is no coincidence that, in relation to the War on Terror, the Pentagon paid for the entire capacity of the only private satellite moving over Afghanistan with high enough resolution to see the bodies of people.[50] Even more starkly, the structure of al-Qa'ida as a technologically-extended 'network of networks' depends heavily upon globalizing communications media, even as it draws heart from the embodied commitment of persons prepared to die for a sensibility.

Table 4.4  Modes of integration

| Modes of integration | Examples of modalities of connection | | Forms taken by those modalities |
|---|---|---|---|
| Face-to-face | consanguinal<br>ritual<br>convivial<br>perceptual | – embodied-communal<br>– embodied-ceremonial<br>– embodied-sociable<br>– embodied-affiliative | ties of embodied genealogy<br>ties of temporal recognition<br>ties of spatial contiguity<br>ties of 'known' affinity |
| Object-extended | inalienable<br>reciprocal<br>commercial<br>financial | – reified-sacred<br>– reified-communal<br>– abstracted-commodified<br>– abstracted-fiscal | things 'beyond the cultural'<br>circuits of gift exchange<br>markets of commodities<br>networks of monetary exchange |
| Agency-extended | patrimonial<br>ecclesial<br>martial<br>institutional | – traditional-bureaucratic<br>– traditional-universal<br>– autocratic-hierarchical<br>– abstracted-bureaucratic | embodied loyalty<br>religious calling<br>military authority<br>corporate placing |
| Disembodied | pictorial<br>aural<br>encodable<br>digital | – analogical-perceptual<br>– analogical-perceptual<br>– symbolic-informational<br>– abstracted-informational | contextualized images<br>contextualized sounds<br>decontextualized codes<br>decontextualized transmission data |

The foregoing discussion of different forms of integration can be summarized in a table. (Table 4.4) The matrix is not meant to be exclusive of all the modalities of social connection, but rather to point to dominant patterns. In real life these different modes are not so easily taken apart, but the analytical moment is important because it allows us to understand both ontological differences between different social formations and ontological contradictions within any given society.

That should be enough on modes of integration to give a sense that what we are doing is providing a method for sensitizing research and political argument. Now, in winding up the chapter, we return to the grounding of theory itself. Through all of this discussion it is important to remember that theory itself, including the kind of social mapping that we have been attempting, is but one miniscule part of the broader historically-changing process of how we see and understand the social and natural world. It is based on what is known in the language of social theory or philosophy as epistemology – ways of knowing. Theory, conducted at whatever level, from empirical to categorical analysis, is already an extraordinarily abstract way of looking at and enquiring about sociality. It works at a level of what might be called analytical enquiry, however, it relies upon an abstract distance from the modernist certainty usually associated with that level. In other words, it follows the postmodern move to recognize the contingent nature of methodology, and then returns to the level of the analytic to rethink reflexively and systematically its own foundations.

The most concrete kind of enquiry is perceptual. It works through the embodied senses and by relatively concrete reference points. Certainly even in the most primary confrontation with another person, or with nature, the senses are mediated, but this does no more than qualify the argument that we can usefully distinguish differently-abstracted levels of epistemology. In tribal society, perceptual enquiry conducted as a form of bricolage (Lévi-Strauss) tends to be set in relation to myth as a dominant level of socially framed enquiry that we might call *perceptual-analogical*. Such enquiry works through analogies between culture and nature; for example, in Mary Douglas's terms taking the body as a natural symbol of the meaning of things. Across human history, perceptual-analogical enquiry itself quickly became conceived in more abstract terms: from the formalism of Plato and his analogy of the cave wall to the universalism of Thomas Aquinas when he determined that the proper form of the City of Man could be understood in terms of the City of God. For the metaphysical philosophers of the Christian, Moslem and Jewish Middle Ages, knowledge was still based on the sensual experience, but what frames the act of knowing is a common ground of the sacred, spiritual and universal. It is what we might call the *cosmological-gnoseological*.[51]

A further kind of enquiry (*technical enquiry*), that has very early roots but comes into dominance with the coming of early modernism, was conducted through media and techniques that extended the range of seeing and abstracted from the perceptual limitations of the body. The most dramatic of these media ranged from ancient lenses used by the Egyptians to Galileo's instrument in the early seventeenth century used for looking at the clock of heaven, to Max Knoll and Ernst Ruska's instrument in the 1930s for casting the shadow patterns of 'things' too small ever to be seen by the naked eye. Such media from the telescope to the electron microscope extended upon much older techniques of recording patterns of natural and social activity from the technique of writing to that of mathematical notation. In its emerging dominance, technical enquiry tended to cut across the customary and traditional presumptions of perceptual-analogical and cosmological inquiry, though not always by replacing those prior levels. As traditional understandings about big things such as the heavens and small things such angels dancing on the head of a pin came to be more and more confined to the world of religion, technical enquiry came together with an epistemological stance that was part of revolution in the way of thinking – *analytical enquiry*.

The point of this for our purposes is that while analogical and technical abstraction, for example, gave rise to complex philosophies and theories, the distance before the material world offered by analytical abstraction made possible social-theory-as-such. That is, to be blunt, in the nineteenth century, and only for a few intellectuals, the mode of enquiry shifted to a new dominant level of interpretative analytical enquiry that for the first time made possible a particular kind of theory – theories of the social that explain social life in terms of itself rather than through natural laws or sacred givens. In summary, social theory became possible at a certain level of epistemological abstraction – what I have been calling *analytical enquiry* – as intellectuals from Marx to Freud began to abstract from perceptual, analogical, cosmological and technical understandings of the social world. In these terms, writers such as Hobbes and Rousseau were political philosophers, not social theorists. They tended to explain the social world in terms of analogies and metaphors such as 'the law of nature' and 'the body politic' and activities rather than analytically break the social world down into constituent parts – processes and practices, patterns and structures. A further development in analytic enquiry, one which gave us both post-structuralism and string theory, was the move to 'return' to the use of metaphors and thought-experiments but this time from a highly-abstracted analytic standpoint.

Although there is not the space to do so here, a detailed parallel history and comparative sociology could be written for the changing dominant levels of ethical abstraction: different ways of thinking about what is 'good' and what is 'right'. Put most briefly, it is possible to show that like other social practices, the nature of different deontological systems are patterned upon the nature of the society in which they are lived and contested. At the risk of oversimplifying a long and incredibly complex history of different ethical systems, it is useful to distinguish analytically a number of dominant modalities in relation to different dominant ontological formations: relational ethics, exemplary-universal ethics, codified ethics and reflexive ethics. The first – *relational-particularistic ethics* – is dominant in tribal societies, although it has continuing if subordinate relevance in all societies. Relational ethics emphasizes the right way to sustain particularistic relations between persons; and between persons and things: sacred and valuable goods, places, features on the landscape, animal species and forces of nature. It is the kind of ethics recounted in living narratives by genealogically-related story-tellers on the basis of what has been handed down to them. The interaction of each telling itself works to reconfirm the integrative force of face-to-face relations. A second major form, *exemplary-universal ethics* abstracts from relational ethics by locating the source of meaning elsewhere other than within the perceptually known social and natural relationships themselves. If, for example, in Navajo or Yolgnu tribal culture the life-sustaining relation between mother and child provides the actual foundation for all bonds of kinship, social and natural,[52] then in Christian traditional culture the mother-and-Christ-child image has a double referent. It refers to the sacred life that is at once universal and removed from the lives of mere mortals and, at the same time, actually returned to the flesh as a sustaining lived sign of the exemplary-sacred. Caroline Walker Bynum, for example, provides us with a wealth of medieval evidence of iconographic associations drawn between the lactating Virgin and the eucharist, such that in many images the person of Mary becomes unnecessary to the exemplary-universal tension. *The Saviour*, by Quirizio da Muranano (1460–1478) shows Christ with one hand opening his wounded chest where a nipple would be found, and with the other hand feeding a eucharistic wafer to a kneeling nun.[53] Thus, the painters tell us, He is the way and the life. He *is* exemplary of how relation ethics should work. In this setting, codes of law are given by God or derived from such universal exemplaries, but they do not stand alone.

While exemplary-universal ethics maintains a continuing force to the present, in many areas of life it either shaded into or was overwhelmed by the third more abstract kind of ethics – *codified ethics*. The overlaying of forms can be seen in such movements as Wahhabite Islam, arguably, alongside modern intellectual training, one of the strongest influences on the terrorism of Osama bin Laden.[54] Aziz Al Azmeh sets this out in its complexity showing how all Islamic neo-fundamentalisms look back to an exemplary universalism while paradoxically (flexibly) hardening the scripture as modern codifiable law. Wahhabism, for example,

> purports to detail the exemplary behaviour of the Prophet and his contemporaries, and to utilize this register of exemplaries as a character for reform. The fundamentals of rectitude are contained in this register, and the history that intervenes between the occurrence of the exemplary acts and today is an accident that no more than sullies and corrupts its origin, and which therefore can be eliminated, as history is the mere passage of time, not the work of social, political and cultural transformations ... [The scriptural and the historical-contemporary] are set in parallel registers and are expressed in terms of today's fundamentally right bearings, making the iniquities of today less historical realities than supervening mistakes that can be eliminated by reference to exemplary precedent.[55]

Whether we refer to traditional or modern Islam, Christianity, or Confucianism as examples, the universalizing religions of the book all treat ethics as that which is both exemplified *and* codifiable. The codification occurs through intellectually-mediated reflection upon the meaning of a transcendent God, transcendent Nature or transcendent Law. Sometimes the right and the good were passed on by God-sustained edict, such as when Moses was handed the two stone tablets containing the Ten Commandments, or sometimes they were enshrined in natural law beginning with the Greek philosophers such as Aristotle (384–322 BCE) in his *Nichomachean Ethics*, but they were usually constituted in the overlaying of forms. By the eighteenth century, codified ethics was able, more or less, to stand alone, even if many documents such as Thomas Paine's *The Rights of Man* (1791–92) still appealed to natural law as a back-up. This was the century that began the modern state's emphasis on codified constitutions, even if constitutions tended to do likewise.[56]

*Reflexive ethics*, a fourth bundled form of ethics, came into dominance in the twentieth century as professional philosophers of ethics increasingly began to relativize its old verities and lay-intellectuals increasingly interrogated its grounding assumptions. I will not even try to develop that line of thinking given the constraints on space, but instead attempt to draw all the themes of the whole discussion together – themes of ontology, epistemology and ethics. Keeping in mind all the qualifications about the power and distortion of abstract maps, tables and figures, we are now in a position to present a highly simplified social-relational map of the dominant forms of (1) being in the world; (2) seeing and enquiring about the world; and (3) reflecting upon how we should act in the world (Figure 4.2).

In the context of the previous discussion, Figure 4.2 both sums up the entire approach and shows its profound dangers. If you entered the discussion at this point rather than reading from the beginning, it would show how meaningless a mapping exercise becomes when reduced to a series of concepts-in-relation. Most obviously, it shows that political and social life cannot be more than tentatively sensitized by tables and blueprints. In Figure 4.2, the broken arrows represent the increasing abstraction of different modes of *being, enquiring* and *engaging*. The solid arrows represent different kinds of interrogations of the social – either analytical or ethical interrogations – conducted at increasing ontological depth that have become systematically possible in line with the increasing abstraction and reflexivity of the past hundred years or so. Implicit in the argument is the claim that it is only at the *analytical* level of epistemological abstraction that social theory is able to theoretically take apart its own method and distinguish between levels of *theoretical abstraction*. This was the genius of Marx amongst others, although he did not spell it

| Ontological abstraction | Epistemological abstraction | Deontological abstraction |
|---|---|---|
| Ways of being in relation to others and to nature, understood in relation to the modes of categorization: embodiment and knowing, spatiality and temporality. | Ways of seeing and enquiring about the social and the natural | Ways of thinking about what is 'good' and 'right' |
| e.g. Modes of Integration<br>• face-to-face<br>• object-extended<br>• agency-extended<br>• disembodied | e.g. Modes of Enquiry<br>• perceptual-analogical<br>• cosmological-gnoseological<br>• technical<br>• analytical<br>  – empirical analysis<br>  – conjunctural analysis<br>  – integrational analysis<br>  – categorical analysis | e.g. Modes of Engagement<br>• relational-embodied<br>• exemplary-universal<br>• technical-codified<br>• reflexive<br>  – an ethic of agonism<br>  – an ethic of rights<br>  – an ethic of care<br>  – an ethic of foundations[a] |

Figure 4.2 Different forms of abstraction: a summary of the overall approach

[a]For an argument about how we might conceive of ethics as levels-in-tension, see Chapter 12.

out systematically. It suggests further that only by reflecting upon the complex overlaying of different forms of enquiry can we come up with the kind of approach espoused in this book. Similarly, in relation to levels of ethical abstraction, it is only at the level of *reflexive* ethical abstraction that it is possible to distinguish between levels of ethics. This does not mean however that those different levels of analysis or ethics were unavailable to people prior to the emerging forms of analytical or reflexive abstraction, 'only' that they were not dominant or taken to be self-evident, not given by God or taken from nature.

## Conclusion

By moving back and forth across the levels of analytical abstraction and attempting to understand the ontological changes of our time, it is intended that *Globalism, Nationalism, Tribalism* will illustrate its argument about the emergence of a globalizing and postmodernizing political community as it overlays other continuing forms of community-polity. In terms of the present condition of the world, the most general argument made by the book is that polity and community are increasingly held together at the level of disembodied extension and structured by the emergence of increasingly globalized and abstracted modes of practice. It is these very processes of abstract integration and structuration that, ironically, are giving rise to the sense that the social whole is collapsing into fragments. It is these processes that heighten our sensitivity to the issue that the modern nation-state and contemporary globalization face a series of crises, even as they are being reconstituted along new lines. It is also these processes that in their present form threaten to hollow out human existence even as they excite many people with hopes of liberation from all ontological constraints. In the end, the method is best veiled behind an overt concern to understand the structures and subjectivities, patterns and contingencies of social life, from tribalism to globalism. However, in this period when older methodologies seem anachronistic, and avant-garde approaches leave us floundering for something to say politically, it is well worth being explicit about how the analytical, the political and the ethical are interconnected.

## Notes

1 Michael Hardt and Antonio Negri, *Empire*, Harvard University Press, Cambridge, MA, 2001; Samuel P. Huntington, *The Clash of Civilizations and the Remaking of World Order*, Simon & Schuster, London, 1998; Benjamin R. Barber, *Jihad vs. McWorld: How Globalism and Tribalism are Reshaping the World*, Ballantine Books, New York, 1996.

2 Jason Burke, *Al-Qaeda: Casting a Shadow of Terror*, I.B. Tauris, London, 2003. The term is a relatively common Arabic concept for base, such as a camp or home, foundation, such as a house might have, or method, model or pattern.

3 Anthony Giddens, *Modernity and Self-Identity: Self and Society in the Late Modern Age*, Polity Press, Cambridge, 1991.

4 Louis Dumont, *Essays on Individualism: Modern Ideology in Anthropological Perspective*, University of Chicago Press, Chicago, 1986, p. 207.

5 Flechettes are tiny metal darts within an anti-personnel bomb. In the version used by the Israeli military there are 3,000 flechettes in one shell. In August 2002, a tank crew, deploying weapons of this kind to protect the nearby town of Netzarim, killed a family of fruit-pickers. Flechettes were first used by the French in World War I in bombs dropped from biplanes.

6 Ulrich Beck, *The Risk Society: Towards a New Modernity*, Sage, London, 1992.

7 *Blue Velvet*, directed by David Lynch, 1986; *Arlington Road*, directed by Mark Pellington, 1999.

8 A Nestlé advertisement on Australian television during the 1990s.

9 Karl Marx and Friedrich Engels, *Selected Works*, vol. 1, 1997, p. 502.

10 Georg Simmel, *The Philosophy of Money*, Routledge, London (1900), 1990, p. 59.

11 At the same time it should be said that even as maps are *epistemological* abstractions of the world, they do exist *in* the real world, and as such they are part of the *ontological* (historically, materially and ideationally constituted) abstraction we call social life. The maps that I describe below will never have the ideological power of map-concepts such as 'class', 'nation', 'state', but writing them down puts them in the world nevertheless.

12 Marx, for example, developed the base–superstructure framework as a sensitizing method (albeit one that I think does not work): it was orthodox Marxists who later turned it into an absolutist sign of correct-line methodology.

13 Michel Foucault, *The Order of Things: An Archeology of the Human Sciences*, Tavistock Publications, London (1966), 1970, p. xvii.

14 Pierre Bourdieu, *The Logic of Practice*, Polity Press, Cambridge, 1990, p. 201.

15 Maps and calendars as figural and material abstractions will be discussed in a historically embedded way in Chapter 7.

16 Geoff Sharp, 'Constitutive Abstraction and Social Practice', *Arena*, 70, 1985, p. 64.

17 Pierre Bourdieu, *Outline of a Theory of Practice*, Cambridge University Press, Cambridge, 1977, p. 98.

18 Elizabeth Traube, *Cosmology and Social Life: Ritual Exchange among the Mambai of East Timor*, University of Chicago Press, Chicago, 1986, p. 7.

19 Cited in Mark B. Salter, *Barbarians and Civilization in International Relations*, Pluto Press, London, 2002, p. 45.

20 Ulf Hannerz, for example, works across three levels of abstraction. See his *Cultural Complexity: Cultural Complexity in the Social Organization of Meaning*, Columbia University Press, New York, 1992. In addition to the level of empirical analysis, he has a second level of what he calls 'frameworks of flow' comprising four institutional types: state, market, social movement, and form of life. The third level, in his words, 'involves a more formal sociology, identifying the characteristics of cultural management in social relationships in rather abstract terms of symmetries and asymmetries along several dimensions' (p. 46).

21 This is of course only one way that such a 'levels' approach might be developed. See Appendix 3.1 below on how the levels of analytical abstraction fit into the overall framework of this book.

22 On the other hand, I do derive pleasure from the ordering process having historical antecedents. It takes the same form as traditional taxonomies such as the early-thirteenth-century manuscript that connects embodiment and cosmology thus: 'There are four winds. There are four ranks of angels. There are four times of the year: spring, summer, autumn, winter. There are four humours in the human body: red bile, black bile, blood and phlegm.' See Megan Cassidy-Welch, *Monastic Spaces and Their Meanings: Thirteenth-Century English Cistercian Monasteries*, Brepols, Turnhout, 2001, p. 157.

23 Note how in this sentence the definite articles in '*the* nation-state' and '*the* nation-states' work at quite different levels of abstraction. The first use is as general social form: the second use collects together particular polity-communities.

24 See the critique by Maurice Godelier, *The Enigma of the Gift*, Polity Press, Cambridge, 1999, pp. 19–21.

25 Jürgen Habermas, *Communication and the Evolution of Society*, Beacon, Boston, 1979.

26 Gianni Vattimo, *The Transparent Society* Polity Press, Cambridge, 1952; Poster, *The Mode of Information*, Polity Press, Cambridge, 1990, particularly pp. 64ff. As an aside it is worth noting why I use the term 'mode of communication' rather than Poster's term, 'mode of information'. First, as a concept denoting a social relational practice (communicating through all its various means and techniques), 'mode of communication' is a much broader concept than 'mode of information'. The latter denotes only the outcome of an epistemological practice, not the practice itself. Second, I take information to be only one possible register in a broad epistemological range: wisdom, knowledge, information and data. See Tables 4.1 and 4.2.

27 Described at a more abstract level of analysis (namely, the categorical), these would be called metaphors of *genealogical placement*. See Chapter 5.

28 For example, see Claude Meillassoux, *Maidens, Meal and Money*, Cambridge University Press, Cambridge, 1981. for one possible way of conceiving of the many different forms of domestic mode of production in band and tribal society.

29 Other categories can be addressed at this level, for example, power, risk, etc.

30 Jean-François Lyotard, *The Postmodern Condition: A Report on Knowledge*, Manchester University Press, Manchester, 1984.

31 Fredric Jameson, *Postmodernism or, the Cultural Logic of Late Capitalism*, Verso, London, 1991.

32 Hardt and Negri, *Empire*, p. 12.

33 Susan Strange, *Casino Capitalism*, Manchester University Press, Manchester, (1986) 1997.

34 John Hinkson, 'Postmodern Economy: Value, Self-Formation and Intellectual Practice', *Arena Journal*, New Series, no. 1, 1993, pp. 23–44. Hinkson tends to write of the postmodern economy as substantially displacing the modern economy of time-space rationalization.

35 This section builds upon the earlier volume, *Nation Formation*, Sage, London, 1996, Chapter 2 and Appendix, pp. 198–9.

36 When I use the term 'integration' it is intended to carry with it the sense that processes of integration are always simultaneously processes of differentiation.

37 The implicit argument here is that it is at this level of analytical abstraction (epistemology) that it first becomes inevitable that we will begin to distinguish between different ontological levels. By comparison, conjunctural analysis is a form of analysis that, rather than compelling such a theoretical break with classical social theory, usually continues to be conducted on one plane.

38 Daniel McNeill, *The Face*, Hamish Hamilton, London, 1998.

39 Marc Bloch, *Feudal Society*, University of Chicago Press, Chicago, 1961, pp. 123–5.

40 Robert Browning (1812–1889) from his poem 'The Worst of It'.

41 See, for example, Godelier's discussion of co-initiates, co-residence groups and friends, *The Enigma of the Gift*, pp. 144–5.

42 Such a subjectivity–objectivity disjuncture is itself only reflexively visible from the abstract position of the subjectivity of modernism.

43 This would be a way of adding to the terms of Jacqueline Stevens' insightful book (*Reproducing the State*, Princeton University Press, Princeton, NJ, 1999) without coming to the political conclusions that prompt her to write that 'As long as there are political societies based on kinship forms, there will be far-reaching practices of violence that follow from corollary forms of nationality, ethnicity, race and family roles' (ibid., p. xv). The strength of the book is in showing how the state reproduces itself through practices of familial reproduction.

44 See Chapter 12 on the ethic of care.

45 Godelier, *Enigma of the Gift*, pp. 88–95. See Annette B. Weiner, *Inalienable Possessions: The Paradox of Keeping While Giving*, University of California Press, Berkeley, CA, 1992, on the *kitomu* (the different spelling of the same exchange system is only a geographical with the concept of *kitoum* used on Woodlark Island).

46 C.A. Gregory, *Savage Money: The Anthropology and Politics of Commodity Exchange*, Harwood Academic Publishers, Amsterdam, Chapter 5.

47 Edward Forset, *A Comparative Discovrse of the Bodies Natvral and Politiqve*, Theatrum Orbis Terrarum, Amsterdam, (1606) 1973, p. 8.

48 *Ibid.*, p. 10.

49 Jack Goody, *The Interface of the Written and the Oral*, Cambridge University Press, Cambridge, 1987; David R. Olson, *The World on Paper: The Conceptual and Cognitive Implications of Writing and Reading*, Cambridge University Press, Cambridge, 1994; Thomas Crump, *The Phenomenon of Money*, Routledge & Kegan Paul, London, 1981.

50 Naomi Klein, *Fences and Windows: Dispatches from the Front Lines of the Globalization Debate*, Flamingo, London, 2002, p. 170.

51 Here I draw on conversations with Leanne Reinke. The term 'mode of inquiry' itself comes from conversations with Chris Ziguras. See Umberto Eco and Constantino Marmo (eds), *On the Medieval Theory of Signs*,

John Benjamins, Amsterdam, 1989; Etienne Gilson, *History of Christian Philosophy in the Middle Ages*, Sheed and Ward, London (1955) 1980.

52 See Anna L. Peterson, Being *Human: Ethics, Environment and Our Place in the World*, University of California Press, Berkeley, CA, 2001, Chapter 5.

53 Caroline Walker Bynum, *Holy Feast and Holy Fast*, University of California Press, Berkeley, CA, 1987, plate 2.25.

54 John L. Esposito, *Unholy War: Terror in the Name of Islam*, Oxford University Press, Oxford, 2002, pp. 5-6, 73.

55 Aziz Al-Azmeh, *Islam and Modernities*, 2nd edn, Verso, London, 1996, pp. 151-2.

56 Andrew Vincent, *Theories of the State*, Basil Blackwell, Oxford, 1987, Chapter 3.

# Part II

Rethinking Formations of Practice and Being

# FIVE Constituting Customary Community

We have come a long way since the nineteenth-century representations of the savage – noble or otherwise.[1] However, the view that customary and traditional tribalism is a simple and anachronistic vestige of past ways of life, ways of life that will gradually and inevitably submit to a kind of globalized genocide, still runs deep. Anthony Giddens's writings indicate an instructive split here between theory and ideology. It is a good starting point to this discussion, for he believes that customary community is already irrelevant. From a sophisticated theorist who writes with subtlety about the high-presence availability of tribal societies and the complexity of their time-space edges with other social formations comes a resounding death-knell. 'Those societies', he says, 'in which human beings have lived for all but a fraction of the existence of humankind – tribal societies – have either been destroyed or absorbed into larger entities.'[2] In response we can certainly say that the future of indigenous peoples sustaining tribal ways of life is grim, but it is a gross misrepresentation to say that they have all but disappeared.[3] With Ken Coates, we can call this fascination with the 'last of' phenomenon – the last of a particular tribe or way of life – a global death-watch. It has antecedents going back to James Fenimore Cooper's *The Last of the Mohicans*.[4]

Ringing of analogous misrepresentation, we can find examples of genteel 'primitivism' from other unexpected sources. From Ernest Gellner, a one-time anthropologist who did his fieldwork in the central High Atlas of Morocco,[5] comes the following grossly-simplified distinction between oral and literate cultures: 'the savage kinds [clan and tribal] reproduce themselves spontaneously … without conscious design, supervision, surveillance, or special nutrition. Cultivated or garden cultures [agrarian and industrial] are different, though they have developed from the wild varieties. They possess a complexity and richness.'[6] Even Gellner's ironical style does not explain that description. Again, from Michael Mann, a scholar usually blessed with magisterial understanding of his chosen fields of research, comes a facile discussion of clans and hunter-gatherer tribes as if they have no culture at all:

> their social structure was, *and is*, loose and flexible, permitting freedom of choice in social attachments. They are not dependent on specific other people for their subsistence. They cooperate in small bands and in larger units but, broadly, they can choose which ones. And they can disengage when they wish. Lineages, clans and other kinship groupings may give a sense of identity but not substantial duties or rights. Nor is there much territorial constraint. Despite earlier work based on some Australian [A]borigines, most gatherer-hunters do not possess fixed territories. Given their social flexibility, it would be difficult for such collective property rights to develop anyway.[7]

It is as if Mann is overcome by his own meta-evolutionary thesis that social history is a movement towards greater fixity and complexity of social organization – his liberal story of caging. There is not a sentence in the previous quote that does not cry out for a critical response. If his is a picture of what might have been, based on archaeological findings, then the limits of evidence simply do not sustain its conclusions. There are no artefacts of 'freedom of choice' that have been dug up by archaeologists. If his simple picture is a projection back into the pre-historical past based on what anthropological studies now tell us about contemporary hunter-gatherers, then it is arrantly wrong. With exceptions, the evidence runs strongly to the contrary.[8]

The task of this chapter is to find a way through an impasse in the current debates about tribal society. On the one hand, as the work of such writers as Giddens, Gellner and Mann illustrates, there is projected a Great Divide between structures of traditional tribalism and the structures of modernism (and for that matter, postmodernism) that underpin contemporary formations of nationalism and globalism. Uncritically accepting the terms of this Divide has the effect of distorting theoretical analyses of customary community and polity (yes, tribes can have polities even if they do not have states). These writers do not recognize how tribalism continues even as it is being reconstituted and overlaid by processes of modern and postmodern globalization – except perhaps in terms of tribes being 'absorbed' into the commanding momentum of global change. On the other hand, as we will see in forthcoming discussion of writers such as Bourdieu and Appadurai, there is a tendency to do exactly the opposite, that is, to collapse some quite fundamental differences between tribal and modern societies. This entails a different but equally problematic distortion. However, ironically, one of the effects is the same. Either significant dimensions of the continuing distinctiveness of tribalism as a way of life disappears or 'tribalism' becomes a term of abuse for closed particularistic movements. For example, in the hands of the usually-insightful social critic Zygmunt Bauman, the term the 'new tribalism' is used to refer to the contemporary development of sensibilities of extreme xenophobic intolerance to difference. As a means of countering both directions of analysis, the following turns to a discussion of the structures and practices of tribalism.

The discussion concentrates on the levels of conjunctural and integrational analysis, discussing the dominant modes of practice in tribal communities, and focussing on their dominant mode of exchange (reciprocity) with references to the mode of enquiry (analogy), and organization (kinship). Other modes of practice could have been chosen, but the point here is to show the present method at work, not to provide a comprehensive reworking of existing theory. The intention is, first, to show how the method is no more than a guiding map, and, second, to illustrate how using such a bio-cartography should in no way necessarily lead to a reductive account of the trees in the wood or the blood in the arteries of social life. That is, in saying that there are patterns of structuration, it does not in any way necessitate giving up a hermeneutic exploration of life's messiness. To give depth to the discussion, the focus is substantially on questions about different relations of exchange. What is a gift? What is a commodity? How are these different categories related to the constitution of traditional tribes? How are goods embedded in social relations, even though sometimes a particular object can go through phases of being one, then the other – a gift, then a commodity?

## Reciprocity as a dominant mode of exchange

The argument here is simple, but not necessarily commonsensical. It has three initial steps, though they will have to be carefully qualified: first, reciprocal exchange is the dominant mode of exchange in traditional tribal societies, even if other forms of exchange are actively given ways of coexisting with it. *Reciprocity*, in the sense used here, can be defined as exchange of goods *within a network of exchange relations* that carries the 'spirit' of face-to-face integration between the persons involved in exchange, and which thus require some form of ritual recognition or *social* return. This is a broader definition than that usually used for gift exchange.[9] Reciprocity does not necessarily require a return gift. Using the term 'reciprocity' in this way is a methodologically more abstract way of talking about exchange than 'gifting'. Gifts are simply *goods* that have, for a time, become the symbolic media within the broader and incredibly-complex process of reciprocity.[10]

The second step in the argument is that this form of exchange is basically different from, say, barter or commodity exchange. Without wanting to set up an unassailable divide between *the* gift and *the* commodity, I still want to say that gifts and commodities are set within different relations of exchange, relations that are qualitatively different in *social form*. I remember many years ago sitting in an Italian café in Melbourne having a lengthy argument with a friendly French philosopher about what made gifts and commodities different. His eminently-defensible position, indicative of a predominant tendency in the contemporary literature, was that the difference was only one of degree not of quality. The difference, he said, could only be found in the social fact that commodities tend to travel much greater distances along time-space pathways than gift-exchange objects. My response, which he continued to find unconvincing, was that his was a flat-earth theory of social relations. In addition to his useful empirical generalization about differences of degree, there were ontological differences that need to be taken into account – basic qualitative differences between the two forms grounded in the issue that commodity exchange is more abstract than gift exchange.

Without dichotomizing gifts and commodities, it is still possible to argue that commodity exchange tends to occur between abstracted strangers, based on their mutual usually taken-for-granted confidence in an abstract system of exchange-value, whereas reciprocally-framed gift-exchange demands something else. Certainly in modern settings, people give gifts to strangers, but it tends to be done as an act of benefaction or charity rather than as the initiation of relationships of reciprocity. Analogously, in settings dominated by tribalism we sometimes find circuits of commodity exchange, but these circuits tend to be conducted at the boundaries of the society rather than being central to its dominant modes of integration.[11]

This is the basis of the third step. The difference between reciprocal exchange and commodity exchange is a qualitative one, but not as two ends of a spectrum. It is a question of layers of *social* abstraction. Reciprocal exchange is framed socially by an integrative frame of *embodied* relations that works to both mediate and make people *present* to each other. By contrast, in commodity exchange, despite all the language of pseudo-intimacy, the social frame of the abstract market acts to *disembody*, objectify and rationalize the particularities of the persons in the contract of purchase. Life-times of research could be spent by bevies of functionalist or postmodern ethnographers, following the biographies or networks of particular gifts and commodities, and this difference would either escape their notice or be unavailable to them theoretically.[12]

From the way in which my argument is expressed, it can be seen that the approach does not exclude reciprocal exchange being present as a subordinate mode of exchange in modern or postmodern settings. This occurs, for example during ritualistic events such as Christmas or Hanukkah, and personal milestones such as birthdays; or as gifts of flowers to strangers in the street because you like the smell of their underarm deodorant.[13] Nor does it preclude commodity exchange being practised in tribal settings. However, the argument about layers of exchange – dominant and subordinate, generally framing and socially restricted – hints at why the ontological disjuncture between the reciprocity of gifts and the modern commodification of gift-giving in late-capitalism now makes those old and new festivals so rife with personal tension. It gives us a way of understanding why commodity exchange in traditionally-constituted tribal communities is either peripheral, subject to chiefly decrees of taboo and of prerogative, or limited to trading networks with exotic boundary-crossing strangers, reviled outsiders or lower-caste others. Finally, and most paradoxically, it allows us to make some sense of the evidence that practices of reciprocal exchange, particularly in those tribal settings that are constituted in the contradictory intersection of modern and traditional formations, can flourish even as they are changed by the context of globalizing capital.

In earlier defining reciprocity as 'the exchange of goods that carry the "spirit" of embodied connection between the persons involved in exchange', you will have noticed that the word 'spirit' was marked out for querying and treating with some analytical distance. The notion of the spirit of the gift comes to us from Marcel Mauss and his classic text *The Gift*.[14] Mauss drew on the Polynesian concepts of *hau* and *mana*, suggesting that the gift carried the spirit of the giver with it. The thing being exchanged, he says, has a life, a spirit that demands a return. This comment initiated what has become one of the most sustained debates in the history of anthropological theory. It is a debate that at the end of the twentieth century took a new leap in sophistication, marked by the publication of a remarkably lucid book – Maurice Godelier's *The Enigma of the Gift*.[15] The book was published in the context of a wealth of immediate antecedents, in particular, Annette Weiner's *Inalienable Possessions* and Christopher Gregory's *Savage Money*.[16] We will return to that development in a moment, but there is some groundwork to be done first. It is, at first read, familiar ground to anthropologists – concentrating on a few classical texts from Malinowski to Appadurai – but some critical twists will be added.

### History of the debate

Simplifying the debate for the purposes of brevity, the contest over the nature of the gift became a struggle between two apparently irreconcilable positions. Both were bound up in a wider social politics about the nature of being human. On the one hand, there are those like Mauss who attribute magical powers to gifts, or, more accurately, those who take the observations of the natives that gifts embodied a spirit as an adequate description of the magical power of the reciprocity. This makes gift-giving a part of a culture that is ontologically different from secular commodified modernity. On the other hand, there are those who treat gifts as instrumentally-given goods in a rational network of stone-age economics, and/or as incidental elements in structurally-sustained systems of exchange. This either minimizes the Great Divide or reduces the difference to one of differently-regulated *modes of practice*.

Complicating this summary, some writers held both positions at the same time. Mauss's approach, for example, was unintentionally contradictory. While subjectively treating gifts as shrouded in a perceived living spirit, he also writes along another, less foregrounded (instrumentalist) line. In reciprocal exchange, he writes, 'the form usually taken is that of the gift generously offered; but the accompanying behaviour is formal pretence and social deception, while the transaction itself is based on mutual obligation and economic self-interest'.[17] This tension between the subjective and objective will later come back as the point of departure for writers such as Pierre Bourdieu. Mauss's theoretical work was paralleled by the functionalist ethnography of Bronislaw Malinowski, conducted in the Trobriand Islands off Kaiser Wilhelm's Land.[18] Using a method cast as the level of empirical generalization, Malinowski documents a dual movement of gifts and counter-gifts passed in opposite exchange-circles around a *kula* ring of Massim communities. Both writers describe how 'reciprocal exchange', as it came to known, could still be humanly rational while being fundamentally different from the economic rational*ism* of commodity exchange. Although, in later work, Malinowski was explicitly critical of any Maussian sense that the objects of exchange gained their power as fetishized symbols, in *Argonauts of the Western Pacific* (1922), he had implicitly supported Mauss's developing notion of the *hau*, a notion that three years later was to be elaborated in *The Gift*. (Although it is of no particular relevance, it was those two books, as well as Malinowski's *The Sex Lives of Savages*, that 57 years later drew me to the Trobriands to stay in one of the family houses of the Paramount Chief.)

When Claude Lévi-Strauss entered the fray the debate was well under way. His critique of Mauss stands out as being the most influential. Invoking the spirit of the gift, Lévi-Strauss said, is not an explanation at all: the *hau* is no more than 'the conscious form whereby men [and women] of a given society ... apprehended an unconscious necessity whose explanation lies elsewhere'.[19] He is clearly right. However, Lévi-Strauss went on more dubiously to argue that exchange as *the* 'primary fundamental phenomenon' of all social life (a position that is criticized in Chapter 4 in this book) was based upon the unconscious processes of the mind. The other direction taken by writers such as Pierre Bourdieu was to accept provisionally the description of the natives as subjective reality and then to emphasize the objective rational-calculative side of gift giving as its objective reality. Part of the problem with this is that Bourdieu has to treat the objective reality as something that is suppressed from subjective consciousness: a little strange given that calculation is a pre-eminently conscious activity. Bourdieu's position is part of a family of accounts that reduce the *hau* of the gift to 'its material reward'.[20] These accounts have the effect, perhaps unintended, of flattening the difference between gift and commodity exchange. In his writings on Algeria, Bourdieu is, for example, careful to distinguish between an agrarian and a capitalist economy. In an agrarian economy the cycle of production is timed as palpably seasonal. In a capitalist economy the more arbitrary temporal cycle of production 'presupposes the constitution of a mediated, abstract future, with calculation having to make up for the absence of an intuitive grasp of the process as a whole'.[21]

However, when it comes to gift exchange in the same context, his analysis is sustained by a belief that by moving to this more abstract level of analysis – a categorical analysis of temporality – he has resolved the 'debate' between Lévi-Strauss and Mauss, and the relation between the objective and the subjective. The temporal separation between acts of gift giving, he says, helps to explain how the objective registers of self-interest and honour that codify and force the return of the gift, can be subjectively suppressed. And, indeed, it *sometimes* does so help to explain it. It is an adroit if overgeneralized insight, except that the next proposition leads Bourdieu to the kind of reductive analysis that Geoff Sharp describes critically as 'analysis on one plane'.[22] Bourdieu effectively reduces gift-giving to calculative self-interest. Gift exchange becomes

> an exchange in and by which the agents strive to conceal the objective truth of the exchange, i.e. the calculation that which guarantees the equity of the exchange. If 'fair exchange', the direct swapping of equivalent values, is the truth of gift exchange, gift exchange is a swapping that cannot acknowledge itself as such.[23]

Thus, polity and community, society and group, are collapsed into each other, and gifts become 'symbolic taxes',[24] with the metaphor of 'taxes' screaming out its post-tribal heritage.

It is only a short step from Bourdieu's reflexive modernism to Arjun Appadurai's postmodernism. Here gifts are subsumed into his greatly expanded category of commodities. It is much like Anthony Giddens's discussion of the subsuming of tribes into global capitalism. A sympathetic reading of Appadurai's introduction to *The Social Life of Things* suggests that he did not initially intend for this to happen. There are early passages where he criticizes all-embracing definitions of 'commodities as goods intended for exchange'. However, a couple of pages later, ostensibly looking for a sustainable means of distinguishing commodity exchange, barter exchange and gift exchange, Appadurai says, 'let us start with the idea that a commodity is anything intended for exchange'.[25] This move is the start of a theoretical and political slippery-slope. Before long he starts looking for the 'commodity potential of all things'. This is done without any recognition that while he might be right at a certain level of theoretical abstraction and temporal projection that all things can *in theory* become commodities, it is theoretically dangerous to make this the basis of analysis. For the tribal elder, crying silent tears of ecstasy at the sight of a *kwaimatnie*, this temporally-abstracted potential is unimaginable.[26] This man's sacred set of objects – a polished black stone, some pointed bones and several brown seed cases, all wrapped in a strip of red bark – are not future commodities or even *potential* future commodities. The quality of being potential commodities does not inhere in them as essence or projection. They are in that socially-contextualized moment of sublime ecstasy, *and perhaps forever*, inalienable goods. For them to be trans-*formed* into *being* commodities would entail entry into a qualitatively-different exchange system, and someone would have to carry them there.

Is this splitting hairs? It is only if you think that there is an essential inevitability that the commodity form should always be that form of exchange that is normalized as the teleology of things. Appadurai's definition makes it so, by turning most if not all moments of exchange into commodity situations. 'I propose', he says, 'that *the commodity situation in the social life of any "thing" be defined as the situation in which its exchangeability (past, present and future) for some other thing is its socially relevant feature*'.[27] In this definition, gifts and commodities as exchangeable items become the same kinds of thing. And if not now, then in the social theorist's vision of the ever-possible future, gifts are commodities.

What then explains the reason for Appadurai's unthinking reductivism? Why would anyone characterize 'gift exchange as a particular form of the circulation of commodities'?[28] The first hint of an explanation comes as he traces his intellectual antecedence back through Bourdieu's analysis of the temporal delay of gifting to that line quoted earlier from Mauss. Appadurai makes self-interest the common spirit that underlies both forms of exchange. In Bourdieu's upside-down and ironically inappropriate phrase, tribal subjects in not recognizing this objective reality deny the 'true soil of their life'.[29] Just as Annette Weiner has criticized the way in which an abstracted conception of *reciprocity* was appropriated by classical political economists as being fundamental to capitalism and thus used to justify the rise of the free-market economy,[30] here we can be critical of Bourdieu and Appadurai for a further stage in the collapsing of different levels of abstraction.

The second hint for sustaining an explanation comes in the conclusion to Appadurai's celebrated essay. There, the demand for commodities and gifts is described as being conducted as rigid regulative relations, regimes of social control enacted by the powerful and the elite. However, by contrast to *the* gift, *the* commodity is described as disrupting such closure. The commodity is thus, for an unsuspecting moment, lifted up as the postmodern apotheosis of freedom: 'since commodities constantly spill beyond the boundaries of specific cultures (and thus specific regimes of value), such political control of demand is always threatened with disturbance'.[31] Here the object, abstracted from the context of embodied interchange, and thus more mobile than the gift, is naturalized as the pre-eminent state of things. This is thoroughly confused. The gift is now different from the thing of which it is a subcategory. The politics of this issue will be expanded upon in Chapter 12, but the point to be made now is that Appadurai's position takes us to an apparent impasse where commodities are the pre-eminent good, both in exchange and in politics.

Maurice Godelier's work on the *Enigma of the Gift* offers a way out of this collapsing of categories. Beginning with a critique of Mauss, Godelier give us a social-relational account of exchange showing how different kinds of goods, including commodities, circulate in different ways within traditional tribal societies depending upon how they are socially framed. Over time, goods can move through different social frames, even if the dominant (and most constitutively contradictory) social frame is reciprocity. Unlike Lévi-Strauss, this does not mean Godelier makes exchange the basis of social life and thus he does not need to reduce the materiality of social relations, including relations of kinship and marriage, to *symbolic* interchange. The first analytical point to make then is that for Godelier the gift can be explained in social-relational terms as a social good, connected to others, within changing and complex patterns of interchange. For example, the distinction between alienable and inalienable goods is not coextensive with the distinction between exchangeable and sacred goods. In Annette Weiner's terms, there are some gifts that are not meant to be given away – the paradox of keeping-while-giving. Here Godelier's point is both simpler and easier to sustain. Some gifts, such as those from the Gods, are inalienable and can never be fully reciprocated, nor are they available for passing onto others. They are gifts to be kept out of circulation and are often hidden from the view of the uninitiated. These *sacred goods* sit behind the exchange of other circulating valuable or precious objects as the always-something-more. In the terms of the present argument, *valuable objects* or gifts are thus intimately tied back to, but already abstracted from the sacred. They are exchangeable, but the whole imaginary of the society goes with them in the exchange. They are inalienable, but only until they are reciprocally replaced, and then they have gone. And it is upon this possibility of being lifted out – being replaced and therefore replaceable – that in a different social setting further stages of abstraction are possible, including the possibility of being commodified. Godelier writes:

> The precious objects which circulate in gift-exchanges can do so only because they are substitutes twice over: substitutes for sacred objects and substitutes for human beings. Like the former they are inalienable; but unlike sacred objects, which do not circulate, these do ... While they are substitutes for sacred objects and for the supernatural beings that inhabit them, they are also substitutes for human beings, for their substance, their bones, their flesh, their attributes, titles and ranks, for their possessions, material and immaterial. It is for this reason that they are able to *take the place* of humans ... This twin nature of valuable objects makes them hard to define and therefore to think, in our world in which things are separate from persons. But it also enables us to understand why these objects function as currencies, without having all the attributes, and that they often become a currency by shedding a great portion of their former functions and becoming an impersonal means of developing impersonal commercial relations, an instrument that circulates only once it has been stamped with the seal of the institution representing the community as a whole and which is the source of power and law: the state.[32]

Systematizing this argument and drawing it out with help from other sources we can then say that there are a number of different kinds of objects in traditional customary societies:

1. *Sacred objects*: those which, for all intents and purposes, are inalienable, but involve reciprocity with the gods or spirits in and beyond this world.[33]

2. *Valuable objects*: those which are inalienable until reciprocally exchanged, or have limited alienability within restricted circuits of exchange such as gift exchange. It is these goods that most often in the anthropological literature called *gifts*.

3. *Basic objects*: those available for exchange through mutual use, barter or as currency objects. These goods can even become tribal commodities in the restricted sense of that term. Although basic usefulness is never a criterion for entering formal networks of reciprocal exchange or for being sacred, they are often mutually shared in immediate relations of reciprocity.

4. *Currency objects*: those acting as a kind of money. However, within tribal settings, currency goods such as salt money or kina shells are not available for impersonal exchange as capital until a further process of abstraction occurs.

5. *Commodified objects*: those that circulate in restricted markets, usually carried by kin-related groups of traders.[34]

As a way of taking this position further, the following discussions sets out on two quests. First, in order to understand the ontological framing of value, it travels down an apparent byway into a discussion of differently-valued objects, from the crowns of kings to the testicles of Christian boys. Second, it sets out to give Godelier's discussion of money a different emphasis from his own to show how his argument about 'something needing to be kept out of circulation in order to sustain the objects of exchange' can be rethought in terms of the abstraction argument. Godelier himself raises the abstraction process when describing the necessary characteristics of *valuable goods*. 'The "abstract" character and the deconnecting of these objects from everyday life', says Godelier, 'seem to me to be prerequisites for their being able to "embody" social relations and then to re-present them, to present them back to the social actors in a form which is material abstract and symbolic.'[35] However, he does not relate that insight back to the question of the changing nature of value. Opening up this second issue becomes the basis for our next chapter on money and writing as means of exchange and communication.

### Of crowns and precious stones

Writing in *Argonauts of the Western Pacific*, the seminal book mentioned earlier, Bronislaw Malinowski reflected on the parallel significance of kula shells circulating the Trobriand Islands and the crown jewels he had once seen at Edinburgh Castle. 'The Crown Jewels', he said, 'in fact any heirlooms too valuable and too cumbersome to be worn, represent the same type as vaygu'a [kula valuables] in that they are merely possessed for the sake of possession itself, and the ownership of them with the ensuing renown is the main source of their value.'[36] Malinowski's reflection, written against the context of the early-twentieth-century tendency to overdraw the distinction between traditional and modern exchange, over-accentuates the opposite position and is an early indication of the late-twentieth-century tendency, just discussed, to collapse the difference. This collapsing gives us pause to draw some connections between an Alice-in-Wonderland tea-party of objects: crowns, precious jewels, lumps of old rough-hewn rock and the testicles of young boys. The argument here is that their meanings vary across historically-embedded frames and moments rather than being reducible to the objects *per se*. The embeddedness of the objects has a special relevance – the closer they are to what can be called *enduring nature-culture* the more layers of meaning they can sustain. Few of these *moments* that these objects find themselves in are what Appadurai calls 'commodity situations', even though by the end of the description the goods described will be thoroughly imbricated in a setting where commodity exchange is the dominant mode of exchange. The implicit argument throughout will be that even if providing a cultural biography of things (Kopytoff's phrase) enriches the analysis, the description quickly cries out for a more structural explanation of the place of things in the social relations of communities and polities. The conceptual markers of this will be placed in italics. Thus while the description is conducted in terms of subjective meaning, embedded within almost every sentence are terms signifying different kinds of subjective-objective structuring: different ontological formations from tribalism to postmodernism; different formations of practice from absolutism to capitalism; and different institutions of organization from monarchy to church and state. Malinowski's visit to Edinburgh provides both the metaphor of connection and the post-reciprocal setting that will take us from the medieval crowning of monarchs to contemporary presentations of national spectacle and touristic consumption of inalienable and controlled objects like crowns that were once held back from popular viewing.

There is evidence to suggest that ritual seats or footprints in stone preceded crowns as markers of inauguration. In Scotland, but also Ireland and France, there can be found footprints carved out of rock surfaces on the tops of hills. One example is found at Fort Dunadd, a single rocky massif rising above the Kilmartin Valley. On a rock shelf at the top of the hill there is a rock-cut basin, large enough to act as a water receptacle for hand washing, and two footprints, one shallow and one deep. A detailed carving of what is thought by its characteristic double outline to be a Pictish boar was found on the rock behind in 1904, although I could not find it when I went there in June 2000. Examples like Dunadd are believed to be the places that *tribal* kings stood for investiture ceremonies, and written records exist of later inauguration ceremonies, including those of the MacDonald Lords of the Isles in the late medieval period.[37] The full meaning of those events is, however, only available by archaeological inference, and the value of those places is now completely overshadowed by that of a single moveable stone, once used to invest the *traditional* Scots kings: the Stone of Scone. The first Scots' inauguration to be described in written detail is that of Alexander III, in 1249. In an account by an Aberdeen chantry priest, John of Fordoun, there was no crowning, but rather a churchyard ceremony presided over by the Bishop of St Andrews. The eight-year-old future king sits upon a 'regal chair – that is, the Stone – and the earls and the other nobles place vestments under his feet, with bent knees before the Stone.'[38] The Stone was claimed in later texts to have been invested with *mana*[39] and brought to Scone from the plain of Luz in Egypt via Sicily, Compostella in Spain,[40] the Hill of Tara in Ireland and Argyleshire in Scotland, the place of the footprints of Kilmartin. It was thus placed in a mythological kula ring that connected the Stone of Scone to the origins of the *Scoti* and back to the pillow of stone upon which Abraham's grandson Jacob had once laid his head.

We could similarly trace the more recent history of the golden stool of the Ashanti, a gold-adorned wooden chair that descended from the clouds. It was not to be actually sat upon. On sacred ceremonial occasions, the king would pretend to sit on it three times and then seat himself on his own stool, his arm resting on the sacred Stool. Edwin W. Smith relates the story of Governor Sir Frank Hodgson beginning a war in March 1900 by telling King Prempeh that the Stool belonged to the Queen Victoria. As colonial governor of the Gold Coast and representative of the Queen, Hodgson said that he should be given the Stool to sit upon. Fighting began a week later with 1007 casualties on the British side, and an unknown number on the Ashanti side. Smith writes, 'An excellent example of the blunders that are made through ignorance of the African mind! The Governor regarded the Stool as a kind of Stone of Scone upon which the kings of Ashanti were seated at their accession.' [41]

Crowns, even more symbolically mobile than stools, thrones and cumbrous rocks, were regularly used in Europe from the eighth century to signify *monarchical* ascension. In the period of *absolutism*, they became objects of immense but ambiguously-revered value. On the one hand, they accrued ambiguously sacred value as the objectified reality of the monarchy. In this 'the crown' became the lived synecdoche of the body of the monarch and, subsequently, institution of monarchy,[42] but more than that, each particular crown was afforded cultural depth in itself, carrying the meaning of the monarchs who wore it. There is evidence that those monarchs conceived of their crowns as gifts in the tribal-sacred sense.[43] However that may be, the meaning of being gifted a kingship – variously bestowed, conferred and elected – changed dramatically across history. Crowns were loved, kissed, and looked upon in awe, particularly when they were dug up after being waylaid in some political struggle. On the other hand, out of context they became divisible objects able to be plundered for their valuable coloured stones, just like the cloth and jewels of more profane vestments. In *early modern* Britain, if the frame of a crown became old or weakened, the jewels were taken out and reset in a new frame. Much like the abstract body of the king – the body that in dying lives forever – the discarded frame either ceased to be part of the crown or was melted into the precious metal of the new, but the Crown always lived on, symbol of the regal body politic.

Indicative of this practice of discarding the old frame, the oldest surviving English state-crown dates from as late as 1715. This simple fact qualifies Annette Weiner's argument that crowns as inalienable objects always had and have absolute transcendent value, but more recent history calls it into question completely.[44] The central jewel in the monde on top of that oldest crown, once thought to be the real aquamarine,[45] is a paste of the original that was removed in the early-nineteenth century to be included in Queen Victoria's new crown. Because, until 1725, the only diamonds were mined in India and the few made it to Europe were extraordinarily expensive, it became common practice in the eighteenth and nineteenth centuries to hire diamonds from jewel merchants to enhance the coronation crowns. The sense of the politico-sacred here continued while curiously being driven by commodity value. In the twentieth century, *commodity capitalism* made diamonds sufficiently available for crowns to be unique 'authentic' things. However, by the end of the century and the beginning of the twenty-first, stones such as diamonds had become a girl's best friend, and crowns had become more a source of *postmodern* tourist curiosity than objects of sacred reverence.[46] A Tower of London exhibition guide in the year 2000 notes without further comment on the dour specificity that George IV did not have the 12,314 diamonds 'needed' for his coronation of 1821 so £65,250 worth were hired from commercial *agents*, 'the Crown Jewellers'. In the display case with the crown are 12,314 diamonds – not those diamonds, but any old diamonds – lent to represent the original hirelings by a *globalizing* company out of the old African *empire*. Now that the *abstract state* is taxing the *monarchy*, and royal wealth is declining in relative terms, that globalizing *corporation* De Beers is cheerfully thanked as a sponsor of the royal exhibition.[47] Under these circumstances the awe that attaches to the crown now becomes the awe of immense monetary value and perhaps the awe of historicity, but no longer the unassailable awe of the politico-sacred. The crown becomes a *postmodern commodity*, one that cannot be exchanged and cannot be readily circulated out of the realm.

It was during the very period when the British crowns became unexchangeable commodities that the cultural fortunes of the Stone of Destiny were reinvested with ambiguous but sustainable meaning: traditional *and* modern, religious *and* secular, national *and* civic. It also became a *postmodern* gift, the gift that is not actually given and that few true believers think is the Real Stone anyway. Edinburgh Castle now houses not only the Crown Jewels of Scotland, but also a rough-hewn stone, believed to have been taken by Edward I of England in 1296 and returned to Scotland by the Blair government 700 years later in an act of prestation-hype. I call it prestation only in an ironic sense because if you read the fine print the

British *crown* still legally owns the Stone. In all of those 'And Whereas' clauses prefacing the 1996 hand-calligraphed royal warrant for the 'return' of the Stone, there is no clause enacting the giving. Prime Minister Tony Blair's speech of 3 July 1996 said it more directly: 'The stone remains the property of the crown.' It is a further irony that the *modern* legal document is given authenticity by being hand-written in the traditional manner. Reinforcing this point about the overlay of ontological formations, on the day of the return of the Stone to Scotland, deliberately chosen to be St Andrew's Day, a traditional ceremony was held at St Giles Cathedral to celebrate the modern *national* (Scottish) and *state* (British) occasion. From the Old Testament, a young person read *Genesis*, 28, in Gaelic, telling the story of Jacob and his pillow of stone. From the New Testament, another youth read from *John*, 1, in Doric, describing the calling of Saint Andrew, traditional patron saint of the Scots Kirk, and his brother Simon Peter, the rock. Without interviewing all the participants it is impossible to know if the ironies of intersection were intentional, and even then it is doubtful whether enunciated intentions are ever more than practically conscious, brought to the surface by the asking. Why, for example, in an act of post-modern excess, was *Braveheart*'s Mel Gibson invited to the occasion? What we can say with certainty was that the words of the service were chosen carefully. Crossing the fields of sacred liturgy to nationalist ideology, the Moderator of the General Assembly of the Church of Scotland addressed the congregation: 'During all the long pilgrimage of years, the ideal of Scottish nationhood and the reality of Scottish identity have never been obliterated from the hearts of the people. The recovery of this ancient symbol of the Stone cannot but strengthen the proud distinctiveness of the people of Scotland.'[48] There you have it: even he did not say that *the* Stone had been given back.

The earlier reference to boys' testicles can now be related, but it is not just as whimsy that it is included here. Colloquial reference to the testicles as 'the family jewels' is indicative of the contemporary ironical use of metaphor – even metaphors of once great power, now half-dead – to reinvest the body with meaning. More than that, we have only to read the tracts of religious fundamentalists to feel the continuing power of these embodied metaphors. This is the power of objects that take on sacred meaning, where meanings become 'flesh'. (This is elaborated in Chapter 8.) Without a hint of irony or late-modern humour, the Christian pamphleteer Harold Barrow writes in 1947 that the 'old story of English history', the attempted stealing of the crown jewels in 1671, 'suggests a parable about other crowns and jewels'. It is a parable about something '*far more precious* than the jewels in the king's regalia, for every boy has his own Castle of Manhood to defend, and within that Castle there are wonderful and marvellous possessions all of them bearing a sacred and symbolic meaning in the experience of Life' (emphasis added).[49] Barrow is writing with religious certainty not so much about crown jewels in either sense, as about the sanctity of *embodied life* and the religious meshing of the *universal* and the *particular*. He concludes:

> The Castle in the city of Edinburgh in which the Scottish regalia and jewels are safely stored is built firm upon the rock. So in your life there must be a sure and solid foundation. Then you will be able to say truly:
> 'On Christ the solid rock I stand,
> All other ground is sinking sand.'[50]

Poor poetics, but this is still the foundation of contemporary Christianity. God *gave* to the world his only begotten son as the rock upon which Christians stand. The image of the rock as foundation-of-being is found in cultures across the world, from the cenotaph in Edinburgh castle to the Islamic Dome of the Rock in Jerusalem. The latter is simultaneously the place where in both Jewish and Christian mythology Abraham prepared to *give* his son to God on an altar of sticks. In both places, semi-hewn rock emerges from the ground and is sacralized by surrounding it with inscribed pediments and marble columns. In both places, we also see – countering the overwhelmingly dominant trend in theories of nationalism – the overlaying of traditional forms of the sacred with modern nationalism. Both proceed forth in semi-acknowledged relationship (see Chapter 10).

The foundation of the Scottish Kirk is no different. Over time, it has been given metaphoric power through a manifold process that we find everywhere. First, it comes as an image of *enduring nature* – the stone is continuous with the roughly carved rocks used for the sacred investiture of kings, and it is connected to the reinvestment of national mythologies, for example, in the Stone of Scone as it is returned in 1996 across the Scottish border. Second, it comes in the form of *enduring culture*. In 1249 the Bishop of St Andrews consecrates the traditional ruler. In 1996 a ceremony is held at St Giles cathedral celebrating the national occasion. Third, it comes in the image of an *enduring gift* – the blood of Christ as the kind of gift that as Godelier rightly says cannot be reciprocated. The point of this in terms of a theory of structural levels is that we have to remember that despite all the abstractions of exchange in a post-reciprocal, rationalized, commodified world there are still people who *at one level of their being* continue to live the enchantments of sacred keeping and exchanging, and in a place like Israel, Iraq and East Timor are prepared to die for those beliefs. In later chapters, an argument will be made that this level has been thoroughly overlaid by other more abstract forms of practice and understanding, but it does not mean that this 'prior' level has been thus made void.

When the Scottish National War Memorial was built on the elevated grounds of the medieval Edinburgh castle in 1927, it was placed where once stood the Chapel of St Mary, founded by King David I. It is no accident that highest portion of 'living rock' (a space of enduring nature) is left exposed in the shrine. On the lintel of the inner doorway are carved the words of the imperial poet Rudyard Kipling: 'Lest we forget' (a temporality of sacred recollection). Books of Honour list the names of almost every single Scot who has died in war service from 1914 to the present (an abstract relation of embodied connection). In case somebody has been left out, around the walls of the shrine are carved words that recall the sentiments expressed in many cenotaphs: 'And their names though lost to us are written in the book of God'. In this the abstract Word connects all bodies, remembered and forgotten. Like most shrines, the *modern* Edinburgh Memorial resunds with *traditional* biblical references. One author describes the inner sanctum thus:

> Eyes and feet turn instinctively to the central feature of the Shrine – the heart and core of the whole Memorial – the Stone of Remembrance and the Casket. The Stone is set upon an outcrop of the Rock itself, which here breaks through the flagged pavement as if eager to shoulder its burden ... Upon the face of the Stone, which is of green Corona marble, is cut the Cross of Sacrifice, surmounted by the inscription, Their Name Liveth. On the top, guarded by kneeling Angels like the Ark of the Covenant itself, stands the shining Casket ... It contains the Rolls of Honour which bear the names of Scotland's dead, deposited for the rest of time in the ineffable peace of this mystic, enchanted spot.[51]

In this description, the Word and the stone become mutually supportive. Other examples link the traditional, modern and postmodern, the colonial and the postcolonial. In July 2000, to mark the hundredth anniversary of the passing of the Australian Constitutional Bill – the signing of Australian semi-independence as an imperial colony – five Australian prime ministers, past and present, attended a service at Westminster Cathedral, London. As part of the celebrations Tony Blair agreed to build an Australian war shrine in the heart of London in recognition of the sacrifice of Australian soldiers who died defending Britain. Addressing Parliament the next day and recounting the agreement, Prime Minister Blair by a slip of naming lauded not Australian but 'American servicemen and women'. It was a fitting finale to the ambiguously-successful Australian attempt over the previous decade to make itself unique by revitalizing its memory of those who had fallen in war. A central part of this process included belatedly following other countries of the world to find

Australia's own unknown soldier. In the eulogy, Paul Keating spoke of a nation without modern nationalism:

> This unknown soldier is not interred here to glorify war over peace; or to assert a soldier's character over a civilian's; or one race or one nation or one religion above another; or men above women; of the war in which he fought and died above any other war; or of any one generation above any that has or will come later.

Similarly, the sculptors of the tomb spoke self-consciously of the monument's abstract design as inviting dialogue across times and places. Standing behind the head of the red-marble slab they placed four 10-metre pillars representing the primordial elements of fire, water, earth and air – the stuff of life and death. Here traditionalism met postmodernism. How do we know that the bones lying beneath the red marble, the person exhumed from a cemetery near the French village of Villers-Bretonneux, is an Australian rather than a German soldier? For some this is the question that cannot be asked, and for others is an irrelevancy. Either way, the Word and the stone are still there helping to explain to us the power and immortality of the nation.

And so ends a short biography of some strangely connected things. The description only scratched the surface, but it was intended to show that however deeply the description was pursued, however richly textured the description, it depended upon concepts that described systemic patterns of fundamental difference. Second, the discussion was intended to illustrate how treating all goods as subcategories of the master category *commodities* is unhelpful to understanding this world of intersecting layers of difference-identity. For the moment, this merging of the discussion about modes of exchange into a discussion about contextualized meaning serves to take us to the next sections examining first modes of enquiry and then modes of organization. With this first section in mind – that is, as indicative of a discussion moving between the general and particular – the concluding sections can be brief. All that these next sections are intended to achieve is to set up a point of correspondence from exchange to other modes of practice, and a point of comparison from customary society to the practical and ontological abstraction of social life in other social formations, both discussed in more detail in later chapters.

## Analogy as a dominant mode of enquiry

The material and ideational abstraction of the ways of thinking about, addressing, communicating and ordering the social-natural world is a foundational condition of knowledge in all social settings from the tribal to the postmodern, but that does not make the dominant level of epistemological abstraction the same across all social formations. Can both these arguments be made at the same time? Though not necessarily expressed in this way, it is an issue that has vexed social theory since it finally left behind the assumption held by anthropologists such as Lévi-Bruhl that non-literate societies were characterized by an absence of abstract thought. The debate between Claude Lévi-Strauss and Jack Goody provides a wonderful vignette of the much larger picture. Lévi-Strauss's *The Savage Mind* was, in its time, the seminal text in rethinking the comparison of magic and science. Written in the 1960s, it moved to treat magic and science as two parallel modes of acquiring knowledge rather than as epistemological opposites – 'two strategic levels at which nature is accessible to scientific enquiry: one roughly adapted to that of perception and imagination; the other at a remove from it ... [and] more remote from, sensible intuition'.[52] Despite his subtle radicalizing of the distinction, however, his approach was unable to get beyond a murky duality that is at once expressed as an absolute difference and as two parallel pathways to knowledge.

Lévi-Strauss begins by setting up two descriptive metaphors: the first, describes tribal 'science of the concrete' in terms of *bricolage*, and the second, modern science in terms of exploratory engineering. These are helpful to a point. The tribal taxonomer – for example, in thinking about the relationship between a woodpecker's beak, a person's tooth, and tooth ache – operates within a heterogenous repertoire of signs that are brought into interrelation much as a *bricoleur* might construct a building out of readily available, often pre-used materials. On the other side of the duality, the 'engineer' starts from a given theoretical and practical knowledge, but is pushed by the nature of abstracting *concepts* to question the universe of possibilities. Lévi-Strauss thus concludes: 'The physical world is approached from opposite ends in the two cases: one is supremely concrete, the other supremely abstract; one proceeds from the angle of sensible qualities and the other from that of formal properties.'[53]

While acknowledging Lévi-Strauss's contribution, Jack Goody's *The Domestication of the Savage Mind* criticizes him on this very point. Lévi-Strauss, he argues, succumbs to the very dichotomizing of mythical and scientific thought – concrete perception versus abstract thinking, atemporality versus history, cold versus hot societies – that *The Savage Mind* had set itself to get beyond.

> This dichotomy follows traditional thinking and attempts to account for supposed differences between 'we' and 'they' in a blanket fashion. On the one hand, it takes up a relativistic stance and tries to get around the 'evolutionary' implications by insisting that (a) the courses are 'alternatives',

and that (b) they are 'crossing' in the mid-twentieth century. At the same time it refers to supposed historical changes, that is, to the fundamental discontinuity in human knowledge as pursued up to the end of the Neolithic and as pursued in modern times. This continuity is both temporal (there is a plateau between them) and causal (the inspiration is different).[54]

Having identified the key problem, Goody sets out to show how the changing mode of communication, in particular, the shift from the dominance of orality to writing, helps to explain the changing mode of enquiry – and indeed it does. As we shall explore in later chapters, writing as a means of communication contributes to many processes of social structuring, both subjective and objective. For example, writing is fundamental to state formation as it is to institutionalized religions of the book such as Christianity, Islam, Judaism, and Confucianism. Nevertheless, we have to be careful here. It is important not make the technique of writing *the* determinative and driving force of change. The same can be said for the mode of communication in general. In this sense, the constitutive abstraction method is intended to carry forward Jack Goody's insights by broadening out his emphasis on the mode of communication to explore the intersection-in-dominance of various modes of practice including the modes of communication and enquiry, exchange, production and organization.

We need, however, to take a step back now that this pitfall in the sociology of knowledge has been identified. How can we analytically characterize the mode of enquiry in customary tribal formations without being too reductive or dichotomizing? We can say that the mode of enquiry in customary tribal formations *is* different from those lived under the dominance of traditionalism, modernism or postmodernism, but that it cannot be seen as on the other side of a Great Divide. How can it be characterized in terms of itself rather than in contrast to what it is not? Here, returning momentarily to the previous discussion of reciprocal exchange helps to clarify the dominant mode of enquiry. Tribal enquiry *qua* tribalism (that is, to the extent that it is not done in intersection with other modes of enquiry as happens in most contemporary tribal settings) does not address a world 'out there'. Rather, it treats the social and the natural as an integrated union in which events, moments and perceptible things are understood in reciprocal relation to each other. Enquiry is certainly abstracted beyond direct perception, but the social, including the social understanding of 'knowledge' itself, is not abstracted out of the natural and put into independent explanatory schemas.[55] Elements of knowledge can be lifted out from direct perception and palpable experience but only if they are 'returned' – like the spirit of the gift always carrying the ghost of the giver, never lifted out as an independent thing. This means that knowledge can be used as a medium of exchange but only within a socially-sanctioned setting. It can be held and passed on, but only as something held in trust as one might hold a sacred object or a child.[56] Tribal knowledge always *returns* to places, things and bodies. It cannot legitimately be collected as a fact-by-fact accumulating process. Like yams in a store-house, knowledge cannot be accumulated indefinitely or for one's own edification, but rather aggregates power *for itself* in a cycle of social-natural production, exchange, organization and communication.

The concept of *perceptual-analogical enquiry* is intended to evoke this embodied-integrated form of knowledge. The concept of 'analogy' is a tricky one to the extent that our reading of that concept carries a traditional-modern resonance of things of similarity *brought into* relation to each other. Rather, the concept needs to be understood in this context in the sense that things of ritual and stone, knowledge and embodiment, word and place, *are* in relation to each other. Elizabeth Traube captures this sensibility when she describes the Mambai of East Timor treating the whole of their knowledge, *kdain*, as analogous to a tree, *aia*. Knowledge is the unity of roots, trunk, branches and tips:

> Mambai spoke of [knowledge] as the 'trunk of discourse', and they talked of a treasure of 'words' that certain persons kept 'inside their stomachs' ... 'First', I was told, 'the eyes must see, and then the ears must hear'. For one could, as Mambai often observe with satisfaction, take in everything that occurs in ritual practice and yet have received only the part, or the 'tip' as they call it. But if someone with 'words inside the stomach' would come forward, such a person could 'explain and explain and explain until it reaches the kdain'.[57]

If the tree in this narrative appears to be lifted out as a post-tribal metaphor, then that is only because the reader has already understood the concept of 'analogy' in terms of its traditional-modern etymology. To read it in the way that is intended here is to know that the Mambai speak of ritual knowledge in terms of a constant return to 'Our Mother who is rock/Our Father who is tree'.[58] In different cultures, analogous knowledge and the metaphors of its being, take other forms. For example, Nonie Sharp describes knowledge in the fishing cultures of the Torres Strait and Papua New Guinea as taking the form of spiralling genealogies of fish traps and *wauri* shells. For the Binandere people of Papua New Guinea knowledge 'is woven into a spiral within the limits of six generations from the "head" (*opipi*), the terminal ancestor, to the "tail" (*mai*), who is the youngest living descendant of the clan, to the Binandere cone-shaped fish trap (*sirawa*)'.[59] In these terms, knowledge is caught in a spiral of repetition and renewal, holding and passing on.

Analogous modes of enquiry are not confined to tribal society. For example, David Sutton's book *Memories Cast in Stone* discusses the layer of analogical thinking in face-to-face peasant communities caught between traditionalism and modernism.[60] However, in post-tribal societies this mode of enquiry is lived in increasing tension with other modes of enquiry. It is not the predominant level at which knowledge is associated with power.

The traditional mode of inquiry can be compared to tribal inquiry as – in its various forms – traditionalism abstracts from embodied nature and reframes analogous thinking in cosmological terms. Analogy lingers on as abstracted metaphor into the present, but the signs of its reconstitution are everywhere. In the seventeenth century, for example, terms such as 'system' and 'discipline' began to take over from 'tree of knowledge'.[61] It is not that analogies are absent from more abstract forms of enquiry, but that analogies, including about knowledge itself such as 'fields' or 'domains of knowledge', become an abstract representation of the thing, and the thing is no longer carrier of the analogy. That is, with one absolutely fundamental exception. In traditionalism something else, such as God or Nature, mediates this relation, and this something else itself becomes an Analogy with a capital 'A'. This can be readily seen in pivotal instances of a traditional culture. The central sacred text of one tradition, collected in the transformation from oral to literate sociality, begins with the words, 'In the beginning God created the heaven and the earth'. In this moment, God has been abstracted from the creation of world on which we walk. It takes a later cleric to rewrite this in a way that brings creation and existence back together: 'In the beginning was the Word and the Word was with God and the Word was God'.

Abstraction occurs in manifold fields of traditional enquiry from religion to the early manifestations of science, but religion gives us the most telling instances. For example, the Iberian Jewish poet Solomon Ibn Gabirol (c. 1021–c. 1058) in writing an ode to God, posits a series of spheres extending beyond the first spheres of the globe – of the air, of fire, of the space of heavenly bodies – to the tenth sphere of intelligence. This tenth sphere is 'a thought that defies thinking ... the bridal canopy of your glory ... You set its orbit on the pillars of righteousness, and by your power called it all into existence.'[62] In other words, without ever leaving the realm of theology, Solomon maps all of these spherical systems upon one another at ever-greater levels of abstraction. And then, because it is impossible to live at this level, he quickly re-embodies knowledge itself in humankind – or rather he has God do the reinvesting, the re-creating: 'you invested it in the body that serves it ... imparting wisdom into him and distinguishing him from the beasts. We live on a higher plane, in a higher sphere.'[63] This moving from the concrete to the abstract and back again is a generalized phenomenon in traditional and post-traditional meditations on the sacred. Writing centuries later in a quite different countries and fields of enquiry, Georg Hegel (1770–1831) and August Comte (1798–1857) do much the same thing in positing a movement of the spirit of being from the concrete to the abstract.

To put it as simply as possible, across all spheres of life the dominant *form* of knowledge production becomes more abstract, as we move from societies formed in the dominance of tribalism to those formed in traditionalism and modernism. This is so, even if, as we shall see in later chapters, the dominant *content* of knowledge often follows a strangely contradictory path that leads to an abstract obsession with 'concrete' outcomes or subjective detail. For example, in the uneven transformation from the analogical interrogation of nature to technical science and then to techno-science, scientific content moves back and forth between competing emphases. On the one hand, there develops an overpowering emphasis on 'innovative' knowledge that breaks with once taken-for-granted understandings (an outcome of the abstraction process). On the other, we see an increasing obsession with the application of that knowledge as a technical, practical and commodifiable act (this is, what might be called a re-concretization of abstracted research).

In this change, new modes of enquiry carry older content with them and reconstitute prior forms. For example, the difference between the traditional-modern cataloguing of nature in Linnaeus's *Systema Naturae* (1735) and the late-modern mapping of the human genome provides an extraordinary but complicated comparison of different levels of abstraction. In one sense, they are both abstract taxonomies of nature, siblings in common purpose across the centuries, attempting to organize our understanding of the relationship between things. And old Doctor Linnaeus is clearly still with us in the twenty-first century as we continue to refine the human survey of the animal and plant *kingdoms*. However, in another sense, the historical shift from the dominance of the first taxonomy, based on details of what things look like, to the second, based on theories of the constitutive foundations of biological life, symbolizes an incredible change in the cultural frame. This difference is graphically signified by the gradual disappearance of the dominant metaphor of knowledge in Linnaeus's time – the now archaically concrete metaphor of the 'tree of knowledge'.

The analogy of the tree allows a nice segue into the next section on genealogy as the dominant mode of organization in tribal societies. In the same way that in post-tribal societies, analogous enquiry is overlaid by more abstract forms of enquiry, knowledge of family trees and kinship relations carries on but is overlaid and reconstituted in terms of more abstract modes of the organization of power.

## Genealogical placement as a dominant mode of organization

As an indication of the centrality of the kinship relations in customary communities, anthropologists until recently tended to use the concept of 'kinship-based societies' as coterminous with 'tribe'. This was partly a way of getting around problems associated with the concept of 'tribe' itself. In particular, it avoided two equally-unsatisfactory tendencies. Either the concept tended to be over-generalized to describe any strong affinity group including football followers and loose-knit skinhead gangs, or it was associated with a modernist superiority about the putatively primordial and primitive. As emphasized earlier, the important issue here is not which descriptive word we use but rather how those words are defined and qualified. It is sometimes better to redefine and hone old concepts than to contribute to the ever-expanding wasteland of neologisms. In that sense, the word 'tribe' remains useful, as does 'kinship-based society' – although it is crucial to recognize that they are not co-extensive concepts.

This is the first qualification. As tribes become framed by practices of modernism they tend to be less and less integrated by kinship *as societies*. Kinship in those settings continues to be important at the level of the face-to-face, but as the tribal state of Rwanda exemplifies, more abstract practices of state and power formation contribute to changing the way in which identity and difference are constituted. In the modernization of early-twentieth-century Rwanda, colonialism fixed the identities of Tutsi and Hutu as card-carrying tribe-castes (see Chapters 2 and 10). Thus we see the emergence of *modern tribes* for whom the mode of organization in customary tribalism – kinship as genealogical placement – has become reconstituted.

Even in settings of continuing traditional-tribal or peasant life where kinship continues to be central to the mode of organization – and we can talk appropriately of kinship-based societies – we have to be careful to recognize further qualifications. Other forms of embodied connection are sometimes as basic to the connections between people as kinship. There are associative forms of face-to-face integration where kinship, expressed in the form of being born of another, is on occasions overlaid and 'forgotten' beneath other forms of social (still genealogical) placement. For example, Karen Armstrong's work on the household in the Karelian region bordering Finland and Russia shows how the *house* is the setting through which kinship is mediated and reinterpreted through convivial relations.[64]

The third qualification is that in settings of traditional tribalism or peasant village-life, kinship is rarely traceable as objective genealogies of birth and bloodline. These genealogies are not like the abstract lines of certain and closed connection marked on pieces of paper that contemporary Westerners understand from tracing their ancestors back through the records of state, church and shipping companies. For this reason the term 'fictive kinship' was coined. It is, however, a thoroughly unsatisfactory concept. Just because the lines of kinship are not genetically verifiable does not make them fictions or inventions. Here, Pierre Bourdieu's concept of *practical kinship*, shorn of its exaggerated interest-based emphasis, serves as a subtle way of recognizing the complexity of uses to which kinship can be put without turning the 'almost theatrical presentations' of *official kinship* into fiction. The naming of the relevant structural identity – tribe, group, clan, house – and hence the social identity of the individual who is practically *placing* themselves or others, depends upon the social occasion and the place of the interlocutor. Within social limits, different kinds of practical kinship are maintained, enacted and named according to the situation, whereas official kinship, although always available as an explicit public code, becomes practical only when mobilized publicly. Official kinship as 'Abstract units produced by simple theoretical division, such as [in the case of a marriage ceremony], the unilineal descent group (elsewhere, age groups), are available for all functions, in other words for none in particular, and have practical existence only for the most official uses of kinship.'[65]

With this by way of background, I can now say that just as discussed earlier that a methodological lift in abstraction is required to understand the dominant mode of exchange as *reciprocal* exchange, not just as *gift* exchange, so it is with the dominant mode of organization. Kinship, either by extended consanguinity or direct blood ties, is central to customary society but in order to characterize the mode of organization of social life we have to move to a more abstract concept to describe these very embodied relations. The concept that seems to me to carry the meanings needed most appropriately is *genealogical placement*.[66] How does one account for 'fictive kinship' lineages? How does one understand the induction of some kings and 'big men' to power in traditional polities, quite outside of kinship lines? This will be discussed later in Chapter 9, as will the further abstraction of genealogical placement that contributes to nation formation. In that setting everybody knows, or rather sort-of knows, that nations are not held together by documentable ties of blood,

Table 5.1  Dominant modes of practice in tribal communities

| The mode of practice | The dominant modalities practiced in tribal communities |
|---|---|
| production | • manual<br>  – work of the hand with tooled and natural extensions<br>  – from gathering-hunting to gardening and pastoralism |
| exchange | • reciprocal<br>  – embodied gifts: persons turned into exchange objects by rituals such as marriage<br>  – sacred gifts: inalienable objects given by the 'gods'<br>  – exchange gifts<br>  – valuable objects or traded goods of restricted commercial exchange |
| communication | • oral-symbolic<br>  – face-to-face as projections of voice and body<br>  – mediated by natural and analogical signs |
| organization | • genealogically-placed<br>  – genealogical structures usually expressed as kinship,<br>  – embodied but mediated through lore, mythology and exchange practices |
| enquiry | • perceptual-analogical<br>  – knowing as experiential and held in close relation to the object of knowledge<br>  – 'science of the concrete' (Lévi-Strauss's term) |

nevertheless metaphors of blood continue to permeate the language of even the most civic of nation-states.

This discussion of exchange, enquiry and organization, with all its strengths and limitations, can be extended to cover other modes of practice including production and communication (Table 5.1). By doing so, a picture is gradually built up of the incredible complexity of these so-called 'simple societies'. Abstracting from this complexity may involve some simplification, but this is a necessary simplification for understanding the rich patterns of life. It is not the same as the ethnocentric and reductive tendency in a surprising range of Western scholarship to treat all societies that could not produce Stanley Kubrick's *2001* or chaos theory as somehow simpler than those that could.

In summary, then, customary tribal formation can be understood as constituted in the dominance of a specifiable matrix of intersecting modes of practice: reciprocal exchange, manual production, oral-symbolic communication, genealogically-placed organization and analogical enquiry. To understand these modes of practice in fuller complexity entails setting such analysis within a more abstract analytic framework of integrational and categorical analysis. That is, in the case of tribal formation, the dominant modes of practice can be characterized in terms of the dominant mode of integration in that formation – namely, embodied-extended or face-to-face relations. In turn, that mode of integration can be given more analytical depth in terms of the dominant modes of categorization in that formation – the nature of temporality, spatiality, embodiment and epistemology. The next three chapters begin that task, but at the same time attempt to uncover the foundations of other ontological formations, including the modern and the postmodern.

## Notes

1 On the images of nineteenth-century anthropology see Adam Kuper, *The Invention of Primitive Society: Transformations of an Illusion*, Routledge, London, 1988. However, for a classic twentieth-century example, see Alvin Gouldner, *Enter Plato: Classical Greece and the Origins of Social Theory*, Routledge and Kegan Paul, London, 1965, p. 5: 'the full measure of Greek achievement can be taken only if it is remembered that it was made by people who had not yet fully clambered out of the trenches of tribalism'.

2 Anthony Giddens, *The Nation-State and Violence: Volume Two of a Historical Critique of Historical Materialism*, Polity Press, Cambridge, 1985, p. 255. In the earlier volume he wrote of the 'impending demise of those two over-all types of society in which all human beings have lived until no more than 150 years ago', tribal and traditional class-divided societies. See *A Critique of Historical Materialism: Vol. 1, Power, Property and the State*, Macmillan, London, 1981, p. 169.

3 For example, in Xingu National Park, Brazil, consisting of 2.7 million hectares, seventeen tribes live in relative isolation. However, positing the existence of continuing customary tribes misses the point anyway. Tribal formations – layered in variously intersecting relations of tribalism, traditionalism, modernism and postmodernism – continue to exist in most parts of the world.

4 Ken S. Coates, *A Global History of Indigenous Peoples: Struggle and Survival*, Palgrave Macmillan, Basingstoke, 2004, p. 20.

5 Ernest Gellner, *Saints of the Atlas*, Weidenfeld and Nicolson, London, 1969.

6 Ernest Gellner, *Nations and Nationalism*, Basil Blackwell, Oxford, 1983.

7 Michael Mann, *The Sources of Social Power: Vol. 1, A History of Power from the Beginning to A.D. 1760*, Cambridge University Press, Cambridge, 1986, p. 42, emphasis added.

8 See, for example, Graham Connah (ed.), *Transformations in Africa: Essays on Africa's Later Past*, Leicester University Press, London, 1998; Harry Lourandos, *Continent of Hunter Gatherers: New Perspectives on Australian Prehistory*, Cambridge University Press, Cambridge, 1997; and Coates, *A Global History of Indigenous Peoples*, 2004.

9 This definition, partly through an ambiguity over the word 'spirit', also allows us to talk of different categories of reciprocity from embodied exchange to disembodied exchange. This is developed in Chapter 12 which discusses the contemporary dominance of abstract reciprocity – for example, paying into a World Vision children's monthly-support program in exchange for photographs and letters from the supported child.

10 Here 'goods' becomes the generic concept (as opposed to 'bads') allowing us to talk of different categories of goods, ranging from the inalienable to the alienable. Expressed schematically the different kinds of goods can be taken to include the following: goods that are sacred, gift-exchanged, precious, useful and commodity-exchanged. In this argument a particular good can pass from one category to another, or belong to more than one category at the same time.

11 For an example of a commodity market sustained by outsiders, see Clifford Sather's writing on sea-nomadism (*The Bajau Laut: Adaption, History, and Fate in a Maritime Fishing Society of South-Eastern Sabah*, Oxford University Press, Kuala Lumpur, 1997).

12 This is implicitly a critique of the postmodernists for the missing middle in their analysis of integrative forms and ontological categories as socially structured. See, for example, Igor Kopytoff, 'The Cultural Biography of Things: Commoditization as a Process', in Arjun Appadurai (ed.), *The Social Life of Things: Commodities in Cultural Perspective*, Cambridge University Press, Cambridge, 1986.

13 On the moral economy of modernism, see David Cheal, *The Gift Economy*, Routledge, London, 1988.

14 Marcel Mauss, *The Gift: Forms and Functions of Exchange in Archaic Societies*, Routledge & Kegan Paul, London (1925), 1974.

15 Maurice Godelier, *The Enigma of the Gift*, Polity Press, Cambridge, 1999.

16 Annette B. Weiner, *Inalienable Possessions: The Paradox of Keeping-While-Giving*, University of California Press, Berkeley, CA, 1992; C.A. Gregory, *Savage Money: The Anthropology and Politics of Commodity Exchange*, Harwood Academic Publishers, Amsterdam, 1997. See also his much more technical book, *Gifts and Commodities*, Academic Press, London, 1982.

17 Mauss, *The Gift*, p. 1.

18 Bronislaw Malinowski, *Argonauts of the Western Pacific*, London, Routledge & Kegan Paul, (1922) 1972. Less than a century later, after two globally enforced reincarnations in less than a century, Kaiser Wilhelm Land is now part of the independent nation-state of Papua New Guinea.

19 Claude Lévi-Strauss, *The Elementary Structures of Kinship*, Beacon Press, Boston (1949) 1969, cited by Godelier, *The Enigma of the Gift*, on p. 20.

20 The phrase comes from Marshall Sahlins, *Stone Age Economics*, Tavistock Publications, London, 1974, p. 169.

21 Pierre Bourdieu, *Algeria, 1960: The Disenchantment of the World*, Cambridge University Press, Cambridge, 1979, p. 10.

22 Geoff Sharp, 'Constitutive Abstraction and Social Practice', *Arena*, 70, 1985, pp. 48–82. See also Cheal, *The Gift Economy*, pp. 20–5, 41–2, 57–60, on problems in generalizing Bourdieu's claim of temporal separation and calculation of interest.

23 Bourdieu, *Algeria*, p. 22.

24 Pierre Bourdieu, *Outline of a Theory of Practice*, Cambridge University Press, Cambridge, (1972) 1987, p. 95.

25 Arjun Appadurai, 'Introduction: Commodities and the Politics of Value', in Appadurai (ed.), *The Social Life of Things*, p. 13.

26 The description of the *kwaimatnie* and the man crying comes from Godelier, *The Enigma of the Gift*, pp. 125–7.

27 Appadurai, 'Commodities and the Politics of Value', p. 13, his emphases.

28 *Ibid.*, p. 12.

29 Lukács, cited in Bourdieu, *Outline of a Theory of Practice*, p. 171, cited in Appadurai, 'Commodities and the Politics of Value', p. 12. Georg Lukács is, incidentally, taken radically out of context. Appadurai in turn takes Bourdieu's critique of the subjective out of context, forgetting Bourdieu's double-sided critique of the subjective-objective abstraction. In the next passage on from that cited, Bourdieu writes: 'In reducing the economy to its objective reality, economism annihilates the specificity located precisely in the socially maintained discrepancy between the misrecognized or, one might say, socially repressed, objective truth of economic activity, and the social representation of production and exchange' (p. 172). This critique might equally apply to Appadurai's culturalism. The trouble, however, with Bourdieu's return critique that he is not writing about 'objective truth' at all – and certainly not about the *structures* of exchange. He writes about his own subjectivist version of a 'truth' that runs through modern Western thought, perhaps beginning with John Locke and Adam Smith: the ideology that reciprocity and interest are equally the two sides of every economic exchange.

30 Weiner, *Inalienable Possessions*, pp. 28ff. For an elaboration of what I mean by abstract reciprocity, see Chapter 13.

31 Appadurai, 'Commodities and the Politics of Value', p. 12. Note how despite his injunction about commodity situations, Appadurai turns back to the thing itself: *the* commodity.

32 Godelier, *The Enigma of the Gift*, pp. 72–3.

33 It is only under conditions of social crisis that these kinds of goods *become* commodities, although the example of the restricted medieval trade in sacred relics illustrates how sacred goods can enter, in Appadurai's phrase, into 'commodity situations' without becoming commodities.

34 On mercantile kinship, see Gregory, *Savage Money*, Chapter 5. On the historical depth of tribal and traditional trading, see Henry W. Mutoro, pre-colonial Trading Systems of the East African Interior' in Connah (ed.), *Transformations in Africa*. On the interpenetration of forms of exchange, see Nicholas C. Thomas, *Entangled Objects: Exchange, Material Culture, and Colonialism in the Pacific*, Harvard University Press, Cambridge, MA, 1991.

35 Godelier, *The Enigma of the Gift*, p. 162.

36 Malinowski, *Argonauts*, p. 89.

37 Staff of the Royal Commission, *Kilmartin: Prehistoric and Early Historic Monuments* (An Inventory of the Monuments Extracted from Argyll, Volume 6), Royal Commission on the Ancient and Historical Monuments of Scotland, Edinburgh, 1999, pp. 83–91. Entries for the seventh and eighth centuries CE in the *Annals of Ulster* kept in Iona record the presence of the kings of the Picts and the dynasty of the *Dál Riata* from Ireland (now know as the Dalriadic kingdom of North Britain).

38 Cited in Pat Gerber, *Stone of Destiny*, Canongate Books, Edinburgh, 1997, p. 26. Gerber forgets to tell us that the account is based on oral legend and was first written down over a century after the event. However, for present purposes that does not matter.

39 This use of this Polynesian concept is most certainly a twentieth-century addition to the mythology.

40 During my stay in Diego de Compostella, I could find no reference to the Stone.

41 *The Golden Stool: Some Aspects of the Conflict of Cultures in Modern Africa*, Holborn Publishing, London, 1926, p. 7.

42 For a non-European example, see Godelier (*The Enigma of the Gift*, p. 201) quoting from an eighteenth-century Dutch traveller about the Japanese court of the Mikado. As a sacred personage,

> In ancient times [the Emperor] was obliged to sit on the throne for some hours every morning, with the imperial crown on his head, but to sit altogether like a statue, without stirring ... because it was thought by this means that he could preserve peace and tranquillity in his empire ... But it having been afterwards discovered, that his imperial crown was the palladium, which by its immobility could preserve peace in the empire, it was thought expedient to deliver his imperial person ... from this burdensome duty, and therefore the crown is at present placed on the throne for some hours every morning.'

43 See, for example, Arthur Taylor, *The Glory of Regality: An Historical Treatise on the Anointing and Crowning of the Kings and Queens of England*, Taylor, London, 1820, book 1, on the 'election' of the king. Taylor writes for example: 'In the Will of king Ælfred is a clause which shows that he did not consider his crown as conferred by inheritance from his royal forefathers or by the pope's consecration, but that he held it as a gift which, to quote his own words, "Dues et principes cum senioribus populi misericorditer ac benigne dederunt"' (p. 13).

44 Weiner, *Inalienable Possessions*, p. 37. Certainly most of the frames were melted down in 1649 to be sold off during the revolution, but the question remains, how did this mercenary act occur if the objects were sacred? How, for example, in a 'True and Perfect Inventory' compiled by Parliamentary agents in that year could 'King Alfred's crowne, or gould wyerworke sett with slight stones' be valued abstractly in terms of the number of ounces of gold in it. (Jocelyn Perkins, *The Crowning of the Sovereign of Great Britain and the Dominions Overseas*, Methuen, London, 1937, p. 36.) Nor does the source that Weiner cites really support her contention (Grahame Clarke, *Symbols of Excellence: Precious Metals as Expressions of Status*, Cambridge University Press, Cambridge, 1986). Clarke writes rather of precious objects of *status*, some discarded in favour of more glorious versions and some used as security for loans. It is indicative of the abstracted status of the monarchical crown that Joan Evans (in *Magical Jewels of the Middle Ages and Renaissance, Particularly in England*,

Oxford University Press, London, 1922) writes about many valuables – the rings of kings, the breastplates of high priests, amulets of gold, talismans of silver, and magical jewels galore, from those set with diamonds to those of beaver's teeth – but with ne'er a mention of crowns. The medieval Christian condemnation of engraved talismans that thus limited European crown-making to secular crafting is perhaps part of the explanation.

45 Taylor (*The Glory of Regality*, p. 63) certainly thought it to be real, commenting on its 'exquisite beauty'.

46 The crown as synecdoche for the institution of monarchy continues on today, but more as dead metaphor than as an attribution of power to the object of the crown itself. Perhaps a partial counter to this proposition can be found in the spiritualist side of neo-medievalism, fringe revivalist groups who attempt to relive their sense of the past. This sensibility is evidenced in magic-historical or science-fiction literature such as Raymond E. Feist, *Shards of a Broken Crown*, BCA HarperCollins, London, 1998.

47 'Crowns and Diamonds: The Making of the Crown Jewels', exhibition from 'The Royal Collection © Her Majesty the Queen'. It is indicative that She has to resort to ©, the globalized symbol of intellectual property protection. Going back much further, it should be remembered that in 1761 George III sold seats in the nave galleries for his coronation. James I sold knighthoods and rights to monopolize trade.

48 David Breeze and Graeme Munro, *The Stone of Destiny: Symbol of Nationhood*, Historic Scotland, Edinburgh, 1997, p. 41.

49 Harold T. Barrow, *Guarding the Crown Jewels*, Uplift Books, Croydon, 1947, p. 7.

50 *Ibid.*, p. 8.

51 Ian Hay, *Their Name Liveth: The Book of the Scottish National War Memorial*, Trustees of the Scottish National war Memorial, Edinburgh, 1931, reprinted 1985, p. 100.

52 Claude Lévi-Strauss, *The Savage Mind*, Weidenfeld and Nicolson, London, 1966, p. 15.

53 *Ibid.*, p. 296.

54 Jack Goody, *The Domestication of the Savage Mind*, Cambridge University Press, Cambridge, 1977, pp. 7–8.

55 This becomes dramatically more complicated in tribal settings that, with the interpenetration of other modes of knowledge, explain themselves in terms of modern forms of categorization, for example, in terms of anthropological concepts such as 'tribe', 'moiety', 'reciprocal exchange', etc.

56 Thus, Fred R. Myers (*Pintupi Country, Pintupi Self*, University of California Press, Berkeley, CA, 1991) describes one of the dominant symbolic analogies of Pintupi life as 'holding': 'holding the child at the breast' (*kanyininpa yampungka*), p. 247.

57 Elizabeth G. Traube, *Cosmology and Social Life: Ritual Exchange amongst the Mambai of East Timor*, University of Chicago Press, Chicago, 1986, pp. 6–7.

58 *Ibid.*, p. 14.

59 Nonie Sharp, *Stars of Tagai: The Torres Strait Islanders*, Aboriginal Studies Press, Canberra, 1993, p. 75.

60 David E. Sutton, *Memories Cast in Stone: The Relevance of the Past in Everyday Life*, Berg, Oxford, 1998.

61 See Peter Burke, *A Social History of Knowledge: From Gutenberg to Diderot*, Polity Press, Cambridge, ch. 5.

62 Solomon Ibn Gabirol, *A Crown for a King*, Oxford University Press, Oxford, 1998, pp. 48, 50. The confessional meditation is still printed in Sephardic prayer books for the Day of Atonement and used by North African Jewish communities.

63 *Ibid.*, pp. 48, 50. This has been bestowed on the body in all its weakness: 'I am mud, worms, a bucket of guilt and shame, a mute stone', p. 54.

64 Paper to the Anthropological Association of Finland, May 2000: and her *Remembering Karelia: A Family's Story of Displacement during and after the Finnish Wars*, Berghahn Books, New York, 2004. See also Chapter 3 above on 'Levels of Integration' and different modalities of the face-to-face.

65 Pierre Bourdieu, *The Logic of Practice*, Polity Press, Cambridge, 1990, p. 169.

66 This is one of those exceptions to the injunction against neologism. I am indebted to Jukka Siikala for long conversations about the problems of placing kinship.

# SIX Communication and Exchange, Money and Writing

A fantastic corporeal metaphor that links relations of exchange and communication comes to us in the phrase 'money talks'. In one song called 'Money Talks' from a generation ago, the metaphor is used alongside an image of the power of money to cut deep into the body: 'Money don't grow on a money tree. The more you take leave the less for me. Money don't buy what you really need.' It goes on: 'It make an iceman cry, it make a stone man bleed'.[1] Contemporary songs and films regularly evoke the metaphor of money talking, thus giving this object-of-exchange a life of its own.[2] In John Gerner's song also called 'Money Talks', money says different things to different people:

> His money talks
> It says 'I buy what I see'
> Their money talks
> It says 'the good life'
> But when my money talks
> It just says 'goodbye.'[3]

In the iceman version the lyrics have the metaphor of money talking as the irrepressible expression of a green cyborg-machine that rules our lives: 'In the black, on the rocks, money talks, money talks'.[4] Even the popular attempts to qualify this chattering life-force cannot take its power away. For example, Neil Diamond's song with the words 'it don't sing and dance ... it don't walk'[5] has to acknowledge that money talks. At a time when surveys indicate that Western married couples argue about money more than any other subject and Oprah Winfrey life-style programs tell you in the one breath how to arrange your love-life and your wallet, Neil Diamond sings of a love that is supposed to go beyond concerns about money. However, what does he choose as the metaphor for that special love which does not count the cost of being with another? He chooses one of the pre-eminent over-advertised symbols of commodified globalized culture – blue jeans. 'And long as I can have you here with me/I'd much rather be/Forever in blue jeans.' The song metaphorically intones the connection between money, commodification and communication that now seems natural.

Was this connection always so naturally dominant and has it always taken the same forms? The answer is 'obviously not', but setting out a method to make sense of the differences has largely eluded social commentators. This chapter examines the changing nature of relations of exchange and communication from the tribal to the postmodern, treating exchange and communication as exemplifying the complex matrix of modes of practice that would need to be examined in a more comprehensive analysis of any social formation. The chapter's central proposition is that different social formations are marked by different dominant modes of exchange and communication, framed at different dominant levels of abstraction. Here, as throughout the book, I use abstraction in a dual sense referring to both material and ideational processes of 'drawing away' from the palpably embodied: abstraction is therefore not confined to realm of ideas, nor does the process of dematerialization sum up the process of abstraction. Thus I am using abstraction in broader sense than someone like Georg Simmel who writes (pointedly using the metaphor of talking as an analogy for monetary abstraction):

> As a visible object, money is the substance that embodies abstract economic value, in a similar fashion to the sound of words which is an acoustic-physiological occurrence but has significance for us only through the representation that it bears or symbolizes.[6]

The lineages of social abstraction involve a number of processes that have been much discussed in the literature on social change, but rarely considered as part of interconnected matrix: (1) rationalization; (2) commodification; (3) codification; (4) objectification; (5) mediation; and (6) extension. Karl Marx, for example, takes commodity abstraction as the driving social force of modern capitalism, while Max Weber emphasizes the processes of rationalization, including bureaucratization of management and the secularization of religious life. By contrast, we are not looking for *the* driving force. The many historical journeys of modes of exchange, from the reciprocities and cultural limits of gift exchange to the abstractions and boundary crossing of the electronic market and the commodification of almost everything are without a single determinative base. The pathways of change are long, criss-crossing and tortuous. So too are the many lineages from centrality of oral communication to the dominance of electronic modes of communication. While these journeys can be seen *in retrospect* as being patterned by increasing abstraction across history – and that is indeed what I argue is the case for all modes of practice – they are nevertheless intertwined journeys full of twists and turns and recursions. There is no teleology of development and no easy way of marking the edges of the changes.

Seeing – and attempting to understand – the more general patterns of formational change depends upon the distance of retrospect, as well as something more. To begin to apprehend processes of exchange and communication in their full complexity – clothed as they are in desire, fetishism, anthropomorphism, and story-telling – we need the distancing effect of the abstraction of history as it turns back upon itself. As part of this process we are now placed in a time which, through an abstraction of enquiry, increasingly interrogates processes that were once taken for granted, or at least framed by a different mode of enquiry requiring quite different forms of explanation. We need, in other words, the sceptical analytical distance given to us in the form of reflexive social theory. Under these circumstances, the various anthropomorphisms that simultaneously cover money in mystery, and in its modernist phase offer to disclose its 'true meaning' as a mere instrument of value, become evidence of its layers of sociality rather than simply the excreta of an objective reality. The phrase 'necessary shit' is indicative. The assumption that 'the economy' is a separate sphere of social life is one high point of this abstraction process. Similarly, the communications theory that gave us the metaphor of the hypodermic syringe to explain socialization through television broadcasting can be dismissed for its naïve theorizing, but it is still relevant to illustrating how metaphors of the body keep coming back into any discussion of even the most abstract of media. Let me try to condense the thrust of the chapter into a few summary points:

> *Proposition 1.* More abstract modes of practice tend to overlay rather than replace less abstract modes. Dominant modes of exchange and communication have become more abstract, but this is not to imply that the dominant forms have left the more concrete forms behind in the dusty corners of history or in irrelevant spaces of archaism. Embodied speech is a continuing and fundamental practice of communication. It continues to be basic to being human. However, just as kinship is no longer the integrative form that provides substantial ties beyond the immediacy of personal relations, speech is not the dominant means of communication in modern-postmodern settings. Speech has to be mediated and technologically

extended before it is relevant to the predominant integrative networks that connect what I still want to call 'societies'. In the contemporary politics of George W. Bush, Tony Blair, and Vladimir Putin, the rhetorical influence of techniques of orality, played out since the Aristotle's *Art of Rhetoric* and the classical Greek agora, still have many moments of influence in policy-making. We assess political speeches and debates, attentive to the smallest gestures. However, rather than those 'dialogues' being framed by the modalities of face-to-face relations, contemporary rhetoric – even if intended to effect subjective intimacy and immediacy – is objectively projected as part of an abstract and mediated system of monitored image-messages broadcast to multiple strangers.

*Proposition 2.* As relations of exchange and communication became dominated by increasingly-abstract forms of interchange, reaching a new stage in the late-nineteenth century with international agreements on monetary policy and the installation of globalizing telecommunications links, these relations have had a profound effect on the constitution of polity and community. While changes in the modalities of exchange and communication are not in themselves sufficient to explain the conjunction of the nation and state during this very same period, it is no coincidence that both the modern nation-state and disembodied globalism grew up together in the late-nineteenth century. Changes in the modes of communication and exchange contributed to both formations, just as the consolidation of nations and states contributed to enhancing the new media of exchange and communication.

*Proposition 3.* The abstraction of the modes of exchange and communication – as well as all other modes of practice – is linked to the exercise of power, including the acquisition of wealth and control over others. While power has to be theorized itself as operating in different ways at different levels of integrative abstraction, it is argued that more abstract modes of practice give access to techniques and technologies of power that qualitatively outstrip more concrete modes. This suggests that a politics of communication and exchange entails reasserting the foundational importance of more embodied modes of practice. The ravaging systematic abstractions of monetary and media systems (*mediatism*) should be treated as problems for dragging back to earth rather than allowed to float free under the sign of neo-liberal ideologies and practices that project as the abstract 'freedom' of the market (*capitalism*). This is not to suggest that abstract systems of codification are a problem in themselves, but it is certainly to argue that as uncritically-worshipped dominant systems they have the potential to pervert what it has meant to be human.

## Forms of value: means of exchange

As discussed in the previous chapter, it was Pierre Bourdieu who drew attention to the issue of gift-return as occurring in social time – the time of delay. However, while periods of delay are often evidenced in gift exchange, there are far more telling issues of temporal framing that need to be brought out. In particular, there is the issue of the different levels of temporal abstraction in reciprocal-exchange and commodity-exchange systems. In settings of customary reciprocal exchange, delay does not occur as a lapse of *empty time*. Delay as such is not even always necessary in settings of face-to-face integration. Obvious examples of simultaneous giving and 'returning' range from a potlatch ceremony to a Christmas gift-giving occasion. Rather, we can say that when it does occur, the delay is indicative of *time* being embodied in the existence of the persons-in-exchange and being attended to ritually, carefully, personally. The continuing existence of other persons, in time, matters intensely to the meaning of the exchange itself.

This analysis of temporality will be developed much further in the next chapter, but for the moment I want to set up a comparison with the way in which time becomes empty, rationally calculable and increasingly disembodied within settings dominated by commodity exchange. Within capitalist societies, even in the most simple and apparently unmediated transactions of money for commodities there is usually a temporal immediacy where the 'reciprocity' is emptied of embodied meaning. In the moment of exchange, two persons may stand in face-to-face *interaction*, but in colloquial terms it matters less *who* the other person is, than *what* the colour of their money is. When delays do occur in money-commodity transactions, they are attended to contractually. Time is abstractly figured into the equation of cost-value, whether by specified delay, by simple interest calculations or by complex commodity-futures projections. This question of different forms of time is related, for example, to the different forms of social obligation – for example, between the open moral obligations of gift exchange and the specified contractual obligations of commodity exchange. It also takes us back to a related issue that was also mentioned but not adequately addressed in the previous chapter: the social basis of different forms of social value. It also serves to challenge simplistic notions of the rise of post-reciprocal exchange and post-oral communication.

One of the central insights of Maurice Godelier's approach, as previously discussed, is that reciprocal exchange involves keeping some back from the exchange process. Sacred goods or gifts from the gods are not for exchange. Drawing on the work of Joseph Goux, Godelier then attempts to generalize the implications of this insight to post-reciprocal societies. When illustrated through the example of the gold standard, this extension of the argument appears at least initially to have a common-sense validity. In late-nineteenth-century Europe, money circulated as an abstract medium of exchange, but its value was predicated on reserves of gold that most of the time sat immobile in the bank vaults of the nations' capitals – in both senses of the word 'capital'. Here amidst the apparently free-floating and universalizing medium of paper money, Godelier appears to discover something that acts much like the sacred goods in reciprocal exchange. Gold is 'voluntarily withheld from the sphere and the movement of exchange in order for the mass of market and bank exchanges to be set in motion, for everything that can be bought and sold to begin circulating'.[7]

This extension of Godelier's argument, however, has many problems. If something has to be held back, why was it that the pre-eminent process of holding back – the gold standard system – was only formalized in Europe as late as the 1870s? And why, as I will relate later in the chapter, did it effectively break apart a few decades later with the onset of the First World War? The obverse problem this presents for such an approach is how money had value before this 'something' was held back from exchange. If we come forward to the turn of the millennium, a related problem is elicited by asking what is withheld from the sphere of financial exchange in futures transactions when digital money has, essentially, left behind phenomenally-recognizable reference points of palpable 'materiality'.

An easier way of handling this problem is to return to the spirit rather than the specific content of Godelier's analysis and to examine the social-relational context in which exchange occurs. This entails understanding the abstract materiality of money. The value of money, I suggest, is not intrinsically dependent on whether something is held in reserve. It is based on increasing levels of abstraction that make the original bases of money still relevant but less and less phenomenally important, at least at the level of disembodied exchange. Across human history, objects of exchange are overlaid by material processes abstracting exchange value and exchange use. It is not that something is held back, but rather that exchange works as a layering-in-dominance of different ontological formations.

Money – as a distinct media in the changing modes of exchange – is always materially constituted at a relatively high level of abstraction, though we have to arrive in the twentieth century before it becomes materially abstracted in the form of encoded digital impulses or assumes overriding dominance in everyday life. Writing – as a means of communication – has a very similar genealogy. In both cases, we have to be very careful not to imply a connected single pathway from more concrete to more abstract patterns of interrelation. For example, as Jack Goody discusses in studies on the nature of writing, there is considerable controversy over claims that pictures of objects, then symbols for objects such as cuneiform signs, and then writing are on a *direct* evolutionary pathway. However, as he says in discussing the origins of value transactions, this does not mean that we cannot trace changing patterns of abstraction:

> there is one element in these developments that does lead to abstraction and generalization. Tokens represent the content of transactions in an abstract way, when we compare these operations not only to straight barter, to transfers in kind, but also to the forms of 'money' represented by certain forms of exchange item, such as silver in Mesopotamia and bars of salt in West Africa. Of course few if any societies are limited simply to swapping one object for another at the same moment in time; some transfers involve delays, others some functional generalization of goods as media, whether these be raffia mats or bolts of cloth. But the systematic use of tokens marks a first move towards an economy based on generalized media of exchange that we may refer to as money.[8]

The tokens to which he refers have been found in archaeological sites dating back to 8500 BCE, arguably contemporaneous with the development of agriculture. Tokens were initially not a media of exchange, but were a method of recording transactions involving a separation – an abstraction – of number from its object of reference. The move to a system of coinage takes a further series of steps, including the abstraction of value from the object of exchange itself, but also the development of agencies of regulation and codification. This partly fits with C.A. Gregory's suggestion that the systemization of money as a standard of value was made possible by the emergence of the state.[9] It may be an overstatement, but like the co-relation of writing and the state, money and the development of more abstract forms of polity are bound up with each other. This makes much more sense than the common assumption that the monetary market developed out of functional needs or the desire for profit by exploiting the gap between the 'real value' of a coin and its face value or merely for reasons of conducting long-distance exchange. Long before the rise of the corporation, the 'state' was the primary institution bringing together relations characterized by object- and agency-extension. The Egyptian and Mesopotamian rulers and temples, for example, worked with co-ordinated care to record the patterns of transactions, to codify standards of weight and to facilitate an exchange system enabling centralized redistribution of wealth.

## From tokens to coinage

The transition from weighted or numbered materials of exchange – silver, copper, barley, cattle, and so on – to coinage is another matter again. It occurred as a very uneven process. The conventional explanation in the literature is that long-distance trade was at the heart of the creation of coinage, developing directly out of the phenomenon of weighted materials of exchange.[10] It is probably a factor, but not the most important. An alternative approach puts the emphasis on the rise of the *polis* or the city-state as integrating polity and community. In the words of Sitta von Reden:

> A crucial difference between coinage and other wealth lay in the question of their origins. The recognition of coinage as a recompense meant the acknowledgement of the *polis* as an institution that controlled justice and prosperity. Agrarian wealth and ancestral treasure, by contrast referred to the divine order of justice which could be controlled by humans, if at all, only by religious ritual. The introduction of coinage indicates a shift of authority over social justice from the gods to the *polis* ... The *polis* replaced the divine order.[11]

This *is* an important factor, and one that refigures the long-distance-trade argument, particularly given evidence that some early coinage systems were quite localized. However, with the final claim that the 'polis replaced the divine order', Von Reden's analysis slips and fails to take into account the continuing struggle over the meaning of exchange, including continuing sacred and reciprocal claims over its meaning. Thus, for instance, Leslie Kurke writes that, with the development of coinage, the *polis* came to have more control over the circulation of precious metals moving as what she calls 'top-rank gift exchange'.[12] In other words, we can say that the development of coinage as a more abstract medium of exchange accompanied the abstraction of the mode of organization as practiced through the changing forms of the state. To talk of the *polis* is to talk of generalizable social relations.

The mode of communication was also relevant – writing and money were bound up with each other. In the most obvious sense, symbolic representation including figures, words and numbers, allowed the coinage to be abstracted from gift exchange without anything materially being held back. Apart from written inscriptions, coins were engraved with the figurative signs of objects of value, ambiguously secular and sacred – wine amphora, bulls, owls and lions – or carried the heads of gods and kings, often personifying the authority of the state with literal reference. The gold stater of Smyrna from the first century BCE depicts a head wearing a crown in the shape of walled city. The peculiar issue here is that the more the system of value was abstracted from the authorizing figure of the king, the more an accurate rendering of the particular person portrayed on the coin became culturally important. Portraiture on the head of a coin depicting an actual person was uneven in its realism. For example, in the period of Edward I of England (1272–1307 CE) there was still no attempt at depicting Edward himself. When Henry VIII of England came to the throne in 1509 the coins continued to show the head of his father Henry VII. It was only the figure 'VII' that was changed. Nevertheless, the face of the coin carried its embodied and politically-embedded heritage into a more abstract realm of accounting that at once made the 'realistic' accuracy of that depiction more important subjectively, and, in objective terms, increasingly irrelevant.

The other issue worth noting is the way that increasing abstract systems of value came themselves increasingly to stand behind the value of things, both metaphorically and practically. Systems of value came constitutively to frame the value-in-general of all objects. In the European Middle Ages, currency objects that ceased to be useful as media of exchange continued to be used otherwise. For example, coins and coin-like items such as *bezants* and *guaffres* (coins of Byzantine origin and tokens manufactured with money-like appearance) were used as ornaments to attach to clothing in the late-medieval Western Europe. However, even at this point out of the marketplace, their currency value, judged in terms of precious metal content, had a jostling ascendancy. In fourteenth-century France and England, *bezants* were allowed by law to be attached to clothing only by a single stitching so that their backs could be examined for the existence of coated base metals, used in replacement of the mandated gold or silver.[13]

### From coinage and credit notes to paper money

Over the millennium, the monetary market humped along in the tensions and contradictions of the changing nature of the means of exchange. In parallel to the problem of the king's two bodies, money had many faces. The incipient capitalist market lived off the tensions between these faces, derived profit from exploiting the variability of the abstraction processes, and developed new processes of accounting for value as new techniques engendered new problems and new possibilities. Within domestic economies, coinage continued to be important for local and some long-distance trade, but even here the increasing dominant abstracted social framing of value impinged upon the nature of the exchange objects themselves. In Europe, for example, we saw the development of circulating coins having two values – that is, first, its bullion or commodity value, how much the metal used in the coin was worth for itself, and second, its *specie* or tale value, the amount specified on the coin by the issuing body. For the purposes of our argument – namely, that when there are competing systems of exchange operating at the same level of abstraction, they tend to throw up a more abstract systematization of value that overlays and reconstitutes them all – discussing how the marketeers came to terms with the conflict between commodity value and specie value would be sufficient.

However, there was in addition the strange appearance of a third form of coinage that makes our argument even more intriguing. Cutting across the problem, first, of competing currency systems of coinage and, second, of competing ways of valuing any one coin within the different currencies, there were coins that circulated with a ghosted value (making this process more like the holy trinity than the king's two bodies). These ghost currencies were units of account, either based on coinage that had disappeared from circulation or the notional names of values that became actual coins abstracted from their original reference point. For example, the Carolingian system of pence did not have pounds as a monetary value, but as a reference of weight: Charlemagne had decreed that 240 pennies were to be struck from a pound of silver. This coinage had disappeared from Europe, except for Britain. There the 'pound' – though no longer worth the equivalent of a pound (weight) of silver, nor struck from a pound of silver – became a specie pound, again equal to 240 pennies. By contrast, in Milan during the latter part of the fifteenth century, a ghost 'pound' persisted as a unit for accounting debt even though there was no such coin, only its equivalence in pennies or florins. In Florence, it was different again with a ghost shilling – that is an abstract unit: no existing coin called a 'shilling' actually ever changed hands – being worth different amounts depending on whether it operated in the merchant's system of exchange or the citizens' and retailers' system.[14]

Negotiation between different social realms in the same region was compounded by the problem of variably-valued objects-of-value in different trading realms, and changes in those values across time. This allowed for profit-driven trading in the objects-of-value themselves. It gave rise to the remarkable phenomenon of arbitrage. (It is worth noting that at this stage 'arbitrage' related to the different value of things – whereas when we get to the late-twentieth century it becomes further abstracted as trading in value itself.) Variable values between silver and gold, even in late-medieval and early modern Europe where silver was the *de facto* monetary standard, allowed merchants to carry bullion across trading borders, profitably buying gold for silver in one place and silver for gold in another. In turn, the logistical problems caused by trading over long distances and transporting heavy bullion, together with shifts from the particular (the destabilizing effect of lagged fluctuating prices) to the general (an abstraction of context including the rationalization of the meaning of exchange and relations of production) led to the development of new credit instruments.

These credit bills, dependent upon writing as the dominant power container of communication, were more abstract 'trust arrangements' than, for example, promissory notes that had been tied to kinship trust and the public honour of the family or guild in medieval Florence, or the *Guanxi* family extensions that continued to be important in Qing Dynasty China (1644–1912).[15] In China, bills of exchange, 'flying money' (*fei ch'ien*), had been used since at least the mid-ninth century, but in that case they were secured by the Emperor and depended on the known standing of the person carrying the bill. As Fernand Braudel documents in relation to the rise of the imperial city of Amsterdam, secured and unsecured trade bills, commissions-to-trade and other papers of commerce, crossed Europe in the eighteenth century in an entirely different way. It was a deluge without the necessity of an embodied point of reference. The notes were given a semi-secure standing increasingly based on the trade and credit machinery of the networked *polis* – that is, the 'society-as-market'. Intersecting with the embodied lines of face-to-face or agency relations that had long prevailed, 'Amsterdam' itself and then London, both as financial entrepots, became the basis of the security.[16] In other words, credit value began to be secured not only by trust in persons or in their agents but by the (fragile) prosperity of things that in time would come to be called 'the national economy' or 'the global market'. Moreover, we can say that the movement from local to the national and global exchange system was not based on the object of exchange itself – gold and silver to paper, signed, inscribed or printed – but on how that object was enabled in the context of relations of exchange.[17] Paper money could be as restricted as any other means of exchange. In Shanghai in the late-nineteenth century, for example, the colloquial name 'street notes' suggests the very restricted localizing of some notes of exchange. This was, however, the world-time of the rise of the banking industry in association with the printing industry and the uneven spread of state regulation. The new institutions of money tended to issue notes while retaining deposited bullion as reserve in the context of a largely new institutionalization, rationalization and codification of the mode of exchange.

Money involves a material abstraction of value, but it is important, as I have been hinting all along, not to assume that this means that people treat money as merely an objective unit of measure. There is a subjective dimension as well. Even as that abstraction occurs, money does not float free as an arbitrary signifier of pure value. While the abstraction process occurs at the levels of object and disembodied exchange, those levels are, subjectively at least, constantly being dragged back to the level of embodied relations. Among the ways in which this is done is to personalize the 'spirit' of money and its institutions, to anthropomorphize the objects and institutions of exchange as meta-human (the original meaning of corporate) or even quaintly human entities. Perhaps the most famous example of the objects of monetary exchange being humanized comes from the Danish children's writer Hans Christian Andersen (1805–1875) and a story called *The Silver Shilling*.[18] The story follows the adventures of a coin as it is transferred from pocket to pocket. In this period even the institutions of exchange were anthropomorphized. An example of an institution taking on human qualities comes to us from one of the oldest banks in the world, the Bank of England, founded by an Act of Parliament in 1694. On 24 March 1797, Richard Brinsley Sheridan publicly referred to the Bank of England as an 'elderly lady in the City of great credit and long standing who had lately made a *faux pas* which was not altogether excusable'. He thus began the tradition that continued on in the press thereafter of calling the Bank of England, the 'Old Lady of Threadneedle Street'.[19] In a debate in the late 1960s, at the time when the practitioners of globalism demanded an overhaul of financial practices, there was consternation over whether an American transnational, McKinsey and Company, could adequately handle the restructuring.[20] *The Scotsman*, less concerned about national sensitivities, ran an article entitled 'Can McKinsey convert the venerable "Old Lady"', and, as if in reply, the English *Evening Standard* recorded that the 'Old Lady keeps Mum'.[21] It played on the multiple puns of money talking and the Old Lady remaining discreet. Such use of terms of endearment to institutions is not uncommon. For example in the realm of abstract communications, both the British Broadcasting Corporation (BBC) and Australian Broadcasting Corporation (ABC) continued to be called 'Auntie' even as they became rationalized government corporations financially distanced from the people and defended in terms of their financial efficiency – the ABC advertises itself as costing only eight cents a day per citizen.

At each point in the development of increasingly abstract systems of money or communications, the solving of old problems generated new ones. Paper money solved some of the problems of bringing together global trading lines and local consumptions systems, but this had its own problems. It was uneven in its spread: for example, the Islamic world did not introduce paper money until the mid-nineteenth century. More significantly, the question arose, 'What is meant by money?' When should it be able to be converted into other 'more basic' forms of value? Across the eighteenth century at the leading edge of this process, paper money divided in two systems while coins continued to be used as a further concurrent system. On the one hand, bank notes were intended as indicators of the bullions reserves secured for use in far-ranging trade. On the other hand, they were irregularly redefined and held as 'inconvertible' paper money, a store of abstract exchange value that was, because of some financial crisis such as the American Revolution and the Napoleonic wars, decreed as not convertible into gold or silver. The disembodied system of value had not yet broken free of its objectified relations of integration. Runs on banks generated by lack of trust were common. As the pieces of paper with their regularized inscriptions of value left behind precious metals as the carriers of value, and as the systems of guarantee were still be regularized, something was said to be needed to ground the new system. Gold standards as part of a new negotiated setting for exchange were thus developed in the eighteenth century, and were formalized in the United Kingdom in 1821. However, its arrival as a system depended upon a new global compact of the dominant powers marked by the Paris conference of 1865, the accession to the gold standard of Germany in 1873 and the United States in 1879. This process parallels the setting up of World Standard Time (discussed in the next chapter), except that it did not go far enough to globalize abstract value. Gold Standard Value broke apart in 1914, albeit with a short revival between the wars. Gold standard simply could not carry the contradictions between differently-abstracted modes of exchange. For example, after the First World War the victors were determined to rebuild their stocks of gold traded during the war mostly to the United States as paper money ceased to have international value. However, Germany paid the first massive instalment of its reparations by borrowing in London. A few years later, the October 1929 Wall Street Stock Exchange collapse confirmed that contingent crises and the fluctuations of capitalism could not be stabilized by having, in Godelier's words, something held back from circulation.

On 21 September 1931, the London *Times* reported that Parliament had asked for the suspension of the gold standard because of the amount of money being withdrawn from London: 'Since the middle of July more than £200,000,000 had been withdrawn from London, chiefly, it should be noted, on a foreign account. These withdrawals have been met out of *our* reserves of gold.[22] Here we see the beginnings of a new global system of exchange being explained in terms of protecting the national interest. The kinds of editorials that followed took this further. The *Daily Telegraph* of 22 September 1931 had an editorial called 'Off the Gold Standard: What it means for the man in the street'.

> In the wider sense, to be on the Gold Standard means that a country's money is of the same value anywhere as it is at home. Here 'money' does not include the small change that we carry in our pockets, for that, having only limited legal tender privileges at home, is never acceptable abroad ... FIRST STEPS TO RECOVERY ... Not only luxuries of foreign origin must be eschewed, but everything of foreign manufacturing that is not indispensable ... Whatever may be the earlier or later sequel to the suspension of the free gold market, the duty of the individual cannot vary. Salvation does not depend on the subtleties of the currency exports, but on the self-denial of the country at large.[23]

This appeal to the nation or the residual empire has continued up to the present even as a new layer of exchange has developed that has little reference to Hans Christian Anderson's silver shilling and the money that we still carry in our pockets. In the currency of Australia, still not formally a republic, the British Queen, Elizabeth II, is still portrayed on the lowest denomination note. Higher denominations depict historical figures of note: scientists, inventors, doctors and poets. As low-denomination notes have been taken out of circulation and replaced by coins, rationalizing the printing expense and overcoming wear and tear – first the one-dollar bill was replaced and more recently the two-dollar bill – the Queen's face has risen in specie value. Each time that has happened it has entailed a reshuffling of faces at the top. The higher denomination notes thus irregularly and quite arbitrarily change faces, suggesting not only the symbolic mutability of the individual iconic persons, but the fact that the face of money is now predominantly an abstraction of national-imperial heritage rather than a face of embodied guarantee. Elizabeth still appears as the head on all Australian coins, with the tail-side depicting indigenous animals.

One difference from the past is that the visage of the monarch, though still idealized, gets older as the actual body of Elizabeth II ages. The philosophical problem of the king's two bodies no longer concerns people. Interestingly in Britain itself, where the government holds out against the spread of the generalized Euro, in 2001 the Royal Mint of Britain for the first time consulted the people on the design of a new coin. However, there were only three designs to choose from and each of them celebrated the communications revolution and the Marconi wireless transmission in 1901. Here globalism and embodied iconography came together in traditional, modern and postmodern intersection. On one side of the coin the designs all carried images of the earth's curved surface, and on the other side the people of Britain had no choice. They were presented with the

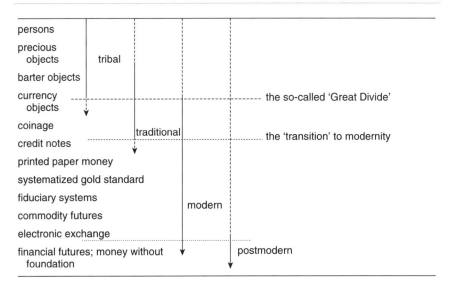

Figure 6.1 Dominant media of exchange in analytically-differentiated social formations

familiar head of state – the slightly aging Elizabeth II·Dei·Gra·Reg·Fid·Def.

A further dimension, completely invisible to the person buying a commodity or watching the daily CNN business report, lies behind the continuing use of coins and notes, materially underwriting this subjective representation of traditional continuity and modern. It is a new mode of exchange that aimed to overcome and more finely control the limitations of time and space – what might be called *electronic exchange*. (See Figure 6.1 for a tracking of these changes.)

### Paper money to electronic exchange

Concomitant with the development of electronic codification as a new dominant means of communication, the overlaying of coinage and paper money by electronic exchange systems was fast, confusing and increasingly integrated with the modes of production and organization.[24] It was something that a classical social theorist such as Marx could not envisage despite his understanding of money as a material abstraction.[25] Although many of the developments had slow antecedents, the changes multiplied quickly. The first globally-linked credit and charge cards such as American Express, MasterCard, and Visa expanded across the 1960s;[26] cheque-clearing systems were developed in the 1970s; and electronic funds transfer systems (EFTPOS) and automatic teller machines (ATMs) came into regular use in the 1980s. For example, in 1985 the Netherlands communications corporation Phillips and the British bank Lloyds announced a joint global funds-transfer system called Sopho-net WAN, spanning countries from Peru to Papua New Guinea. Electronic banking through global browsers such as Netscape and Internet Explorer took hold in the 1990s, as did new schemes for electronic marketing, merchandizing, and computer-assisted share trading. For example, IBM made a corporate comeback across the late 1990s popularizing the new concept of 'e-business' under its slogan 'Solutions for a small planet$^{TM}$'. Incidentally, their advertisements juxtaposed the old and the new: one newspaper e-business advertisement in 1998 showed a contemporary-looking business man pondering over a lap top, sitting next to a giant Egyptian Tutankhamen-figure, itself appearing to hold an ancient ledger book.

Research into this electronic financial revolution – credit and debit cards, smart and loyalty cards, telephone and internet banking, let alone derivative exchanges, futures trading and the like – suggests that although it came with a whirlwind of hype about freedom and self-management, it also became a source of anxiety or unsustainable financial risk-taking for those with lower incomes,[27] and concerns about security and data protection for those who were affluent. These anxieties were well founded, even if the changes were barely understood. The phenomenal world of going into a shop and buying a bunch of bananas or a mobile phone had now been framed by a layer of the economy that operated beyond the legislation of nation-states and far beyond the reach of democratic influence. Traded derivatives – that is, 'contracts specifying rights and obligations which are based upon, and thus derive their value from, the performance of some underlying instrument, investment, currency, commodity or service index, right or rate'[28] – developed from the 1970s and grew exponentially from the mid-1980s. By the turn of the century, they amounted to an estimated US$70 trillion or eight times the annual GDP of the United States. Hedge-funds also increased significantly over the first years of the new century, growing annually at approximately 15–20 per cent to an estimated US$1 trillion. The vagueness of the figures are testament to both the abstraction of the process and the superseding of older forms of institutionalization: derivative exchanges are conducted 'Over the Counter' on private digital networks as the exchange of the temporally projected value of value-units that do not yet exist except as projections; hedge-funds effectively gamble on the future. Both collapse time into an eternal present and trade in fine calculations about what might happen.

I will elaborate on the objective structures of the new forms of electronic global exchange in Chapter 11, but at the moment all I want to do is to conclude the narrative description by returning to our central line of argument about the increasingly-abstract nature of the dominant mode of exchange by making two interlinked points. First, the new exchange system has become re-institutionalized along global lines as technologically mediated and long-abstracted from the production and exchange of things such as cantaloupes and missiles. While it remains deeply institutionalized in codes, conventions and trading systems, it is neither dependent on a 'object' referent such as the gold standard – the New York Mercantile Exchange instituted gold futures trading in 1974 – nor an 'embodied' referent such as Queen Elizabeth II. Second, this is a patterned process. The dominant metaphor for the system, 'the free market' suggests an open fluidity of movement, but what I have been trying to narrate is a systematic pattern of material abstraction, a dominant system of exchange. Thus, in an apparent paradox, the material abstraction of the mode of exchange allowed the means of exchange to be increasingly 'dematerialized' (not necessarily the other way round). Misunderstanding this point has led many commentators to an unsustainable post-structuralism. Arjun Appadurai has problematically described this material change as a removal from the social relations of production and exchange:

> the logic of trade in commodity futures is, following Marx, a kind of meta-fetishization, where not only does the commodity become a substitute for the social relations that lie behind it, but the movement of *prices* becomes an autonomous substitute for the flow of commodities themselves. Though this double degree of removal from the social relations of production and exchange makes commodity futures markets very different from other tournaments of value, such as these represented in the kula, there are some interesting and revealing parallels.[29]

I want to suggest to the contrary that commodity and monetary exchange is neither a 'substitute for the social relations that lie behind it', nor is it removed from the social. Rather, post-reciprocal exchange systems involve new levels of the social. They are certainly very different kind of trading from the reciprocity of the Kula ring, but these differences can be specified socially and analytically.

## Forms of interchange: means of communication

Just as we have sketched above the changing dominant modes of exchange, it is possible to outline a genealogy of the dominant modes of communication, recognizing how older means of communication continue to have profound relevance in the world today. While the conventional distinction made in the literature is between oral and written communication as two distinct modes of communication, it is also possible to trace a complex intertwined lineage from oral-symbolic communication to electronic disembodied communication without either turning the difference between them in a Great Divide or by concluding that it is all just a complex mess. There are some clear distinguishable forms of communicative interchange:

- orality (symbolic interchange);
- writing as lists;
- writing as script, manuscript (often held back as sacred);
- print;
- writing-encoded transmission (for example, Morse code);
- voice-encoded transmission (for example, telephone and radio);
- voice-image encoded broadcasting (television);
- writing-voice-image encoded electronic communication (email, digital-mobile telephone, digital television);
- cyborg communication: encoded digitally for mobile, 'everywhere' and 'anytime' transmission linked to the body as cyborg (postmodern).

There is the space here only to hint at what a fully-fledged analysis might look like. In the earlier discussion of the modes of exchange, we saw how the changing modes of communication wove in and out of the dominant lines of exchange. The work of writers such as Jack Goody, Walter Ong and Elizabeth Eisenstein provide inspiration here, but insight into this process of abstraction is not confined to social theorists, anthropologists and historians. Mambai oral poetry from tribal-traditional East Timor repeatedly contrasts the book and the pen as symbols of European (both traditional religious and modern secular) identity and the sacred rock and tree as the embodiments of their own systems of enquiry. Elizabeth Traube describes a Mambai myth-complex that in effect explains how abstract power held by the non-Timorese or *Malaia* is generated by speaking in the presence of power tokens:

> The walk of the rule follows upon the primordial earth-walk and begins with the activity of Father Heaven. As sovereign god, Heaven's role is to articulate boundaries and divisions. He orders the cosmos by distributing signs of difference, and his first act is to divide his children into opposed

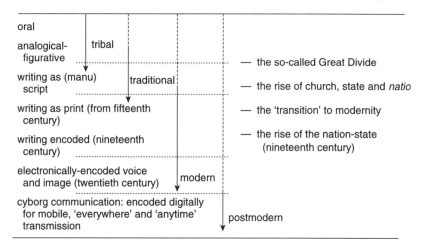

Figure 6.2  Dominant forms of communication in different ontological formations

Note: The modalities of communication are ordered here in terms of their formal abstraction of time, space and embodiment. In practice, they are lived as levels-in-intersection, framed by the dominant mode of communication.

categories of silent and speaking mouths. The primordial enunciation of sovereignty removes the power of speech from Heaven's first born ... Then Father Heaven, the great divider, distributes a patrimony between his two sons. To the eldest, Ki Sa, he gives the sacred rock and the tree, tokens of the original ban and signs of ritual authority over a silent cosmos. Upon the youngest, Loer Sa, he bestows the book and pen ... the younger brother appropriates power over 'speaking' humanity and carries it away to the outside [to Portugal the imperial power in pre-1975 East Timor], leaving behind him an elder brother who is the custodian of a silent cosmos.[30]

Here identity and power are bound up with the question of who controls the means of communication, as well as the nature of that communication. Here the *silence* of the rock and the tree embodies a different form of communication (which as we shall see in a moment is interpreted by the Mambai as now needing power tokens to elicit 'fear and trembling'). Putting this is a global context, one of the means by which this 'lifting out' of identity and the extending of power occurs historically is through what can technically be described as the abstraction of the dominant mode of communication (see Table 4.1 and Figure 6.2). Put in a more elaborate way, we can say that as orality was overlaid by script as part of a more general change in the dominant modes of organizing political community, the nature of polity and community was either transformed in the case of *Malaia* cultures or, such as in the case of the Mambai, new content was incorporated into the myth complexes of tribal-traditional peoples to explain why this change had consequences for their own systems of authority.

Scribes and interpreters of the word were at the centre of this emergent mode of practice. They were drawn into a new relationship to genealogical connection, sacred time and enduring nature. In this process, books such as the Bible – in a double ontology as both words of codified meaning and The Word of Truth – gained a doubly-powerful purchase on the literati, momentarily lifting them out of the here and now, and enabling them to look back upon that world. This would explain how the Old Testament scholars find textual evidence to suggest that the Israelites were a *traditional* nation. Working on an even broader canvas, Jack Goody takes this point further.[31] The technique of writing as a means of communication and storage of information is simultaneously a necessary condition of the formation of bureaucratic states and of the emergence of universalistic religions, namely those institutionalized religions such as Judaism, Islam, Christianity and Confucianism. It enabled a clear measure of separation of polity and religion from kinship as the dominant mode of organization.

I do not think that it is stretching this argument too far to say that just as religious and state institutions came into being though the same world-historical processes, so too did the possibility of abstracting a community of people such as the nation beyond the relative immediacy of face-to-face relations. This does not mean that framing of a society in terms of written and electronic communication depends upon everybody in that society being 'literate' in the usual sense of that term. In early-modern Europe, literacy was not generalized even though authority operated as much through the power of the pen and sword as the power of the embodied word. Coming forward to take an example from the present, each day in the teeming Indian metropolis of Mumbai an illiterate bureaucracy of delivery agents – *dabbawalas* – manage to distribute thousands upon thousands of stainless-steel cylindrical lunch-boxes to workers who have previously placed individualized monthly food-orders. The non-textual *dabbawalas* manage this feat of organization through an intricate colour-coded pattern printed on the tins. At the same time as the overall system relies on more abstract forms of memory-storage and organization. That is, codification can take different forms within a dominant mode of communication characterized as a 'writing culture'.

In the past couple of decades, despite continuities of older communicative forms, writing, script and print have been overlaid by digitalization. As Bill Cope and Mary Kalantzis have argued, it was not the technological possibilities of digitalization *per se* that made the difference, but rather how it came to be used:

The Gutenberg discourse of typography even survived the first iteration of Hypertext Markup Language or HTML, the engine of the World Wide Web ... The truly significant shift away from the world of Gutenberg commenced in the second half of the 1990s and is eptimomised by the rapid emergence since 1998 of XML or Extensible Markup Language [based on the technique of abstracting the information architecture from the rendering of meaning through typographical representation]. In this respect, its conceptual bases are fundamentally different from HTML. Its main distinguishing feature is that it marks up for structure and semantics, instead of for presentation. This represents a truly revolutionary shift away from the practices of text manufacture that had predominated for the last half-millenium.[32]

In other words, even though as ordinary readers we cannot see XML, as a meta-markup language it has the potential to reframe completely the mode of production and communication that makes the text that we continue to rely upon whether in printed or digitalized form. XML is a system that marks the marking of meaning in a text with a framework of tags or Document Type Definitions. It can place and re-place text according specifiable fields of meaning, and specifiable contexts, times and spaces. For example, a text produced within this architecture could be set to be rendered differently according to the specifications of who is reading or listening to that text, at what given time it occurs, and in what location. This is potentially postmodern text-made-text, or even context-made text, 'a technology for the automated manufacture of text from a self-reflexive and abstracted running commentary on meaning function'.[33]

## Consequences for tribalism, nationalism and globalism

This discussion has the effect of qualifying how we think about tribalism, nationalism and globalism. For example, it entails a reworking of the dominant ways of setting up a theory of the nation, including the work of Benedict Anderson and Ernest Gellner. While what I have been describing is a layered dialectic of continuity-and-discontinuity, a layering of ontological formations, that qualifies the pivotal emphasis on an epochal shift from traditionalism to modernism. Moreover, Anderson focuses on a historically-later shift in the mode of communication – print – as it intersects with a new mode of production – capitalism. A fuller response to Anderson's path-breaking work would require working through the significance of other changing modes of practice beyond production and communication, including layers of transformations in the modes of exchange, organization and enquiry.

However, for present purposes, all I want to do is qualify the epochal tone of his argument that the national consciousness becomes possible only when 'three fundamental cultural conceptions, all of great antiquity, lost their axiomatic grip on men's minds'.[34] The first was the conception that a particular script-language such as Church Latin offered privileged access to the ontological truth; the second that monarchs ruled naturally as the divine legatees; and the third that religious cosmology and history were indistinguishable. In beginning to qualifying this proposition, it is worth remembering that it was Church Latin that gave us the connected concepts of *natus* and *natio*. The Bible, for example, is replete with the naming of peoples, communities who at one level continued to live as twelve tribes long after they were named, at a more abstract level, as an interconnected whole. Similarly, in the case of the Mambai myth-complex of the rock-and-tree and the book-and-pen, new social forms such as national community were laid over existing and continuing tribal and traditional relations. To continue the Mambai story I began relating earlier, the elder brother travels to Portugal to ask for a new token of status to replace those that his younger brother has stolen. The younger brother Loer Sa responds by handing over gift objects that include a flag pole, promising to return to East Timor with the national flag at a later date. Ka Sa returns to East Timor with the flag pole and finds that his community now responds by revisiting the sacred rock and tree with 'fear and trembling'. In other words, new formations most powerfully arise in the intersection of social practices and ontologies, not in their epochal replacement.

The parallel argument, developed further in the next section of *Globalism Nationalism*, (particularly Chapter 10), is, first, that none of Anderson's three conceptions were ever uncomplicatedly axiomatic even in traditional community-polities. Second, struggles over the (contingent) dominance of these conceptions continued long after the emergence of print-capitalism. As Benedict Anderson himself says, the Bible was at the centre of the printing and marketing furore associated with the sixteenth-century Reformation and Counter-Reformation. If Gutenberg's invention made the Bible into the first major print-commodity, it also extended the relationship between church and state. The less obvious point is that Martin Luther may have been challenging the sanctity of Latin, but his theology was based on a continuing sanctity of the word, albeit the word couched at a more abstract level as The Word of Communication Himself. God did not just express himself through a communicative language: he was Communication.[35] Luther's point of departure was *John* 1: 'In the beginning was the Word, and the Word was with God, and the Word was God.' This is a remarkable statement of abstract universalism: words from the first century, carried through into the sixteenth century with a new technological drive and social passion.

We should also note that for some time to come the Bible continued to sit comfortably in the hands of the monarchs as their power was projected into the indefinite future. An etching by William de Passe (c. 1598–1636) called 'Triumphus Jacobi Regus', c. 1623, depicts the extended family of the English King, James I. His seated Queen, Anne of Denmark, and eldest son, Henry, hold skulls to signify that they are dead; Charles, the heir to the united thrones, stands with hand resting on the Bible. The book sits in profile with the word 'Biblia' inscribed on it to make sure that we know what we are looking at. In the same way that the skull motifs allow Anne of Denmark and Henry to be present to the contemporary viewer even though their bodies lie rotting in the ground, the Bible acts as a signifier of future sanctification. Charles will be king. The embodied king is yet to rule: long live the abstract King. We are actually not far from the coming of Cromwell and the English Revolution against the monarchy, but here again Cromwell offers the Bible as the sign and wonder of a new chosen people, the English.[36] The English revolutionaries may no longer need to draw a genealogical continuity from the Israelites brought out of Egypt to themselves as the new chosen community of England. Nevertheless, as we will see later in relation to the Puritans of *New* England in Chapter 10, what connects this chosen people to those of Israel is the Abstract Word.

Liah Greenfeld gets carried away at this point, proclaiming incredibly that the birth of the English is not only the first of its kind but the 'birth of all nations'.[37] Adrian Hastings agrees and goes further: 'Britain, for long the prototype of modernity, pioneered the nation-state, it also pioneered the non-national world empire.'[38] This is bizarre, but it has some strengths in that it recognizes, for example, that nation formation and globalization were bound up with each other. In Hastings' writing – and keep in mind that he is Emeritus Professor of Theology at Leeds – the Bible becomes unnecessarily elevated as the central text of nation formation, whether it be the original formation of the English nation or the coming to nationhood of the parts of its empire. While I am sympathetic to his attempt to show the continuing relevance of religious sensibilities to nation formation, we have to question his one-dimensional overstating of the power of the Bible itself. It is simply reductionist to say as he does that

The specific root of [African] naxtionalism does not lie in the circumstances of post-Enlightenment modernity. On the contrary. It lies rather in the impact of the Bible, of vernacular literature and of the two combined in creating a politically stable ethnicity, effectively 'imagined' by its members across a unique mythology.[39]

Despite what Hastings argues, much more was happening in Africa than the translation of the Bible. That book as part of an emergent-dominant mode of communication – print – was only one part of a general overlay of new modes of practice carried by a globalizing series of empires. As we have seen, the dominant mode of exchange was also changing across the world and this also contributed to the formation of nations and extended relations of globalization, not the least in the colonial world through the savage extension of global capitalism.

## Notes

1 Eric Woolfson and Alan Parsons, 'Money Talks', 1985.
2 See, for example, the movie *Money Talks*, 1997, directed by Brett Rattner.
3 John Gerner, 'Money Talks', 1988.
4 Woolfson and Parsons, 'Money Talks'.
5 Neil Diamond and Richard Bennett, 'Forever in Blue Jeans', 1979.
6 Georg Simmel, *The Philosophy of Money*, Routledge, London (1907) 1990, p. 120.
7 Maurice Godelier, *The Enigma of the Gift*, Polity Press, Cambridge, 1999, p. 28.
8 Jack Goody, *The Logic of Writing and the Organization of Society*, Cambridge University Press, Cambridge, 1986, p. 53.
9 C.A. Gregory, *Savage Money: The Anthropology and Politics of Commodity Exchange*, Harwood Academic Publishers, Amsterdam, 1997, p. 223.
10 Jonathan Williams, (ed)., *Money: A History*, British Museum Press, London, 1998.
11 Von Redden (1995) cited in Leslie Kurke, *Coins, Bodies, Games and Gold: The Politics of Meaning in Archaic Greece*, Princeton University Press, Princeton, NJ, 1999, p. 16.
12 Kurke's interpretation in *ibid*.
13 Stella Newton, *Fashion in the Age of the Black Prince: A Study of the Years 1340–1365*, Boydell Press, London, 1980, pp. 25-6, 36ff.
14 John F. Chown, *A History of Money: From AD 800*, Routledge, London, 1994, pp. 17–19, 39–40.
15 Richard John Lufrano, *Honorable Merchants: Commerce and Self-Cultivation in Late Imperial China*, University of Hawai'i Press, Honolulu, 1997.
16 Fernand Braudel, *Civilization and Capitalism 15th–18th Century:* Vol. III, *The Perspective of the World*, Collins, London, 1984, Chapter 3.
17 For a more thorough tracking of this process, or what he calls a history of 'general conjunctures', see Pierre Vilar, *A History of Gold and Money: 1450–1920*, Verso, London (1960), 1976.
18 Hans Christian Andersen, *The Silver Shilling*, Fabbri Publishing, Milan, 1990. I chose this edition because it illustrates the lines of globalism. It is published by an Italian publishing house (which also publishes the *Star Trek* magazine) in conjunction with the Japanese publishers, Gakken, Tokyo. The accompanying tape was recorded at the Redwood Studios and the package is distributed from East Sussex, England.
19 File ADM 10/1 688_1, Bank of England Archives.
20 Public relations managers at the Bank had concerns about responses to the Bank of England employing an American consulting company, *per se*. They therefore prepared answers to possible press questions about McKinsey's American origins including the reply that 'Our understanding is that McKinsey is more an international than a purely American firm'. Briefing papers dated 22 October 1968, from File ADM 10/1 688_1, *idem*. There was in fact subsequent discussion in the British House of Commons about what steps were taken to secure a 'British consultant'.

21 The *Scotsman*, 30 January 1969; The *Evening Standard*, 17 July 1969.

22 Bank of England archives: ADM 10/45 Going off the Gold Standard, 1931 Press Cuttings 1931-32 (emphasis added).

23 *Ibid*.

24 While the electronic means of communication made a difference, again it depended upon an extensive development in the relations of exchange. Thomas Crump's discussion of the 'pure-money complex' (*The Phenomenon of Money*, Routledge & Kegan Paul, London, 1981, Chapter 12), that is, of transactions performed 'purely in terms of time and money', goes too far to suggest that such complexes characterize all societies, but it is instructive.

25 Indicatively Karl Marx (*Capital: Vol. 1*, Progress Publishers, Moscow [1887], 1977, p. 129), writes 'Only insofar as paper money represents gold, which like all other commodities has value, is it a symbol of value'.

26 Lewis Mandel (*The Credit Card Industry*, Twayne Publishers, Boston, 1990) shows for example how the credit card developed over the period from local bankcard experiments in the 1940s, but the shift really took off with the systematization of computerized codification.

27 Jan Pahl, *Invisible Money: Family Finances in the Electronic Economy*, Policy Press, Bristol, 1999.

28 A. Cornford, cited in Susan Strange, *Mad Money*, Manchester University Press, Manchester, 1998, p. 30.

29 Arjun Appadurai, 'Introduction: Commodities and the Politics of Value', in Appadurai, (ed.), *The Social Life of Things*, p. 50.

30 Elizabeth Traube, *Cosmology and Social Life: Ritual Exchange among the Mambai of East Timor*, University of Chicago Press, Chicago, 1986, pp. 55-6.

31 Goody, *The Logic of Writing*; also his *The Domestication of the Savage Mind*, Cambridge University Press, Cambridge, 1977; and *The Interface between the Written and the Oral*, Cambridge University Press, Cambridge, 1987.

32 Bill Cope and Mary Kalantzis, *Text-Made Text*, Common Ground Publishing, Altona, 2003, pp. 10-11.

33 *Ibid.*, p. 11.

34 Benedict Anderson, *Imagined Communities*, Verso, London, 2nd edn, 1991, p. 36.

35 Hagen Schulze, States, *Nations and Nationalism: From the Middle Ages to the Present*, Blackwell Publishers, Cambridge, MA, 1986, p. 129.

36 On the concept of 'chosen peoples', see Anthony D. Smith, *Chosen Peoples: Sacred Sources of National Identity*, Oxford University Press, Oxford, 2003.

37 Liah Greenfeld, *Nationalism: Five Roads to Modernity*, Harvard University Press, Cambridge, MA, 1992, p. 23.

38 Adrian Hastings, *The Construction of Nationhood: Ethnicity, Religion and Nationalism*, Cambridge University Press, Cambridge, 1997, p. 7.

39 *Ibid*. p. 151.

# SEVEN Time and Space, Calendars and Maps

The god associated with time was a blood-thirsty savage. Kronos, son of Uranus (Sky) and Gaia (Earth) castrated his father to become ruler of the universe during the first Golden Age of humanity. This was the age before humans lived in families, generations or states. The universe went backwards. Humans did not give birth and then, in turn, die. They came to life *autochthonously* as the classical Greek concept, and now anthropological term, would have it – that is, out of the earth itself. Kronos is informed by his parents that he will be dethroned by one of his own sons, and so begins devouring his offspring at their birth. His wife tries to save one of their newborn, Zeus. She deceives Kronos with a stone wrapped in baby clothes. Some versions of the myth have Rhea pressing the stone to her breast, and her flowing milk creating the stars known as the Milky Way. Zeus grows to godhood and does overthrow his father. In doing so, he sets the clock of mortality, which for the first time allows humans to experience the pain and pleasure of the succession of generations.

How different is that sense of *cosmological time* from the abstracted *empty time* which obsessed the modern/postmodern world at the end of the second millennium of the Common Era? This was the time of the Y2K global panic, *One Minute Bedtime Stories*, and machines that measured temporal change in nano-seconds. A hundred years had passed since Guglielmo Marconi had sent the Morse letter 'S' across the Atlantic, and quite new regimes for regulating, exchanging and communicating across time and space were being promoted. On 1 January 2000, a consortium of European and US corporations, the Interactive Media in Retail Group (IMRG), launched a software system to provide a global web-based standard-time. Supported by British Prime Minister Tony Blair, IMRG proposed a system that overlaid Greenwich Mean Time, and extended the Co-ordinated Universal Time protocol to create what they called Greenwich Electronic Time (GeT). GeT was intended to be a common international standard for electronic communication and commerce.¹ It was aimed squarely at rationalizing and systematizing the global market. Also around the turn of the millennium the idea of a common, global, standard map based on satellite-imaging was being mooted. A commercial satellite called Okonos swept the world, taking spatial photographs with a one-metre resolution. Its digital images were available for sale on the World Wide Web, and such images were being used for global climate-change forecasting relevant to the agricultural futures markets and for selling packages of temporal risk. Time and space at the turn of the millennium were thus dominated by classical *modernist* concerns about efficiency, profit, movement, speed and control, but this was complicated by other co-existing temporal and spatial modalities. This was the year 1420 according to the Muslim calendar, the year 208 according to the calendar of the French Revolution and the year of the Dragon according to the Chinese calendar.² The range of alternative possibilities included those in settings where the millennium was as irrelevant as Father Christmas. It also included *neo-traditional* forms of millenarianism such as espoused by the Japanese sect Aum Shinrikyo who released nerve gas into the Tokyo subways in order to speed up the time of Armageddon; or as held by the Concerned Christians who fled to the holy city of Jerusalem in 1999 just in case the doomsayers were right.

The discussion in this chapter moves the emphasis of *Globalism, Nationalism, Tribalism* from modes of practice such as exchange and communication to categories of being-in-the-world – time and space. In previous chapters, the concept of *ontological formation* was introduced. The formations of tribalism, traditionalism, modernism and postmodernism were listed as providing the simplest adequate range of the categorical frames for understanding the human condition. They were treated as provisionally useful ways of naming the dominant formations in which people are framed by generalized patterns of interwoven ontological categories, and much more useful, for example, than epochs named in terms of how people produce food and objects of exchange: namely, hunter–gatherer, agricultural, and industrial societies.

We now need to give some detail to that complex interweaving of formations. How do communities constituted in the framing of tribalism *tend* to live their categories of temporality, spatiality and the embodiment? What does it mean to live in modern time and space? Is it possible to talk of postmodern time or postmodern space? In answering these questions, it is not the expressions of time or space or their content that mark the difference. We are trying to address issues of social form. This means setting up the conditions for explaining how, for example, while both the *traditional* medieval Order of Matins and a *postmodern* neo-tribal film *Highlander IV* make much of the phrase 'world without end', they are set in completely different temporal and spatial frames. The overall argument can be summarized in three main propositions, although I will add more points as the chapter proceeds.

> *Proposition 1.* Time and space are deeply-embedded social-relational categories. They are ontological categories constituted as both the context and the outcome of patterns of social practice and meaning. In short, time and space can only be understood socially.[3]
>
> *Proposition 2.* Different social formations live their dominant or *framing* senses of time and space in fundamentally different ways. For example, the notion that time passes at one-second-per-second is a tautological and modern convention rather than being either intrinsically natural or scientifically verifiable. It is abstracted from nature, and verifiable only within a particular mode of scientific enquiry – the Newtonian treatment of time as unitary, linear and uniform. It reached its culmination in 1974 when the second came to be measured in atomic vibrations, allowing the post-phenomenal concept of nano-seconds – one-billionth of a second. The time of postmodernity, including the time of relativity and quantum physics does not move in this way. In the late-modern/postmodern case of Einsteinian relativity it moves in relation to the speed of the participant through space.
>
> *Proposition 3.* Across history, more abstract modes of living in time and space have become layered across more concrete modes, reconstituting rather than replacing those 'prior' forms.[4] To give a simple example, the 'telling of the time' has moved from knowing the patterns of nature – for example, the movement of the sun across the sky, seasonal changes, or the movements of the stars – to reading off increasingly abstracted forms of measurement: from sands through the neck of an hour-glass, the movements of hands on a mechanized clock to digital readouts based on the unseen oscillations of quartz crystals. Despite historical shifts in the dominant ways of telling the time, modern/postmodern persons don't always wear digital watches and they occasionally check out the height of the sun to work out what time it is. Most people are blithely unaware of an existing global internet time developed by the Swiss company Swatch which uses a meridian in Biel and divides the day into 1,000 divisions of 1 minute and 26.4 seconds. Nor do they care that the Swatch digital watches they wear, although abstracted from analogue time, themselves tend to use a form of temporal presentation that harks back to the medieval sundial. (The first circular faces or dials on clocks, with pointers visually indicating the hour of the day, date back to the fourteenth century.)

## The abstraction of time

It is a dangerous analytic task upon which we embark. The possibilities of being misunderstood are endless. I originally intended to begin the chapter by simply describing the dominant nature of time in social formations framed by tribalism. However, rather than taking such a direct route, I will begin more strategically by first underlining Proposition 3 through using an example of the complex layering of ontologies of time in a particular tribal-traditional-modern community.

The Tokelau, a Polynesian community living on a narrow island of land flanked by ocean, have two co-existing calendrical systems. The first is a celestial 'night-time' calendar based on the positions of the stars and connected to tribal subsistence activities, particularly fishing. The second is a modern 'day-time' calendar. With the abolishing of traditional kingship in 1915 and the later establishment of a Tokelau public service, the way that time was traditionally lived – day and night – has been overlaid by a second modern system of day-time reckoning, 'office time'. In other words, with the institutional abstractions of the polity through the coming of the institutions of church, public service, school and hospital – one set of processes in a more general shift – natural or embodied time has been reconstituted. This has profound consequences for tribal-traditional time even if continuities from the past are still carried on. This change is connected not only to the abstraction of institutional authority over the authority of kinship relations, but also, recalling previous discussions about the intertwining of modes of practice, to the abstraction of exchange and the increasing centrality of money:

> What one could then call 'subsistence time' denotes activities centred around the production (including hunting and gathering activities), distribution and consumption of food. 'Office-time' activities are those that involve the running of various departments of the Tokelau public service. These activities are to a greater extent (although this may be said only to be a matter of degree) outward oriented, and have their roots in the monetary sphere ... The two systems conflict in several respects, and there are many signs to indicate that they have opposing consequences with respect to social reproduction. In short, whereas subsistence-oriented activities are geared towards reproducing large extended families and a very tight network of inter-family cooperation, monetary based activities tend to produce smaller, more independent units and do absolutely nothing to generate village cooperation. On the other hand, the monetary sphere is also closely connected with the demands for closer inter-atoll and national co-operation on a formal institutional level.[5]

Thus, as Ingjerd Hoëm's research illustrates, face-to-face integration becomes more privatized as the dominant level of integration is both extended and abstracted. This, in intersection with the commodification of the economy, makes 'national co-operation' across the three Tokelau

Islands more thinkable, even desired. The subjective consequences of this go very deep, challenging something as basic as how one looks at another person. As traditionally understood, in public contexts the Tokelau face is made as a 'fragrant presented surface', adorned, oiled, perfumed, and attentively demure – the 'day' side of things. Looking at another is framed by careful codes of social engagement. For example, to directly 'face' another person is to assume a posture of social equality. The new infrastructures confuse this sense of the public face. It adds another layer-in-tension to the day: the public post-gendered face required by the public service; the direct voice elicited by modern pedagogy.

Similarly, the modality of communication shifts. In traditional Tokelauan ways of speaking, relationships tend to be represented in spatial terms rather than through direct personal pronouns, and great care is taken in either ascribing or avoiding the implied attribution of agency. The sensitivities here are linked to one's *place*, understood in both spatial and social terms. Hoëm writes:

> We can see here a way of thinking which is deeply rooted in the forms of sociality which produce and are produced by it. To switch ways of thinking and forms of sociality associated with the *palagi* [the modern Westerner], or to live in various combinations of the two is certainly possible. What I wish to point out here, however, are the discrepancies between two frames of reference. In terms of the linguistic representation of agency presented above, such discrepancies are apparent on the syntactical level. In the modes of communication associated with the making of the nation-state (education, official documents, etc.), there is a markedly different pattern of communication. The syntax shows more resemblance to the patterns of English: the pronouns (especially ego-orientation) enter, the spatial reference is backgrounded and the typical pattern of verb-initial sentences, is left in favour of noun initiation (achieved through topicalisation). This is significant in that the ego- or I-orientation is traditionally heavily sanctioned and downplayed.[6]

Confirming these changes are shifts in the content of traditional songs. At the now-regular administrative meetings of representatives of the three atolls, songs are sung as tribute and 'confirmation' of tribal-traditional culture. However, instead of the songs beginning with particularistic lines of placement such as 'Atafu my beautiful island ...' the words are changed to stretch the sense of belonging across the atolls-as-a-unity. Atafu turns into 'Tokelau, my beautiful homeland ...', and the song itself, as repository of oral knowledge, is redirected to play a quite different role of national unification.[7]

In this example, relations of time and space are analytically distinguishable even as they are embedded in everything else. Tribalism is an ontological formation, a layer of being, not a totalizing description of communities we call 'tribes'. Now, I can make the bolder Propositions 1 and 2 again – the argument here is that, despite this overlaying of formations, we can still examine what it means to live in the dominance of tribalism, or any other ontological formation, as a specifiable way of living. Put simply but in more theoretical terms, the argument is that we can analytically abstract the generalities of that ontological formation and distinguish it from other formations. The pitfalls besetting this journey are rife. For example, when Anthony Giddens uncritically quotes Evans-Pritchard on the Nuer having no 'concept of time', he needs to be much more careful about how he frames such a move. Writing in 1939, Evans-Pritchard says:

> Strictly speaking the Nuer have no concept of time and consequently, no developed abstract system of time-reckoning ... there is no equivalent expression in the Nuer language for our word 'time', and ... they cannot, therefore, as we can, speak of time as though it were something actual, which passes, can be wasted, can be saved, and so forth.[8]

The sentence that Giddens uses to frame that claim, on the surface, is weak: 'Most small-scale "primitive" societies seem to lack such an abstract conception of time (or of space either).'[9] He is very careful to distinguish between the general human category of historical consciousness and the modern notion of *historicity* – the reflexive control of linear time. However, in accepting Evans-Pritchard's assessment, the weak qualifier falters and Giddens carries forward the unsustainable dualisms between timeless cultures and cultures with linear time.[10] We can say in reply that contemporary tribes have tended to acquire a powerful sense of their own historicity, that the slow acquisition process of that sensibility can in many cases be traced to the clash of ontologies that came with colonization or culture contact, and that Giddens has picked out what is one of the most misleading quotations from Evans-Pritchard that it was possible to find.

Another common and equally-unhelpful version of this differentiation is to say that tribal societies live in circular time and modern societies live in linear time. It is not that cyclical time does not exist in *tribal* and *traditional* thought and practice – for example, we find it in the Hindu law book of *Manu*, or in the *Books of Chilan Balan* from the Maya Indians of Yucatan in southeastern Mexico, although there we also find a coincidence of circular and linear time.[11] It is rather that a metaphor of linearity, even when it bends back upon itself, is an inadequate way of describing the rich complexity of dominant temporality in customary *tribal* cultures. This limitation applies to all variations on the modern linear metaphor: circular, pendulum-like, reversible, and even rhythmic time.

This inadequacy of all modern metaphors of time when describing tribal time has led at least one contemporary commentator to go back to the claim that there are cultures where time does not exist. 'Having disposed of cycles, I want to dispose of time itself', writes Tony Swain in relation to the Aborigines of Australia. 'This is not as difficult as it first might appear', he says: 'Ricoeur argues, correctly, that numbered intervals are necessary to open-ended linearity, but I would go further and say they are indispensable to time itself ... Significantly, the rhythms of Aboriginal life are totally unnumbered, as Aborigines traditionally used no counting at all.'[12] There is not the space here to debate the dubious claim that pre-contact customary Aboriginal people did not have counting procedures, but it is important to question Swain's claim that a tribal ontology of time depends upon a form of mathematics, associated with traditional and modern cultures. Why is time restricted to those cultures that differentiate and count things in the manner of stones on an abacus frame? This claim appears to be the opposite of that which we encountered earlier (Chapter 5) when Arjun Appadurai reduced tribal gift exchange to traditional and modern commodity-exchange. However, the effect is the same. In the earlier case (Appadurai), a tribal category-of-being is reduced to a traditional-modern category, and disappears, or, as in this case (Swain), the capacity to deal in a category-of-being is stolen from tribal people directly, and ... disappears. Funnily enough, what Swain offers us back instead of 'time' is the concept of 'rhythmed events'. Call me simple, but it seems to me that we are back to a sense of time with his concept of 'rhythmed events'. It is a different sense of time from the temporality variously posited by Plato (cosmological time), Newton (empty time) or Einstein (relative space–time). It is time that is not talked about *in itself*, but it is *time* nevertheless.

One way of handling this problem, as already strongly hinted at in the examples used above, is to distinguish different forms of temporality without necessarily treating them as confined to different ontological formations. This still allows for a more specific proposition that argues that the nature of those formations can be characterized by their dominant temporal forms (see Figure 7.1).

> *Proposition 4.* Tribalism can be characterized by the intersection-in-dominance of *analogical*, *genealogical* and *mythological* time; traditionalism can be characterized by the overlaying of *cosmological* time; modernism by the overlaying of *empty* and *relative* time; and postmodernism by the overlaying of *virtual* space–time. Analogical, genealogical and mythological modes of temporality are also available in post-tribal settings constituted in the dominance of traditional

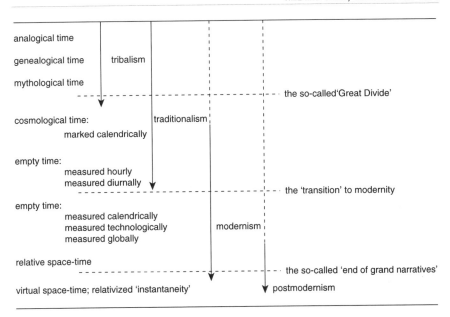

Figure 7.1  Dominant ontologies of time in different social formations

or modern ways of life – available particularly at the level of the face-to-face – but they tend to either be confined to moments of remembering and ritual or treated as archaic, residual or quaint.

*Analogical time* treats temporal movement as analogous to changes in nature (where nature is always-already cultural). The most obvious examples are seasonal changes (the English words 'time' and 'tide' comes from the Anglo-Saxon, *tid*, meaning season); lunar cycles, the basis of the Islamic calendar; and circadian rhythms including the diurnal birth and death of the sun. In the time of the Mambai of East Timor, past, present and future are located along the axis of the tree, from the trunk – base, source, origin, beginning – to the top, the end, the present-future.[13] In the time of the oral poetry of Hesiod (from the seventh century BCE) that has come down us in written form as *Works and Days* (from the fifth century BCE), the activities of Gods, persons and the nature of things are bound up with each other: 'when powerful Zeus brings on the rains of autumn, and the feel of a man's body changes, and he goes much lighter, for this time the star Seirios goes a little over the heads of hard-fated mankind.'[14] This, by the way, is the right time to have sex. Analogical time is thus also bound up with embodiment (and, as we will see in a moment, it is linked though mythological time), but the time related to the human body has a rhythm of its own that can be analytically distinguished as *genealogical time*.

*Genealogical time* is time embodied in significant life-moments, life-histories and genealogies – periods of speaking, periods of pregnancy, passages of life-periods, life-times of birth and death: all marked by ritualized and profane social moments. There is no concept of time-in-itself in this conception: it is temporality enframed by face-to-face relations as a mode of integration, and projected accordingly. Genealogies within customary tribal settings are held in embodied memory, but in other settings they are also stretched beyond memory and are abstracted as lists and (family) trees showing connections to past times and places. In tribal settings, genealogical time is abstracted from immediate embodiment, however, it is not as abstracted and rationalized as Pierre Bourdieu suggests in his dualist treatment of genealogies, mappings and calendars as intellectual abstractions opposed to local generative schemes that just happen to occur in practice (introduced in Chapter 4 above):

> Just as genealogy substitutes a space of unequivocal, homogenous relationships, established once and for all, for a spatially and temporally discontinuous set of islands of kinship, ranked and organized to suit the needs of the moment and brought into practical existence gradually and intermittently, and just as a map replaces the discontinuous, patchy space of practical paths by the homogenous, continuous space of geometry, so a calendar substitutes a linear, homogenous, continuous time for practical time, which is made up of incommensurable islands of duration, each with its own rhythm, the time that flies by or drags, depending on what one is doing, i.e. on the *functions* conferred on it by the activity in progress.[15]

In the present approach, Bourdieu's description of genealogical-calendrical time (as well as what he describes as 'practical time') fit into what can be called, 'homogenous empty time'.[16] I will discuss this below in relation to modernist conceptions of time. However, before doing so I want to argue that, in tribal societies at least, analogical and genealogical time both tend to be drawn unevenly together in what might be called 'mythological time'.

*Mythological time* narrates the medium of life, a medium that is 'beyond' but also informs and is part of what happens here. It originates before but frames the experiential world now, both temporally and spatially. Mythological time keeps getting drawn back to analogical and genealogical instances – for Hesiod, time is implicitly the narrative space of all being, but it is also embodied in Kronos and the story of the generations. We find the same process exemplified in that most extraordinary form of mythological time, the Aboriginal 'Dreamtime' or 'The Dreaming'.

One of the complications of getting at this form of time is that the concept was first named by anthropologists – from Baldwin Spencer and F. Gillen at the end of the nineteenth century to W.E.H. Stanner in the mid-twentieth century. This Western-introduced appellation was then thoroughly incorporated into various Aboriginal interpretations of their own being-in-time. It now connects different mythologies about the lives of Ancestral Beings across different tribes and clans that were once either discontinuous or only loosely connected. Notwithstanding this process of translation from one language-group into the conception of Aboriginality, the forms of the Dreaming myths, though not its content, have similarities across indigenous Australia – it is the ground of past and present. It is not conceived of a single totalizing creation-story but as a series of sacred stories that differ from place to place and from story-teller to story-teller depending upon their knowledge. As Fred Myers puts it in his work on the Pintupi people, The Dreaming can only be understood as being both a given condition and an interpretative projection in relation to the placement of those who live and tell it:

> For the Pintupi, at least, particular attention should be paid to the precarious achievement of Society within the constraints of life in dispersed local groups as a construction that transcends the present and immediate. Essentially, the form taken by The Dreaming among the Pintupi represents this dilemma. Its structure is a product of the way Pintupi society reproduces itself in space and time. Indeed, the distinction that the concept of The Dreaming establishes between two levels of being reflects the structuring of Pintupi space. Such a view sustains the intuition that two other constructs of major importance in Pintupi social life – *ngurra* meaning 'camp', 'country', or 'place', and *walytja*, referring to 'family', 'relatives', or 'kin' – are fundamentally linked to the concept of The Dreaming. It is in relation to this practical logic that space and time, defined by the Dreaming, acquire their value.[17]

In this instance, and many others, mythological time is inextricably bound to relations of place (for the Pintupi, *ngurra*), embodiment (*walytja*) and knowing (*ninti* – in Pintupi, 'holding'). The elements of being are in this setting not abstracted out of each other. However, with the colonial encounter it was brought sharply into focus as new pressures of time-discipline, displacement and codified knowledge hit people in the face. In this one tectonic process of confronting white colonizers from a different world-time, these older forms of time-space were brought under great pressure *and* brought to the attention of indigenous peoples themselves as the ground of their nameable ways of life.[18]

*Cosmological time*, by comparison, is time that is abstracted from mythological time by processes of universalizing and synthesizing myths and practical logic. It is time beyond history but expressed only through it. It is beyond sensible human knowing, but expressed through material instances, mediators, shadows on cave walls, or signs of God on earth. Unlike in the case of the ancient Greek Gods or the Ancestral Figures of the Dreaming, cosmological time is not embodied, but rather instantiated in its omni-presence. It is the whole truth, the One Truth and the only Truth, however contested. This kind of temporality includes what Anderson, drawing upon Benjamin, calls 'Messianic time', temporality that brings past, present and future together connected in the sight of God. However (leaving aside the blatant ethnocentrism of a concept that names the dominant traditional form of time in terms of the religions of the Torah), confining the time of traditionalism to the Messianic would be to accept that the *sacred* traditionalism is an all-encompassing frame of that ontological formation. To the contrary, even if the sacred is extraordinarily important, it was not all-encompassing. From the ancient Stoics and Epicureans to their Renaissance brethren, temporal connection did not always depend upon a god or gods. In some conceptions, 'What has happened has happened and it is no longer possible to undo whatever has happened. Lazarus does not rise, Iphigeneia does not live on after her fiery death, nor does the sun stand still in the sky at Joshua's command'.[19] In the present argument what secular traditionalism still depended upon, however, was something beyond itself, usually Nature as cosmology.

*Empty time*, the *leitmotif* of modernism, gradually overlays the power of cosmological time, particularly in Europe across the period of the late-medieval and after, and eventually carries through the dethroning of both God and Nature as dominant categories. Empty time is time-in-itself, natural with a small 'n'. It is time self-consciously abstracted as a category of existence, able to be mapped day by day onto empty calendrical grids. Time in this setting is often described metaphorically – it travels like an arrow, it is spaced like knots on a long string, and it flows like a river – but it is not part of these things in the way that analogous time would have it. This is the form of temporality that allows for historicity. That is, it leaves the space for reflection upon 'historical time' as it is measured (tautologously) across time and space. The emergence of such a level of temporality leads us in two simultaneous directions: the first is subjectivism, for example, as expressed by Immanuel Kant for whom time was the foundation of all experience. The second is objectivism, expressed by Isaac Newton in 1687 as giving the possibility of 'Absolute, true, and mathematical time, of itself, and from its own nature, [flowing] equally without relation to anything external'.[20]

Empty time emerged in the cracks of cosmological time, particularly, as Richard Sennett documents, through processes of agency or object-extension: through corporations being given a life-time of their own, abstracted from the lives of persons, or objects of exchange including money being used to secure time or deferred salvation. Using an example of economic contractual obligations being rewritten in thirteenth-century Paris, Sennett writes:

> If a charter could be revised, the corporation defined by it has a *structure* which transcends its *function* at any one time ... In Humbert de Romans' Paris, measured time was just beginning to make its appearance in the guilds: guild contracts, especially in the manufacturing trades, specified the hours of work and computed wages on this basis.[21]

Empty time allows many practices, and brought much contestation. It is this kind of time that frames the possibility of conceiving of *usury*, lending money at interest, in effect 'buying time'. Despite being prohibited at various times by Judaism, Christianity and Islam, it legally escaped the strictures of cosmological time by being allowed in dealings with persons from a different cosmology – a medieval Muslim, for instance, could borrow with interest from a Jewish lender. This can be compared to *usance*, a form of lending over variable time discussed by Chris Gregory in *Savage Money*.[22] Usance involves repayments in kind after the exchange-use of goods such as grain and land, and is not interest in the modern sense. For example, when a farmer is lent seed, contracting to pay back some time after the harvest that amount of seed and an additional contracted proportion, the rate of usance has a value, but there is no abstraction of common temporal measure in that calculation. There is no sense that a certain amount of time equals a certain level of return. The temporal point called 'after the harvest' remains a socially-negotiated horizon. The return is embedded in the fate of nature and the continuing embodied relationship between lender and borrower.

This is not to say that usance cannot be rationalized in the modern sense, but it did not begin life that way. In Gregory's words, 'As such it has its value in the historically contingent relationship between the lender and the borrower. Temporality, as the reciprocally recognized relationship between lender and borrower, determines the language used to describe the transaction – use? interest? usury? – and values it as good or bad.'[23] In a world of strangers conducting business in an increasingly-abstract market, usury quickly became normalized. Time-measured capitalism emerged powerfully through the eighteenth into the twentieth centuries, aided by time-industrialization – the industrial production of the mechanisms for telling the time. In 1760, the production of watches averaged one time-piece per worker-month. In 1960, a decade after the United States Time Corporation made the first Timex watch, the company was making eight million of them annually. A further decade on, and it had globalized its production base and was making thirty-million time-pieces in plants around the world.[24]

This period of the eighteenth into the twentieth centuries was also the time of intensifying *historicalism*, the propensity to globalize a single temporal system and a singular sense of 'world-time'[25] across a singular world-space. Homogenous empty time became the first kind of time that allowed for the global extension of time without becoming beset by internal contradictions – mostly because it relativized other temporal systems in terms of itself as the normalized ground of everyday practice. In empty time, the high priests of cosmological time could have their holy days (quickly becoming holidays), but the calendar they added their days into was rationalized in terms of relativized nature. Inside the sacred houses, time was gradually reworked. The sacred concept of the *hora* (hour) became regulated in empty time as reformists including John Calvin and Martin Luther argued for limiting sermons to a consumerable abstract time-measure.[26] Holy days were a longer-term problem. For centuries, philosophers, astronomers and mathematicians had attempted to reconcile analogical time (the time of nature) with different versions of cosmological time (religious renditions of the time of the sacred): the Greek astronomer Ptolemy in the second century, the Hindu astronomer Aryabhata in the sixth century, the Venerable Bede in the eighth century, the Arab mathematician Mohammed Ibn Musa al-Khwarizmi in the ninth century and the Oxford Franciscan Roger Bacon in the thirteenth century.[27] The problem was that the days of their calendars were out of step with the lunar months and the solar year. In 1582, Pope Gregory VIII finally issued a papal bull to realign sacred and analogical time in terms of a new calendar, but this was the beginning of the end of the dominance of cosmological time, at least in Christendom.

This intersection of cosmological time and empty time continues to the present. For example, the hands of the clock at the front of the Baiturrahman Grand Mosque remain at 8.47 a.m., the time that the tsunami struck Aceh on 26 December 2004. Seven-thousand people attended the Eid al-Adha holy day service early in 2005 to honour the tsunami victims across Indonesia. However, empty time nevertheless frames these holy events as the rest of the world squabbled over which high-technology early-warning system would be used in the future to simultaneously warn nations in the Indian Ocean about impending disasters. Extending upon the preceding discussion we can add a further proposition.

*Proposition 5.* The extension of a generalized connection across an abstracted world-space – namely, globalism – is associated with a parallel temporal process of generalizing connection across world-time: historicalism.

Empty time is also associated with modern globalism. The great revolution of empty time culminated in the nineteenth century with political and scientific debates around the introduction of standard world-time. In 1884, at the Prime Meridian Conference, agreement was finally reached to link the world temporally, counting 24 hours around the globe with each hour aligned to zones marked by longitudinal meridians east and west of Greenwich. It was symbolically the last gasp of traditional 'Rule Britannia'; even if the conference was held in Washington, D C. This was time as globalized and practically relativized in relation to the locality on the globe where one stands. There are many theoretical ways of coming at this development – from the level of empirical generalizations about the detail of the debates and technological developments, through conjunctural and integrational analysis to categorical analysis about the changing nature of time itself. Most often the history of time has been written at the level of collecting details for making empirical generalizations. In the story told by Clarke Blaise, standard time began in the mind of the chief engineer of the Canadian Pacific Railway, Sandford Fleming, in June 1867 when in Bandoran, Ireland, he missed the Londonderry train because of a basic temporal discrepancy.[28] At that time, across the world, railway times were set separately and only in rough relation to each other, usually taken from solar readings. However, at a more abstract analytical level, it is possible to tell the story as a world-history of the emerging dominance of a new mode of temporality. As we have seen, this revolution was neither immediate nor totalizing and universally accepted. It is indicative that in Joseph Conrad's novel, *The Secret Agent* (1907), the central character, a Russian anarchist, was sent to England to blow up the Greenwich Observatory, the site of the prime meridian.

Unlike the attempt to standardize the basis of money in the gold standard (see Chapter 5), however, standard time has become an enduring institution. It is not that it rules supreme, but it meets the requirements of what Bourdieu calls the practical logic in relation to the complex *habitus* of *capitalism* (based on an accelerating electronic, just-in-time mode of production and an expanding mode of commodity and financial exchange), *mediatism* (the systemic interconnectivity of a mass-mediated world based on a mode of electronically-networked communication that emphasizes instaneity), and *techno-scientism* (based on a new intersection between the mode of production and the mode of enquiry that rationalizes time). Other modalities of time have since emerged. *Relative space–time* grew up in the era of empty time, and although it has been around for nearly a century it does not look like displacing empty time as the dominant ontology of contemporary temporality. It is time connected and relativized in the expression $E = mc^2$ (matter-energy determines the curvature of space–time) that is, it is time relativized in relation to one's place and movement through the universe. In the field of physics, this kind of time has itself been 'superseded' by quantum physics, and more recently by notions of *virtual space–time* in which time has become the times of parallel universes and time-warps. This is time best expressed in science fiction and superstring theory.[29]

In the present then, we can find across the world all of the forms of temporality that we have been discussing, from the analogical to the virtual, and from the tribal to the postmodern. Empty time, the dominant temporality of this period has become filled with the possibilities of other times and other sensibilities, but dominant it remains – a dominant and savagely demanding ontology that frames objective and subjective relations in the twenty-first century.

## The abstraction of space

The abstraction and extension of spatiality across history and across different social formations arguably follow the same patterning as that of temporality (as do other modes of being from epistemology to embodiment – though, as we will see in Chapter 8, there are some parting distinctions with the emergence of modern modes of embodiment, mostly because human beings still find it culturally impossible to treat the body as 'empty'. As I will argue there, the social body under these conditions tends to be abstracted metaphorically, for example, in the case of the body politic.) In the case of spatiality, the patterns of change are even more closely linked, despite a number of theorists of modernism claiming that, since the nineteenth century, time has replaced space as the dominant motif of social relations (or vice versa) (Compare Figures 7.1 and 7.2).

Just as in the case of analogical time, the ontology of *analogical space* involves treating social places as analogical to sites in nature. For example, the Yolngu place of *ganma* is the confluence of two waters, fresh and salt water, that meet in a particular mangrove lagoon, as well as the power and danger of such a fertile life-giving place.[30] Place is bound up

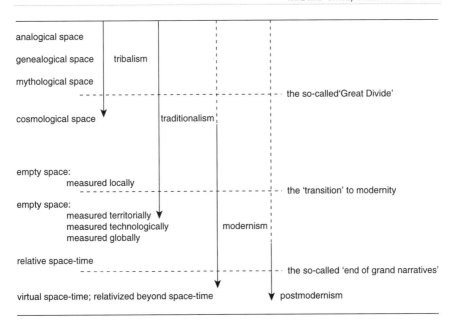

Figure 7.2  Dominant ontologies of space in different social formations

with time, embodiment and knowledge. Related to this, *genealogical space* is embodied in life-histories and genealogies – life-times of birth and death marked by ritualized and profane social moments (bound by the face-to-face as a mode of integration). *Mythological space* treats spatiality as the narrated life-world. This medium of the mythic is 'framing' and yet constantly permeates the whole experiential world without being singular. Mythological space is condensed in meaning at particular sites as places carrying the recognition of change or stability in time such as stones, rock formations, and trees, mountains and rivers, burial sites and other places marking life-passages. By comparison to mythological space – which is grounded in a landscape of meanings, unevenly drawing together places by analogy and genealogy – *cosmological space*, the dominant spatiality of traditionalism, is universalizing, proclaiming itself as metaphysical and totalizing. Particular sites are anointed as signs of the cosmological, and although these sites do not carry the cosmological in themselves, they are seen as expressive of it.

If, as discussed earlier, modernism is characterized by the overlaying of prior forms of time by empty time, we can say similarly that empty time walks alongside *homogenous empty space* as it leaves behind or reconstitutes prior forms of spatiality. Just as with the development of empty time, conceptions of empty spatiality developed in the fissures and contradictions of cosmological subjectivities and practices, emerging to overshadow the mysteries of earlier mythological space. Frank Lestringant, for example, shows how, in the Renaissance world, different forms of mapping continued side-by-side despite the dominance of ontologies of cosmological space:

> The topographer's landscape-map was a profuse and indefinitely fragmented receptacle of local legends and traditions that were rooted in the vagaries of relief, hidden in the folds of terrain, and readable in toponymy and folklore [analogical and mythological space]; whereas the reticular and geometrical map of the cosmographer anticipated the conquests and 'discoveries' of the modern age. No doubt the marvellous [the mythological representation of fantastic creatures] was not absent from it; but it subsisted there only by special dispensation. If for example, the Le Havre pilot Guillaume Le Testu placed at the margins of the known world, in his *Cosmographie Universelle* of 1556, monstrous populations inherited from Pliny, St Augustine and Isidore of Seville, it was only to establish provisional boundaries for a knowledge in a perpetual state of progress. 'Progress' means here that enlargement of a space that was pushing out on all sides and stitching together as, as voyages allowed, the remaining gaps in it.[31]

In Lestringant's words, cosmological space during this period 'anticipated' empty space. That is, cosmography continued to treat cosmology as foundational – many map-makers from Sebastian Münster to Jodocus Hondius were geographer-theologians – however, the new forms of mapping displaced God to the textual and ritual mediations that accompanied the maps. Empty spatiality, in allowing space to be measured by new techniques and processes of technological mediation, set up new spatial perspectives such the Mercator projection that put humankind as the viewer of the globe rather than God. It is no coincidence that by the sixteenth century, the Garden of Eden had largely disappeared as a mapped place.[32] Conceptions of empty space were framing the transition from frontiers to borders as abstract lines on a map and were linked to the emergence of institutionally-extended spaces such as state-organized territory and private property.

Commodified space – private property – developed across the same period as institutionalized space. Both were dependent upon the institution of the state to set up juridical, military and administrative surveillance systems to establish their dominance and to regulate their reproduction, but they were also part of a shift in the dominant ontological frame that was to have an increasingly powerful effect on all the peoples of the world. The colonization of other frames of space and time occurred with brutal excess as a sailor-soldiers headed out in ships with guns, germs, and steel to fill the world's 'empty spaces'.[33] New kinds of abstract mapping carved up the landscape of the New World. Only a few years after the American Revolution had decided who was going to dominate North America, the US Congress in May 1785 authorized the survey and sale of over a billion acres stretching from Canada to Mexico in an immaculate abstract grid of straight lines. Thomas Jefferson's plan included US states that were yet to be named and some that never came into existence – Assenisipia and Metropotamia.[34] Across the other side of the globe, Edward Gibbon Wakefield set out to do the same thing for Australia and South Africa. Into those 'empty spaces', and not just colonial spaces, people poured their sense that they were making new worlds, and in some senses they were – in Benedict Anderson's phrase, those spaces became 'saturated with ghostly national imaginings'.[35] Recall the song of 'Tokelau, my beautiful homeland ...'. States and nations were coming together:

> *Proposition 6.* The modern abstraction of time-as-history and space-as-territory (in empty time-space) was foundational to the formation of modern state sovereignty, the nation-state and the 'take-off phase' of modern globalism. This is related to the argument in the last chapter that both the modern nation-state and disembodied globalism grew up together in the period of the late-nineteenth century as relations of exchange and communication became dominated by increasingly abstract forms of interchange.

The modern struggle over the globalization of one form of generalizing empty spatiality – metric measurement – occurred during the same period. Over the period of the eighteenth to the twentieth centuries, metric measurement (that is, post-embodied measurement) was taken up by all the countries on the earth except for the United States, Burma and Liberia. *Relative space–time* emerged out of the limits of empty regulated space as the measurement of very large and very small things – from universes to atoms and light waves – failed to succumb to two-dimensional measurement techniques. In the late-eighteenth century, the search for the length of the metre as one ten-millionth of the distance from the pole to the equator had been posited on the belief that because the globe was eternal and perfectly spherical it would generate a measurement that would be 'for all people for all time' (Cariat de Condorcet).[36] However, when finally the metre was generalized and confirmed at the Convention of the Metre in 1875 (paralleling the 1884 Prime Meridian Conference), it became an exercise in modern paradox. By that time, science had stripped measurement of its any analogical certainty. The metre had become no more than a relative measure preserved as a unit of convention in a platinum-iridium bar. And it gets more bizarre. In the mid-twentieth century, soon after the second became defined as the duration corresponding to the transition between 'the two superfine levels of the ground state of the Caesium-133 atom', or 9,192,631,770 periods of its radiation, the metre was redefined as the distance travelled by light in a vacuum in 1/299,792,458 seconds. Concurrently, postmodern notions of *beyond space–time* had entered the human lexicon with hyperspace, parallel universes and multiple space-time dimensions (again mostly handled as science fiction and avant-garde physics-philosophy).[37] Ontologies of empty space remained dominant, much as had empty time, not because it was the newest, but through being embedded in the globalized practices and subjectivities of what I have been calling *capitalism*, *mediatism* and *technoscientism*.

Out of this discussion, there is a final proposition that I want to put tentatively, but without developing it here:

> *Proposition 7.* The reconstitution of time and space has political consequences, with more abstract means of connecting time and space giving increased potential for power at a distance. As the dominant way in which we live time and space has become more abstract, it has become more open to processes of rationalization, objectification and commodification. Thus the way that power is generated has itself become both (potentially) more extensive in its reach and intensive in its depth, as it has become more abstractly constituted.

This proposition will be part of the warp of the three chapters in Part III on the state, the nation and globalization. Before we turn to this final section, we still have to come to terms with the changing nature of embodiment, the subject of the next chapter.

## Notes

1 BBC News Online, 1 January 2000, 09:11 GMT; http://news:bbc.uk/i/low/sci/tech/580334.stm.

2 David Ewing Duncan, *The Calendar: The 5,000-Year Struggle to Align the Clock and the Heavens*, Fourth Estate, London, 1999.

3 For a different version of this proposition, see Barbara Adam, 'Social Versus Natural Time, A Traditional Distinction Re-examined', in Michael Young and Tom Schuller, *The Rhythms of Society*, Routledge, London, 1988.

4 This proposition thus addresses a couple of throwaway sentences in Norbert Elias (*Time: An Essay*, Blackwell Publishers, Oxford, 1992): 'One of the difficulties one encounters in an essay on time is the absence of a developmental theory of abstraction' (p. 41), and in a footnote: 'I deliberately avoid speaking of a level of abstraction. For from what is the concept of time abstracted?' (p. 201).

5 Ingjerd Hoëm, 'Processes of Identification and the Incipient National Level: A Tokelau Case', *Social Anthropology*, vol. 7, no. 3, 1999, p. 291.

6 *Ibid.*, p. 290.

7 *Ibid.*, p. 292.

8 Cited in Anthony Giddens, *A Contemporary Critique of Historical Materialism*, Macmillan, London, 1981, p. 36. Giddens frames his discussion through Heidegger, saying that, 'The temporality of Dasein, the human being and that of the institutions of society in the longue durée are grounded in the constitutive temporality of all Being ... there are at least five features of the human subject that distinguish human existence as peculiarly historical' (p. 34).

9 *Ibid.*

10 For an illuminating discussion of the lineages of this dualism, see Peter Rigby, 'Time and Historical Consciousness: The Case of the Ilparakuyo Maasai', in Diane Owen Hughes and Thomas R. Trautmann eds, *Time: Histories and Ethnologies*, University of Michigan Press, Ann Arbor, MI, 1995.

11 Thomas R. Trautmann, 'Indian Time, European Time', and Nancy M. Farriss, 'Remembering the Future, Anticipating the Past: History, Time, and Cosmology among the Maya of Yucatan', both in Hughes and Trautmann (eds), *Time*.

12 Tony Swain, *A Place for Strangers: Towards a History of Australian Aboriginal Being*, Cambridge University Press, Cambridge, 1993, p. 18.

13 Elizabeth Traube, *Cosmology and Social Life: Ritual Exchange among the Mambai of East Timor*, University of Chicago Press, Chicago, 1986, pp. 14–15.

14 Discussed in Anthony Aveni, *Empires of Time: Calendars, Clocks and Cultures*, Basic Books, New York, 1989, Chapter 2, citation from p. 48.

15 Pierre Bourdieu, *Outline of a Theory of Practice*, Cambridge University Press, Cambridge, 1977, p. 105, (his emphasis).

16 Using the phrase that Ben Anderson brought to the fore in rewriting Walter Benjamin's work on temporality. Benedict Anderson, *Imagined Communities*, Verso, London, 2nd edn, 1991.

17 Fred R. Myers, *Pintupi Country, Pintupi Self, Sentiment, Place and Politics among Western Desert Aborigines*, University of California Press, Berkeley, CA, 1991, p. 48.

18 For an illuminating illustration of this process of confrontation, see Chinua Achebe's novel, *Arrow of God*, Heinemann, London, 1964; discussed as length in Elias, *Time*, pp. 164–84.

19 Agnes Heller, *Renaissance Man*, Schocken Books, New York, 1978, p. 125. See also Chapter 6 in the same book, 'Time and Space: Past Orientedness and Future Orientedness'.

20 Both examples, including the quote, are from Stephen Kern, *The Culture of Time and Space, 1880–1918*, Harvard University Press, Cambridge, MA, 1983, p. 11.

21 Richard Sennett, *Flesh and Stone: The Body and the City in Western Civilization*, Faber and Faber, London, 1994, pp. 204–5.

22 C.A. Gregory, *Savage Money: The Anthropology and Politics of Commodity Exchange*, Harwood Academic Publishers, Amsterdam, 1997, pp. 213, 224–31.

23 *Ibid.*, p. 226.

24 David S. Landes, *Revolution in Time: Clocks and the Making of the Modern World*, Belknap Press, Cambridge, MA, 1983, pp. 241 and 340.

25 The concept of 'world-time' is adapted from Wolfram Eberhard, *Conquerors and Rulers*, E.J. Brill, Leiden, revised edition, 1965.

26 On preaching time, as well as merchant, market and schooling time from the end of the late-medieval period see Gerhard Dohrn-van Rossum, *The History of the Hour: Clocks and Modern Temporal Orders*, Chicago University Press, Chicago, 1996, chs 8–9.

27 Duncan, *The Calendar*; Arno Borst, *The Ordering of Time: From Ancient Computus to the Modern Computer*, Polity Press, Cambridge, 1993.

28 Clark Blaise, *Time Lord: Sir Sandford Fleming and the Creation of Standard Time*, Vintage Books, New York, 2000.

29 Michio Kaku, *Hyperspace: A Scientific Odyssey Through Parallel Universes, Time Warps, and the Tenth Dimension*, Oxford University Press, New York, 1994.

30 Helen (Verran) Watson, *Singing the Land, Signing the Land*, Deakin University, Geelong, 1989, Chapter 1; and Helen Verran, 'A Story about Doing "The Dreaming"', *Postcolonial Studies*, vol. 7, no. 2, pp. 149–64.

31 Frank Lestringant, *Mapping the Renaissance World*, University of California Press, Berkeley, CA, 1994, p. 4.

32 Alessandro Scafi, 'Mapping Eden: Cartographies of the Earthly Paradise', in Denis Cosgrove, *Mappings*, Reaktion Books, London, 1999.

33 Jared Diamond, *Guns, Germs and Steel: A Short History of Everybody for the Last 13,000 Years*, Vintage, London, 1998. On the colonial geo-political imaginary, see Walter D. Mignolo, *Local Histories/Global Designs: Coloniality, Subaltern Knowledges and Border Thinking*, Princeton University Press, Princeton, NJ, 2000.

34 Andro Linklater, *Measuring America: How the United States was Shaped by the Greatest Land Sale in History*, HarperCollins, London, 2002.

35 Anderson, *Imagined Communities*, p. 9.

36 Ken Alder, *The Measure of All Things: The Seven-Year Odyssey that Transformed the World*, Little Brown, London, 2002, p. 1.

37 Kaku, *Hyperspace*; Martin Dodge and Rob Kitchin, *Mapping Cyberspace*, Routledge, London, 2001; Margaret Wertheim, *The Pearly Gates of Cyberspace: A History of Space from Dante to the Internet*, Doubleday, Sydney, 1999.

# EIGHT Bodies and Symbols, Blood and Milk

Even in this world of mass media, futures markets and Patriot missiles, the body-as-natural-symbol continues to contribute to how social groups create boundaries of identification. This process of identity formation takes various contradictory forms. For example, under conditions of late capitalism, cultivating one's identity has become increasingly commodified, objectified and individualized, with the dominant subjective emphasis turning on the individual as autonomous, self-active and self-forming. At the same time, under certain circumstances, we can still feel ourselves to be part of something palpable or beyond the self. In contemporary Western societies, even the most gregarious individual could not be said to have a meaningfully-textured relationships with more than a few dozen others, yet as Benedict Anderson describes in writing about the nation-state, there is a 'remarkable confidence of community in anonymity'.[1] In this abstraction of community, embodiment as a universally-shared experience creates bonds across settings of anonymity that are not completely discontinuous with those found in the more concrete settings of reciprocal tribalism. Bodily symbols and signifiers – from the signs of blood, bile, semen and milk to representations of Unknown Soldiers, national heroes and religious figures – draw on the power of symbolism to make sense through linkage and remembrance. It is significant that recently George W. Bush had to defend Defense Secretary Donald Rumsfeld for using a computer-simulated signature to sign letters of condolence to the families of more than 1,000 troops killed in Iraq. We all know that Donald Rumsfeld does not know the families personally, but it remains *symbolically* important in the social world of mediated relations that he attends to the death-letters with his own hand. 'I know Secretary Rumsfeld's heart', George W. Bush responds, 'I know how much he cares about the troops.'[2]

In focusing on the body, this chapter continues the discussion of the categories of being-in-the-world that we began with in the previous chapter on time and space. The present chapter is wrapped around a basic question. In what ways are embodiment and bodily symbolism part of the processes of socially defining the self, and how are they relevant to integrating community and polity? This question is approached comparatively. The chapter compares forms of embodiment in different contexts from customary tribalism to postmodern capitalism. The discussion leads to the broaching of a second more politically-charged question. Is the reconstitution of embodiment in contemporary Western society stripping the body, our bodies, of their capacity to enrich the social connection between people except as limited sites of immediate intimacy or as residual culturally-managed symbolism? A background concern here involves thinking about what might be an alternative way of framing the current practices of social relations. This ethically-driven concern is elaborated in more detail in the final chapter, but as pointer to the direction to be taken, the approach can be summarized as proposing a reflexive politics of embodied socially-negotiable limits. In other words, considerations about the value or otherwise of the various modes of disembodied extension should be bound within a framework of condensed and complex limitations on the transcendence of embodiment. These limits are not simply 'given'. They require regular public debate over their meaning. This should not be read as an argument for a return to kinship-based or close-knit geographically-insular parochial communities. It *is* nevertheless an argument for the ontological importance of relations of embodied or face-to-face integration at a time when more abstract relations of integration and differentiation are globally predominant. It is an argument for relations of continuity, reciprocity and co-operation in the reflexive establishment of overlapping, intersecting communities. It is to suggest that the constraints of embodiment are not simply impediments to be left behind as soon as is technologically possible, but, like ontological limit of human mortality, are good basic starting-points for social life. These are limits that make the excitements of restrained boundary-crossing and moments of transcendence meaningful in the first place.

Overall, then, the chapter presents four main propositions:

> *Proposition 1.* Embodiment is lived across all forms of community as a deeply-embedded social-relational category. It is an ontological category constituted as both the context and the outcome of patterns of social practice and meaning.
>
> *Proposition 2.* Different social formations are framed in terms of fundamentally-different dominant senses of embodiment. These

dominant modes of corporeality may be dominant but that does not mean that nothing else lives in their shadows.

*Proposition 3.* Across history, more abstract modes of living our bodies have become layered across more concrete ways of doing so, reconstituting rather than replacing those 'prior' forms. That is, across world-time and world-space, bodies are constituted in differently-intersecting levels of abstraction. This argument has the effect of substantially qualifying propositions that assume that bodies are just natural, as well as challenging the obverse – the counter-propositions that turn practices of corporeality into discursive formations. Social meanings are not just signs written on individual bodies.

*Proposition 4.* This reconstitution of embodiment has political consequences intimately connected to the abstraction of time and space. As the dominant ways in which we live have become more abstract, our bodies have become more open to processes of rationalization, objectification, commodification and political-cultural management. The importance of bodily symbolism continues throughout this reconstitution, but it draws now for its subjective power on subordinate relations of embodied connection that have largely retreated into the realm of the privatized and personal. It is politically projected through the power of changing modes of communication

## From natural symbols to techno-machines

Symbols connect by drawing on the creative human ability to interpret the unfamiliar through imaginative connection with the known. The term 'symbol' (in Greek, *symbolon*) itself carries its own dead metaphor of face-to-face contractual connection: a 'symbol' originally referred to a metal object broken in half and carried separately by two people as a material sign of their pledge to each other.[3] In one example of symbolic connection from the 'concrete to abstract', the intimate familiarity of the body laid to rest in a war memorial relates individual citizens to the Body Politic. In another, the transubstantiation of bread and wine relates Christians to the Corpus of the Church community. Order, continuity, integration and depth of meaning are gained through symbolic bridging of this distance.[4] While the bridging made by symbolic expression is in *one* sense arbitrary (that is, in *one* of the senses emphasized by post-structuralists), it nevertheless gathers meaning and thus becomes culturally non-arbitrary when it is interpreted by a person or a community who lives its meaning. A rich interweaving of practices, values and sense-messages forms the background against which symbols can yield meaning. Hence, bodily symbols reveal as much about their cultural setting, and the practices and perceptions which constitute attitudes to the body, as they do about that which is being signified.

The social need to develop and define relationships with others does not decrease as the means of societal integration become increasingly extended across space and time. However, the form in which it is expressed grows increasingly abstract as it is reconstituted. This abstraction is paradoxical. While it continues to reproduce the desire for group identification, drawing together the faces of the nation, the ethnic community or the global network, it also seems to weaken the embodied depth of the connection. The faces of George W. Bush, Fidel Castro, or Cathy Freeman, integrate an amorphous mass of individualized strangers (the nations of the United States, Cuba and Australia respectively), despite the fact that we have no relation to them at the level of the face-to-face. On the other hand, President Bush's Christmas card list grows by hundreds of thousands of people each year. Thus modern-global, national and even local communities 'stretch' the sense of integration found in the reciprocal kinship network of tribal or traditional societies. This stretching, this abstracting of the social horizon, has virtues in that historically it has formed part of the basis for the enriching possibilities of a universalizing ethic, highlighting the *needs of strangers*. However, it is this same stretching which thins out the connection which is so crucial for maintaining a depth of ontological security. The fragility of social identity in late capitalism already suggests a possible answer to the issue of how the constitution of persons differs across historical and social settings. This will be considered in more detail later in relation to the image of the body in contemporary culture. First, a little more needs to be said about symbols in general, natural symbols, and more particularly about the culture of the body as a natural symbol (Mary Douglas's term).

Symbols work to integrate societies and express the meaning of social relations. A society's sense of community, whether tribal, traditional, modern or postmodern, becomes knowable in part through the representations made by symbols. As carriers of richly-condensed networks of meaning, symbols are part of this multi-layered complexity. They secrete the memories and codifications of our various histories in layers of possible interpretations and reference-points. They are energetic tools in cohering and ordering social relations, expressing life in richly-dramatic sequences of imagery. Like the continuing power of the photograph of 9-year-old Kim Phuc running away from a US napalm-attack in 1972, symbolic imagery can thus be palpable and intense despite its inevitable representational abstraction or distance from what it portrays. All meaningful symbols are thus always caught in a meshing of cultural contradictions between more concrete and more abstract levels of social integration.

The body can be used in integrating a community and defining its social relations as both a universalizing experience – the human body as common to all of us – and as a particularizing experience: the body as a marker of difference – gendered difference, ethnic difference, differences of age, family, and so on. Paradoxically, both these relations of embodiment – universalism and particularism – find their richest and most stable expression in contradictory intersection with each other. In other words, embodiment is most pregnant with meaning when, first, the universalizing and more abstract modalities of social relations qualify the differentiating, exclusionary, inwardly-turned and more concrete modalities of symbolically likening the community to a body. It is most sustainable when, second, the cultural infuses with the embodied without rationalizing the body as biologically given. It is richest when the nature/culture contradiction – that is, the tension between being culturally reflexive about what it is *to relate* to nature as a human being, and being *part of* nature as a embodied being – is not so stretched by the possibilities of techno-science that we (our bodies) become increasingly reduced to pliable social constructions. At the point when, in the dominant culture, 'we' become the 'soft infrastructure' of our dreams for liberation from our mortal, defective and socially-demanding flesh and blood, then the contradictions rebound in potentially-damaging ways. One the one hand, they frame desires for embodied perfection or transcendence including through designer procreation, foetal stem-cell experimentation, extreme surgery and cloning. On the other, they naturalize romantic and even reactionary attempts to reclaim embodied authenticity through appropriating older traditions of asceticism, body-policing and even martyrdom.

More broadly, ontological contradictions inevitably arise in the intersection of different levels of integration, and in the intersection of the cultural practices conducted at those different levels with the world-as-given, 'the natural'. Understood this way, it follows that such contradictions, including the nature/culture contradiction, are enriching insofar as any one level does not come to constitute the dominating mode of living-in-the-world, thereby thinning out prior levels of human interrelation (see Table 8.1).

Valorizing either the more abstract universalizing forms of disembodied integration or the more concrete forms of face-to-face integration has

Table 8.1 Levels of integration as levels of embodiment and abstraction

| Levels of integration | Degree of abstraction | Contradictions between nature and culture | Societal forms given the dominance of a particular level of integration |
|---|---|---|---|
| face-to-face | decreasing ↑ | condensing ↑ | tribal |
| object-extended | | | tribal to traditional |
| agency-extended | ↓ | ↓ | traditional to modern |
| disembodied | increasing | stretching | modern to postmodern |

worrying consequences. At its most politically disturbing, the heightening of a sense of external boundaries-as-given can be lived in terms of carefully guarding against the poisoning of foreign intrusion and the protection of social 'orifices'. Internal cohesion, allegiance and familiarity can be reduced to the harmony of the essentially-bounded, fully-closed, interconnected human body. For example, long before the period of the 1994 Rwandan genocide, discussed in previous chapters, Liisa Malkki documents the naturalizing of 'body maps' differentiating Tutsi and Hutu persons down to the colour of their tongues and the whites of their eyes.[5] According to Malkki's Hutu informants, these understandings served as means of working out who among them were to be killed in the massacres. These understandings were articulated with other maps that interpreted the reasons why Hutu were killed in certain ways. Instances of pushing a sharpened bamboo stick through the anus and up into the brain of a slain Tutsi, for example, were possible reversals of the putatively ongoing Tutsi attempt to humiliate the Hutu intellect. Here Arjun Appadurai provides a thought-provoking intervention:

> The question is, how can forms of identity and identification of such a scope – ethnic labels that are abstract containers for the identities of thousands, often millions of people – become transformed into instruments of the most brutally intimate forms of violence? One clue to the way in which these large numerical abstractions inspire grotesque forms of bodily violence is that these forms of violence – forms that I have called vivisectionist – offer temporary ways to render these abstractions graspable, to make these large numbers sensuous, to make labels that are potentially overwhelming, for a moment, personal. To put it in a sanitized manner, the most horrible forms of ethnocidal violence are mechanisms for producing persons out of what are otherwise diffuse large-scale labels that have effects but no locations.[6]

Appadurai's analysis opens up major questions, but it does not quite work. What he misses out on are the different levels of analysis necessary to understanding such a complex process as *modern* genocide. Abstract maps of embodied difference *are* ways of generalizing from the particularities of persons, but that does not mean that sharpened bamboo sticks serve to produce persons out of these generalized maps. To the contrary, I would suggest that the bamboo sticks are used symbolically as a means of carrying through the process of dehumanizing and objectifying others. This is not despite, but rather because of, the contradictions involved in actually killing persons face-to-face. These contradictions intensify as murderers are confronted by the repeated flesh-and-blood concreteness of particular deaths. They bleed like us; they die like us. How can we show the Otherness of their ugliness and evil? The levels that need to be held in tension here include the projections of necrographic maps across the modalities of abstract codification, institutional projection and face-to-face engagement. Thus, we can distinguish what it means to project generalized racist images of the Tutsi as cockroaches in repeated radio transmissions and what it means to kill actual persons in repeated acts of bloody violence. Appadurai gets closer to the complexity of this when he says 'real bodies in history betray the very cosmologies they are meant to encode'.[7] It is a useful qualification to make so long as we are clear that we are talking about societies formed, at least at one level, in the intersection of post-tribal ontologies.

The human body provides readily-available and dangerously-manipulable images for communities that treat issues of identity and differentiation as if communities were singular Bodies of Difference; as if they draw their disparate elements into mysterious organic cohesion. The grasping hands of the Jew in Nazi Germany, the Scheduled Caste ascription of the Untouchable in postcolonial India and the fecund womb of the Palestinian or Bedhouin woman in contemporary Israel are all traditional-modern forms of this process. The fact that treating the body as a natural symbol can be part of generating cultures of narrowly-bounded exclusion and racism should not, however, lead us to conclude that we need to be liberated from all boundaries and modes of exclusion *per se*. Moreover, we should not be deluded by the deconstructionist implication that 'seeing through' processes of meaning formation makes us the master of it. Symbols express socially-constructed practices but, in their framing of meaning, they also gain the power to structure and over-determine processes of social formation. In Mary Douglas's words, they sometimes 'lash back at the people' who create them.[8] It is a dual and reflective process of structuring – people create the symbols which in turn define their society, social behaviour and relationships, and even their sense of body, from which the symbols are derived. As Douglas and Bourdieu have helped us to understand, bodily symbols form an elaborate code that variously regulates dress, posture, etiquette, social contact, expressions of respect, and an innumerable list of other social behaviours. Each codification in itself is of limited consequence but, as part of a generalized code, they define and affirm the social order. These proscriptions are particularly applicable to face-to-face relations and so are most easily identifiable in communities in which historically such relations have formed the dominant level of integration – tribal, kinship or close-knit parochial communities in traditional settings – but they are relevant to all.

## Forms of social embodiment

There are many different forms of embodiment, social forms that come together in varying intersections in different social formations. The following discussion is not meant to be exhaustive, but rather to offer a useful list that reveals the historically-changing complexity of how we live corporeally (see Table 8.2). *Analogical embodiment*, for example, involves the body and nature/culture being treated as analogical expressions of the meaning of existence. It is where the body is treated as a sign of the cultural/natural rather than a metaphor for it. (Here the concept of 'sign' is used in Lévi-Strauss's terms.) In other words, the condition of the body *is* the meaning of the analogy, and any reference-point beyond the body is drawn into the broadest social matrix of meaning without stretching the nature/culture contradiction very far. In this sense, lack of care for menstrual blood *is* the basis for the dissention, for the illness in a marriage or for the pain across a broader social relation, rather than just a metaphor for such conflict and pain. A traditionally-sacralized emperor sneezing during a ritual moment *is* a sign of inevitable dissention in the empire rather than just a pointer to it. Jesus Christ *is* both an embodied man and omnipresent God.

Closely related to analogical embodiment, *genealogical embodiment* is carried in the life-histories and life-times of birth and death. It too is marked by ritualized social moments. Within customary and traditional tribal settings, genealogies are held in living memory, but in other social formations as soon as they are lifted beyond the immediately intimate they tend to be abstracted as lists showing lines of connection to past persons, times and places. A related but inverse form of genealogical embodiment is the practice of carrying one social history inscribed on one's body as tattoos. Moreover, the fact of whether a person is tattooed or not becomes a marker of social identity and difference. In traditional

Table 8.2  Different forms of embodiment

| Forms of embodiment | Expressions of those forms |
| --- | --- |
| analogical | where the body and nature are treated as analogous; the body is a natural symbol or sign rather than a source of metaphorical referents. |
| genealogical | where the body is carried in life-histories and genealogies, life-times of birth and death, and marked by ritualized social moments linking to past bodies. |
| mythological | where bodies are framed by stories of origins and meanings, by mythologies, not so much the medium 'beyond' as the enframing of the experiential world. |
| cosmological | where the body is abstracted from mythic embodiment by a process of universalizing and unifying it beyond history and nature. |
| metaphorical | where bodies are extended metaphorically as secular bodies and Bodies Politic beyond the ontological boundaries of face-to-face and drawn into the service of 'society'. |
| bio-technological | where the workings of the body are treating as able to wrought technologically, mechanically dismembered and extended, bionically |
| cyborg-technological | where the practices of embodiment are abstracted even from the technologized body based on the claim that the body is a digitally, medically-reproducible human-machine. |

Bosnia, for example, elaborate tattooing was common among Catholics and abhorred by the Orthodox Christians. At the beginning of the twentieth century, Catholic girls going through puberty were marked on the backs of their hands with the same signs that appeared on old gravestones: rayed suns, moons and crosses – the signs of the pre-Christian sun and moon cults.[9] In an example from contemporary Australia, in one group of Vietnamese migrant women – some poorly-educated villagepeople, some city-dwelling colonial cosmopolitans – all shared a history of having the umbilical cords that once connected them to their mothers buried in a clay pot at the family home. To all of them that was their 'real' home. Not the country, not the city, but the house and surrounding land where their cord was buried. Many wanted to be taken back to that place to be cremated and interred.[10]

*Mythological embodiment* is more abstract than analogical or genealogical embodiment in that it involves some recognition of its own enframing: it tends to draw together the elements of analogical-genealogical into a larger whole. For example, for the Zaramo of Tanzania, like many other tribal groups, life has three basic *analogical* elements: the red of blood (with menstrual blood being particularly potent), the white milk of a woman and the semen of a man, and the black of death and dying bodily substances. These are not, however, just elements in themselves.[11] Marja-Liisa Swantz's works shows how mythologies are wrapped around these analogical elements. Mythologies involve not so much the medium 'beyond' as the enframing of the experiential world. For example, to continue my obsessive interest in the social meaning of trees, the seasonal cycle of the Zaramo *mkole* tree as its fruit turns from white to greenish red to black provides the basis for myths about female elephants that hid in the *mkole* woods when they had their periods, and about young girls who turned into elephants during rituals associated with their first periods because they were secluded in the *mkole* woods for too long. The elephants no longer come to that part of Tanzania, but the stories are still told as mythological expressions of the Truth. Thus, the *mkole* tree is situated both analogically and mythologically. In living longer than a single human life-time a mkole tree literally binds generations together as the site of repeated ritual practices; it is the site of stories about the origin of life; and it gives its name to the process of connecting lives – *lukolo* is the Zaramo word for clan while *mkolo* means 'one with the clan'.

*Cosmological embodiment* takes mythical embodiment to another stage of abstraction, even if in practice they are often bound up with each other. Cosmological embodiment is abstracted from mythological embodiment by a process of universalizing and unifying it beyond social time and nature/culture and then re-embodied in liminality: 'In the beginning was the Word' becomes 'the body of Christ broken for *you*'. The latter phrase refers both to the particular 'you' and to any generalized 'you' that has faith. As this last example shows in layering upon previous examples of Christian theology, Christianity thus draws on the intersection of analogical, mythological and cosmological embodiment even as it individualizes the relation of the person to the universal.

In the emerging dominance of modernism, other forms of embodiment become more prominent. *Metaphorical embodiment* extends and secularizes the body beyond the ontological boundaries of face-to-face community and draws it into the service of 'society' by the using images of the body as metaphors for the social: for example, in the recent use of Saddam Hussein's face on the front cover of *Time*.[12] The classic metaphor is that of the body politic that was so important to the French Revolution as the body of the king gave way to the body of the citizenry. Antoine de Baecque writes of the revolutionaries as persons using metaphor as a political-historical tool:

It would be more correct to say that they thought abstractly by means of metaphor and that they gave to their comprehension of the individual, and of the human community, and even the universe, the figure of the human body. Their language, even at its most philosophical and legalistic, was charged with these images. The Abbé Sieyès, to take the example of someone highly suspected of 'metaphysics' [replete with what I have been calling a subjectivity of *cosmological embodiment*] conceived of his ideal legislative system ... in terms of pure geometry: 'I imagine the Law in the center of an immense globe; all citizens, without exception, are at the same distance upon the circumference, and all occupy equal places.' This symbol of perfection traced by the bodies of all citizens joined together in a circle is the quintessential metaphor with Sieyès, but similar images are found throughout the pamphlets, giving body to the story of the revolution.[13]

In this description we can also see the intersection of a related form of embodiment *bio-technological embodiment*, a subjectivity-practice that abstracts the body through the natural and social sciences, treating it as extendable and manageable by technological means and social techniques. This is the modality that Foucault appropriately refers to as being open to the modern techniques of bio-power – a changing mode of organization that takes populations and their 'welfare' as the locus of concentrated institutionalized activity.[14] One step beyond that subjectivity-practice of embodiment *cyborg-technological embodiment* reduces the body to a bio-machine. Bodies in this regime of practice and meaning are not just technologically manipulable. They are digitally and bio-reproducible, able to be reconstituted in ways that promise/threaten to lift us free of the constraints of given nature. This is the world of stem cells being treated as abstract biomass.

## Tribal bodies, traditional bodies, modern bodies

Through this discussion there have been hints that the dominant forms of embodiment, just as with the dominant forms of temporality and spatiality, can be associated with the dominance of different ontological formations: tribalism, traditionalism, modernism and postmodernism. Describing this association is the task of the following discussion.

### Tribal bodies

To the extent that practices of customary tribalism prevail, tribal bodies, I argue, are constituted in the dominance of analogical, genealogical and/or mythological relations. In this argument none of these modes of embodiment are reducible to each other, and tribal formations are no less complex for having less immediately available ways of taking social hold of embodiment. Overall, within such formations, processes of integration and differentiation are framed at the level of the face-to-face, or what Anthony Giddens calls 'high presence-availability'.[15] However, this does not mean that customary tribal formations are one-dimensional. In other words, the body is used in tribal societies as the basis for a symbolic order that orients people in particularistic relation to each other, spatially and temporally, but the various dominant modalities drawn upon by tribal practices of embodiment – analogy, genealogy and mythology – are always-already in tension. Face-to-face embodiment tends to set the limits and possibilities of remoteness and nearness, but even in these apparently most concrete of settings a primary level of abstraction occurs.[16]

For example, in relation to *consanguinal relations* (discussed in Chapter 4 as one of the modalities of the face-to-face),[17] the analogical-genealogical conception of the body is already abstracted beyond the biologically-extant lines of kinship. Pierre Bourdieu's comparison of two forms of tribal kinship, official and practical, opens up an aspect of this propensity to live across the lines of the analogical and mythological. He argues that while 'actual' genealogical kinship organizes and legitimizes on official occasions, more often kinship relationships are cultivated (only existing, he would maintain, through and for the practical interests they serve). Leaving aside the way in which Bourdieu reduces the distinction to the constitutive primacy of self-interest, it draws our attention to the way in which even such primordial relations as blood ties are lived as already abstract relationships.[18] That is, even something as thick as blood is part of a cultural, rather than simply a natural, relation. Bourdieu's distinction can be paralleled with Douglas's comparison between tribal rituals that are just commemorative and those in which the symbolic action is considered to be efficacious.[19] Efficacious rites rely on the participants' receptivity to extension of 'logical' principles beyond their immediate settings so that they might be imagined to effect change on a person, occasion or environment. Tribal sorcerers rely on this abstraction of direct agency in their performance of magic.

In relation to *ritual relations*, people affirm, imagine and live modalities of co-presence across lines of spatial extension, across temporary absence and even across the temporal parting brought by death. In spatial terms, ritual relations order social arrangements into a meticulous separation of pure from polluted, sacred from profane, male from female, or initiated from child or stranger. An example of how the gendered body is basic to the physical structuring of place is given in Maurice Godelier's description of the Baruya family house or Pierre Bourdieu's description of the Kabyle.[20] The Baruya house is divided by gender as though an imaginary line ran through the hearth at the centre of the house. The wife and children sleep and eat on the side closest to the door, while the husband – and any other man entering the house – takes up his place on the other side, beyond the hearth. No woman may enter the male part of the house, and she must avoid stepping over the central hearth less she pollute the place where the husband's food is prepared. The hearth itself, built by men from the husband's family, is symbolic of kinship and lineage. This spatial practice is at the same time taken to be literally analogical to the 'nature' of male–female relations and bathed in mythological stories that explain why it is so. Beyond these tensions, customary tribalism does not exist in the present as a pure form. With the abstraction of public-versus-private spaces and with the development of a gendered distinction around the contradiction between nature and culture, the positive virtues of a partial separation between men's and women's cultures, for example, including rituals and exchange cycles, has in many cases hardened into public traditional patriarchy. Women of the Baruya, a New Guinea mountain tribe, stop, turn their heads and draw a flap of their bark cloak across their faces when passed by a man journeying on the roads between villages.[21] Women's subordinate public placement in relation to men is thus abstracted-concretized as a pattern of bodily gesture.

At a very basic level the human body is always treated as an image of society – interest in its apertures reflect the social preoccupation with entrances, exits, escapes and invasions; it is impossible to consider the body as natural with no sense of its social-cultural dimension. The emergence of what we have been referring to as the nature/culture contradiction was integral to the process of hominids becoming human. This is part of the basis on which it is possible to say that even in a tribal setting there is a form of abstraction of the body. Victor Turner's study of the Ndembu in Zambia reveals how people experience society as an intricate arrangement of descent groups, structured by the bodily inscriptions of age, gender, and genealogical hierarchy. The cultural colours of the human body – black bile, red blood, white milk – form a vivid symbolic centre for the patterning of complex representations of male and female spheres, of nourishing and destructive powers of purity and pollution.[22] However, the images of integration and differentiation are not straightforward. Blood is not always thicker than milk, and the milk is not always human. For example, in the Rwandan myth of origins, it is milk that provides the master metaphor for distinguishing the blood of kinship. Kigwa who had descended from heaven had three sons from whom to choose his successor: Gatwa, Gahutu and Gatutsi (read these names carefully in the light of earlier discussions of the twentieth-century Rwandan massacres). One night he gave them each a pot of milk to look after. When dawn came it was clear that only Gatutsi had stayed awake. Because Gahutu had fallen asleep and spilt his milk he was destined to be always a serf. Gatwa having drunk his milk was destined to be always a pariah.[23] Thus we have a mythology explaining the reality of a community-polity than was to last until Rwandan independence when the metaphor and reality of spilt blood became much more important than that of spilt milk.

## Traditional bodies

In post-tribal traditional societies, analogical, genealogical and mythological relations remain relevant, but are overlaid by cosmological and political-metaphorical relations. For example, the sense of face-to-face attachment to dead loved ones carries through, but it does so in different forms depending upon the techniques of depiction and its social framing. Writing or artistic representation lends itself to treating persons as both deeply-intimate relations *and* stylized icons that are linked to cosmological frames such Christianity. Representations of monarchs or public figures and their families, for example, extend this tension because of the crossings of public-political records and private consolation. The depictions of the family of James I of England provide graphic examples.[24] William de Passe's 'Triumphus Jacobi Regus', c. 1623, discussed earlier (Chapter 6) shows Anne of Denmark and her eldest son, Henry, holding skulls to signify that they are dead. Similarly an etching done slightly later by Gerrit Mountain (c.1623–1635) called 'The progenie of the most renouned Prince James King of Great Britaine France and Ireland', c.1633, has James's dead family members again present to the live members. Again the dead are marked as distinct by holding skulls. The skulls are symbolic – not literally their skulls in an analogous relation of life and death, but *memento mori*. It is a common trope in European court paintings at least going back to Henry VIII's time. Holbein's 'The Ambassadors' is based on the possibility of seeing a skull from one angle of viewing. Continuing the same point, an oil painting by David des Granges depicting the Saltonstall Family painted around the same time as the etching of James I, *c.* 1636, depicts both the current wife and his late wife in the same conjugal scene. The dead woman lies with her eyes open on a death-bed, reaching out her hand as her husband extends his gloved left hand towards her. His ungloved right hand, this time flesh to flesh, holds the hand of his son.[25] It is significant that it is his ungloved right hand. In this symbolically-charged action we see the simple gendered extension of patriarchal power.

If we move from public–private families to polities framed by relations of traditionalism, we can see how ontologies of kinship fade into those of kingship. In relation to traditional polities it is worth reasserting the half-forgotten but obvious point that in the ascension of kingship, the bloodlines of tribal and post-tribal kinship continued to be vigorously defended and later religiously sanctified, even if that 'bloodline' sometimes took the form of genealogical placement rather than documentable kinship ties (in the modern sense). This is discussed in more detail in the next chapter on state formation, but we can note here that one major difference was that agnatic bloodlines became codified and legally defended. Embodied patriarchy was inscribed onto the bleached skins of calves and lambs as legalized knowledge and expressed in the language of the Latin jurists, *ob sanguinis continuationem*. By contrast tribal and tribal-traditional bloodlines were part of embodied memory rather than written contract and could be either patrilineal or matrilineal.

Recalling the earlier description made of the inauguration of the 8 year-old Alexander III seated on the Stone of Scone in 1249 (Chapter 5), it is relevant that the king's official poet read out in Gaelic a complete genealogy of the boy-king. Like the begetting sequences in the sacred books of the Bible – he begat *him* who begat *him* who begat *him*, and so on – the genealogical served to link orally-transmitted tribal traditions to the line of actual sovereigns, the one living to the many dead. Rather than just making up a fabulous sequence of successive male bodies, it inscribed the connection between the historical record and the mythological understanding. Back went the historical genealogy through Malcolm III (died 1093) to Fergus mor mac Erc of the early sixth-century, a king of Irish-Gaelic origin who allegedly settled as the founding Dalriadic king of Scots in the Kilmartin area, the place where the carved footprints I discussed earlier are found. Further back went the genealogy into the mythological embodiment of Iber Scot, son of Gaedel Glas and grandson of Scota the Egyptian princess at the time of Moses' exodus. Depending on the version of the ancient lineage, Scota married Nel, himself son of Fenius the Scythian (descended from Noah) who, according to an early medieval Irish poem, brought the 'People's Speech' – presumably Gaelic, the same language used to read Alexander's lineage – from the Tower of Babel as it toppled over.[26] These are extraordinary mythological-genealogical connections that travel an analogous path to that of the Stone of Scone.

Three points can be made explicit. First, in relation to Chapter 6 on the abstraction of written record out of oral transmission, here we have an example of the intersection of different ontological forms, the oral genealogy of traditional tribes and the written genealogy-cosmology of such sacred texts as the Torah Bible, and Qur'an. Even though there is not sufficient detail of evidence or contemporary commentary to say which prevailed it is possible to generalize that in both of these media – oral and written – history and mythology intertwined. Related to this, there is a second point to be made about the importance of embodiment. Here we have a genealogical list serving a number of simultaneous purposes. The genealogies proclaimed the embodied connection of the living king to dead kings and to the originating tribes of their common kinship. They proclaimed the oral-embodied mythological history of the abstracted community of the realm. At the same time the genealogies had to make sense of the written documentation about the origins of humanity contained in the sacred text of a new over-bracing cosmology – in this case, Christianity. Ironically this had to be done through the oral-into-written tradition of a group of quite different of tribes that were once exiled in Egypt. The connection at this point became the body of the daughter of the Pharaoh – biblical in origin but not of the tribe of Israel. As William Ferguson writes, 'the ingenuity of the genealogists and the vivid imaginations of the bards combined to accomplish the task of reconciling tribal traditions with Holy Writ'.[27]

Moreover, by the time we get to Alexander III, the genealogies were written through and against other genealogies of origin and other claims to sovereignty. In other words, the genealogies came to be abstracted as political-metaphorical embodiment. Chronicles abounded, sagas of origin as diverse as Isidore of Seville's *Chronica de Sex Aetatibus* (early seventh century), Nennius of Bangor's *Historia Brittonum* (early ninth century), Geoffrey of Monmouth's *Historia Regum Britanniae* (c.1136), and Ari Thorgilsson's *Islendingabók* (*Book of the Islanders*, early twelve century). Alexander III's authority rested on a genealogy that had to stand up against that of Henry III and later Edward I (the king who 'stole' the Stone of Scone) as those rival kings drew on Geoffrey of Monmouth's genealogy of the English kings to stretch their kinship back to Brutus of Troy. All of this serves to underline a third point. This 'ingenuity' of connections is not simply a case of the invention of history, but an attempt to make sense of the question of origins against the proclaimed origins of others. Written lists of embodied connection had to be documented from prior written texts, historical and mythological. They were contested. Inventions of tradition, if they did happen, were either quickly lost in the midst of the greater task of forging a continuous traditional narrative or were challenged by more ingenious chroniclers.

By the time we get to conceptions such as the king's two bodies – sovereign and personal – political reworkings of analogous embodiment allowed new meanings of state to emerge that were meant to be taken as metaphors (though with analogical power): the sovereign as the soul and the state as the body. In Edvvard Forset's account of the 'bodie politiqve (as of the naturall)' the sovereign gives life to the body of the state, with the state itself made up of four natural elements related to each other as fire, air, earth, and water: first, the 'generous' or policy-makers to maintain the state, second, the 'learned' to instruct and direct, third, the 'yoemen' to 'worke the commodities of the land', and lastly the 'trafiquers' or traders to bring in things from the outside.[28] In the early modern period, political-metaphorical embodiment within the dominance of traditional ontologies of time and space also allowed for reworkings of existing representations. In the late-seventeenth century the 'French' engraver Peter Lombart (1613–1682) etched a complicated equestrian image based upon Anthony van Dyck's 1633 portrait of Charles I, 'King of Great Brittaine France and Ireland'.[29] Sometime later, the same image of man and horse was re-etched with Oliver Cromwell's head on the same body. Cromwell is still dressed in most of the King's magnificent garb. It is only the King's medallion and part of his garter that have been erased. The body astride the stallion and the detailed background are exactly the same – exquisite line for exquisite line. In part, this can be explained by reference to the expense of the engraver's copper plate. However, this leaves out the question 'Why, even in such publicly charged circumstances as the post-execution period of Charles I, image-makers were comfortable to reissue anachronistic versions of the original?' Going beyond the 'mere' act of regicide, Cromwell had abolished the office of monarchy itself, but in the code of image-making of the time the replacement of the old King's head was a sanctioned and relatively-common practice. With the Restoration, Charles II came to the throne, and in a reversal of the trajectory of change at the time, traced his lineage back to Moses. In a sequence of commissioned portraits, all of the previous kings, including Robert the Bruce were painted with Charles' facial features.

## Modern bodies

The capacity for the body to be the figure of an integrating, organizing symbolic form is greatly diminished in late-modern/postmodern societies. This should not be taken as implying an argument that embodiment becomes irrelevant to post-tribal and post-traditional processes of structuration or ontological security. There are continuities. For example, just as for the Baruya of Papua New Guinea embodied place is important, in a typical Victorian to 1960s' working-class English home the body defined the lay-out of space and structured 'appropriate' behaviour within specifically bounded places. The back of the house contained the kitchen, bathroom and toilet – providing privacy for body functions – while the front of the house, containing the parlour, was given over to public, social relationships where the body was required to present itself with formal decorum.[30] Despite these continuities, the basic differences from tribal and traditional forms of embodiment to modern forms still have to be made very clear.

The emerging dominance of modernism has involved an increasingly self-conscious acculturation of the 'excesses' of the body as a natural symbol. In the broader sphere of the contemporary nation-state, changing one's national identity still involves one's own body. It requires a ceremony of symbolic boundary-crossing. Ironically, however, it is a ceremony of *naturalization* which self-consciously subordinates the significance of birth-place to transform an 'alien' into a citizen. The ceremony treats the nationally-naturalized body in a more abstracted way than the rituals of tribal boundary-crossing or identity transformation, which call for the bodies of the initiates to be physically and subjectively changed. National naturalization assumes, almost perfunctorily, an abstract overlay that has reconstituted the cultural meaning of birth. By contrast, for example, Aboriginal initiation ceremonies usually entail a bloody renaissance, a *rebirth* of the initiate's actual body.[31] Analogical embodiment is not irrelevant to naturalization in the modern context but it is reworked metaphorically. In any case, actual bodies still have to be there. In most countries, any would-be citizen must attend the ceremony in *person*, swear an oath, and receive a document confirming his or her transition out of the old cultural inscription of what birth means to identity. Similarly, leaving one's homeland is still not entirely straightforward. In Australia during its Bicentenary year, expatriates like the late Peter Allen as proud recipient of the Order of Australia and Rupert Murdoch, a little sheepish at becoming an American citizen, were confidently voicing that sentiment of postmodern nationalism, 'I still call Australia home'. Notwithstanding this layer of sentimental attachment, however, Rupert Murdoch is now an abstracted global citizen. The streets of New York serve as well as anywhere else for his constitutional walks (although he did come home for his sister's funeral).

The *modern* nation thus becomes an abstract community of strangers, but one that metaphorically (powerfully) draws on the subjectivities and ideologies of attachment to embodied others (blood-become-sacrifice) and actual places (soil-become-territory). Unlike Christianity where Jesus is simultaneously God the Spirit, God-Incarnate, and an embodied mortal man, no *one actual* person can stand in for the nation. National community, or more particularly each 'ordinary person' with in it, potentially carries that embodied connection. Certainly the nation throws up abstracted icons. Female figures lifted out of history were the most serious contenders for this role. Boadicea, Joan of Arc, Liberty or Marianne became iconic figures with their historical and particularized bodies left behind. However, contemporary figures do not stand in the same relation to the nation, even if body metaphors continue to be important. In June 1971, Margaret Thatcher, as Education Secretary in the Heath government ended the provision of free milk in the mainstream primary schools in Britain. She became know as Thatcher the Milk Snatcher, and later, in the context of the Falklands War, satirical cartoons showed her with armour-plated, sharp conical breasts. However, she never became 'the New Britannia'. Her breasts never lactated as the mother of the nation, nor were they depicted as full of the milk of human kindness in the way that Marianne's bosoms were illustrated in the French Revolution.

It is indicative of the contradictory nature of the abstraction of the modern nation that its only lasting iconic representative is the 'person' whose name we will 'never' know – the Unknown Soldier. This abstracted soul, who, like Jesus, dies for us all, preferably has no recognizable remains or personal effects, no bones that would identify *him*. However, unlike Jesus with his body gone and the stone rolled away, the soul and preferably some of the bones of the Unknown Soldier dwells beneath massive slabs of stones, firmly located in place. Even the postmodern versions of these tombs, including the Australian tomb discussed in Chapter 10, depend on the symbolic stability of eternal nature-culture. And despite cyborg-technological interventions, such as DNA-testing of the Arlington Unknown Soldier, the power of the tomb is still revisited in ritual moments.

## To the body as an individualized postmodern project

The culture of late capitalism is overcome by an extraordinary fascination with the body. Concomitantly, our relationship to our bodies is being mediated and penetrated to its core by a myriad of technological incursions. Our relationship to others is becoming dominated by increasingly disembodied modes of social engagement. Whether it be sex without the embodied presence of another person or the technological enhancement of the sexual body, the broad range of practices from telephone sex to cosmetic surgery illustrate an emergent but already-pervasive development in these postmodern times. They are part of the broader phenomenon of techno-disembodiment – an increasing abstraction in the way in which we live our bodies and a generalizing of the technological mediation of social relations. These contradictory developments – on the one hand, the reflexive fascination with taking control of our concrete bodies, and on the other, the abstraction and disembodiment of social integration – are thoroughly bound up with each other. They reinforce each other in an intimate spiral of externalized desire and an internalized sense of incompleteness. In the face of the contradictory nature of this process, contemporary social theory, from psychoanalytic approaches to structuralist and post-structuralist accounts of the present, seems unable to take up its full complexity.

Our own bodies have become increasingly problematic to ourselves. The modern/postmodern body has pushed the 'I am body, yet I have a body' paradox to its limits.[32] The body has been abstracted as a malleable form. It remains important to the constitution of identity but more as the constructed image through which the self is presented to others than as a locus of the simultaneous connection and separation from others. The experience is one of an individualized tension – the 'disembodied embodiment' in which the body is part of a 'creative project', an objectified container for effecting appropriate style. The body no longer is a reassuring entity from which relatively stable metaphors can grow, but rather the site of momentary personal and political metaphors: from photos of Lyndie England with an Abu Ghraib prisoner on a dog-leash, to 'The New Face of America' feature on the front-cover of *Time* for its special edition on immigration – a computer-simulated racially-composite face.

For the most part we feel our corporeality personally. Caught in the expectation that one's body should be constantly monitored and reformed, through diets, aerobics, plastic surgery and clothes fashion, the body becomes an immediate but abstracted 'experience'. It becomes, *at one level*, what Donna Haraway calls the *cyborg body*.[33] The fetishism of breast enlargement is only the most controversial example of those possibilities listed in books with titles such as *Cosmetic Surgery: A Consumer Guide*. The symbolic significance of the body has thus been changed by capitalist developments grounded in personalized consumption. The body becomes a cross-gender industry, with mass consumerism ascribing the signs of appropriate identity.[34] It also becomes a science with medicine ascribing the frame for viewing our corporeal defects. Reflexivity about the body in contemporary society has offered, through technologies that transcend embodied form, the opportunity to be liberated from the dictates of nature. Yet the image of the body as a package to be manipulated by the 'looking-glass self'[35] of consumerism and techno-science has hollowed out our sense of social connection. Brian Turner aptly characterizes these contemporary contradictions in his description of the body as 'at once the most solid, the most elusive, illusory, concrete, metaphorical, ever-present and ever-distant thing – a site, an instrument, an environment, a singularity and a multiplicity'.[36]

In a step beyond the way that George Bernard Shaw's heroine in *Pygmalion* had her identity synthetically built by mastering the appropriate insignia of the upper class, in George Mead's terms, the contemporary body 'internalizes the external'.[37] We become objects not just of the gaze of others but also of ourselves. Our body becomes self-monitored as body parts. At the excessive end of this process, Lolo Farrari, the 'Eurotrash' model listed in the Guinness Book of Records for her surgically-enhanced breasts, talked of revelling in the knowledge that she was being remade by plastic surgery. 'I love the feeling of general anaesthetic', she said in an interview, 'falling into this black hole and knowing that I'm being altered as I sleep'.[38] Tragically, she died at the age of 30 after taking her nightly dose of antidepressants. Even at the more banal end of the process, as Rosalind Coward identifies, a sense of fragmentation develops when different parts of the body are referred to in the third person as 'problem areas':

> If the ideal shape has been pared down to a lean outline, bits are bound to stick out or hang down and these become problem areas. The result is that it becomes possible, indeed likely for [people] to think about their bodies in terms of parts, separate areas, as if these parts had some separate life of their own.[39]

The contemporary image of the body would seem to have lost its capacity to offer deep ontological grounding to individuals. Along the way, modern body metaphors such as 'the body politic', 'body corporate' or 'body of people' have become shallow or procedural senses of group or association. The complex analogue the body once provided for an intricately-structured social system has been increasingly 'hollowed out' as it has been segmented and commodified. The symbolism that in tribal settings provided knowledge of the structures and consonance of society – knowledge inscribed in the body's natural-cultural patterning – is being increasingly lost to late-modern/postmodern society (Figure 8.1).

The status of the body in late capitalism reflects a paradox characteristic of the disembodied level of integration. While there has been the consolidation and generalization of a universalized perspective of the

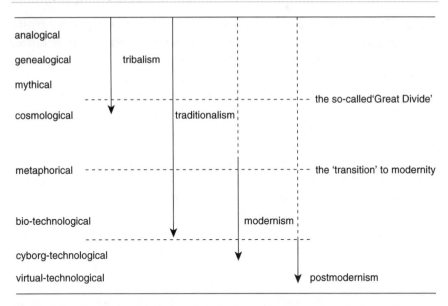

Figure 8.1  Dominant ontologies of embodiment in different social formations

Other, witnessed in the extensions of globalization, there is also a heightening of the sense of the particular and local. A parallel tension constitutes the body as an abstract homogenized form: the changing but universalized standard to be attained, yet also the physical space into which one can retreat to experience the inner, more real self. New Age meditation, yoga and similar mind/body communion experiences use the body as a capsule into which the weary postmodern mind can crawl to be rejuvenated. Yet even this intimate retreat has become thoroughly commodified, individualized and privatized. The example of Tokyo's night-life district offering Brain Mind Gymnasiums full of machines that, according to their promoters, 'help you find yourself' may seem bizarre, but it is only a step beyond the now-naturalized Walkman™ radio. The strategy behind the Japanese manufacturer's design of the Walkman was to provide insulated space for people by providing a way of listening to music privately-in-public, a public privacy located literally within the confines of one's own body-space. The popularity of Walkman radios and iPods among the world's commuting populations, like that of the mobile telephone, confirms the 'need' that this product first met. A benign example – maybe – but once again, one in which the body is presented ambiguously, accentuating embodiment but interceding in what it means to walk around together or share a public space.

In the face of this withdrawal into the private self, critics as diverse as Richard Sennett and Julia Kristeva argue that the only way out is becoming 'strangers to ourselves', fragmenting our inner sense of unity.[40] In Sennett's view, this would be achieved through our acknowledging of the place of pain:

> Such pain has a trajectory in human experience. It disorients and makes incomplete the self, defeats the desire for coherence; the body accepting pain is ready to become a civic body, sensible to the pain of another person, pains present together on the street, at last endurable – even though, in a diverse world, each person cannot explain what he or she is feeling, who he or she is, to the other. But the body can follow this civic trajectory only if it acknowledges that is no remedy for its suffering in the contrivings of society, that its unhappiness has come from elsewhere, that its pain derives from God's command to live together as exiles.[41]

The irony here is that in rightly recognizing our late-modern desire to escape pain and mortality, Sennett argues for an exacerbation of one of the very processes that is bound up with what he wants to ameliorate. His concern is the increasing privatization of social relations, but because he fails to recognize that this is only one dimension of the broader process of the abstraction of social integration, he ends up advocating another of its associated dimensions, the fragmentation of self.

## Conclusion

We have seen how the body is always-already abstracted, even in the most bounded of face-to-face settings. However, the argument of this chapter has been that the abstraction that occurs in tribal settings has a condensed depth that is rarely found in late-modern/postmodern society. Our bodily symbols and images are constituted in a very different way. More abstract modes of social interrelation have come to overlay and, very often, to change the nature of our embodied interactions. The electronic screen brings impassioned faces of Chinese students pleading with each of us to support their struggle, despite most of us having never stood where they stand in Tiananmen Square or spoken to them in person. It allows us to see the devastation of a tsunami sweeping across Sri Lanka, Thailand and Indonesia. For a time we may respond with public outrage to the inhumane way the students were treated, or with compassion for the families of those killed by the tsunami, but we cannot know these people as more than encapsulated, time-frozen images. The unnamed young man who stood in front of an oncoming tank becomes an abstracted symbol, but one with much less cultural resonance that Liberty baring her breast as she leads a charge in the French Revolution. We cannot obtain a sense of him as a historical figure, let alone as a complex, multi-dimensional person. The shallow objectified image consumes the subject and the person fades away. While we can celebrate the expansive sense of humanity that mediation creates, we should not forget that the processes of abstraction through which this is possible places our relationship with the abstracted 'other' under shearing strain. Unlike the tribal form, this abstraction has stretched so far beyond the more concrete face-to-face experience that it has buried the layers that texture and amplify it. As quickly as we were first drawn to empathize (although the more abstract concept 'sympathize' is a more accurate term here), we become inured, bored, hardened or even resentful of the repeated intrusion of the iconic images onto our television screens. Having given money to one of the many appeals for the 2004 tsunami disaster, the issue of reconstruction comes to be deemed as the province of intellectually-trained experts. These experts are not even experienced as acting on our behalf. In this sense, abstraction is no longer just an extension of a relation previously or potentially experienced as embodied presence. It has created a completely new form of interaction that can draw only on our sense of what a fuller relationship *might be*.

The implicit argument here (and developed in Chapter 12) for a renewed politics of ethically-reflexive embodiment obviously does not entail a return to the *content* or *modalities* of relations found within tribal reciprocity, the kinds of enactments that we have just been describing. Rather, it is an argument for a politics of embodiment that reasserts the social forms of engagement with others expressed by those modalities.[42] It asserts the importance of recognizing that our bodies are not just our individualistic self-creations. It supports the value of retaining a respect for cultural (embodied) boundaries insofar as they enhance the dialectic of difference *and* interconnection. This is a slow politics, but just as revolutionary in its implications as the calls for sweeping aside the current oppressions and injustices of the contemporary world.

## Notes

1 Benedict Anderson, *Imagined Communities: Reflections on the Origin and Spread of Nationalism*, Verso, London, 2nd edn 1991, p. 36.

2 Reported in *The Australian*, 22 December 2004.

3 C.A. Gregory, *Savage Money*, Harwood Academic Publishers, Amsterdam, 1997, p. 35.

4 Abner Cohen, *Two-Dimensional Man: An Essay on the Anthropology of Power and Symbolism in Complex Society*, Routledge & Kegan Paul, London, 1974, p. xi.

5 Liisa Malkki, 'Context and Consciousness: Local Conditions for the Production of Historical Thought and National Among Hutu Refugees in Tanzania', in Richard G. Fox (ed.), *Nationalist Ideologies and the Production of National Cultures*, American Ethnography Society, Washington DC, 1990.

6 Arjun Appadurai, 'Dead Certainty: Ethnic Violence in the Era of Globalization', in Birgit Meyer and Peter Geschiere (eds), *Globalization and Identity: Dialectics of Flow and Closure*, Blackwell Publishers, Oxford, 1999, pp. 318-19.

7 *Ibid.*, p. 311.

8 Mary Douglas, *Natural Symbols, Explorations in Cosmology*, The Cresset Press, London, 1970, p. xiv.

9 M.E. Durham, *Some Tribal Origins, Laws and Customs of the Balkans*, George Allen & Unwin, London, 1928, Section III, 'Tattooing and Symbols Tattooed'.

10 Personal correspondence, Kate Cregan, November 2000.

11 Marja-Liisa Swantz with Salome Mjema and Zenya Wild, *Blood, Milk and Death: Bodily Symbols and the Power of Regeneration among the Zaramo of Tanzania*, Bergin & Garvey, Westport, CT, 1995.

12 Mentioned in Chapter 4 in the discussion of the face-to-face.

13 Antoine de Baecque, *The Body Politic: Corporeal Metaphor in Revolutionary France, 1770-1800*, Stanford University Press, Stanford, CA, 1997, p. 2. The image also serves as a prelude to the contemporary images of globalization discussed at the beginning of Chapter 11 below.

14 Michel Foucault, *Discipline and Punish: The Birth of the Prison*, Penguin, Harmondsworth, 1977.

15 Anthony Giddens, *The Constitution of Society: Outline of the Theory of Structuration*, Polity Press, Cambridge, 1984, pp. 122ff.

16 Geoff Sharp, 'Constitutive Abstraction', *Arena*, 70, 1985, pp. 48-82.

17 Analogical, genealogical and mythological relations are differently abstracted modes of embodiment (situated, if you like, on a vertical axis), while consanguinal, ritual, perceptual and convivial relations are modalities of the face-to-face (situated on a horizontal axis of different social settings).

18 Pierre Bourdieu, *Outline of a Theory of Practice*, Cambridge University Press, Cambridge, 1977, pp. 34-8. While this distinction is useful, using it here does not imply any sympathy for Bourdieu's over-emphasis upon self-interest or group-interest as the motivating *basis* of action.

19 Douglas, *Natural Symbols*, p. 8.

20 Maurice Godelier, *The Making of Great Men: Male Domination and Power Among the New Guinea Baruya*, Cambridge University Press, Cambridge, 1986, pp. 10-11; Pierre Bourdieu, 'The Kabyle House or the World Reversed' in *Algeria 1960*, Cambridge University Press, Cambridge, 1979.

21 Godelier, *Making of Great Men*, pp. 9-10.

22 Douglas, *Natural Symbols*, pp. 10-11.

23 René LeMarchand, *Rwanda and Burundi*, Pall Mall Press, London, 1970, p. 33. On the importance of milk in Rwandan tribal society including gift exchange and marriage ceremonies, see Jacques J. Maquet, *The Premise of Inequality in Ruanda*, Oxford University Press, London, 1961.

24 From the collection of Queen Elizabeth II, England: 'The Kings Head: Charles I. King and Martyr'. Interestingly, and commonly, James is named as 'James VI and James I'. Because James I ascended to the throne of England as James VI of Scotland, the modern curators of the travelling exhibition in Scotland, shown at the Palace of Holyroodhouse, Edinburgh, March 2000, felt it necessary to accent his Scottish heritage.

25 Tate Gallery collection, London (T02020).

26 William Ferguson, *The Identity of the Scottish Nation: An Historic Quest*, Edinburgh University Press, Edinburgh, 1998, Chapter 3. See also Alfred P. Smith, *Warlords and Holy Men: Scotland A.D. 80-1000*, Edinburgh Press, Edinburgh, 1984, pp. 70ff. on the complexity of genealogy in the 'Pictish King-Lists'.

27 Ferguson, *ibid.*, p. 5.

28 Edward Forset, *A Comparative Discovrse of the Bodies Natvral and Politiqve*, Theatrum Orbis Terrarum, Amsterdam, (1606) 1973, folio 38.

29 From the collection of Queen Elizabeth II, 'The King's Head', Palace of Holyroodhouse.

30 Douglas, *Natural Symbols*, p. 158. For a discussion of the way in which in France this separation of private spaces, first limited to the bourgeoisie, spread after World War II to the working class, see Antoine Prost, 'Public and Private Space in France', in Antoine Prost and Gerard Vincent (eds), *A History of Private Life*, vol. 5, Harvard University Press, Cambridge, MA, 1991.

31 Fred Myers, *Pintupi Country, Pintupi Self: Sentiment, Place and Politics among Western Desert Aborigines*, University of California Press, Berkeley, CA, 1991, pp. 228–33.

32 Bryan S. Turner, *The Body and Society: Explorations in Social Theory*, Basil Blackwell, Oxford, 1984, p. 7.

33 Donna J. Haraway, *Modest_Witness@Second_Millennium.FemaleMan©_Meets_OncoMouse™: Feminism and Technoscience*, Routledge, New York, 1997.

34 Anne Balsamo, *Technologies of the Gendered Body: Reading Cyborg Women*, Duke University Press, Durham, NC, 1996; and Turner, *The Body and Society*, pp. 30 and 109. For an interesting confirmation of this development by one of its defenders see Bob Mullan, *The Mating Trade*, Routledge & Kegan Paul, London, 1984, p. 2. He says: 'Finally, the critics seem to forget that the introduction industry is an *industry*; the primary terms are supply and demand, and profit ... it is not a social service, except indirectly, but not by intention. The introduction industry is no more inherently wicked than, say, ... the car trade.'

35 Turner, *The Body and Society*, p. 110.

36 *Ibid.*, p. 8.

37 See Kenneth Burke, *The Philosophy of Literary Form: Studies in Symbolic Action*, Vintage Books, New York, 1957, pp. 96–7.

38 *The Guardian*, 16 March 2000. Her last single, released just before she died, was called 'Set Me Free'.

39 Rosalind Coward, *Female Desire: Women's Sexuality Today*, Paladin Books, London, 1984, pp. 43–4.

40 Julia Kristeva, *Strangers to Ourselves*, Harvester Wheatsheaf, New York, 1991; Richard Sennett, *Flesh and Stone: The Body and the City in Western Civilization*, Faber and Faber, London, 1994.

41 *Ibid.*, Sennett, *Flesh and Stone*, the last sentences of his book, p. 376.

42 For one example of this see Reinke, Leanne, 'Utopia in Chiapas? Questioning Disembodied Politics', in James Goodman (ed.), *Protest and Globalisation: Prospects for Transnational Solidarity*, Pluto Press, Sydney, 2002.

# Part III

## Rewriting the History of the Present

# NINE State Formation

## From Kingdoms and Empires to Nation-States

The structures and subjectivities of polities changed dramatically from tribal-traditional kingdoms to traditional empires and traditional-modern monarchical states. Just as incredible was the transition to the dominance of the modern empire and the modern nation-state.[1] Given that states have dominated post-traditional world history, this chapter is about the changing form of the state. It sets up some of the historical background to understanding the formation of nation-states and the processes of globalization discussed in the next two chapters. We are now entering the conventional terrain of political theory, but with a more explicit emphasis on the ontological issues that underlay questions about the formation of political institutions, including the constitution of the modern nation-state. The discussion takes the form of a top-down narrative, but the account is always intended as social relational in method. The next chapter traverses some of the same ground as this one, but with an emphasis upon forms of community rather than forms of polity.

The argument of the chapter is based on the following propositions:

> *Proposition 1.* States exist as more than the sum of their parts. That is, states cannot simply be understood as collections of persons exerting political power individually and severally, although they are that too. It is this question of the 'more than' of the state-as-polity that has caused so much anxiety in the political and social theory of the state. The state as defined here is a very particular form of corporate body. It is both an abstract administrative body and a complex of abstractly interconnected bodies – from persons to apparatuses – that exert legitimized and enacted power over a people or peoples within a designated

territory. Crucially, each of those notions – legitimation, people, and territory – are taken to vary in meaning according to the cultural definitions of their world-time, and relative to the community or communities in question.[2] This allows us the breadth to examine different kinds of state-as-polity set within different dominant formations from the traditional to the postmodern.

*Proposition 2.* The state as an institution of ritualized political organization is more abstract, for example, than the ritualized kinship systems of organization in tribal societies. Pre-traditional tribes did not develop state-based polities until they found ways of abstracting from kinship as the dominant mode of organization. In many circles this argument appears to be a statement of the obvious, but it necessary to say it explicitly because of a contemporary tendency to reject all hints of any 'Divide' between social formations. On the one hand, the present argument counters, for example, the suggestion that states did not emerge until all significant practices of tribalism were left behind. It equally counters the opposite-leaning suggestion that the 'nation-state bureaucracy is directly analogous to the ritual system of religion'.[3] It is not the presence of ritual or otherwise, sacred or secular, which defines state formation. This is not to deny that many parallels can be drawn across different formations in terms of similar-looking practices (from routinized to sacred rituals) and subjectivities (from the superficial content of different belief structures to some of their deeper subjectivities). It is to argue that state formation depends upon a constitutive shift in the nature of political organization and power.

*Proposition 3.* With the emergence of state formation, first occurring in the intersection of tribal and traditional formations, qualitatively different forms of state can be distinguished. For example, the genealogically-placed hierarchies of 'kinsfolk' named by a traditional-tribal king or the patrimonially-defined traditional servants of the traditional monarch can be distinguished as qualitatively different from the civil servants or the bureaucratic agents of the modern nation-state. Implicit in this argument is the less secure claim that states can be formed in societies formed in the continuing dominance of tribal traditionalism. As already expressed, this entails processes of abstraction that lift the carriers of office, at one level of their being, out of the immediate organizational dominance of kinship ties. Examples of this abstraction can be found in the ritual ceremonies of ascension in the earliest monarchies. Similarly, the agents of this corporate body, when they are acting in that capacity of agents, are in a sense lifted out of their personal bodies to represent something beyond themselves. This point leads directly into the fourth argument.

*Proposition 4.* The difference between different modes and institutions of organization can in part be understood in terms of their changing dominant constitutive levels of abstraction, but this does not mean that there are not continuities across different forms. For example, the authority of monarchy – whether it be tribal-traditional, classical-traditional and, even in increasingly trivialized ways, modern and postmodern monarchy – is at one level continuous with the customary modes of organization of kinship and genealogical placement. It emerged from tribal associations of lineage. At another level, the development of the rituals and institutions of monarchy involves a lift in abstraction that takes the polity along a series of steps away from kinship. The king has to be lifted, both practically and metaphorically, out of the known and everyday rounds of social life, even as that person acts as a mediator back on its social and sacred divisions.

Putting the arguments this way is more contentious than appears on the surface. There is a pressure in social theory – whether it be mainstream empiricism, modern systems theory or postmodern expressions of poststructuralism to say that it is not possible to theorize the state as such, let alone systematically distinguish its different forms. All we can do, they say, is examine 'its' micro-practices of power or 'its' patterns of organization. The first challenge for the chapter is to get around this impasse.

## Bringing the state back in – as social form[4]

The 'state' as a concept of theory and analysis has always had a difficult history, no more so than in the middle of the twentieth century as its changing form, particularly the perceived waning of its sovereignty, led some writers to say that the concept was useless. In this *first retreat* from theorizing the state, a prominent political scientist David Easton argued for striking out the very concept of 'state' from the vocabulary of political science.[5] In doing so – tellingly – he seized upon the more abstract term: 'political system'. He had three major objections to using the term 'state': first, it was too difficult to define. Since political science supposedly now required precise orienting concepts to direct empirical research, a term like 'state', which lacked an operationally-precise definition and fomented conceptual confusion, should be jettisoned. Second, it was too political. It carried too much ideological baggage. Especially, it was over-imbued with the symbolism of order: 'it was an instrument to achieve national cohesion', a crucial myth in the struggle for national unity and sovereignty.[6] Third, it limited the scope of political research. It appeared to prevent the study of political processes in acephalous tribes or non-state societies. It was used too simplistically to give the appearance of the polity as a homogenous and singular entity. Taken away from their structural-functionalist underpinnings the points that Easton makes are ones that any approach has to take seriously.

The force of this kind of move to discard the concept of the 'state' was so powerful that in the 1980s it was felt necessary to publish an anthology called *Bringing the State Back In*.[7] The book marked the intensification of period of increasing interest in theorizing the state, an interest renewed in a variety of quarters. *Daedalus* devoted a special issue to the state in 1979, while the American Political Science Association took as its theme for the 1981 Conference 'Restoring the State to Political Science'. Interest in state theory was further stimulated by two emerging realms of debate: first, over the nature of the capitalist state. This became a central focus of neo-Marxist theory – key writers included Nicos Poulantzas, Jürgen Habermas, Claus Offe and Bob Jessop. Second, historical sociologists began to debate the causes of state formation and the reasons why some states and state systems grew and prospered – particularly the European states – while other state systems collapsed. Leading writers here included Charles Tilly, Theda Skocpol, Michael Mann and Anthony Giddens. Their work both drew on and overlapped with very extensive research carried out by political anthropologists and, in particular, by American cultural anthropologists, into the origins of states, classes and the beginnings of socially-differentiated 'complex' societies. Their collective output highlighted the nexus between state and war, identified several distinctive trajectories of state formation, and showed that it was possible to use the term 'state' to draw attention to a different set of structural regularities within the processes of social and political evolution, complementary to those for which empirical-behavioural scholars had previously understood themselves to be searching.

Much of this literature is of very high quality and reading it, especially the material dealing with the way in which states establish themselves and change in their social form, should be sufficient to counter the kind of doubts and criticisms that Easton expressed towards the 'operational utility' of the concept of 'state'. The volume and quality of this research are the main reasons for one text on the state beginning thus: 'the period in which social science "lost interest" in the state ... is now over'.[8] However, the flood of research upon the state creates new drawbacks. There is so much of it, a synthesis is lacking, and because much of it is historical and anthropological, it seems to have passed by the political mainstream. Moreover, by concentrating on the state-in-history and the transformation from the traditional to the modern state rather than on more contemporary developments, those theorists who wanted to 'bring the state back in' inadvertently left the way open for a new theoretical challenge to sneak in the front door. It quickly took over the front rooms in the house of state-theory.

### The second retreat

During the 1980s and 1990s we saw the development of a second and much more theoretically-sophisticated retreat away from directly addressing the state as a general institution and structure of power. It was not that the orthodox core of the discipline of politics needed to find new reasons for *not* studying the state-as-such. A glance at even the most recent university political-science textbooks confirms that the state continues to be prominent in its absence. Under the heading of 'Government', the state continues to be the implicit subject of political studies, but it is hardly ever directly mentioned. The texts rarely broach questions about the historical form of the state or its changing institutional practices. As a Derridean deconstructionist might express this peculiar absence–presence, the writers of politics textbooks in effect treat the state as a hidden signifier, a master concept that could be said to connect all of their analysis but is always under erasure. The texts cover almost every aspect of the state from the conduct of government enacted via the party system, the public face of politics fought out in the houses of parliament, through to the role of bureaucracy and other agents of the state involved in the implementation of policy directives. However, they consistently and comfortably avoid ever talking about broad structural continuities and transformations in the state as a whole.

In the disciplines of sociology, criminology and social welfare, studies of the state in the guise of the welfare-surveillance state had been given a new lease of life during the 1980s. However, in the 1990s these disciplines too began to come under the influence of the *second retreat* influenced by trends outside them all. It is a retreat with many apparent similarities to the first. The central difference, which might be described in terms of a shift from an emphasis on 'Government' to a concern with 'governance', is based on a methodological aversion to considering the state as anything other than a contingent collection of contingent processes. This moves the debate an epistemological step beyond the pre-1980s' propositions that all state decision-making processes are messy, no more than a matter of muddling through. If some neo-Marxists had responded to the first retreat by re-emphasizing, and sometimes over-emphasizing, the state as structured whole,[9] by contrast, the new trend goes further along old pluralist lines: it involves understanding the state as always dissolved into multiple and changing sites of micro-power. The theoretical rationale for this move comes from field of post-structuralism, particularly influenced by Michel Foucault. Its political orientation ranges from left-liberal to postmodernist.

The contemporary theoretical retreat from the state is taking three main forms. First, it treats the concept of the state as a useless or over-generalized abstraction. Second, it implicitly characterizes the state as everywhere and nowhere, the metaphoric naming of one of the discursive closures in the flow of ubiquitous power. And, third, it understands the postmodernization as comprehensive process contributing to fragmenting, decentring and deterritorializing the modern state. As becomes readily obvious when listed in this way, these trends contradict each other.

The first form of retreat is part of the backlash against all structural theories of the state, whether Marxist or Weberian. As one of the postmodern turns there has emerged a tendency to treat the state as either a useless abstraction – that is, as an abstraction in the sense that it is not real – or as a discursive abstraction, where it is only real to the extent that it discursively names a set of 'shifting and temporary connections'. For example, the postmodern feminist Judith Allen gives voice to this turn when she writes:

> 'The state' is a category of abstraction that is too aggressive, too unitary and too unspecific to be of much use in addressing the disaggregated, diverse and specific (or local) sites that must be of most pressing concern to feminists. 'The state' is too blunt an instrument to be of much assistance (beyond generalizations) in explanations, analyses or the design of workable strategies.[10]

Writers of these kinds of statements are reacting to an earlier tendency to treat the state as a monolithic whole, as an institution that was given unproblematic anthropomorphic agency. In this tendency, a state was said to be able to act as if it had a life beyond the people who made it up. Sometimes it was even invested with a personality, usually masculine. There are deep problems with classic and modern theory insofar as it treats the state in this way. However, by refusing to make generalities about the state-in-history the alternative (postmodern) approach simply turns the problem on its head, and in the process the state has had to 'disappear'. It has come to exist as a concept under erasure.

The power of this move inveigled its way into both the Marxist and liberal tradition alike. In his book on state theory, the Marxist Bob Jessop finds it necessary to include a section entitled 'Does the state exist?' He concludes that as a social relation it does exist, but along the way he presents as one of his major theses the problematic proposition that 'as an institutional ensemble the state does not (and cannot) exercise power: it is not a real subject'.[11] Similarly, commenting on the liberal tradition, Clyde Barrow writes:

> the ambiguity in the boundaries of the state concept is compounded by the analytic requirement that, for political authority to achieve stateness, there must be a relative unity to the apparatuses exercising that authority within the boundaries of what we call the state. However, as a result of its internal development and expansion during the twentieth century, Poggi argues that it is now 'totally unrealistic ... to conceive the state as making up *an* organization', as suggested in the definitions proffered by Skocpol, Skowronek, and others. In fact, their emphasis on the unevenness of state development suggests a research agenda in which it is possible to talk about organizations that wield state powers, but in which one cannot any longer talk realistically about *the* state or *a* state.[12]

In both these cases we find the assumption that an entity can wield no power if it is a material abstraction.

There is a simple way out of this problem, simple at least in its saying. It can be addressed in terms of the main themes of the present book. States do exist and they are much more than transitory discursive formations. However, the way in which they are described depends upon the level of generality *and* at what level of theoretical abstraction we want to begin the description. While at the level of empirical detail and process they may be contingent and changing, at the most abstract generalizing level, they have tended historically to be relatively-stable structures of governance. They operate as a more or less co-ordinated ensemble of agents who draw on sets of juridical procedures to administer (by consent and coercion) a given territory and people. The state may be an abstraction, but it is a material abstraction, a lived structure of unevenly-integrated and patterned practices and ideologies.

Viewed from a more 'concrete' epistemological level, the state in practice *is* messy. The closer one gets to the ground the more the state does disappear into a disorganized ensemble of individuals battling it out over micro-issues in their micro-settings. Such analyses do help us to avoid the problem of treating the state as a homogenous, undifferentiated whole. However, it makes no sense to valorize less generalized and less abstract descriptions if by doing so we can no longer talk about the state-as-such. To modify a common aphorism, a detailed description of every leaf in the forest is not sufficient to come to an understanding of the forest, and those leaves are no more real than the forest itself. These different levels of description are useful in combination. Ranging across different levels of theoretical abstraction, and qualifying each level of analysis by other levels, serves to enable a much more nuanced understanding than does heading off in the direction of either empiricism or theoreticism.

The second postmodern trend which has made it hard to 'bring the state back in' is a tendency to treat the state as simply a nodal point in the ubiquitous circulation of power. In this move, the state is at once treated as having enormous power and reduced to nothing but a symptom of the circulation of power in general. This is a bit confusing. The following quote from the poststructuralists Gilles Deleuze and Félix Guattari will need translating into language that is more accessible; however, with careful reading it does give a direct rendition of this double move:

> the modern nation-States ... take decoding even further [than traditional and early modern states] and are models of realization for an axiomatic or general conjunction of flows (these States combine social subjection and the new machinic enslavement, and their very diversity is a function of isomorphy, of the eventual heteromorphy or polymorphy of the models in relation to the axiomatic).[13]

In this description, the modern state is said to offer a place for the temporary slowing down of abstract capital. Their phrase, the 'axiomatic of flows', is used to metaphorically name global capitalism. When they describe the state as 'models of realization for an axiomatic' they are trying to understand why, despite the fact that capitalism can do without states, states are given new strength by the deterritorializing flow of capitalism. In other words, they see states as contradictorily an expression of the global flow of power even though they inhibit it. States become megamachines of enslavement just as globalism contributes to a generalized regime of 'voluntary' subjection. The effect of all of this is to overstate the role of the state as a comprehensive machine of internal control, and at the same to over-reduce it to a residual effect of grander external processes.

Michel Foucault makes something of a parallel move when, on the one hand, he says that we live in the era of 'governmentality', but then, on the other, he reduces the form of state we experience today to an effect of the whole discursive formation – 'a society controlled by apparatuses of security'.[14] Accordingly, he writes:

> the state is no more than a composite reality and a mythicized abstraction, whose importance is a lot more limited than many of us think. Maybe what is really important for our modernity – that is for our present – is not so much the *étatisation* of society, as the 'governmentalization' of the state.[15]

Foucault wants to take the state out of the centre of discussions of contemporary power and replace it by governmentality, but ironically his own analyses centre upon state apparatuses – such as the prison and the clinic – and upon state practices such as policing and welfare provision, all seen as key institutions in the globalization of bio-power. It is no wonder that some commentators have accused Foucault of underestimating the state, while others have said that he makes the state everything.[16]

As with the first problem, there is a relatively simple way out within the constitutive abstraction approach. It is possible to say that the state is a central institutional ensemble with enormous actual and potential power at its disposal without either demonizing it as the source of that power, or reducing the state to the kinds of power it uses. We have choices about the ways in which the state will act. What Foucault calls modern 'governmentality' is part of what I have been calling 'the legal-rational mode of organization', that is, the means, techniques, procedures and cultural assumptions or ideologies practiced in administering the movement of objects such as commodities and the activities of people – increasingly aggregated under the categories of 'the population' or 'the citizenry'. Legal-rational bureaucracy is arguably the dominant mode of organization across the late-modern world. Economic rationalism or neo-liberalism is an ideology of that mode of organization. In this sense, the institution of governance, the dominant mode of organization and the dominant ideology of that mode of practice are not the same thing. The state, just like the multinational corporation, is an institutional structure through which its agents enact various modes of organization governed by ideological presuppositions about what is 'right' or efficacious. The state is not reducible to a 'model of realization' of something beyond itself: it is a real, patterned, materially-lived abstraction. Similarly the variously directed categories of persons that the state comes to administer – 'the population', 'the body politic' and 'the nation' – are categorical abstractions of actual people, and real to the extent that they are lived as constitutive categories of identity and practice.

The third element of the postmodern retreat from the state arises out of flawed attempts to understand the very real transformations of the modern state into what John Hinkson calls the postmodern state. Hinkson argues that, 'A dualism between modern "totalizing" forms ... and a postmodern specificity and decentredness leaves little conceptual space for a post-modern state.'[17] One book called *Postmodernization* attempts to look into this space, however, in doing so the authors in their enthralment with their own theoretical apparatus lose sight of some of the continuities of the modern state even as it engages with processes of postmodernization. They conclude that the state is devolving into a postmodern 'disorganization complex':

> the general direction of change can be charted with modest accuracy. It involves a general shift away from corporatist centralism and towards a more decentralized and fragmented minimal state. More

specifically, the vector of change involves shifts from centralized to decentralized state apparatuses and from authoritative to manipulative forms of control. This may prove to be the best *temporary* survival strategy for the state ... The current process of devolution seems to follow logic of ironic reversals ... differentiation and centralization [under modernity] give way to fragmentation of domains, each with fuzzy boundaries and unspecific functions .[18]

Any empirical force the argument might have is undermined by its radical overstatement. Crook, Pakulski and Waters set up a totalizing view of the nature of the transformation, and treat real and emergent-dominant trends including privatization, corporatization, deregulation, and globalization as harbingers of the end of the state as we know it. It all becomes so fuzzy that they have to employ unhelpful oxymorons to label the 'disappearing' state – the postmodern state as a 'disorganization complex'. While *Globalism, Nationalism, Tribalism* also argues that we are witnessing a transformation of modernity and the development of an emergent layer postmodern structures and sensibilities, it attempts to do so without setting up a dichotomous schema for understanding historical change. To carry this argument through, the chapter now turns to analyse the dialectic of historical continuity and discontinuity through which we can understand the state as a continuing pre-eminent form of polity.

## Empires, kingdoms and monarchical states

In embarking upon the historical discussion, a number of definitional issues need to be clarified. The concept of *kingship* is used here despite the complicated array of synonyms, all meaning something slightly different. Conventionally, it is used as a generic term for a particular kind of sovereign leadership where authority is socially conferred but in such a way as to mask its origins in the realm of the polity. It is conventionally used as including pharaohs, tsars and other monarchs but as distinguished from 'big men' and chiefs, to the extent that kingship is abstracted from immediate kinship ties – kings supposedly presided in Europe, and chiefs in the colonies. However, it is more complicated than that.

First, we have the issue that the concept of *kingship* should be able to embrace different forms of ascension to power: emperors in some traditions such as that of the Roman Empire were elected by proclamation, whereas other were rather than more ambiguously proclaimed by consecration. Michael Mann, for example, describes how, in the early empires, kingship was legitimated as absolute rank continuous with genealogical ties rather than as sacred mediation.[19] Second, the concept of *king*ship has to be understood in all its quietly-assumed gender specificity. This is because that is historically the way that it has mostly been – an institutional agency normalized as patriarchal, but treated as if the very gendered body of the prince has been left behind once *he* (or she) is made king. As Patricia Springborg writes, even though kingship was mimetic with fatherhood in most forms of kingship including Pharaonic Egypt, women were given a unique power to recognize legitimate and illegitimate kin, 'to make and unmake kings'.[20] Genealogy is so important that when a suitable man was not available, women born as female were invested with male persona and abstracted as kings. From the Egyptian monarch Hatshepsut to the British monarch Elizabeth I, the gender of queens was ambiguously overlaid by the universalizing category of (male) kingship.

*Kingship* as a concept, in the sense that I want to use it, thus stretches the conventional use a little, emphasizing the ambiguous ontological status of all 'kings' in terms of gender and genealogy, power and transcendence, embodiment and abstraction. Kingship crosses quite different relationships to embodiment and power – from tribal-traditional kings whose power is only partially lifted out of the *organizational* structures of kinship to postmodern monarchs where kinship determines only the genealogy of election and the stories of cultural legitimation. Historically, it has only been under conditions of the dominance of traditionalism – emerging, ascendant, or waning – that kingship in its various forms can be associated with the clear sovereignty of the polity. However, this does take away from the ambiguous status of such formations. Similarly, postmodern monarchy, despite its abstraction as a pastiche of language games, still draws upon layers of the modern and traditional. When the Prince of Wales is jokingly pronounced by *The Scotsman* as the Scottish king-for-a-day,[21] or even when some political scientist writes of the irrelevance of monarchs, their engendered genealogical-elected power continues to engage commentators. Kings may be largely irrelevant to the modern polity – and, in many societies, so say most of us – but ambiguous intrigue still runs deep for historically-embedded reasons.

### Kings mediating persons and gods, nature and culture

There is a striking homology here between the ambiguous status of tribal-to-traditional kings and the ambiguous status of gifts discussed earlier.[22] Just as gifts are precious goods caught between and connecting sacred goods and useful goods, kings are elevated above the people into the realm of the sacred, but are still beholden to the embodied world. In one way, the nature of this quality of being beholden changes dramatically from tribal-traditional to classically-traditional kingship but there are still generalities to be made. Kings, and less often queens, are lifted out as something special, chosen by God(s), elected by Holy Spirit(s), and called to sit on high thrones of stone or lifted up on shields of wood. Even in the case of imperial Japan, where the first emperor Jimmu (660 BCE) was said to have descended from the Gods, subsequent emperors had to be inducted into office. However, for all the rituals of elevation – investiture, ascension, anointing, sanctification, veiling and crowning – the early chiefs, *sayyid*, caliph, khans, emir and emperors were still, in effect, confirmed in their position by the people around them.[23] For example, the Mandate theory of kingship in China seems to have developed after the Shang dynasty in the period after the late Egyptian dynasties. Moreover, for all the acculturation of kings they were still caught in a mediating position between culture and nature as a link in the various versions of the Great Chain of Being. If the theories about the footprints and swords in stone are right, then the king is simultaneously anointed for ascension and symbolically tied down into enduring nature. These ambiguities meant that for all the anointing of their sanctified bodies, they could still be looked upon in moments of crisis and contradiction, in nature or culture, as persons embodied in mortal flesh and blood. In the Chinese context, the very meaning of the Mandate of Heaven, probably going back to the western Chou Empire (1122–771 BCE), was that the mandate could be withdrawn. Even in the Old and Middle Kingdoms of Egypt, an extraordinary instance of a relatively-continuous and unitary polity-community ruled by pharaoh as gods, failures in the expected cycles of nature were interpreted as signs that the king was no longer sacred.

The possibility of 'seeing through the veil' of eternal monarchical sanctity obviously does not occur in the fabulous manner described in the story of the innocent child who exclaimed, 'the Emperor has no clothes'. Nevertheless, that story – published by Hans Christian Anderson in 1837 with sources traceable to a Spanish story recorded by Don Juan Manuel (1282–1384)[24] – is indicative of an ever-present issue that vexed the hierarchy of traditional courts. A particular monarch may prove to be no longer truly sacred even if that person had been properly sanctified. Similarly, as discussed in Chapter 5, gifts are abstracted from the run-of-the-mill objects, but they do not become unambiguously sacred or eternally inalienable. They are invested with the *hau* or *mana* of the sacred *in the social process* of reciprocal exchange: it does not just inhere in the object. Furthermore, gifts can return to being ordinary when exchanged with the wrong person, exchanged out of time or out of place, or worse, left languishing outside the circuits of cultural attention. Similarly, kings had to be *made* sacred. Sacredness was not just a birthright, a status inherently dwelling in the next lump of flesh in the royal bloodline, even if this was most often a necessary condition of that status. If sacredness were inherent, we would not find the heavy ritual emphasis on the sovereign's elevation that we in fact do find throughout history and across different social formations.

In the Christian West from the early-medieval period, holy anointing became crucial to the ceremony of *lifting* a person to monarchical status. This simple statement has the effect of substantially qualifying the Weberian emphasis on the special charisma of the king. Charisma was substantially conferred, not a personality trait. The ceremony became at once genealogical and sacral-political (see the previous chapter on forms of embodiment), bestowing on the monarch an ecclesiastical sense of self, akin to papacy, and an elected power akin to that of emperor. This was to change subtly in the post-medieval period. In French, this rite called the *sacré*, was to become *sacré et couronnement*. In a similar secularizing abstraction from the sacred, the English-language concept of *coronation* gradually took over from the concept of *consecration*. As C.A. Bouman points out, it was until well after Shakespeare's time that people asserted that, 'Not all the water in the rough rude sea, can wash the balm off from an anointed king',[25] but nevertheless a change was occurring. The sacred, like tradition itself, had increasingly to be defended. Bouman like others uses the concept of *sacring* to discuss the custom of regal anointing, with the first unequivocal European evidence of the process appearing in relation to the Visigoth king, Wamba (672 CE).

In Northern Africa (Egypt) from c.1500 years BCE, and in Europe by the ninth century CE, the rituals were becoming textually elaborate. In the later European Middle Ages, formularies on how it should be done crossed the boundaries of empire and kingdom. In Europe, they travelled as inter-related manuscripts and manuals, circulating in a globalizing field called Christendom. Writing had its own formalizing effect on practical tradition as scribes copied down the rubrics and practices in as full a manner as possible, recording even antiquated and obsolete details of rituals that became again available for current use.[26] By the time we get to the famous example of Louis XIV (1643–1715), absolutist ruler of France, the ritualistic splendour of the court had increased to an extraordinary level, but then so too had both the distance between the king and people, and the tension between the king's two bodies – personal and sacred. If it was literally believed that the king of pre-colonial Rwanda should not bend his knees, lest the kingdom shrink, by the time of Louis XIV it was only metaphorically true that if the king sneezed, the whole country caught a cold.

By this time, the form of the state was caught between traditional and modern practices and sensibilities. On this point, writers as diverse as Ellen Meiksins Wood, Perry Anderson and Anthony Giddens come together to emphasize the tensions of the absolutist state as a hybrid form. Wood, for example, in her discussion of the absolutist state in eighteenth-century England, describes how the state used modern techniques of extracting surplus value, taxing the propertied class rather than applying feudal rent. This occurred even as the traditional aristocracy gained, for a time, renewed sources of power and sinecure in the turmoil of the Old Corruption and the agrarian revolution. The same could be said about the rise of a reflexively-monitored system of administration through abstract codes of law, an impersonal bureaucracy and institutions of sequestration:

> It is, then, misleading to treat the common law as a token of antiquity on the grounds that it represents ancient principles of custom as against the modern conceptions of legislative sovereignty. The evolution of common law was intrinsic to the process of state-centralization, and as such it belongs to the same processes that dissolved feudalism and established the reality, if not the conceptual clarity, of a unitary sovereignty in England. In that sense, the common law, even when it embodied ancient customs, stood in direct opposition to antique principles of custom in both the scope and modalities of its application. Its claim to enshrine age-old custom could even confer legitimacy on what amounted to the suppression of particular customs and their subordination to the legislative power of the state.[27]

However, when Anthony Giddens traces what he presents as a lineage from the European traditional state through the hybrid absolutist state to the emergence of the nation-state, his analysis loses sight of his own well-articulated rationale. At the beginning of his analysis, he emphasizes that we should not be setting up a 'progressivist' or 'single pathway' interpretation of historical change. This too easily turns into a futile search for *the* 'missing link' – whether it takes the form of a hybrid state-form, or a pivotal practice that is said to make *the* difference. In Giddens' argument, we should be showing how 'modern states can be contrasted in a generic way to traditional ones'.[28] Alternatively, in terms of present approach, we should be setting up an approach that allows us, firstly, to analyse the layers-in-dominance of different ontological formations. In relation to the recent history of polities, this means taking seriously the layers of traditionalism and modernism (and later, in some cases, postmodernism) in all 'modern states'. Second, we should be able to map both the very different pathways to modern statehood taken by particular polities, *and* the generalizing processes that eventually contribute to naturalizing the dominance of the nation-state as the highest order of polity-communities in all those particular instances.

## Nation-states

The phenomenon of nation-state formation similarly continues to trouble all of us who want to go beyond descriptive documentation and attempt an explanation of its formation and transformations. It is indicative of this lack of resolution that the major debates of the past three decades remain contentious. One of the key debates is implied in the question, 'Are nation-states natural or invented, expressions of perennial interests or uniquely modern?' Perhaps the best response is that question itself is misconceived. 'Either/or' questions rarely get to the heart of explanatory issues. Nation-states are historically-produced social entities existing within a system of nation-states, each with discontinuous histories and elements of invented or reconfigured content, but which in an uneven process of consolidation come to be experienced as naturally extending out of the past and into the future. That is, we *can* say that *nation*-states are objectively modern (even as state formation crosses all 'post-tribal history'[29]) and that modernist processes of cultural invention did sometimes occur in legitimation of a particular nation-state. However, to leave it at that belies the complexity of explaining how nation-states can be both objectively understood as modern and subjectively experienced as primordial, reaching back into pre-modern history. The invention, fabrication and reworking of the past have to be understood against the deep embeddedness of the cultural forms which were drawn upon to symbolize the connection of each nation to its past.

Without having a way of saying both these things at the same time, we get caught in the dead-end debate between the so-called 'primordialists' who argue that nation-state formation is based upon deeply-embedded human traits and the 'modernists' who tend to emphasize the recent history of the coming together of state and nation. What the modernists need to explain is how the objective conditions and dominant way of conceiving of modern national identity came to support the subjectivity that either a nation-state is a continuous polity-community going back to the past or a young nation that will acquire such maturity by acts of authenticity and connection to enduring nature. What the primordialists need to explain is how nations and states came together so late in human history. In this spirit, we can draw out the following proposition extending upon the list at the start of the chapter:

> *Proposition 5.* The nation-state is a very peculiar community-polity that involves the intersection of state and nation. This intersection involves the historical coming together of a particular form of the

state – as objectively an increasingly-rationalized, modern bureaucratic apparatus – and a particular form of the nation – as an increasingly-abstracted community of strangers, experienced subjectively as a community a distinct form of perceived foundational connection.

Another related set of debates has been over methodological issues. One standoff occurs between those who would emphasize the importance of cultural expression and iconography (or *content*) in the formation of nations and those who emphasize structural processes that underpin the transformation from earlier *forms* of statehood to nation-statehood. Similarly, there are debates between those writers who emphasize the particularity of the processes and the uniqueness of the pathways, to the formation of each nation-state and those who work at a higher level of abstraction and give priority to generalizing processes. Hence, in coming to an adequate approach to nation-state formation, as for understanding any social formation, it is crucial to find a way of handling considerations of content and form, of the subjective and the objective, and of the particular and the general.

By working self-consciously across different levels of analytical abstraction, these problems arguably fall away, or at least can be seen for what they are: usually, confusions about the status of a particular claim. In beginning seriously at the level of empirical generalization, we are forced to engage with on-the-ground details of material or cultural grievances, the particularities of different histories, the various practices of different persons, groups and institutions. At this level, the patterns *and* anomalies of *content* come to the fore. Each particular nation-state can be seen for its uniqueness. Over-zealous generalizations can be constrained.

At this level, particular histories tend only be abstracted into generalizing claims to the extent that those claims acknowledge contingencies and counter-examples. This is the level at which writers such as John Breuilly work when they set up extended typologies of the nationalism and the nation-state.[30] Writings concentrating on this level of analysis, often have considerable strengths – setting up typologies, for example, is one of many useful orienting techniques – but it also has dangers. The core problem arises when an empirically-oriented writer becomes aware of the limitations of their own empirical generalizations, and then concludes that abstract theory *per se* is problematic just because it takes the process of generalizing even further. For example, Anthony Smith says:

> This brings me to perhaps the most fundamental difference between my approach and that of Ernest Gellner. For Ernest, it is possible and desirable to have a general theory of nationalism, one that

derives from the postulates of modernity. For myself, no such general theory is possible. Though I prefer a certain kind of approach, which may be termed 'ethno-symbolist', I feel that the differences between nationalisms across the periods and the continents are too great to be embraced by a single Euclidean theory.[31]

Some empirically-oriented writers also seem to forget that despite their avoiding of abstract theory, they commonly use abstracting concepts such as 'modern', 'power', 'state', or *ethnie* without having a more abstract methodological frame in which to make sense of them. For example, John Breuilly is adamant that nationalism is, above all else, a political doctrine with the objective of attaining control of the state. Nation-states are no more than the outcome of that consolidation of power. The irony here is that, while eschewing theory, Breuilly's conclusions depend upon a conceptual category – namely, *power* – that stretches from the apparently self-evident to the most abstract theoretical order of analysis. Put more generally, when a method has no way of putting a concept such as 'power' both into a systematic methodology and into a broad social and historical context, the concept comes to explain everything and nothing. Writers caught in the thrall of this level seem ironically to conclude that it is impossible to have a generalizing theory of the nation-state, even as they continue to make sweeping generalizations about nationalism and nation-state formation hidden in definitional claims and taken-for-granted concepts.

There is not the space here to write an empirical history of the various tracks of nation-state formation, but the present approach can be made very explicit. Nation-states were much more than power containers – even if power is an important consideration – that were formed by common structural processes out of very different kinds of polities including republics such as the United States of America, old empires such as the United Kingdom; absolutist states such as France, and colonies such as Venezuela and Mexico. In other words, many different kinds of traditional polities took different tracks in converging on a single dominant form of modern polity-community – the nation-state. To understand how these different historical tracks were framed by common processes, we need to take the discussion to a level of abstraction beyond empirical analysis. Three propositions, extending upon previous summations, provide a bridge to the discussions of conjunctural analysis and its contribution to understanding this uneven process.

> *Proposition 6.* While we should always keep in mind the unique particularities of any one country, it is equally important to generalize the explanation to broader changes in the nature of the relation between community and polity across the period of the eighteenth

into the twenty-first century. Modern nation-state formation occurred in a very specific historical conjuncture of change.

*Proposition 7.* The consolidation of the nation-state did not sweep all before it. (This same point will be argued later – Chapter 11 – in relation to globalization.) The nation-state was not completely normalized across all levels of community, even if it did become the dominant polity-community framing both the organization of power and the legitimation of political-cultural meaning. This point qualifies the writings of scholars such as Ernest Gellner who, despite recognizing the importance of uneven development, treats nation-states as being built on a single epistemological space that covered the world like a tidal wave. What we can say is that the nation-state was constituted in the emerging dominance of new modes of practice.

*Proposition 8.* Across the world, nation-states were constituted in the uneven intersection of globalizing changes in the dominant modes of practice that included a combination of the following: (1) modern state formation as the outcome of a changing mode of organization bringing with it new ways of organizing authoritative power, including the means of violence; (2) print as the emerging dominant mode of communication; (3) capitalism as an intersection of changing modes of production and exchange; and (4) secular and scientific rationalism as expressive of a changing mode of enquiry that brought with it new forms of education and cultural standardization. Expressed this way, we can say that these changing modes of practice tended to overlay and reconstitute traditional subjectivities and structures of polity and community without necessarily replacing them. This is not to argue, for example, that each society that became a nation-state was dominated by capitalist modes of production and exchange, but rather to say that capitalism as a globalizing framing context was fundamental to abstracting social relations in such a way that made the nation-state system possible. For example, as discussed in the next chapter, there is a strong relationship between the structures of modern capitalist imperialism and the subjectivities of nationalism.

This theory of the nation-state uses quite different language from writers such as Gellner, Anderson, Nairn, Giddens and Smith; nevertheless, it generalizes aspects of their approaches. For example, whether we take Gellner's emphasis on the shift from agrarianism to industrialism or Nairn's on the uneven spread of capitalism, both effectively give priority to transformations in the dominant mode of production. In emphasizing the intersection of print capitalism, Anderson gives priority to the changing modes of production *and* communication; and Giddens and Smith (at least in the latter's early work) focus on the rise of the scientific state as a new mode of organization. All that I am suggesting here is that we need a more integrated theory of changing dominant modes of practice – production, exchange, communication, organization and enquiry – to give *one* layer of explanation for the rise of the nation-state. The language of 'modes of practice' used here is most distant from Anthony Smith's ethno-symbolic method with his focus on myth-symbol complexes. He does attempt a broader understanding of the structural setting when he theorizes the desire to become a nation-state in the context of what he calls the three Western revolutions – 'a revolution in the sphere of the division of labour, a revolution in the control of administration, and a revolution in cultural co-ordination'.[32] However, in effect, his analysis focuses on only one of the modes of practice that others have shown to be also crucial:

> These three revolutions, then, revolved around the fashioning of centralized and culturally homogenous states; and by the early twentieth century, the whole European continent was divided into a network of bureaucratic 'rational' states, and the concepts and practices of state-making were being deliberately transplanted overseas to the various colonial territories. It was within this crucible – the European and colonial inter-state system – that nationalism emerged and nations were formed.[33]

The quote is also worth dwelling upon because it marks a point of profound but easy misunderstanding of his position. Anthony Smith is being extraordinarily careful in this rendition of his argument. Leaving aside the problems associated with too-easily calling the triple revolution 'Western' and confining the discussion to the mode of organization, each step that Smith takes is unswervingly accurate at the level of empirical generalization. First, the changes *did* 'revolve around the fashioning of centralized homogenous states' – though this involves understanding that the term 'homogenous' relates to states and not nations. In light of this it should not taken to assume that cultural homogenization had actually been forged, but rather that a political struggle by centralized states to assert such a cultural unity had ensued. Second, modern ideas and techniques of state-craft *were* 'being deliberately transplanted overseas to the various colonies' – though this should not be taken to mean that 'deliberate transplantation' explains the process of nation formation in the colonies, nor that we can automatically assume that the structures and subjectivities of nationhood came from the West. Third, it *was* within the crucible of 'the European and colonial interstate system' that nationalism emerged as a political practice and nations were self-consciously affirmed by *the people* – though this should not be taken to mean that the colonies simply took up what was being exported from the West. Nor should be this taken to mean that non-Western countries such as Thailand, countries that were never colonized, were outside this globalizing process of nation-state formation.

All of this is to suggest that explaining such social formation entails exploring the practices and ideas, both traditional and modern, that developed in the uneven but systemic matrix of integrating connections formed as a modernizing Europe reached out across the globe with other communities and polities responding. This matrix simultaneously had a profound effect upon the West. Even the most powerful of the old European empires and kingdoms found themselves caught in its contradictory logic. Nation-states developed in various places across the entire world from the beginning of the nineteenth century (even though a century later there are many examples of states other than nation-states in both Asia and Europe). This occurred as part of a globalizing process that linked different kind of states, Western and otherwise, into a lines of imperial or asymmetrical relationship. We should not assume that all Third World nation-states developed after those in Europe, even if some states such as Indonesia and Rwanda clearly did so. For example, Mexico was by the usual definition a nation-state before Italy or Germany. Similarly, I argue against the conventional Western-centric argument that Europe provided the blueprint for the transformation of the geo-social map of the world in the image of the first nation-states – putatively, England and France. This theme will be taken up again in the next chapter when we come to elaborate on the formation of nations. The language of 'modes of practice' involves a complete rewriting of Anthony Smith's categories of the triple *modern* revolution to the extent that he would see the changes as a series of background factors, whereas the present approaches uses them as an interconnected matrix of determinants. To further elucidate this difference, and to set concepts such as 'the modern' in a broader framework, we now need to move to yet more abstract levels of analysis.

Benedict Anderson is the writer who does most to elaborate a theory of national community that works at a more abstract level. As discussed earlier, he does this in terms of a ground-breaking argument about the development of what he calls, following Walter Benjamin, 'homogenous empty time' or abstracted time. In his argument, the possibility of nation formation only arose when it became possible through print capitalism for the members of a community to imagine themselves simultaneously moving through the kind of time that they could fill with their own collective experiences and aspirations. It effected a separation of cosmological time and historical time, and 'the search was on, so to speak, for a new way of linking fraternity, power and time meaningfully together'.[34] However, as his book *Imagined Communities* implicitly recognizes – with additional chapters in the second edition on censuses (embodiment), mapping (spatiality), memory and forgetting (knowledge) – this approach needs to broadened out in relation to explaining nation formation – and this becomes even more obvious in relation to nation-state formation. Nation-statehood required the dominant abstraction of categories of existence such as time, space, embodiment and knowledge. In a sense, all that *Globalism, Nationalism, Tribalism* is doing here is providing a possible methodology for Benedict Anderson's theory to come together as a consistent explanation of the constitutive frame that made possible the *modern* nation-state. The constitutive abstraction thesis also provides an analytic method for understanding how this relates the quite different emphasis in the Foucauldian literature on the emergent practices of governance in the modern state as polities begins to administer peoples abstracted as 'populations' or 'citizenries' through such techniques as the regularized gathering statistics of the patterns of activity or procedures of democracy.[35] At the same time, it helps us understand why there is such an emphasis on the modernity of the nation-state in most of the writings, and how we can define what it means to talk of the dominance of modernist processes. In the terms presented here, they can be defined in terms of the nature of an ontological matrix that includes but goes beyond the nature of time to discuss the nature of temporality, spatiality, corporeality and epistemology.

As a way of linking into the next chapter, let me add a couple of additional propositions:

> *Proposition 9.* Movements arguing for the congruence of nation and state are in the first instance carried predominantly by certain classes of people – in particular those abstracted in some way from the ontological frames of tribalism and traditionalism. This occurred, for example, through those who work at the level of disembodied extension such as through print as the dominant means of communication rather than through orality or script.[36] However, for the nation-state to come into being, this way of being had to be generalized to a broader population than just the intellectually trained, for example. This brings together Tom Nairn's point about the pivotal place of intellectuals in calling people to the recognition that nation-statehood offered them a way forward, Ernest Gellner's emphasis on the importance of the state (as a means of agency extension) organizing a generic education system that generalizes the capacity to communicate through disembodied means, and Benedict Anderson's argument about print-capitalism.

*Proposition 10.* Belonging to a nation-state has classically involved contradictory cultural subjectivities, as much as it has been projected through contradictory political ideologies. This can be seen in a number of ways. Although, as an ideology, nationalism can be used instrumentally to integrate and legitimate state power and state violence, contradictorily it often runs deeper in people's consciousness than an instrumentalist explanation can allow. From Ho Chi Minh, and Xanana Gusmão to George W. Bush, even those political elites who have attempted to harness its magical brutal powers have not stood outside its subjective power. Expressed theoretically, the magic of nation-state is that while objectively it is based upon practices of abstract interrelation – modes of practice that are abstracted at the level of agency and disembodied extension, and therefore open to instrumentalizing – it is simultaneously *experienced* as grounded in the level of the face-to-face in subjectivities of embodied relation to relevant others and to place.

One of the issues given theoretical space here is the peculiarity that, though the ideologies of the nation-state are distinctly *modern* in form, modern nationalists characteristically draw upon prior cultural mythologies, including traditional cosmologies and collective stories of origin. In 'new' nation-states the search for cosmological origins is carried often as the naming of moments of national blood sacrifice. In the peculiar but consistent case of Australia, the tragic World War I battle of Gallipoli is evoked – where 'far from home' on the coast of what is now Turkey, Australian soldiers were slaughtered in defence of the British way of life. Now, 'returned servicemen' and Australian backpackers alike make their way on annual modern-postmodern pilgrimages to experience the moment of Anzac Day. Linking those two themes together, these stories of origin can be invented or culturally managed. However, even in the case of new nations from Indonesia and East Timor to Australia where scholars routinely talk of the invention of heroes, it is unlikely that the process can be explained simply by recourse to asserting that the cultural scribes of the national spirit were (and are) straight-forwardly manipulating the sense of the past. Thus, we can say that the carriers of nationalism are modernizers drawn into contradictory kinds of modernism. In one manifestation we find a modernism obsessively aware of looking backward to tradition. More recently, we find new kinds of modernizers drawing upon the cultural aesthetic of postmodernism to argue that we should leave the archaic traditions of the past behind. These lines of argument anticipate the terms of the next chapter as we turn to questions of the nation as a contradictorily-abstracted community.

## Notes

1 The use of qualifiers such as tribal, traditional and modern continues to be done here as ontologically defining rather than just as loose adjectives. This is more than a matter of definitional consistency. When Feliks Gross (*The Civic and Tribal State: The State, Ethnicity and the Multiethnic State*, Greenwood Press, Westport, CT, 1998) uses the term 'tribal state' to apply to states such as Nazi Germany espousing racist ideologies, he confuses ideology with social form and uses the term 'tribal' as politically pejorative. Thus, when we get to his chapter on 'African Tribal Traditional States' he has to distinguish them as tribal-traditional even when they are dominated by modernism, and to acknowledge that they were not always characterized by racism.

2 For an account of different rationalities of the state in ancient Greece, Renaissance Italy and Absolutist Europe, see Christian Reus-Smit, *The Moral Purpose of the State: Culture, Social Identity, and Institutional Rationality in International Relations*, Princeton University Press, Princeton, 1999, Chapter 3.

3 Michael Herzfeld, *The Social Production of Indifference*, University of Chicago Press, Chicago, 1992. p. 10.

4 An earlier draft of this passage appeared as part of a chapter written with Hugh Emy in Paul James (ed.), *The State in Question*, Allen & Unwin, Sydney, 1996.

5 David Easton, *The Political System: An Inquiry into the State of Political Science*, Alfred Knopf, New York, 1953, p. 108.

6 *Ibid.*, pp. 112–13.

7 Peter Evans, Dietrich Reuschemeyer and Theda Skocpol (eds), *Bringing the State Back In*, Cambridge University Press, Cambridge, 1985.

8 John A. Hall and G. John Ikenberry, *The State*, Open University Press, Milton Keynes, 1989.

9 Most of the well-known neo-Marxists bent over backwards not to over-generalize their claims and not reify the state, not to treat the state structures as things. For example, going back to Nicos Poulantzas, he writes: 'it is precisely one of the merits of Marxism that ... it thrust aside the grand metaphysical flights of so-called political philosophy – the vague and nebulous theorizings of an extreme generality and abstractness that claim to lay bare the great secrets of History, the Political, the State, and Power' (*State, Power, Socialism*, Verso, London, 1980, p. 20). However, as later Marxists pointed out, Poulantzas somehow thought he could do this in the abstract, hardly referring to actually existing states to illustrate his general arguments.

10 Judith Allen, 'Does Feminism Need a Theory of "the State"?', in Sophie Watson (ed.), *Playing the State*, Verso, London, 1990, p. 22.

11 Bob Jessop, *State Theory*, Polity Press, Cambridge, 1990, p. 366.

12 Clyde Barrow, *Critical Theories of the State*, University of Wisconsin Press, Madison, WI. 1993, pp. 144–5.

13 Gilles Deleuze and Félix Guattari, *A Thousand Plateaus: Capitalism and Schizophrenia*, University of Minnesota Press, Minneapolis, 1991, p. 459.

14 Michel Foucault, 'Governmentality', in Graham Burchell, Colin Gordon, and Peter Miller (eds), *The Foucault Effect: Studies in Governmentality*, University of Chicago Press, Chicago, 1991, p. 104.

15 *Ibid.*, p. 103.

16 Jean Cohen and Andrew Arato, *Civil Society and Political Theory*, MIT Press, Cambridge, MA, 1992, pp. 280–6.

17 John Hinkson, 'The Postmodern State', in P. James (ed.), *The State in Question*, Allen & Unwin, Sydney, 1996.

18 Stephen Crook, Jan Pakulski and Malcolm Waters, *Postmodernization: Change in Advanced Society*, Sage, London, 1992, pp. 103–4.

19 Michael Mann, *The Sources of Social Power*: Vol. 1, *A History of Power from the Beginning to A.D. 1760*, Cambridge University Press, Cambridge, 1986, Chapters 3 and 4, with the one outstanding exception to this generalization being the Egyptians, 'the one near-unitary society in the ancient world' (p. 108).

20 Patricia Springborg, *Royal Persons: Patriarchal Monarchy and the Feminine Principle*, Unwin Hyman, London, 1990.

21 *The Scotsman*, 22 May 2000.

22 See Chapter 4 above, in the section entitled 'Reciprocity as the Dominant Mode of Exchange'. If this right, it explains why mythologies of kings bearing gifts, such as to Bethlehem, take on a double ambiguity, and in this case a spectacular condensation of meaning.

23 On the election of the king, see Arthur Taylor, *The Glory of Regality: An Historical Treatise on the Anointing and Crowning of the Kings and Queens of England*, Taylor, London, 1820, book 1. On the simultaneously sacred and secular foundations of kingship, see Reinhard Bendix, *Kings or People: Power and the Mandate to Rule*, University of California Press, Berkeley, CA, 1978, Chapter 2. This classical book, although written with different themes of focus to the present study, provides an overview of field of kingship with its empirical descriptions and careful generalizations providing an excellent counterpoint to my tendency to overgeneralize.

24 See D.L. Ashiman (ed.) *Folklore and Mythology* website, University of Pittsburgh, accessed 2003. There are published other tales of the Aarne-Thompson type 1620 about kings and images of 'invisibility' sourced from Sri Lanka, Turkey and India.

25 William Shakespeare, *Richard II*, Act II, Scene 2, cited in C.A. Bouman, *Sacring and Crowning: The Development of the Latin Ritual for Anointing Kings and the Coronation of an Emperor before the Eleventh Century*, J.B. Wolters, Gröningen, 1957, p. ix. The assertions of that statement did not, of course, mean that the sacredness of the monarch was unambiguously unassailable, but such statements nevertheless did continue well into the twentieth century. See, for example, Jocelyn Perkins (*The Crowning of the Sovereign of Great Britain and the Dominions Overseas*, Methuen, London, 1937, p. 15) where in describing the crowning of Edward VII in 1902, she says, 'the tie uniting King Edward VII to the hearts of his subjects was something more enduring, more sacred than had ever existed before'. However, keep in mind that at the time of writing she was the Sacrist of Westminster Abbey.

26 Bouman, *ibid.*, pp. 71ff.

27 Ellen Meiksins Wood, *The Pristine Culture of Capitalism: A Historical Essay on the Old Regimes and Modern States*, Verso, London, 1991, p. 48.

28 Anthony Giddens, *The Nation-State and Violence*, Polity Press, Cambridge, 1985, p. 83.

29 'Post-tribal history' in this instance is understood as particular histories rather than as a generic concept. It refers to the history of those particular societies that are no longer formed in the dominance of *tribalism*. Thus, for example, in parallel with the argument made earlier in relation to kings, states develop in tribal-traditional societies that develop some form of abstracting technique for recording and codifying memories such as listing or writing. Thus the mode of organization of the state depends upon a more abstract mode of communication than orality.

30 John Breuilly, *Nationalism and the State*, University of Chicago Press, Chicago, 2nd edn, 1994.

31 Anthony D. Smith, 'Memory and Modernity: Reflections on Ernest Gellner's Theory of Nationalism', *Nations and Nationalism*, vol. 2, no. 3, 1996, p. 386.

32 Anthony Smith, *The Ethnic Origins of Nations*, Basil Blackwell, Oxford, 1986, p. 131.

33 *Ibid.*, p. 134.

34 Benedict Anderson, *Imagined Communities*, Verso, London, 2nd edn, 1991, p. 36.

35 Graham Burchell, Colin Gordon, and Peter Miller (eds), *The Foucault Effect: Studies in Governmentality*, University of Chicago Press, Chicago, 1991.

36 On the abstraction of print and its relation to intellectual practice see Geoff Sharp, 'The Idea of the Intellectual and After', in Simon Cooper, John Hinkson and Geoff Sharp (eds), *Scholars and Entrepreneurs*, Arena Publications, Melbourne, 2002.

# TEN Nation Formation

## From the Medieval to the Postmodern

Just as the nation-state did not die at the end of the twentieth century – despite premature claims about its imminent demise – its emergence as a social form in the nineteenth century was not a creation *ex nihilo* and immediate. Social forms such as these can only be understood in the long run of world history and in relation to the changing matrix of social practice and categorization. This chapter suggests that nationalism, the nation and the nation-state can only be fully understood in terms of the slow and emerging dominance of more abstract social relations across all the modes of practice from communication to enquiry, and across all modes of categorization, including time, space and embodiment. It is the galloping and overt dominance of these very processes of abstract structuring – experienced as global flows of capital and culture – that, ironically, is giving rise to the sense that the nation and nation-state face an impending crisis, and that the social whole is collapsing into fragments. However, this does not mean that the nation as a form of community is about to disappear. In fact, national identity is being vigorously reasserted, whether it is in the classically-modern form of a million soldiers massing on the India-Pakistan border or as autonomous individuals walking the postmodern streets of Hip Hop Nation. Nations, like other post-tribal territorial communities, are changing fundamentally – with the placement and relationship between persons at the level of the face-to-face becoming more contingent and fragmented – but rather than becoming anachronistic vestiges of a passing world, nations are becoming more contradictorily stretched between traditional, modern and postmodern ways of living.

Although the narrative of the chapter will not follow a straight line, the underlying propositions, expanding upon those in the previous chapter, provide points of guidance:

*Proposition 1.* Polities and communities, once formed as networks of association between known persons, became increasingly abstract across history in an uneven process of world-historical change. The modern nation as the pre-eminent form of abstract community of the past two centuries was, and is, held together by relations of disembodied extension. From the beginning it was structured by abstracted modes of practice in the context of an increasingly-globalized world, however, this abstraction has intensified and generalized in the current period while its contradictions have become increasingly stark.

*Proposition 2.* The conjunction of nations and states first occurred during the period of heightening modern globalization. In other words, modern nation formation and modern global formation were born during the same period out of the same processes – that is, through the same abstracting modes of practice. This simple historical reality should at least give pause to those who would argue that globalization is in *essential* opposition to the nation-state.

*Proposition 3.* Just as the nation-state is not about to disappear, this kind of community-polity did not suddenly appear in history. There is no first nation-state, no first nation, and there is no date that marks the beginning of the nation-state or the nation as a social formation. The best that we can say is that a small motley collection of modern republics and constitutional monarchies emerged as system of self-conscious nations and nation-states in the late-eighteenth and early-nineteenth centuries, and that this collection had consolidated by the beginning of the twentieth as the dominant system of polity-communities.

*Proposition 4.* Across the globe, nation formation as we know it developed with the changing modes of practice associated with the dominance of modernism, however, though modern nations are modern constructions (note the apparent tautology) they are not simply so. Nation formation involves *both* deep continuities and radical discontinuities with traditional and sacredly conceived ways of life. This is easier to say than to theorize.

Making these arguments precise in their most general expression thus involves going in two simultaneous directions. The first is to suggest that the discontinuity can be understood as a process of objective abstraction and reconstitution of prior ways of living in and understanding community and polity. The second direction runs alongside the first but emphasizes the subjective continuity. It suggests that the nation as an abstract community of strangers – secular and horizontal – contradictorily *grounds* its subjectivities in the very categories that at another level of abstraction have been substantially reconstituted. Three such grounding categories are particularly relevant here: relations of embodied connection, times of sacred or secular-condensed recollection, and places of enduring nature. The use of the concept of *grounding* here is intentional. It marks a clear distinction from the prominent modernist theorists of nationalism such as Ernest Gellner, Anthony Giddens, and even Benedict Anderson, who tend to treat these categorical elements as the mere traditional *content*, refabricated for a modern context.[1] By contrast, I am suggesting that these things still have categorical meaning as part of the contradictory form of the nation-state as an abstract political community. This continuity has become clearer as the modern connection between nation and state has become problematized. In the contemporary world, I argue, embedded ontological categories have continuing significance for the nation, even as such evocations become less and less relevant to the state.

## Across the traditional–modern divide

Whereas in the last chapter we focused upon the question of nation-*state* formation, we now turn to elaborate the problem of explaining *nation* formation, its changing form and its various contradictions. This section carries forward the discussion from the last chapter on the relationship between traditionalism and modernism; second, it questions the notion of 'territorial nation' and 'ethnic nation' even as ideal types: and, third, it elaborates upon the critique made earlier of those theorists who still pose the idea of Europe as the 'blueprint' for postcolonial nation formation.

The traditionalism–modernism question continues to dominate the literature; however, there has been little progress beyond the debates over deep ethnic origins versus fabricated modern structurings. The most revealing example of this debate is that between Ernest Gellner and Anthony Smith in the pages of *Nations and Nationalism*,[2] but in the end it did not get anywhere. On the one hand, radical modernists overplay the break between traditional and modern societies. When Ernest Gellner says that nationalism was possible only through the changes wrought by modern industrialism, the evidence suggests that his theory is more applicable to the nation-state than to the nation as a long-run but fundamentally-changing form of community. On the other hand, ethno-symbolists tend to give a descriptive and factorial account of the continuities, without providing us with a way of theorizing the discontinuities. When Anthony Smith says that the basis of the modern nation is usually a long-run ethnic community, the genealogical accuracy of his position depends upon treating the national recovery of a unified ethnic past as a one-dimensional matter of retrieving symbolic content. It missed out on the matter of subjectivity being unevenly reconstituted in the context of changing social form. When Benedict Anderson says that the nation has to be understood in terms of the faltering grip of the great religious communities upon people's imagination, what he is describing is the rise of a subjectivity of *modern* national reflexivity – not the full sense of nation formation as it simultaneously carries forward and reworks traditionally-located subjectivities. Hence, the fifth summarizing argument of the chapter can be expressed as follows:

> *Proposition 5.* Rather than replacing traditionalism in a revolutionary and epochal shift, modernism emerged unevenly and across a long period of change and upheaval as the dominant ontological formation.

As any area-specialist would understand, there is a deep and contradictory relationship between traditionalism and modernism, both in the past and in all contemporary national societies. The current 'revival' of nationalistic Islam in Aceh, for example carries all these tensions. The 1976 Achenese Declaration of Independence carries an archetypical modernist claim for a primordial past:

> We, the people of Acheh, Sumatra, exercising our right of self-determination, and protecting our historic right of eminent domain to our fatherland, do hereby declare ourselves free and independent from all political control of the foreign regime of Jakarta and the alien people of the Island of Java. Our fatherland Acheh, Sumatra, had always been a free and independent sovereign State since the world began.[3]

There you have it: a modernist argument for an essentialism of traditional identity, one that contradictorily cuts straight across the rational interpretative relativism of the modernist mode of inquiry. Modernist claims for the deep continuity of nations are rarely now made in such stark primordialist terms – 'since the world began' – nevertheless even when historical/primordial claims come mediated by more rationalized enquiry they still tend to look back to a pre-modern continuous past. For example, for their rendition of the Acehnese chronology showing that their nation began before the colonial incursion, the writers for the *atjehtimes.com* website draw upon the *Encyclopedia Britannica* and the populist *Encarta Encyclopedia*. Without a notion of levels – that is overlaying levels of tribalism, traditionalism, modernism, and most recently postmodernism – the problems of explaining this intersecting set of contradictory claims to knowledge remain intractable.

As an abstract community, at least in the form that we currently understand it, the nation calls back upon the embodied subjectivities of more traditional forms of community, including traditional 'ethnic' community (or *ethnie* in Smith's terms); however, it only comes into being under conditions of the emerging dominance of modernism. To make more sense of the question, let us shift the terms of the debate to the theme of genealogy. Ernest Gellner would rightly say that it is rare for nations to be seen as objectively connected by a verifiable genealogy linking the whole society – the act of census data-collection just documents the already-existent civil nation and in*corporates* ethnicity as one marker of modern nationality. This is true; however, that is not the point. Community beyond the immediacies of family is never formed along one to-one bloodlines. Even persons set within tribalism do not understand extended genealogies in that way.

The examples of the genealogical mapping of nations give an indication of what *is* important. The nineteenth-century author of the *Scottish Nation*,[4] a limited-edition genealogy of the 'great families' of the Scotland, confides to his dear readers that his compilation, more than just a collection of names and immediate forebears, perhaps represents the true nation. After all, Scotland has only a small population, he says – spoken like a true national aristocrat, leaving out all those of no station or standing. Ethnic completeness is an afterthought to that author, not the purpose that drove the mapping. It confirmed what he already knew, a truth that is not really helped by empirical verification. Compare this to the listing of names read by children related to those who died in the September 11 terrorist attack on the New York Twin Towers. In 2003 the reading took three hours. There was no sense that this list represented everybody in the United States, but at the same time the names are both individuals and representatives of the nation.

An equally-complicated example comes from Somalia where, according to Islamic tradition, the whole of the nation is linked by one intricate genealogical tree. However, when Abdalla Omar Mansur sets out to interrogate the authenticity of such a claim by looking at its epistemological logic, he completely misunderstands the nature of this mythology.[5] It does not matter that different tribal groupings have different narrative versions of the creation story of the stranger coming down from the sacred tree, or that the Qur'anic version links the motif of the man in the tree to Moses whereas others do not. What we have here is an intersection of tribal forms of enquiry (including the Daarood and Ajuuran clans) and traditional forms of enquiry and knowledge (the Islamic religion), together with modern nation formation (the Somali nation). The tree from which the ancestor-king descends is both mythological and doubly abstracted. It is abstracted as an icon – the sacred tree, sycamore – and as the genealogical tree that can be memorized graphically or drawn as lines on paper: an abstract but lived *tableau* (see Chapter 4 above).

In this way the modern nation can leave genealogical placement behind or carry traditional genealogical placement to a further level of abstraction – and carry it, it most often does. National genealogy can thus bear two forms of truth: old and new, traditional and modern. Persons can believe as *practical consciousness* that the mythology is, in the tribal or traditional sense, *true*, and at the same time, if pressed, accept as *reflexive consciousness* that nations are not literally held together as a single documentable tree of blood-by-birth. Moreover, even at a reflexive level the categories of life and death continue to inhere in the modern nation. They do so not as the putatively kinship-based idea of a single founding family[6] but as the ideas of living in the territorial place of one's forebears and at times of crisis self-actively putting one's life on the line for one's nation. The verities of blood and soil become the metaphors of the modern nation, and these metaphors, though not so directly expressed as under Adolf Hitler's Germany, continue to permeate the language of even the most civic of nation-states.

A tragic contemporary example is the discourses of the martyrs/suicide bombers of Palestine as they confront the modern militarized state of Israel. Anthony Smith would say that this shows that a *specific* ethnic embodiment is often important to the sense of nationhood. And of course in many cases – though not including Indonesia, Singapore, Australia, Canada, the United States of America and others – he would also be right. However, it tells us little about the structural changes, objective and subjective, that make ethnicity a symbolic marker to be drawn upon in nation formation. By contrast, I have been pressing to have these themes of traditionalism and modernism understood in terms of an argument about ontological formations as unevenly layered across each other, rather than as epochal replacements of prior formations. The themes of extended genealogies and abstract bloodlines point to the continuities and discontinuities across different ontological formations, and it suggests that a levels argument might provide a way out of the 'ethnic roots/modern structures' dilemma.

There are methodological traps here for the unwary. The most obvious trap is to treat the constitutive foundations of tribalism and traditionalism as *the* basis of the modern (contradictory) nation. This, in other words, entails forgetting a primary insight of comparative social theory: nations are not tribes, even if tribes can become nations. (We'll come back to this issue in the next two sections on Rwanda and the United States.) By the same argument, ethnicity is not *the* basis of the modern nation. Moreover, 'ethnicity' is itself a modern phenomenon, not a pre-modern expression of genealogical connection. That is why Anthony Smith has to use the French term *ethnie* rather than 'ethnic community'. 'Ethnicity', in the argument of this chapter, is the modern name given to *one* way of subjectively embedding the more abstract relations of the modern nation in more concrete ontological categories of embodiment, temporality and spatiality. Ethnicity is important and relates to subject/objective relations of embodiment, but it is not so important that it warrants lifting above other ontological categories such as tradition and future common fate (temporality) or place and territory-in-common (spatiality). Modern empire-nations as diverse as Indonesia and the United States are cases where issues of temporality and spatiality have been officially emphasized over and above questions of ethnicity. This relates to a further major issue on which this chapter departs from the mainstream writings, the question of the relationship between ethnicity and territory.

> *Proposition 6.* The distinction between territoriality and ethnicity is useful, but the distinction between 'territorial nation' (Western) and 'ethnic nation' (Eastern) collapses into a heap of qualifications.

There is a tendency, following a long tradition from Hans Kohn onwards, to treat the analytic distinction between 'territorial nations' and 'ethnic nations' as the basis of two distinct models of nation formation. This leads to a tortured narrative about the sequence of nation formation. In this story, first came the 'territorial nations' in the West. Supposedly, for some unspecified time, territoriality formed the only concept of the nation. Then, those European states found that it only worked if they also developed a shared culture of myths and symbols. Alongside this development but more gradually there emerged ethnic nations on the basis of pre-existing ethnic ties: Germany, which was also a bit territorial; and Eastern Europe and the Middle East, more prominently ethnic. Later, when the political elites of Asia and Africa decided to create nations, they first tried the Western model, but were compelled then by the 'logic of the situation to form new myths and symbols'.

Who were these first 'territorial nations' that could take their ethnic elements for granted? First, it should be said, going back to the discussion of the previous chapter, that they were territorial *states*, not territorial *nations*. Second, these states could take ethnicity for granted before the nineteenth century because ethnicity as distinct from blood ties (genealogy) was not for anyone at that time an active category of self-identification. The 'ethnic revival' was not a revival. The new positive use of the concept of 'ethnicity' occurred in these states *as* they became nation-states. If we take one of the oft-used examples, the French, we find an amalgam of cultures and regions (*ethnies* if you like, but only as a retrospective appellation) brought together through changing modes of practice across the nineteenth century. Discussed at the level of empirical generalization, nation formation was evidenced in such apparently banal processes as military conscription (beginning in the late eighteenth century), railways (from the 1850s), compulsory and secular education (from the early 1880s) and the generalization of print distribution and radio broadcast from the end of the century. However, even despite the self-conscious territorial organization of the nation-state it was not until the beginning of the twentieth century that this could be taken for granted. Even then we can list the continuing ethnic-territorial cultures that could have become nation-states: (1) the Burgundians in eastern France, a people of Scandinavian origin whose language had died out since their incorporation in the French state at the end of the fifteenth century, but who have carried forth a regional identity to the present day; (2) the Basques from the south-west border of France and Spain who have asserted for themselves the national legitimacy of a government of Euskadi; (3) the Bretons, from the north-west peninsular of France, who revived the Breton language at the end of the nineteenth century as a response to Francification, not the other way round; (4) the Provençals, who still use the language of Occitan or *langue d'oc*, though as a private rather than public language, and sustain a sense of cultural difference through folk revivals and tourism; (5) the Corsicans, who from the late-1960s have sponsored strong movements for regional autonomy or semi-autonomy; and (6) the Catalans, from the south-east border of France and Spain (including Andorra), who still feel a strong cultural, though not political, nationalism drawing upon the distinct and old language of Catalan.

This tendency to treat patchwork Western territorial states such as France as if they were already territorial nations is related to a tendency to treat the features of being a nation as intrinsically Western. This is simply a category mistake. There is nothing about the notions of 'territoriality' or 'political culture' or 'legal codes', for example, that makes them 'Western'. Certainly the dominant Western mode of organization involves a certain form of abstract territoriality and sovereignty over the landscape, however the absolutist states (or what some writers too easily calls 'the nations') of England and France did this by virtue of their transition to modern forms of juridical framing – not by virtue of being 'Western'.

We only have to compare these to the approaches to territory and culture in the 'Eastern' state of Japan to see how shaky the categories become.[7] Japan, like China, had long been a territorial state with established legal codes and conceptions of sovereignty. The Tokugawa modernizing revolution of the late-nineteenth century was certainly influenced in part by Western-educated intellectuals, but it also restored the traditional emperor as the essence of the national polity, or *kokutai*. This carries through our theme of the contradiction of traditionalism and modernism.

> *Proposition 7.* European expansion, in the context of fundamental shifts in the modes of practice, was fundamental to nation formation, but this does not mean that Europe provided the blueprint for nation-state formation.

When some writers argue that the earliest cases of territorial nations were in the West – England, France, Spain, the Netherlands, and later Russia – there is a further question of analytical anachronism here that needs to be addressed. So far I have argued that though these polities were certainly long-run territorial entities that later became nations, it does not make them continuous nations, or at least it does not make them nations back then. It should, however, be said that there *were* 'nations' prior to the nineteenth century, but they were not nation-states, and they were not 'territorial nations' as such. As a short-hand response to the existence of nations prior to the nation-state, the different 'stages' in the history of nations, nationalism and nation-states can be set out as a series of moments:

1. The concept of *natio* existed in the medieval period and earlier, but it meant something completely different from the modern sense of the word 'nation': first, in archaic definitions the concept of *natio* was used as coextensive with 'tribe' (or what has been referred to as *ethnie*); secondly, it referred to *traditional* communities of erstwhile strangers who found common purpose with each other under conditions of being lifted out of their locales into new settings of face-to-face *interaction*. This occurred in places such as monasteries, universities and military barracks. The only commonality in this second case with the *modern nation* is that these communities – groups that we can *traditional nations*, assuming all the unusual ontological weight that the adjective 'traditional' has to carry in this context – were abstracted communities forced to examine basic issues of embodiment, temporality and spatiality. They were communities of fate but they were not territorial nations.

2. From the sixteenth century in England, and to a lesser extent in other places such as the Netherlands, the concept of the 'nation' went through a stage of politicization. However, it was associated with the genealogically-connected, aristocratic ruling classes or the emergent groupings of *men* of learning, the new intellectually trained of a country or region. Despite the

language of 'nation'-ness, the predominant political structure remained from the top firmly that of *traditional* kingdom or empire, and from the bottom, village or parish. The unwashed masses did not care to be part of any putative nation, nor were they invited to be so. In this third manifestation of traditional communities of common fate, *traditional nations* were territorial only to the extent that they were coextensive sometimes with kingdoms, sometimes counties, and sometimes empires.

3   From the late-eighteenth century we started to get intellectual and political creeds about the 'nationalism' as European philosophers, theologians, poets, composers and artists 'discovered' the concept. However, as I have been implicitly arguing, naming the thing does mean that the thing is exclusive to the places that first name it. Nevertheless, this period marked the rise of *modern* nationalism as a self-conscious European philosophy.

4   The late-eighteenth to mid-nineteenth centuries saw the emergence of explicitly nationalist movements in the Americas, Europe and parts of Asia. These movements rose *before* most of the old absolutist states, kingdoms and empires began to see themselves as territorial nations.[8] This simple fact is an important challenge to the idea of pre-nineteenth century, pre-nationalist territorial nation-states.

5   Across the nineteenth century across the world, public spheres developed that broadened beyond the court or town square. This development occurred in association with different ideologies of public sovereignty, democracy or national citizenship, and was an important ideological backdrop to the still emerging nation-state system. They depended upon a changing mode of communication that drew a reading public into political consequence.

6   It was not until the late-nineteenth-century that the uneasy conjunction of national citizenry and abstract state really became established, forming in some cases what can be now called the classical *modern* nation-states. It is important to remember that the old empires carried through into the next century as viable polities.

7   The short twentieth century featured the 'great wars' of territorial nationalism, and the liberation movements of *modern* tribalism and neo-traditionalism. During this period new nation-states emerged in the African and Asian Third World, but they also formed in Europe including Yugoslavia, and its subsequent breakaways.

8   The late-twentieth century and early twenty-first century saw the rise of a new subjectivity of nationalism – postmodern nationalism – where the emphasis moved to an aesthetic of choice. While there may still be no postmodern nations as such, during this period, particularly in the West, postmodern subjectivities of ephemeral intensity came to overlay the continuing modern foundations of the contemporary nation.

The first point to draw from this genealogy is that the history of nation formation is one of continuity *and* discontinuity. *Traditional* national sentiment is qualitatively different in many fundamental respects from the *modern* nationalism of horizontal and generalized compatriotism.

Nevertheless, despite this difference, is it a subjectivity that demands a broader explanation of nation formation than the modernist theorists currently allow. In the sense in which I am using these terms, modern nationalism is associated with a self-conscious politicization of the relation between community and polity, usually with the desire for a state for one's nation, whereas traditional national sentiment has no such associations. On the other hand, modern and traditional national subjectivities are related in that they both entail a process through which persons are, *at one level*, lifted out of the integral connections of face-to-face community, and abstracted from messianic time and sacred place (see Chapter 7). It is this process that enables certain persons still living within the ontological formation of traditionalism – namely. intellectuals, clerics, and poets – to name territorialized places or genealogically-connected peoples as a distinct and demarcated entities, bounded in territorial space and historical time, and separable from other such similar entities.

The second point is that this chapter parts company with any implicit argument in the mainstream literature that Europe provided the blueprint for modern nation formation, except in regard of the philosophical naming of the idea of nationalism. One step in this revision is to qualify fundamentally any implication that Europe is *the* birthplace of the nation-state. Certainly, as has already acknowledged above, Europe was central to the emergent system of capitalist production and exchange relations that through imperial expansion affected fundamental changes in the societies of the 'periphery'. These changes became the context for the first wave of emergent nation-states in the nineteenth century.[9] However, even in relation to the last wave of Third World nation-states we have to be careful, for example, of too quickly agreeing with Benedict Anderson's emphasis on the export of the *idea* of nationalism when he draws attention to the surface phenomenon that 'twentieth century nationalisms have a profoundly modular character'.[10] In one sense, it is a useful description. However, questions remain: why, and in what way, was the blueprint of the civil nation-state taken up? (I'll come back to this question shortly.) Moreover, we need to ask whether in fact it is the case that the Western European nation-states simply came first as a model to copy.

The context to this concern is a prevalent Eurocentrism in the literature. Ernest Gellner is so Eurocentric in his approach that when he sets up a political geography of nation-state formation it begins with Western Europe – though without needing to name it as such – and moves eastward across a series of spatial-temporal stages without ever leaving a European (Eurasian) continent that begins with France and ends with the Russian empire. Greater Europe is thus the assumed setting of all nation-state formation. Gellner's 'final stage' of nationalism – completely ignoring colonial nationalisms in Southeast Asia and Africa that occurred well before the more recent ethnic revival in Eastern Europe – begins in 1945 and involves the defeat of the 'romantic cult' of ethnicity and the convergence of mass culture around consumption-based prosperity and self-satisfaction.[11] Anthony Giddens is just as explicit: 'The European state system', he says, 'was not simply the "political environment" in which the absolutist state and the nation-state developed. It was the condition, and in substantial degree the very source of that development'.[12]

Examples that qualify the focus on Europe as the proximate source of the nation-state are not hard to find. As I wrote in *Nation Formation*, profoundly influenced by Benedict Anderson's thesis on the nations of the new world, the Thirteen States in North America had instituted the internal pacification of its indigenous inhabitants; they had fought a war of independence against a European power which brandished absolutist doctrines of the indivisibility of sovereignty (1775–1781); they had worked out a system for parcelling, commodifying and administering the 'empty' frontier territories; and, in the name of the People of the United States, had ratified a unifying constitution (1789) – all before the August Days of 1789 saw Louis XVI's *ancien régime* brought to an end by his erst-while royal subjects. If we travel south to the colonies of Spanish America, Anderson asks: 'why was it precisely *creole* communities that developed so early conceptions of their nation-ness – *well before most of Europe?*'[13] The apparent anachronism cannot be explained through a straightforward diffusionist or modular argument. I would argue that the gradual and uneven consolidation in Europe, and elsewhere, of developments that framed the transition from the imperial or monarchical state to the abstract state, also contributed to a changed world-time, a changed constitutive setting in which across the globe, and bearing back upon Europe, states and peoples began to assert their political and cultural identity. In short, nation-states were formed in the over-determined and uneven context of modern globalization. This, I suggest, was the generalizing frame for the formation of nation-states, both in Europe and elsewhere. Even the nation-states that were formed later during the second wave of decolonization after the late 1950s could not simply copy the Western blueprint. The decolonizing communities may have been pressed to take up what was by then a global model, but the more important issue was a globalizing pressure of social change that was integrated and accommodated from within. In other words, as the nature of the dominant layer of their internal societies changed, modern nation-state status was contradictorily naturalized: at one level as an expression of a traditional continuity, and at another as an expression of modern progress and complete discontinuity.

## In the context of empire

A further step in distancing the present argument from the idea of a Western blueprint or 'modular export' approach involves examining the process of how the colonies responded to the imposition of a modernizing administration. In explaining how the development of nationalism in Spanish America could arise earlier than in the heartlands of Europe, Benedict Anderson describes a manifold process that helps us to qualify his own 'modular' argument. In the first place, creole administrators, clerically-trained men (women were excluded) who were often white but born in the Americas, found themselves as administrators on common 'journeys' that took them across time, status and place. In the language of the present chapter, through a new rationalizing mode of organization they were abstracted from relations of traditional embodied temporality and spatiality. Moreover, unlike European and East Asian feudal nobles who ascended genealogically, or absolutist 'men of learning' and Confucian functionaries who climbed through talent, the creole functionaries of the New World climbed to a certain level only to find themselves barred vertically and horizontally. They shared the embodied cultural-racial marks of trans-Atlantic birth, bound within the geographical limit of their particular colony, but unable to be masters of it. Finally, in the context of a changed mode of communication in intersection with capitalist trade relations, they began to imagine themselves as a horizontal community. My condensed description of the process may not be immediately clear, however, Anderson presents it with a brilliantly lucid word-picture:

> Early gazettes contained – aside from news about the metropole – commercial news (when ships would arrive and depart, what prices were current for what commodities in what ports), as well as colonial political appointments, marriages of the wealthy, and so forth. In other words, what brought together on the same page, *this* marriage with *that* ship, *this* price with *that* bishop, was the structure of the colonial administration and market-system itself. In this way, the newspaper of Caracas quite naturally, even apolitically, created an imagined community among a specific assemblage of fellow-readers, to whom *these* ships, brides, bishops, and prices belong.[14]

This description provides us with the means of qualifying Anderson's own claim about modularity. However, I want to emphasize that it is only a qualifying and a resetting of the argument, not a rejection. I say this because Partha Chatterjee, the theorist whose work I intend to use to carry my argument one step further is more critical of Anderson than is warranted. Chatterjee rightly describes Anderson as problematically setting up three distinct and chronologically-ordered models of nationalism: (1) creole nationalism in the Americas; (2) linguistic or so-called 'popular' nationalism in Europe; and (3) official nationalism in Europe. It is from the third variant that nationalism develops a modular quality that in the twentieth century can be drawn on by the Third World. Chatterjee concludes that:

> instead of pursuing the varied, and often contradictory, *political* possibilities inherent in this process, Anderson seals up his theme with a sociological determinism ... What, if we look closely, are the substantive differences between Anderson and Gellner on twentieth century nationalism? None ... In the end both see in third-world nationalisms a profoundly 'modular' character. They are invariably shaped according to the contours outlined by given historical models: 'objective, inescapable, imperative'.[15]

Here Chatterjee has overstated his objection to Anderson, particularly given our earlier discussion about the importance of his work on endogenous structural processes such as the journeys of the creole elites. Nevertheless, Chatterjee's critique of most modernist theory, including that of Anthony Smith and Ernest Gellner, is telling. On political grounds, it challenges the liberal modernist approach as treating Third World colonial resistance and postcolonial politics as pre-determined by a universalizing modern West. And on factual grounds, he criticizes the approach for misreading the nature and timing of nationalism as it developed in Africa and Asia. For example, during the second half of the nineteenth century a new elite-driven education system was developed across Bengal (not too dissimilar to the examples of Japan and Germany in the 1870s). Thus, the beginning of *modern* and *public-political* Indian nationalism was marked symbolically by the formation in 1885 of the Indian National Congress. At this point he adds a subtle and unexpected twist. We might have expected him to say that the mainstream position forgets that the process parallels the timing in much of Europe when it argues that Indian nationalism is said to have emerged *after* the period of modernization and 'social reform' from the 1820s to 1870s. On this he would have been right, but he sets out to establish a much more difficult and important point, one that allows us to illustrate the 'levels' argument left hanging a couple of paragraphs ago.

Chatterjee comes to argue that 'anti-colonial nationalism' develops culturally long before its overt political manifestations.[16] It does so by dividing social life into two domains: first, the (traditional) spiritual or the 'inner' domain of deep cultural identity – language, religion, family. It is at this *level* that we see the earliest resistance to the intervention of the colonial state, and later the reinterpretation of the nature of the traditional spiritual domain in national terms: subaltern politics becomes more than 'numerous fragmented resistances'. The second domain is the 'outside' (modern) domain of economy, state and science. For the indigenous intellectually-trained groupings, this involved study and imitation of the acknowledged Western 'superiority', including 'its' notions of rule of Law and State. Later, drawing upon the resources of Western Enlightenment universalism, they challenged colonialism and its differentiation between the outsiders as rulers and indigenous peoples as ruled, thus completing the project of the modern state. These two domains, or what I would call the two ontological formations of traditionalism and modernism, were in a contradictory relationship, though with mutual historicities and interwoven practices. In the histories of the late-nineteenth century written by Bengali scholars, the narrative style located in 'homogenous empty time' was interwoven with mythic and sacred time. Concurrently, the bilingual intelligentsia embarked upon a cultural project to make Bengali a standardized language outside the influence of the state, and in doing so they wove together two versions: a formal and standardized prose influenced by European syntax, and a poetic idiom self-consciously drawing upon 'rustic' Indian preachers and philosophers. Thus, says Chatterjee:

> In fact here nationalism launches its most powerful, creative and historically significant project: to fashion a 'modern' national culture that is nevertheless not Western. If the nation is an imagined community, then this is where it is brought into being. In this its true and essential domain, the nation is already sovereign, even when the state is in the hands of the colonial power.[17]

Much more could be done to draw out the implications of both Anderson's and Chatterjee's work for the argument being developed here – for example, through the work of Ashis Nandy[18] – however, enough has been said to indicate that the emphasis of the present chapter is as much on social form as it is on social content. This takes us back to where we started: Anthony Smith's attempt to find an intermediate position between the two problematic positions of theoretical modernism and primordialism. However, as this chapter has been concerned to argue, the trouble with his intermediation is that it has significant costs. Smith effectively gives up on the possibility of a broad theory of nation formation and emphasizes what he calls the driving force of *mythomoteur* with specifically 'ethnic' content. This takes away from the deeply-materialist sense of the basis of identity formation and puts the emphasis primarily on ideas that can be dredged up from the past.

To summarize the discussion thus far, I want to suggest that despite obvious differences, there were patterned and materially-based similarities in the formation of nations, Western and Eastern, First World, Second World and Third World. First, nation formation involved a predominant, if uneven, shift in the nature of each society based upon changes in the dominant modes of practice – production, exchange, communication, organization and enquiry – not just the taking up of an imported idea. This is not to suggest that change was comprehensive, that it involved the reconstitution of all those modes of practice, or that it permeated all the way down to day-to-day life of all people. Whether we are talking about the Netherlands and Portugal or Indonesia and East Timor, older modes of practice continue(d) long after nation-state status was declared.

Second, it involved an abstraction from traditional social relations through such processes as cultural upheaval, geographical mobility and education. Thus the difference of emphasis between different theorists on different actors – Anderson on the importance of local 'creoles', Nairn on 'intellectuals' and Gellner on 'clerks' or what I was generically calling earlier, following Geoff Sharp, the 'intellectually trained' – can be understood in this common framework where the process of forming abstract communities can take many pathways on the same map. Third, nation formation is rarely based upon a homogenous population, even if mythologies of common ethnic connection are forged. This has the effect of qualifying rather than rejecting Smith's argument. It is important to remember that whether we are talking about France, the United States, East Timor or West Papua, nations were, and are, being quilted together out of patchworks of culturally-distinct peoples. Fourth, nation formation is rarely consensual, even if it does over a couple of generations become deeply constitutive of social identity. In this, Rwanda and India, Britain and the United States have much in common, even if the violence had different expressions, different adversaries and different ideological rationales.

I want to take the discussion further through two case studies: the first examining the formation of the tragic nation-state of Rwanda in global-colonial context; the second tracking the formation of a nation-state out of the republic of the United States of America. This simultaneously allows us to follow up an earlier theme. At the beginning of *Globalism, Nationalism, Tribalism*, I began to ask questions about how abstracted communities of identity – the nation, and even the *modern* tribe when it too becomes a post-genealogical community – could generate such powerful embodied personal and social loyalties unto death. This is a continuation of that theme. It is crucial to understanding one dimension of the sources of insecurity in the contemporary world.

## The (dis)continuities of tribalism in a postcolonial nation-state

Understanding what happened in Rwanda across the course of the twentieth century, leading to the period of genocide and beyond, entails looking at much more than the empirical particulars of unfolding events. One dimension of patterned change involves the colonial polity and the way in which traditional processes of communal identity were simultaneously institutionalized as modern (legitimized) and as traditional or customary. In other words, as part of the global extension of colonialism to Africa in the late-nineteenth and early-twentieth centuries the very nature of tribal difference was reconstituted. Although in relative terms nineteenth-century Rwanda was linguistically and culturally interconnected – and this makes the explanation harder – it was nevertheless divided into three main 'tribal' groupings: the majority Hutu, the Tutsi (officially, a minority of 9 per cent of the total population before the massacre), and tiny group called the Tua.

Understanding the relevance of this apparently unremarkable constitution of identity for the coming genocide, involves understanding how the nature of cultural division was hardened, and thus fundamentally changed by colonial edict long before that period. The pre-colonial polity, or at least one layer of it, was from the end of the eighteenth century a highly-centralized kingdom based upon the semi-sacredness of its leaders – as far as we know, all pastoralists.[19] Only in the nineteenth century as the identities of pastoralist and Tutsi became synonymous did this become a double domination: pastoral aristocracy over agriculturalists and Tutsi over Hutu (and Tua). However, even then a process called *kwihutura* qualified the boundary between Tutsi and Hutu. It allowed the possibility, through accrual of pastoral wealth, of leaving behind Hutuness and becoming a Tutsi. Under German and then Belgian rule, Tutsi identity, associated with traditional power, and Hutu identity, associated with subjection, were made into a strict caste-like division. Identity cards were issued and the Belgians used the traditional structure of chiefdom as the apparatus of (savage) mediated administration.

As Mahmood Mamdani subtly argues, the colonial state depended on this meshing of the modern and traditional: 'these powers were justified as "customary", and custom was proclaimed by the very authority sanctioned by the colonial power as "customary". This tautology was crystallized in the legal institutions.'[20] The European power thus ruled through the Tutsi, now a modern tribe-caste-class[21] who at the same time looked to embodied expressions of their 'essential' difference: greater height, longer noses and so on – and thus at one level continued to treat themselves as tribes in the old way.[22] As I began to argue in Chapter 1, the fixing of tribal identity involved modernization, as both sides, colonial and native, called for different reasons upon the subjectivity of customary continuity.

Before moving to the second point, one issue has to be made clear. While it is my argument that precolonial 'Rwanda' included a complex polity framed by what has been defined most broadly as *traditionalism* intersecting with *tribalism* this is not to imply that traditional leaders were themselves completely quarantined from processes of modernization, or that they did not use both tribal and modern influences to their own ends. In the late-nineteenth and the early-twentieth centuries, the 'newly-redefined Tutsi aristocracy' was sensitive to the modern 'scientific' confirmations that could be put up as evidence of their noble heritage. This parallels the way that the nineteenth-century Kings of Siam used modern cartography to confirm their place in the world. In attempting to use modern methods to stave off incursions the British on their borders they inadvertently reconstituted their traditional kingdom as an abstract nation.[23] 'Even today, amongst exiled Tutsi, the myth of Egyptian origins still survives in the heads of people who are now its victims after having thought they were its beneficiaries.'[24] As Gérard Prunier adds, the story of Rwanda's past became 'closer to H. Rider Haggard's realm of heroic fantasy in *King Solomon's Mines* that to the humbler realities of a small East African Kingdom'.[25] The story also belied the complexity of the situation. Small though it may have been, Rwanda was as complex as any comparable *traditional* European kingdom. In the nineteenth century, King Rujugira institutionalized the integrating tribal-traditional cosmology of Ryangombe (the Lord of the Spirits, thought to be of Hutu origin) into the royal court and set up army corporations with enduring institutional identity (some of which were Hutu).[26]

The second related point of explanation is simple but important. With independence from the Belgians in 1962, and after a short period of formal power-sharing, the hierarchy of power was reversed. The global community had deemed that democracy was the best immediate form of rule to be instituted in Rwanda, and this time by the weight of civic numbers the Hutu assumed administrative power. However, the colonial cultural heritage carried through into the new nation-state, with the Hutu still feeling that oppressive weight of traditional-modern history. This resentment was confirmed by an invasion by two or three hundred Tutsi refugees from Burundi. It was called the 'invasion of the cockroaches'. Politically-driven country-wide killings of targeted Tutsi followed, with global bodies such as the United Nations reporting between 1,000 and 14,000 deaths. Thus, as the newly-independent polity attempted to achieve what the development theorists of the time called 'nation-building', a run of return pogroms began. In 1988 a Hutu uprising in the north of neighbouring Burundi was followed by mass killings of Hutu; and, in 1990, Tutsi militia from Uganda invaded as the Rwandan Patriotic Front.[27] From this bloody history, some tentative conclusions can be drawn. The months of April and May 1994 were horrific, but 1994 was 'only' the most horrific episode of the many such episodes of violence that arose in the context of globally-mediated deep uncertainty about the identity of the 'other' Rwandans. They were defined as being a threat to the nation. The new violence, in part, was based on a process of ideologically and administratively fixing that identity in an unsustainable modern hierarchy of power layered across modernized and changing tribalism.

Why was the fixing unsustainable? Why, rather than providing for cultural security as it might have under the ritualized conditions of traditional or customary tribal society, did locating this difference within a national state set up a history of *ressentiment*? This leads us to a further dimension of patterned change. Parallel but counter-developments, such as the changing nature of power in a 'democratic' and militarized postcolonial world, rendered that 'fixing' as increasingly fragile and crumbly. The backdrop to the 'reversal' of the hierarchy with formal independence in 1962 included, for example, more than a decade of UN decolonization missions to take apart the fixity of Tutsi dominance. Other modern counter-processes to the fixing of identity – counter-processes which I will do no more than mention here – include the role of school-based modern education and the development of monetary exchange system (see Chapter 6 above). These loosened the taken-for-granted certainty of traditional-then-colonial forms of identity without establishing anything workably solid in its place. Thus, we have manifold kinds of tensions. There are tensions between the intersecting ontological formations – tribal, traditional and modern. Moreover, there are tensions within modernism itself: tensions between heightened sensitivity and studied indifference to difference; tensions between the colonial fixing of identity around reconstituted older forms and postcolonial processes of its undermining, both incremental and revolutionary.

## From traditionalism to postmodernism in a modern nation

This section takes up the theme of ontological tension by tracing the faltering but continuing traditionalism of the United States of America from the eighteenth century, when the USA broke away from British colonial rule, to the present, when we are seeing a new layer of postmodern sentiment and practice overlaying a continuing process of modernization.

In the period prior to the formal constituting of the United States in the eighteenth century, the Puritan 'settlement' of the Americas was defended, in Perry Miller's phrase, as the act of a 'Bible Commonwealth'. Many new settlers saw themselves as forging a covenant with God. Miller is worth quoting at length to compare with what comes later:

> Long before they came to America, [the New England theologians] had become members of a school of doctrine now know as the 'federal' or 'covenant' theology. They revised or amplified pure Calvinism by defining the relationship between the predestined elect and his God not merely as the passive recipient of grace, as did Calvin, but as an active covenant, after the model of that between Abraham and Jehovah in the Book of Genesis. According to this doctrine, the saint was redeemed not simply by an infusion of grace, but by being taken into a league with God, an explicit compact drawn up between two partners, wherein the saint promised to obey God's will and God promised infallibly to grant him salvation. Starting with this notion of a personal and inward covenant, the theologians extended it to the church and state. They argued that a nation of saints, all of whom were personally in covenant with God, would also be in covenant with Him as body politic.[28]

Thus, the New Englanders *as a community* had by a double act of free volition – migrating to North America and submitting to the laws of the Bible – made themselves into a chosen people in a promised land. In their religious-political tracts they, or at least their political scribes, expressed the belief that had forged a covenant that could be enacted in a state. By the time of the American Revolution, the notion of a covenant with God was being overlaid by a self-instituted modernizing contract, sustained through the post-traditional laws of nature. The 'citizenry', or rather their ruling and writing classes, had discovered natural rights – God-given (sacred-traditional), but nevertheless 'self-evident' laws of nature (post-traditional). These were laws that just required writing down by God-fearing gentle*men* and rational scholars in order to become laws of state. Thus, completely contrary to the claims of the modernist theories of the nation, here we find two modes of enquiry, the traditional-cosmological and the early modern rational coming together – albeit in contradictory and overlaying ways. Perry Miller says with muted irony Americans had succeeded, 'where the Jews did not, in recovering something of the pristine virtue ... Yet once the machinery of national humiliation proved effective in producing the providential victory of the Americans, were they not bound to the prophecy that by their utilization of the form, they, and they alone, would bring about a reign of national bliss?'[29]

In other words, the 'citizenry' now written into existence by the Declaration of Independence were now, at the level of their communion in the abstracted state, set free from God to make their own way in the world.

The constitution (in both senses of the word) of the abstract state became, as it did in many other places at the same time, the highest expression of that freedom, and the republic of 'these United States' (plural not singular) was about to be born. At this point, Liah Greenfeld gets carried away again (cf. Chapter 6 above), this time into enjoining us to celebrate the civic purity of this beginning: 'in a certain, analytic, sense', she says only partly covering her partisan tracks, 'the American nation is an ideal nation: the national element in it is challenged by the fewest counterinfluences; it is a purer example of *national* community than any other'.[30] She confirms this in a second book that ties nationalism to capitalism and argues that the United States was the birthplace of capitalism or what she calls 'economic civilization': 'the unprecedented position of the economic sphere in modern consciousness is the product of American society, in turn shaped by the singular characteristic of American nationalism'.[31]

The evidence regarding the formation of the United States of America, including her own beautifully detailed narrative, suggests otherwise. The USA was born not as a nation or a nation-state but rather as a republic in a complex intersection of continuities with the past and discontinuous new beginnings. It was born in the blood of civil war in the context of global change, including around embodied slavery. The projected covenant with God waited until the middle of the nineteenth century to become the cultural evocation of an emerging nation and, during the same period, the contract with men (no women were there for the writing of the Constitution) became the political codification of the federating unitary state. The state, in effect, rejected any such covenant while the forgers of the nation made it a contested expression of piety.[32]

It is indicative of this tension that in the highest written document of state, the Constitution, the Bible is absent, as is the concept of 'the nation'. Even in the Declaration of Independence – written by a secret congress of strangers meeting in the home of a lecturer in scientific obstetrics – God is reduced to 'nature's god' (lower case). Nature's god is embedded within the first couple of paragraphs of the Declaration as it begins by naturalizing the break with the British Crown: 'in the course of human events it becomes necessary for one people to dissolve the political bands which have connected them with another, and to assume among the powers of the earth the separate and equal station to which the laws of nature and of nature's god entitle them ... '.[33] This accords with Thomas Jefferson's contradictory modernism. He calls upon the Bible but writes, for example, with extraordinary relativism of the 'family God of Abraham, of Isaac and of Jacob, and the local God of Israel'.[34] Here we are at the end of the eighteenth century and while the postcolonial republic has been formally signed into existence as the United States, there is a long way to go in establishing a nation-state.

While there is no demarcation point, no calendrical marker at which time we can say that the United States became a nation-state, it is possible to give some symbolic high points in the connecting of the secular-state/sacred-nation. In these, the Bible is present, even if as rhetorical evocation rather than as indicative of the hopes for a Bible Commonwealth. Gary Wills, despite the postmodern title of his book *Inventing America*, is wonderfully insightful here in his discussion of the traditional overtones in Lincoln's Gettysburg address of 1863. The speech begins: 'Four-score-and-seven years ago, our Fathers brought forth ... ' Why such a stilted style? Why four-score-and-seven? To hear the phrase in the context of Victorian America is to hear the biblical overtones, says Wills. There is no reason to immediately start counting back eighty-seven years from 1863 to get to 1776. It allows Lincoln, in effect, to get around the issue that the date 1776 is no automatic marker of the beginning of the nation-state. In fact, the thirteen original colonies had instructed their delegates to sign the Declaration of Independence on the basis that it did not imply a unified polity. Even more pointedly, Lincoln was talking in the middle of a war of states that would by its end kill over half-a-million people. Why centre the nation on the phrase 'Our fathers brought forth'? President Lincoln is drawing on the deeply-gendered biblical references to Our Father and the faith of our fathers. As Wills puts it:

> Lincoln is talking about generation on the spot. The nation is rightly called new because it is brought forth maieutically, by midwifery; it is not only new but newborn. The suggested image is, throughout, of a *hieros gamos*, a marriage of male heaven ('our fathers') and a female earth ('this continent'). And it is a miraculous conception, a virgin birth. This virgin birth is brought forth by those, who in an embodied sense, cannot give birth.[35]

At the very time of Lincoln's calling upon the language of redemption to connect a nation-at-war-with-itself, the Bible had ceased to be substantially more than a legitimating *signifier* of the state-nation. Though, as I argued earlier, the bureaucratic state and the religions of the written word grew up together, by the nineteenth century this had fundamentally changed. The state and the sacred had ceased to be symbiotic. Individuals continued to have faith, but the state-nation as a polity-community of liberal individuals was assuming a more urgent calling that the Kingdom of God. In the middle of that century as Congress voted to put the phrase 'In God We Trust' on the nation's currency and to recognize officially Thanksgiving Day as one of the nation's holy-days, the Bible had become a book to wave around at public meetings, cite passages from and swear upon, but not a book of instruction to guide the practices of the increasingly abstract state. In short, while the Word continued to be relevant to the nation, it became less and less important to the state. This development would reduce the Bible to a thing of national evocation as the nation and state were drawn together at the end of the nineteenth century.

### The United States as a tribal nation?

Although we should acknowledge continuities of social form and subjectivity, it is crucial not to treat the constitutive foundations of tribalism or traditionalism as *the* basis of the modern (contradictory) nation. Most starkly, it bears repeating the proposition that nations, whether they are traditional or modern, are not tribes. This is the case even if tribes, as we have just documented in relation to Rwanda, can become nations. However, a surprising number of writers ignore this injunction and use the concept of 'tribalism' to describe graphically the depth of pain or division that lies behind contemporary nation formation. Harold Isaacs gave us its apotheosis in *Idols of the Tribe*.[36] More recently, for example, in response to the outpourings of Americans after the metaphysical trespass of September 11, Mark Slouka writes: 'a few facts seem to be taking shape. A few truths even. The first is that, despite the muzzy pap of the globalists, who never tire of limning their vision of a borderless friction-free world, we remain strikingly – even shockingly – tribal.'[37] Lest you think that he is referring to the terrorists as the tribals, he follows immediately with a further 'truth': 'The second is that the source of this tribal identity – the three-century-old myth of American exceptionalism – is alive and well'. He is of course accurate about American exceptionalism, but what that has to do with tribalism remains a mystery.

A recent tome, *Blood Sacrifice and the Nation: Totem Rituals and the American Flag* published by one of the world's most respected university presses, provides a fantastic example of bad theory that takes us down the same path.[38] The book's thesis – that, the nation is a tribe founded on a civic religion that demands the blood sacrifice of its children – is again dramatized by taking as its example the United States, a highly-differentiated nation without a singular ethnic genealogy let alone tribal-national roots. Let the authors first set out their approach in their own words:

> What binds the nation together? ... This book argues that violent blood sacrifice makes enduring groups cohere, even though such a claim challenges our most deeply held notions of civilized behaviour. [This is defensible so far, as long as the concept of sacrifice is not taken in the modern

> metaphoric rather than traditional literal sense.] The sacrificial system that binds American citizens has a sacred flag at its centre. Patriotic rituals revere it as the embodiment of a bloodthirsty totem god who organizes killing energy. [This is going to be hard to sustain without contorting the available contradictory evidence that leads other writers such as Michael Billig to write of the banal nationalism of the United States.[39]] This totem god is the foundation of the mythic, religiously constructed American identity. Our notion of the totem comes from Durkheim, for whom it was the emblem of the group's agreement to be a group ... We intend to show totem dynamics vigorously at work in the contemporary United States. We lay out the practices and beliefs that furnish the system without which the nation is in danger of dissolution. Their focus is the magical and primitive use of the flag, the totem object of American civil religion.[40]

At first I thought this was the metaphoric excess of the introductory page, used to draw in the reader before settling down to the serious analysis. However, for all the wealth of empirical description the book never gets beyond detailed description and methodological mire. The most important insight for our purposes is that the pre-eminent civic nation, the USA, still uses the rhetoric and subjectivity of blood sacrifice. This goes against the modernist argument and supports my seemingly outrageous claim, made earlier, that the cry 'for blood and soil' is not just the sentiment of a deranged fascist dictator in the 1930s. However, *Blood Sacrifice and the Nation* leaves us with too many questions. How can such a differentiated nation, a nation that does not believe that embodied genealogical kinship is the means of its integration, be considered a tribe? Through its totem system, answer Marvin and Ingle – the kinship form is exogamy. There is no postmodern irony here, only poor extrapolation. Exogamy, they say, actually organizes popular elections and reconciles potentially violent political-clan differences:

> Two major clan groups bearing animal identities are descended from the flag, the tribal ancestor, for whom the totem eagle is occasionally substituted. During seasonal festivals called elections, representatives of the elephant and donkey clans form an exogenous mating pair that produces a reincarnated savior king, an embodied totem president who bears a sacrificial charge ... The cross-fertilized membership of the two great non-exclusive electoral clans deflects potentially murderous struggle. It reorganizes the identities of contending groups by focusing away from irreconcilable differences associated with exclusive affiliation by blood and subordinating these differences to blood ties of totem sacrifice.[41]

The tensions in the method abound and show themselves in obvious ways. America is in their analysis both one large differentiated tribe, and a nation of tribes in the plural. The totemic fathers of the nation are those established by sacrifice in war, but their list singles out as 'the most significant totem avatars for living Americans' the venerated war heroes (not) of Franklin D. Roosevelt and John F. Kennedy. Roosevelt did not enter the

Second World War until forced to in December 1941; and Kennedy presided over the Bay of Pigs fiasco, the Cuban Missile back-down and kept 16,000 troops in Vietnam under the guise of being advisors. The evidence is ambiguous as it is for their description of the flag. For Marvin and Ingle, the flag is simultaneously the god of nationalism, the totem emblem, a body, a representative of the violently sacrificed body, and the 'baby' that came from Betsy Ross's body. It is both an artefact based on an oral, not textual, culture and the intimate subject of poems, novels, advertisements, and newspaper and television programs. It is the totem 'whose mission it is to organize death', the object that must not be used for commercial purposes, and it is also the motif on everything commercial from table linen to condoms. It is the *male*, transcendent totem that is taboo to touch (even though the Old Glory Condom Company ran advertisements around the slogan 'never flown at half-mast), and the *female*, popular totem that expresses itself in the 'messy, rutting shoving, people' who know the answers to questions about baseball.[42]

While the analysis conducted by Carolyn Marvin and David Ingle is confused and confusing, their empirical evidence is indicative, first, of the condensation of meaning around icons such as the flag, and, second, of the contradictory intersection of levels of integration from the subjectively embodied to the abstract disembodied in the constitution of the nation. In terms of the present approach, we can take this further to show the contradictory intersection of levels of ontological formation in the formation of the modern nation – of traditionalism, modernism, and much later (as the ironic advertisements of the Old Glory Condom Company illustrate), of postmodernism.

We can begin our discussion of the postmodern nation state in the realms of subjectivities, making use of contemporary popular-cultural and academic descriptions; not using the descriptions as direct support for our thesis but more as evidence in spite of themselves. Surely something is happening when a right-conservative American journal heads its cover-page with the question 'Is America still a nation?' and publishes an article entitled 'The post-modern state'[43] no question mark or interpretative insecurity here); when a left-wing Australian speech-writer and prime-ministerial adviser gives a speech at one of Melbourne's ruling-class restaurants, advocating that Australia become the first postmodern republic;[44] and when an Indonesian poet writes the following half-defensible, half-risible sentiments:

> I began to imagine Australia being the first country in the world to separate the idea of a 'nation state' from the desire to have one centre, one logos, one myth. Perhaps this is a post-modernist concept of

nationhood. Maybe this is something feasible in a lucky country, where people can jump easily from one place to another, whose self-perception is not threatened by the 'Other', and whose horizon moves among buildings, cars, holidays and consumables.[45]

Something is happening, but not necessarily in accordance with the descriptions put forward by the proponents of postmodern nationalism themselves. The first thing to note is a kind of postmodern, even (post)national, 'exceptionalism'.[46] In the past, nationalist intellectuals working within the frame of modernism tended to claim exceptional status for their *own* nation *as a nation* – even if this lay paradoxically in seeing that nation as further than others down the evolutionary pathway to true cosmopolitanism. In the new setting the temptation to see one's own nation as exceptional continues but it is opened to the possibility of eulogizing other nations, and of seeing the exceptional nation as passing beyond nationhood. Here an American academic is calling Germany and Japan the 'perfect nation-states' but still claiming a (*post*-national) exceptionalism for the United States as the 'prototypical postmodern society, ... no longer a nation-state'. An Indonesian poet is extolling the virtues of the exceptional confusions of identity in Australia. And an Australian speech-writer (who incidentally used to work as a satirist writing scripts for a comic impersonator of Australian prime-ministers) is both advocating a 'new inclusive nation' and projecting the possibility of Australia becoming an exceptional post-nation: 'it might be the first post-modern republic, and I mean that in the nicest possible way. I mean a republic that exalts the nation less than the way of life'.

The second point is that such 'post-national' evocation requires an intellectual abstracting, a distancing position of emotional and political safety. It tends to be expressed through four main modes of operation: a critical, though not usually self-critical, separation of the author from what is being described; a pragmatic and sometimes crudely-instrumental calculation of possible benefits; a tendency towards the 'vision' being content free; and an ironical self-protective use of wit and pastiche. Don Watson's speech combines all four. It is critically heartfelt while shying away from the often all-consuming passion of modern nationalism. It is unashamedly instrumental, espousing a national interest in becoming a post-nation: how better to ride with the tide of global capitalism and enhance 'our competitiveness ... our posture and status abroad, especially in Asia'. It lacks content about the meaning of becoming a republic. And it has the safe distance of hyperbole. The speech begins with an address to the poultry in his backyard (keep in mind that the novelty of this address derives in part from the influential backroom-status of its author):

> I say to them – and imagine the tears running down their beaks like perspiration on the nose of a Baptist when he's telling a fib – I say to them after all this, when you have seen the age of the fence posts, the ruins of farms which are after all as much ruins as the ruins of ancient Greece, and the human cost the same, surely this country has been through, seen enough ... surely, I say to them, Australia can be a republic.[47]

The third point to emphasize, at least as important as the preceding points, is that although postmodern nationalism is an ideology with generalizing pretensions, it is still only an emergent sensibility, actively lived only by the intellectually trained, and actively espoused only by certain individuals of that class. It is an ideology whose name is still to enter the common lexicon. It is presented as 'a recollection of an absence that can appeal to anyone'. More precisely, postmodern nationalism recollects an absence that appeals particularly to people formed within the apparently open structures of globalizing capitalism. It incorporates some of the traces of modern nationalism such as a ritualistic sense of embodied solidarity – evidenced in the return to Australia of an 'unknown soldier' from the battlefields of France. The exercise was full of contradictory cross-currents. The designer of the tomb, Janet Laurence, talked explicitly of the desire to appeal to all: 'its abstract nature could speak about other losses and absences to future generations who would not have an immediate link with World War I'.[48] However, it is without any of the demands of ultimate sacrifice and unquestioning loyalty implicit in the older, more comprehensive identity conferred by the modern nation-state. If the modern nation-state was experienced as both publicly and intimately structuring one's life-world then the postmodern *nation* (even when it is not named as such) is increasingly *experienced* as an unstructured, and at times even optional, background choice. At the same time, under conditions of postmodernism, the *state* is most often viewed either as a baleful institution to be minimized and deregulated or as a necessary, if intrusive, organ of public administration, as a provider of essential services for the vulnerable.

To say that under conditions of postmodernism the nation state is *experienced* as becoming less structured is not to suggest that our subjective sense of the present provides us with an accurate picture. The image of the nation-state as an aging leviathan, more comfortable lumbering amidst the inglorious structures of the past, is belied by the alacrity with which 'it'[49] has recently taken up various administrative techniques such as electronic information storage and other forms of disembodied surveillance.[50] Rather than collapsing into disorganized, decentred micropractices, the structures (the dominant *modes of practice*) are changing. Life at the face-to-face level may be becoming more fragmented in the sense that personal relations have less certainty, but social life is being restructured *and* reintegrated at a more abstract level. This restructuring offers new, and potentially dangerous, possibilities for political practice.

## Conclusion

Drawing the themes of this chapter together, we can say that the modern nation came into being across the globe through the overdetermination of changing dominant modes of practice, integration and being – modes associated with the upheavals of modernity in the context of extended global confrontations, imperial and otherwise. However, though the modern nation was made possible by these patterned changes, it had to be made by people acting politically. We can say that as a consequence of this process of change, not as a cause, the formation of nation-states came in late-modernity to be experienced as natural. That is, to the extent that they thought about it, most of the population came to assume that nation-statehood, whether consensual or striven by blood sacrifice, is the normal form of community-polity. From the bottom, some individuals and peoples may have thought they wanted to live under a different nation-state, but usually this meant wanting a state for their own self-proclaimed subordinate nation.

Throughout the book, I have being arguing about the dialectic of continuity and discontinuity. Viewed though the flickering screen of the contemporary globalizing and postmodernizing nation-states of the West with all their contradictions, it is hard to see any continuities-of-form here. The continuities at most appear as surface content, and even then only as points of reference: a Jewish Wailing Wall, a Christian burial site, the Islamic Dome of the Rock, the Stone of Destiny, a slab of engraved marble, or a coloured piece of calico. However, the postmodern/late-modern nation has all the ontological vulnerabilities of the earlier dominant forms of polity – from traditional kingdom and absolutist state to the classical modern nation-state – with new tensions heaped on top. Despite unprecedented technical power, it still has to legitimize itself, at one level, through basic categories of human existence such as embodiment, placement and the temporal transcendence – the transcendence of the community-polity despite the assured mortality of all who live within it. Polities and communities will continue to do so, for good and evil, so long as we remain embodied persons living with others. Unfortunately and grotesquely in the current period of human history, this process has seen the contradictions of social meaning and practice within and across existing polity-communities stretch to breaking point. This is why its politicians and its people have returned again with renewed intensity, even if in changing ways, to draw on writings about faith, existence and transcendence. It is also why the newest 'evil empire' of Islam is another sodality of the Book; why Catholics and Protestants in Ireland are struggling to sustain the Easter Friday agreement; and why the Palestinians continue to die heroically throwing stones at armoured vehicles or, tragically by strapping their bodies with explosives and martyring themselves to slaughter Israeli civilians who do not deserve to die.

## Notes

1 Benedict Anderson, *Imagined Communities: Reflections on the Origins and Spread of Nationalism*, Verso, London (1983), 2nd edn, 1991. Ernest Gellner, *Nationalism*, Orion Books, London, 1998; Anthony Giddens, *The Nation-State and Violence: Volume Two of a Contemporary Critique of Historical Materialism*, Polity Press, Cambridge, 1985.

2 Ernest Gellner, 'Do Nations have Navels?', *Nations and Nationalism*, vol. 2, no. 3, 1996, pp. 366–70; Anthony D. Smith, 'Memory and Modernity: Reflections on Ernest Gellner's Theory of Nationalism', *Nations and Nationalism*, vol. 2, no. 3, 1996, pp. 371–88.

3 Cited in Gareth Knapman, 'Regionalism, a Form of Proto-Nationalism in Acehnese Politics', Honours Thesis, Department of Politics, Monash University, 2001, p. 9.

4 An apology: I started to read this book in a second-hand bookshop in Edinburgh, but did not have enough money to purchase the volume at this time. By the time I had accrued enough money to make the book mine, the capitalist market had already whisked it away, along with all its publication details. The university libraries of Edinburgh and Melbourne do not have a copy.

5 Abdalla Omar Mansur, 'The Nature of the Somali Clan System', in Ali Jimale Ahmed (ed.), *The Invention of Somalia*, Red Sea Press, Lawrenceville, 1995.

6 It is actually the projection back upon originating social formation from (different) positions of abstraction within (different dominant ontological formations). Compare the biblical creation story of Adam and Eve and the Freudian creation story of the totem and taboo: the first is sacred traditional Truth, the second is metaphorical modern 'truth' with a hint of pre-anthropological myth-making.

7 Benedict Anderson, 'Eastern and Western Nationalism', *Arena Journal*, New Series no. 16, 2000/1, pp. 121–31.

8 'England' might be one counter-example, but prior to the nineteenth century I would still call it a traditional nation (genealogically extended but bound by class-based delimitations) rather than a modern nation.

9 This is the thesis put forward by Tom Nairn in *The Break-Up of Britain: Crisis and Neo-Nationalism*, Verso, London (1973), 2nd edn, 1981. It also bore back on the empires themselves. For an elegant exposition of the case of England, see Krishan Kumar, *The Making of English National Identity*, Cambridge University Press, Cambridge, 2003.

10 Anderson, *Imagined Communities*, p. 135.

11 Ernest Gellner, 'The Coming of Nationalism and its Interpretation', in Gopal Balakrishnan (ed.), *Mapping the Nation*, Verso, London, 1996.

12 Giddens, *Nation-State and Violence*, 1985, p. 112.

13 Anderson, *Imagined Communities*, p. 50.

14 *Ibid.*, p. 62.

15 Partha Chatterjee, *Nationalist Thought and the Colonial World*, Zed Books, London, 1986, p. 21.

16 Partha Chatterjee, *The Nation and its Fragments*, Princeton University Press, Princeton, NJ, 1993.

17 Partha Chatterjee, 'Whose Imagined Community?', in Gopal Balakrishnan (ed.), *Mapping the Nation*, Verso, London, 1996, p. 217.

18 Ashis Nandy, *Time Warps: The Insistent Politics of Silent and Evasive Pasts*, Permanent Black, Delhi, 2001.

19 Mahmood Mamdani, 'From Conquest to Consent as the Basis of State Formation: Reflections on Rwanda', *New Left Review*, no. 216, 1996, pp. 3-36; Jacques J. Maquet, *The Premise of Inequality in Ruanda*, Oxford University Press, London, 1961, pp. 124-8, 148-52.

20 Mamdani, 'From Conquest to Consent', p. 12. See also Wm. Roger Louis, *Ruanda-Urundi: 1884-1914*, Clarendon Press, Oxford, 1963, part 2.

21 See René LeMarchand, *Rwanda and Burundi*, Pall Mall Press, London, 1970, on the complications of using the terminology of caste and class in relation to the Tutsi.

22 Despite these putative embodied differences, witnesses after the 1994 massacres talked of the executioners often demanding identity cards to determine if they were killing the right people.

23 Thongchai Winichakul, *Siam Mapped: A History of the Geo-Body of the Nation*, University of Hawaii Press, Honolulu, 1994.

24 Jean-Pierre Chrétien cited in Gérard Prunier, *The Rwandan Crisis: History of a Genocide*, Columbia University Press, New York, 1997, p. 36.

25 *Ibid.*, Prunier.

26 See David Newbury, *Kings and Clans*, University of Wisconsin Press, Madison, WI, 1991, Chapter 4. The significance of these interrelations between Hutu and Tutsi should not be lost in the modern confirmation of caste-tribe difference.

27 The RPF, which again reversed the power hierarchy and returned the Tutsi to government in the wake of the 1994 genocide, had been formed in 1987 in Uganda. The unevenness of the process and how it spread beyond the borders of one nation-state is indicated by the fact that the RPF leader, Paul Kagame, had up until the early 1980s considered himself Ugandan. To carry the story forward: in August 1998, Tutsi-led rebels backed by Rwanda, claimed control of two-thirds of the Democratic Republic of the Congo. Angolan, Namibian and Zimbabwean troops sent in to support President Kabila. The European nations, including former colonial power Belgium, organized a foreign evacuation. In Rwanda, there are still rumoured to be Hutu rebel movements in the jungle.

28 Perry Miller, *Nature's Nation*, Harvard University Press, Cambridge, MA, 1967, p. 17.

29 *Ibid.*, pp. 103, 105.

30 Liah Greenfeld, *Nationalism: Five Roads to Modernity*, Harvard University Press, Cambridge, MA, 1993, p. 403.

31 Liah Greenfeld, *The Spirit of Capitalism: Nationalism and Economic Growth*, Harvard University Press, Cambridge, MA, 2003, p. 1.

32 Gaines M. Foster, 'A Christian Nation: Signs of a Covenant', in John Bodnar (ed.), *Bonds of Affection: Americans Define their Patriotism*, Princeton University Press, Princeton, NJ, 1996.

33 Quoted in Gary Wills, *Inventing America: Jefferson's Declaration of Independence*, Vintage Books, New York, 1979, p. 374.

34 Quoted in Steven Grosby, 'The Nation of the United States and the Vision of Israel', in Roger Michener (ed.), *Nationality, Patriotism and Nationalism in Liberal Democratic Societies*, Professors of World Peace Academy, St. Paul, MN, 1993, p. 62.

35 Wills, *Inventing America*, p. xv.

36 Harold R. Isaacs, *Idols of the Tribe: Group Identity and Political Change*, Harper & Row, New York, 1975.

37 Mark Slouka, 'A Year Later: Notes on America's Intimations of Mortality', *Harper's Magazine*, September 2002, p. 35. It is an otherwise splendidly provocative article.

38 Carolyn Marvin and David W. Ingle, *Blood Sacrifice and the Nation: Totem Rituals and the American Flag*, Cambridge University Press, Cambridge, 1999.

39 Michael Billig, *Banal Nationalism*, Sage Publications, London, 1995.

40 Marvin and Ingle, *Blood Sacrifice*, p. 1.

41 *Ibid.*, pp. 22–3. This is the subject of their Chapter 9.

42 *Ibid.*, compare, for example, pages 22 and 192; 19 and 22; 29, 25, 42, 43 and 11; 42–3 and numerous discussions of the flag's textual representations; 20 and 29; 32, 54 and 215.

43 James Kurth, 'The Post-Modern State', *The National Interest*, no. 28, 1992, pp. 26–35. The article is full of historical distortions and methodological *faux pas*. (With thanks to Andy Butfoy for this reference.)

44 First reported in *The Age* (26 March 1993), and later reproduced in full as Don Watson, 'Birth of a Post-Modern Nation', *The Australian* (24 July 1993).

45 Goenawan Mohamad, 'Australia by Name, Postmodernist by Nature', *Sunday Age*, 12 July 1992.

46 For a further example see Jacques Derrida's discussion of how France assigns for herself the exemplary' task and avant-garde position in advancing the subsumption of the European nations within the post-national setting of `*Europe': The Other Heading*, Indiana University Press, Bloomington, IN, 1992, pp. 49–54.

47 Watson, 'Birth of a Post-Modern Nation'.

48 *The Australian*, 4 November 1993.

49 It almost goes without saying given the previous chapter that 'it' is shorthand for the patterns of practices and discourses of the many persons (intellectually-trained agents) who work in the many apparatuses which we call the 'state'. Using the shorthand references is not necessarily to imply that 'the state' operates as a single homogenous entity, nor to reify 'it' as a hypostatized object acting organically or anthropomorphically. As I argued in Chapter 9, contrary to some of the more pedantic postmodernists, such designations as 'state' and 'society' continue to be useful.

50 David Lyon, *The Electronic Eye: The Rise of the Surveillance Society*, University of Minnesota Press, Minneapolis, 1994; David Lyon, *Surveillance after September 11*, Polity Press, Cambridge, 2003.

# ELEVEN Global Formation

## From the *Oecumene* to Planet Exploitation

Images of war, terrorism, tsunami floods and stock-market fluctuations seem to dominate our sense of the globe in the twenty-first century. The images are connected to dramatic events: the attack on the World Trade Center, the wars in Afghanistan and Iraq, protests across the world against the World Trade Organization or the 'Coalition of the Willing', and scenes of the space shuttle exploding above the earth. They have completely overshadowed the superficially peaceful image of planet earth that carried the mainstream sense of the global from the post-Vietnam 1970s, symbolized in the Apollo 11 moon-landing. Back then, David Attenborough was making *The Tribal Eye* (1976) a series concerned with art in so-called 'primitive' societies, and then *Life on Earth* (1979), a series which attracted an estimated 500 million viewers world-wide. These kinds of images continue into the present, but simultaneously, through the late-twentieth century, images of planet earth were themselves simultaneously globalized and commodified as corporate icons. They all tended to link the global to the putatively local or to embodied expressions of the human.

At the turn of the century, the telecommunications transnational Nortel turns the globe into a spongy human brain divided into eastern and western hemispheres: 'To guarantee our success, we source intelligence from both hemispheres'. Energex's naked baby reaches towards a blue heaven, sitting on corporate cloudy-blue earth. Barclays Global Investors uses an image of the globe with the words, 'Events here. Affect your investments here ... and here ... and here.' Lines of penetration, pointing to nowhere in particular, are used to indicate the multitude of places where your investments might be affected. Lockheed Martin presents a globe that has been broken into a thousand facets of localized colour or globalized significance. And perhaps in the most strikingly derivative connection of the embodied and disembodied, NEC, under the slogan 'C&C for Human Potential' uses a peacenik-style water-colour-rendered globe around which floating people – all Western, all white – linked their bodies to form a kind of global garland. Such advertisements, as bizarre as they are, act as distorting representations within the dominant matrix of representations that has the globe getting smaller and the people becoming more interconnected.[1]

In this context, many commentators took that experience of globalization and made it into the basis of their definitions. The problematic process of defining globalization is a good place to begin in order to set up an alternative approach to the whole question of what does globalization mean. This alternative emerges as a series of hints with references back to Chapter 2, before later being developed more formally. For the moment, we begin with one deeply flawed example. Malcolm Waters writes that we can define globalization as *'A social process in which the constraints of geography on economic, political, social and cultural arrangements recede, in which people become increasingly aware that they are receding and in which people act accordingly'*.[2] This definition sounds helpful on the face of it. However, against such a definition, the first response is that the geographical constraints do not simply recede across *all levels* of interchange. The English Channel has not dried up, and the executives of the world's communications-connected corporations still experience jet-lag as they fly to an ever-increasing number of 'face-to-face' meetings.

Reading backwards, without the 'increasing awareness' qualification, the definition would quickly fade into an over-generalized claim that globalization includes every process of abstracting mobility across space. For example, the use of wheeled vehicles in the ancient world after 3000 BCE, spreading across Eurasia from the Fertile Crescent, would fit a definition based on the criterion that the practice contribute to overcoming spatial constraints. Only in a completely-overgeneralizing sense can this be said to be *a practice* of globalization *per se*. That is, even if we need to take seriously the issue that from abstract distance of the present we can 'see' a tableaux of global human activity emerging as humans moved out of Africa over the course of millennia to effectively colonize planet earth. This issue has at its heart the question of objective globalization. It suggests that we cannot find the magical starting point of globalization, at least as understood in objective terms, but an objective dimension needs to be built in that puts the emphasis on the extension of social relations across world-space. That is, it is lines of interconnecting *relations* across world-space, whether embodied or disembodied, that makes for globalization.

To avoid such issues, Malcolm Waters' definition pivots on a subjectivist dimension, however, this dimension becomes so central that it makes the definition unworkable. It remains as an under-theorized claim that implies that people need to be aware of processes of globalization for it to exist. Again, reading backwards, this means that if they do not believe that the constraints of geography are not lifted, globalization does not exist. In other words, objective globalization cannot exist without its subjective recognition. This clearly is as untenable as Bishop Berkeley's claim that nothing exists that he cannot see, and thus a few pages later Waters finds himself arguing two contrary points at the same time: first, that 'some measure of globalization has always occurred', and, second, that 'globalization could not begin until [the early modern period] because it was only the Copernican revolution that could convince humanity that it inhabited a globe'.[3]

Put in more theoretical terms, what it suggests is the need for a layered rather than one-dimensional approach to understanding the spatial integration of social relations from the local to the global, and from the embodied to the disembodied.

Discussion of Malcolm Waters' approach is worth continuing here because he attempts to use a kind of 'levels' metaphor to attempt to get out of the very problem that his definition of globalization initially sets up. In the end the move utterly fails, but it is instructive for considering what kinds of pitfalls a *levels approach* needs to avoid. Part of the problem is that he reduces the metaphor of levels into a series of ideal types. He begins by distinguishing three types of exchange: *material exchanges* from trade to capital accumulation (linked to the economy); *power exchanges* from elections to the exercises of military control (linked to the polity); and *symbolic exchanges* from oral communication to data transfer (linked to the culture).[4] Already we have a problem here, because, as theorists as dissimilar as Michael Mann and Michel Foucault have suggested, questions of power are relevant across all spheres of social life. Power reaches far beyond the political. Similarly, material relations cannot be limited to economic exchange relations. Both projections of power and symbolic interchange always have a material dimension.

According to Waters, these three types of exchange tend to be associated with three different types of spatially-organized social relations: local, international and global. First, ignoring the obvious point that 'material exchanges' such as trade (using his definition of 'material') are in the contemporary period central to the process of globalization, Waters concludes that commodity and labour exchanges tend to bind social arrangements to localized settings. What about long-distance trade, a seminal exchange-relation of our time? Waters blithely settles that problem by redefining traders as intermediaries 'who stand outside the central relationships of the economy'. Second, 'power exchanges', he says, tend 'to tie social arrangements to extended territories ... indeed they are specifically directed towards controlling the population that occupies a territory'. This is the sphere of nation-states engaged in international relations. Again by a peculiar definitional closure, international relations are treated as not globalizing. The third of his forms of exchange, symbolic exchange, thus becomes the arena of globalization. Such exchanges 'release social arrangements from spatial referents'. He has already forgotten that on the previous page he defined symbolic exchange as including, alongside more abstracted or mediated forms of communication, forms of communication that are often conducted as face-to-face interchanges: oral communication, performance, oratory, ritual and public demonstration. In a reversal of his argument we can say that these forms of exchange often act to bind social arrangements to localized places and to localized persons. The act of talking to someone is a form of symbolic exchange, but it is not usually the stuff of globalization.

How can such a confused book become an academic best-seller? It is because it appears to have an explanatory complexity expressed with simple directness. Moreover, it never stops taking new methodological turns to solve the problems of the last turn, and thus has an initial impressiveness. 'In summary then', he writes, 'the theorem that underpins the new theoretical paradigm of globalization is that: *material exchanges localize; political exchanges internationalize and symbolic exchanges globalize*' (his emphasis) – all of which is both empirically unsustainable and theoretically unhelpful. To get out of the set of problems that this proclamation entails, Waters' approach takes another helical turn. He writes:

> We need to make a point here which is subtle and complex but which is extremely important. The apparent correspondence between the three arenas of social life – economy, politics, and culture – and the three types of exchange – material, power and symbolic – should not mislead us into thinking that each type of exchange is restricted to a single arena.

Warning bells ring. When someone says that they are going to make a 'subtle and complex point' it is time to assess very carefully and very critically what they are up to. In this case, the writer is onto something, but has twisted himself like a cartoon super-hero in a spiral of increasingly powerful confusion. The key implicit insight – though never made explicit – is that processes of embodied integration tend to tie people to localities while disembodied or more abstract processes are potentially associated with the crossing of spatial and temporal boundaries. This relatively simple point is rarely made in the literature on globalization.

In terms of the present approach, we can say that in the contemporary world the more abstract the form of relation the more it seems to transcend borders. Put more precisely, the more materially abstract the process of globalization, the more it has in the contemporary period been deregulated and allowed to cross the borders of locales and nation-states. While the movements of bodies, objects of exchange and processes of disembodied interrelation are all increasingly globalized, what most commentators miss is the relatively obvious point that they are globalized in different ways. In empirical terms, finance capital flies across deterritorialized borders while refugees are administered by states with a new vigilance unknown in human history. Drawing upon the method of the 'constitutive abstraction' approach, this point can be taken further as part of a systematic series of propositions.

## Arguing about globalization

*Proposition 1.* Globalization involves extensions of social relations across world-space, defining that world-space in terms of the historically-variable ways that it has been practised and socially understood through changing world-time. In other words, long before that stunning satellite photograph of the globe hit us in the face with the obviousness of planet earth, there were different practices and conceptions of world-space (see Chapter 2). We may not have previously come close to the current condition of self-conscious globality – an unprecedented development in human history – but processes of globalization and the subjectivities of globalism were occurring, both intended and unintended, to the extent that social relations and subjectivities (together with their ecological consequences) were being given global reach. For example, *subjective* projections of the globe (globalism) emerged with the incipient development of a technical-analytical mode of enquiry by the ancient Greek philosophers. An understanding of the inhabited world-space (the *oecumene*) began to be debated during the sixth and fifth centuries BCE, combining information both from phenomenal experience such as oral testimony and from abstract principles such as geometry.[5] Early classical maps were intended to encompass the whole earth beyond the *oecumene*, and even if that was more limited in practical terms than the lines of *objective* extension that later developed in the traditional empires, it involved nevertheless a subjective globalization of *terra cognita*.

*Proposition 2.* The form of globalization has been, and continues to be, historically changing. This can be analytically understood in terms of globalization taking fundamentally-different forms across world history, or even within one historical moment. In any particular period, globalization ranges from embodied extensions of the social, such as through the movements of peoples, to the disembodied extensions, such as through communications on the wings of textual or digital encoding. In terms of the present argument, across human history, and carrying into the present, the dominant forms of globalization range from *traditional* forms (primarily carried by the embodied movement of peoples and the projections of traditional intellectuals) to *modern* and *postmodern* forms (primarily carried by disembodied practices of abstracted extension, in particular the projections and practices of an emergent cosmopolitan class of the intellectually trained).

*Proposition 3.* The driving structural determinants of contemporary globalization are *capitalism* (as I wrote earlier, based on an accelerating electronic mode of production and an expanding mode of commodity and financial exchange), *mediatism* (based on the systemic interconnectivity of a mass-mediated world, based on a mode of electronically networked communication), and *techno-scientism* (based on a new intersection between the mode of production and the mode of enquiry). Contemporary globalization has reached its present stage of relative globality under conditions of the intersection of each of these modes of practice: production, exchange, communication, organization and enquiry. For example, satellite transmission, cable networking, and the internet were all developed techno-scientifically as means of communication within state-supported capitalist markets that rapidly carried globalization to a new dominant level of technological mediation.[6]

*Proposition 4.* Globalization is structured as relations of power. If it can be argued that disembodied power, borne across the various modes of practice, has the greatest capacity to effect generalized change at a distance, this proposition can be made more explicit. The dominant form of contemporary globalization is structured as relations of disembodied power that bear back upon the bodies of the people across the world with increasing intensity and systematicity.

*Proposition 5.* One of the driving ideological determinants of contemporary globalization is the contested philosophy of neo-liberalism. However, the ideological-subjective grounding of globalization also goes much deeper and wider than economic ideologies. Globalization is carried forward through the relatively uncontested territory of the taken-for-granted assumptions of our time. Ideologies of economic globalism from notions of market freedom to the joy of a 'borderless world' have naturalized the techniques and technologies of global extension as the inevitable outcomes of material progress. However, more than that, globalism partakes of the excitement that surrounds generalized notions of autonomy, mediation and interconnectivity.

*Proposition 6.* Globalization does not inevitably sweep all before it. All that is solid does not melt into air. For example, processes of globalization may eventually undermine the sovereignty of the nation-state, but there is no inevitability about such an outcome, neither in logic or reality. It is salutary to remember that the institutions and structures of modern globalization and the modern nation-state were born during the same period; they were formed through concurrent processes, with the tension between these two phenomena being over boundary formation and sovereignty rather than in general. (See Chapters 9 and 10 for an elaboration of this argument.) This argument goes directly against those who would treat nation formation and global formation as the antithetical outcomes of respectively a 'first and second modernity', or those who would narrowly define globalization as that which undermines the nation-state.[7] In the context of contemporary globalization we have seen both nationalist revivals and reassertions of tribalism. As Michael Freeman argues:

> The impact of technological and economic globalization is more complex than simplistic 'end-of-nation-state' prophesies allow, but it is reordering of the world in such a way that many feel excluded and insecure. In this situation the so-called 'new tribalism' (which we have seen is not really new nor tribalism) appears to offer security and a measure of self-determination. As decision-making power moves away to trans-state or supra-state agencies, so sub-state ethnonationalist groups are encouraged to bypass what they perceive to be their unresponsive nation-states and seek solutions either at higher levels, where the real power is thought to be located, and/or at more local levels, where autonomy seems possible. Globalism and 'tribalism' may, therefore, not only co-exist but mutually support each other.[8]

All this suggests a very different approach from positing a 'world of flows' – of ethnoscapes, mediascapes, technoscapes, financescapes and ideoscapes – such as presented by Arjun Appadurai.[9] It also suggests the need to go beyond the claims about a one-dimensional 'network society' as described by Manuel Castells.[10] Globalization is not simply a process of disorder, fragmentation or rupture. Nor, on the other hand, is it simply a force of homogenization. Writers as sophisticated and concerned about the structures of the 'social whole' as Fredric Jameson and David Harvey have found themselves arguing that the postmodern world has become increasingly fragmented without having an account of the level at which fragmentation takes place and the level at which reintegration is occurring.[11]

A similar problem of positing a social whole based on fragmentation is found in the argument about a shift from 'organized' to 'disorganized capitalism'.[12] World capitalism has not recently become disorganized – and it was not uniquely organized in the first place; certainly not when Rudolf Hilferding first coined the term at the beginning of this century. It is true that the pace of change has accelerated and the life-world is experienced as increasingly in flux, but this does not mean that generalizable patterns cannot be ascertained. Both the critics of postmodernity and the postmodernists themselves may be right to point to the subjective *experience* of fragmentation. However, they have done very little to theorize the relationship between the increasing interconnection of social relations at a more abstract level (able to be generalized when viewed from afar) and the confusing, variable pastiche of fragmented practices and counter-practices apparent when viewed at close hand.

By explicitly recognizing how the nature of our analysis depends upon the place from which we begin the analysis (in other words, the level of abstraction taken by the theory), we can usefully move across a manifold of theoretical levels from on-the-ground detailed description to generalizations about modes of practice and forms of social being without privileging any one level. In doing so, it becomes possible to say that the world is becoming increasingly interconnected at the most abstract level of integration – for example, by the disembodying networks of electronic mass communication – even as social difference and social disruption at the level of the face-to-face is accented in and through that same process.

## Structures of globalization

### Empirical analysis

Many writings on globalization start with an anodyne ode to the new patterns of interconnection. Books usually begin with a series of quaint anecdotal market-linked instances that evidence the globalizing of the life-worlds of ordinary people like you and me. They begin with someone getting up in the morning to a diet of global cornflakes, followed by a day of global consumption and communication. One of the strangest variations on this genre was presented at a recent Australian-American Leadership dialogue in Washington by the United States Trade Representative Robert Zoellick:

> Consider the life of the typical American, 19,000 km from Australia. Jeff gets up and reads his favourite paper, the *New York Post* [owned by a network of global companies chaired by ex-Australian

> Rupert Murdoch], while eating an omelette made with Surprise Bay cheddar [an Australian cheese]... Afterwards, he turns on the Fox News Channel [also in the Murdoch stable] for a quick check of the weather and goes to the Looksmart internet search engine to locate plans for an outdoor barbecue that he wants to build. He prints the directions and heads outside to make use of a newly delivered load of Boral bricks. When he stops for a break, he grabs a Coke ... Jeff's hypothetical all-American day was touched by an Australian product or investment at just about every turn. Even his classic Coca-Cola and treasured Ford were produced by Australians ... testament to the amazing reality of globalisation.[13]

This particularly ideologically-charged version of the anodyne ode is intended to show that globalization does not equal Americanization. Rather, we are all participants in an amazing process. Unfortunately, too many of these quotidian calendars are skewed this way and that. There is nothing intrinsically wrong with adding incommensurable empirical instances together and calling it 'globalization'. However, the value of empirical work depends very much on what drives the choice of examples and what is meant by globalization. Similarly, in order to understand globalization, we need all the work that has been done in amassing statistics on the extent of world interconnection. In order to make any sense of the processes at all, statistics can be helpful. However, in both cases – anecdotal patterns and statistical patterns – the usefulness of the description depends on how it is done and what is claimed.

Any theory of globalization has to be built on a foundation of extensive empirical research. However, problems usually arise over either describing different things or partial versions of the same thing – hence the aptness of Manfred Steger's use of the Buddhist parable of the blind scholars attempting to describe an animal they have never encountered before by groping at its various body parts.[14] As such the debates over the process of globalization are full of unhelpful proclamations. Either it is said that it does not exist *as such*,[15] or that it is all-embracing or epochal;[16] that an earlier stage of globalization was brought to an end by the Great Depression,[17] or that the dominance of market globalization ended with the attack on the World Trade Center towers.[18] By moving to a more abstract level of analysis, the all-or-nothing style of these interpretative claims can be avoided.

## Conjunctural analysis

At the more abstract level of conjunctural analysis, I have been suggesting that one useful way of examining the nature of globalization is through tracking the networks of social interchange in relation to analytically-distinguishable modes of practice. Many writers already make this move partially and implicitly, some more successfully than others. Richard Langhorne's writing is usually quite subtle, but it illustrates the limitations of concentrating on one mode of practice. He begins with the tautologous claim that globalization is made possible by '*global* communications' (my emphasis). This is expressed dramatically as a single determinative: the 'communications revolution is *the* cause of globalization' (my emphasis).[19] Descending into reductionist technological determinism, he writes: 'the real beginning of the globalizing process came when the steam locomotive revolutionized the transport of people, goods and information, particularly newspapers, and at much the same time, the electric telegraph first divorced verbal communication from whatever was the speed of terrestrial transport'.[20] Anthony Giddens vacillates between the same emphasis on communications technologies as the key and saying singularly vague things such as 'Globalisation is thus a complex set of processes, not a single one ... Globalisation not only pulls upwards, but also pushes downwards ... Globalisation also squeezes sideways.'[21]

Working from a quite different perspective that at once avoids the tendencies in the literature to overemphasize the mode of communications and/or lose specificity of focus, Susan Strange takes the categories of security, credit, knowledge, and production as her basis for analysing the systems of power in globalization.[22] Strange's categories are adequate for what she wants to understand – namely, the control of who-gets-what in the world of finance capital – but her categories leave out too much for a broader understanding. Even if it is not the single determinative basis of globalization, changes in the mode of communication have to be recognized in the matrix of explanation somewhere. Arguably, by working across modes of production, exchange, communication, organization and enquiry we are in a better position to engage in a fuller range of questions across the spectrum of concerns about globalization and localization. A summary of the dominant determinative pressures in the world today would thus look something like the following. In the contemporary period, the dominant *mode of production* has become computer-mediated and less dependent on labour-in-place or single-site integration; *exchange* has become increasing dominated by the manifold processes of commodity marketing and abstracted capital trading; *enquiry* has become techno-scientific and rationally decontextualizing of locality and specific nature; *organization* has become abstract rational-bureaucratic and centred on the institutions of the state and the transnational corporation; and *communication* has become dominated by electronic interchange, including mass broadcasting with the content sourced across the globe, but control either centred in corporate America or organized relative to it. All of these processes contribute to the extensions of globalization.

Focusing for a moment on the mode of communication, we can bring together empirical and conjunctural analyses. Going back to the Murdoch media empire example touched on earlier, in April 2003 Rupert Murdoch closed a $US6.6 billion contract to buy US pay-television group DirecTV, thus giving the News Corporation–Fox Entertainment nexus the first global pay-TV satellite network, including Star Asia, Star Plus (India) and British Sky. This is empirically a powerful illustration of globalization in action, but it does not tell us much about the nature of the process. What does it mean in relation to evidence that this globalizing corporation is part of promoting the new nationalism? Fox News succeeded in winning the largest cable-audience share in the United States during 'Operation Freedom for Iraq' predicated on presenting the war through the matrix of gung-ho nationalism. The stars-and-stripes fluttered in the top left-hand corner of the screen and presenters such as Bill O'Reilly spoke in the language of 'us' and 'them', the 'good' and the 'evil'. *The O'Reilly Factor* had a daily American audience of 5.4 million viewers in the first week of April 2003. Despite the global reach of Fox News, this is evidence that might be equally taken as substantiating claims about counter-globalization tendencies and suggesting a return to the boundaries of the nation-state. The point here, however, is that we are not talking about content, but about the social form of communication. Whatever the force of the content – localizing, nationalizing or globalizing – the form of the media is globalizing in its interconnections, points of reference and technological sourcing. Whether it is Fox News, CNN, or even Al-Jazeera, the dominant telecommunications systems are satellite-based, cross-referential, and watched by more than their local or national audiences. Fox News, like all of the news groups, has a globally-accessible website. Neilsen/NetRatings reported that in the week ending 23 March 2003, over 2.3 million persons accessed Fox News, 8.3 million persons accessed MSNBC and over 10 million persons accessed CNN. Across the month of March 2003, Nielsen gave the 'active internet universe' as 247.5 million users, a massive expansion from that time in March 1994 when the US Vice-President Al Gore presented 'his' project for a network of networks – the Global Information Infrastructure.

The world-wide internet population is now variously estimated at between 580 and 655 million persons, with, for example, starting with the letter 'A', 10.5 million internet users in Australia, 3.7 million in Austria, 2.0 million in Argentina, 24,000 in Aruba and no information on

Afghanistan.²³ This is an indicative list showing how the take-up of such technologies is related to the economic and political standing of the populations concerned. Nevertheless, we can say that the immediate reach of those media of communications is global. A person can now stand anywhere in the world from Aruba to Afghanistan to Australia and, through satellite-linked communications systems including the Global Positioning System (GPS), be technologically and globally networked in some way or other. 'Welcome to your new office', proclaimed an advertisement in 1998 for iridium.com, introducing the world's first hand-held global satellite phone – 'it measures 510,228,030 square kilometres'.

### Integrational analysis

It is only at this level of analysis that the argument about power being carried by the most abstract forms of global movement and global interconnection can be directly addressed. We can distinguish between different dominant kinds of globalism expressed in terms of modes of integration.

- *embodied globalism* – the movements of peoples across the world, the oldest form of globalism, but still current in the movements of refugees, emigrants, travellers and tourists.

- *object-extended globalism* – the movements of objects, in particular traded commodities, as well as those most ubiquitous objects of exchange and communication: coins, notes, stamps and postcards. It is no small irony that Nike is at once the (traditional) Greek goddess of victory and also the name of a (modern/postmodern) globalized consumption object. Traded global commodities today range from pre-loved pairs of Levis to the relics and treasures of antiquity such as Cleopatra's Needle and the Ram in the Thicket from Ur, a statue representing a deity from 2,600 BC, stolen from the Iraq National Museum during the collapse of Saddam Hussein's regime.

- *agency-extended globalism* – the movements of agents of institutions such as corporations and states so prominent today, but gaining ground quite early in the first millennium with the expansionist empire of Rome and the proselytizing of the agents of Christendom.

- *disembodied globalism* – the movements of 'immaterial' things and processes including images, electronic texts and encoded capital. This is the really new phenomenon with its beginnings in the late nineteenth century, but only taking off with the development of electronic communications and computerized exchange.

It is at this level of analysis that Proposition 2 elaborated at the beginning of the chapter can best be understood. Put most directly, the argument here is that embodied globalism is not the defining dominant condition of contemporary globalization, although it is still present and, in some cases, dramatically increasing. Migration is one area that has not increased. Despite interesting work by writers such as Stephen Castles and Robin Cohen on the post-war changes in migration patterns,[24] the statistical evidence suggests that in terms of sheer numbers and proportions the century after 1815 rather than the present century was *the* period of embodied global resettlement. The century from 1915 saw a sharp decrease in transnational migration between the world wars and then an upsurge after 1945, however, in relative terms, global migration was constrained by increasingly restrictive immigration laws.[25] What is new in relation to migration in the past few decades, I would argue, is the increased diversity and spread of immigrant destinations across the globe, not the fact of massive movement. Other movements of people, particularly in the areas of tourism and refugees, have increased exponentially across the same period. However, in the case of the refugees, monitoring and surveillance systems, border guards and military patrols make state-organized processes still the framing condition of the flows of the wretched of the earth. Similarly the movement of tourists is predominantly framed by disembodied management systems related to the rise of the abstracted category of 'the population' rather than by following genealogical pathways, pilgrimage lines or *wantok* connections.[26] Travel agents and airlines now depend upon Global Distribution Systems and inventory management systems to schedule the millions of flights each year, and travellers depend upon those agents and their abstract systems. For example, Qantas Airlines' booking engine on its website, e-Travel Planitgo, processed more than six million online bookings between 2000 and 2005.

## Categorical analysis

This level of analysis emphasizes the changing nature of the various categories of being including temporality and spatiality, embodiment and epistemology. Here we are interested, for example, in the *nature* of the space that people move in, relate across, and set up systems to manage or transcend. I want to elaborate upon just one point, an issue raised in a different context in Chapter 2. While globalization by definition involves the extension of social relations across world space, it does not mean that globalization can be explained in terms of the abstraction of spatiality in itself. This point parallels Justin Rosenberg's argument:

> It is not only space and time which partake of these qualities of uniformity and abstraction. On the contrary, for classical social theory, it was precisely the generalising of these properties across the

totality of forms of social reproduction (mental and material) which define the key question – the question of modernity itself. Abstraction of individuals as 'individuals', of space and time as 'emptiable', of states as 'sovereign', of things as 'exchange-values' – we moderns, wrote Marx, 'are now ruled by *abstractions*'.[27]

One of the most telling processes of abstraction of space can be illustrated by linking back to the early discussion of the changing patterns of the mode of exchange. As Saskia Sassen documents, the foreign-currency exchange market led the way with increasingly globalized transactions from the mid-1970s with a daily turn-over of US$15 billion. The escalation in itself was extraordinary: $60 billion in the early 1980s; US$1.3 trillion in the late 1990s. Over and above this, however, the point is that these more abstract forms of exchange outpaced more concrete exchange transactions such as commodity trading, which itself was greatly increasing in volume: foreign currency exchange was ten times world trade in 1983, sixty times in 1992 and seventy times in 1999.[28] For all the substantial facts and figures that Paul Hirst and Grahame Thompson accumulate in order to dismiss the significance of this change and to show the continuities in the international integration of the economy from the 1870s to the present, they reduce the differences in form to the kind of empirical generalizations that an accountant might make. For example, the change in character for them is reduced to 'a switch to short-term capital' from the longer-term capital of the gold standard period. Some of 'the capital flows of the present, they suggest, 'could thus be accounted for by significant differences in the pattern of interest rate variation'.[29] This hides so much, including the recurrent themes of contemporary globalization: the speed of transactions (at one level, challenging the modern idea of regulating temporality for social return) and the transversal of jurisdictional bases (at one level, challenging the modern idea of the nation-state regulating territoriality). The volume of traded derivatives, in this respect, abstracts from and carries forward the power of older kinds of capital movement such as direct foreign-currency exchange.

This conversation, as brief as it is, is intended to be only indicative of the kind of research needed in relation to the changing forms of globalization and how they are bound up with the most basic conditions of how we live spatially and temporarily. There is a concurrent task to which we still have to attend – namely, to put into theoretical context what is happening to the wretched of the earth in these changed circumstances as capital flies around the globe. If you read the tracts put out by conservative think-tanks and governments, globalization is simply a 'great force for good'.[30] According to a recent Australian government report, 'Over the past 30 years, mainly due to strong growth in globalising East Asia, world poverty has declined. However, poverty increased significantly in more inward looking economies, many of which also were poorly governed economies.'[31] Presumably the second sentence of that pronouncement is intended to cover the fact that over the 1990s more than 50 countries suffered declining living standards as measured in conventional terms. This is conveniently forgotten in an accounting system that works on population measures dominated by the marginal success of China. The following section of this chapter addresses these concerns as one dimension of what in Chapter 4 was called a crisis that 'goes to the heart of being human in the world today'.

## Globalism, empire and the politics of structured subjection[32]

Each day, around the world, 30,000 children die of preventable diseases. This is savage globalization at its most stark. Across the last decade 13,000,000 children were killed by diarrhoea, a number that exceeds the count of all the people killed in armed combat since World War II.[33] However, despite an increasing global division of wealth and poverty, mainstream theory and practice in its various guises – conservative, neo-liberal, libertarian and social liberal – now takes for granted the very structures of global capitalism, structures that earlier theories of dependency and imperialism, in all their faltering overconfident dogmatism, tried to criticize as the source of the problem. Some of the mainstream approaches have responded that indeed something can be done about global poverty – we need an intensification of the very same processes that may, for a generation or two, harden those inequities. The rest stay strangely silent. Meanwhile, avant-garde theory tends to be consumed by post-structural questions about globalism as a chaotic process and neo-colonial identity as an ambivalent subject-position.

In general, amorphous conceptions of 'interdependency' and 'the borderless world' have tended to replace the hard-edged connotations of imperialism, dependency, underdevelopment and structured subjugation.[34] This two-fold softening of the theories of structured subjugation is mirrored darkly by Western mass-cultural representations of the Third World.[35] The images take two major forms: first, as an aestheticized theatre of horror in which only a few can be rescued from among the mass of unredeemable; and second, as a romanticized location of Otherness. The global electronic media has enhanced the possibility of us witnessing famines and floods on the other side of the world, but in one of those tragic contradictions of globalism, the images of Third World poverty and exploitation are far more likely to be anaesthetized in the form of advertisements for World Vision, the Body Shop or the Italian clothes manufacturer Benetton,[36] than they are to be systematically examined on the evening television news.

The second form taken by popular images, romanticization, can be found everywhere. They range from the ridiculous – for example, IBM's postmodern advertising campaign 'Solutions for a small planet'™, depicted Buddhist monks in saffron robes meditating on the side of a mountain and telepathically anticipating the joy of being able to communicate globally – to the commodified sublime, including the marketing of World Music and the conferencing of novels by Salman Rushdie. One issue of *Studio Bambini*, 'Out of Africa', featured a hundred pages of winter fashion photographed in Africa, with its front-cover image depicting an African boy dressed in safari leather-gear protectively embracing a European girl wearing a delicate turtle-neck knit. Hermes Paris advertised its silk twill scarf featuring African masks using a photograph of a European woman bearing an African baby on her back: 'Africa. Mother and Earth.'

With the problems of the dispossessed of the Third World brought into soft focus in our mediated memory banks, the virtues of the poorer regions of the world as sources of interesting anguished literature, as producers of rainforest timber, and as tourist destinations (that is, at least the unspoilt, unlogged bits), can be presented without fear of too much guilt. Commentators such as Peter Bauer no longer write tomes of expiation on 'Western guilt and Third World Poverty'.[37] Instead, in the late twentieth century a conservative liberal, Francis Fukuyama, comfortably pronounced the victory of market-oriented liberal democracy and wrote a book on *Trust: The Social Virtues and the Creation of Prosperity*. Why are significant parts of the Third World poverty stricken? Implicitly in Fukuyama's account it is because they have low levels of trust in strangers, the '*spontaneous sociability*, which constitutes a subset of social capital'.[38] It is no wonder we feel that the plight of the Third World is all too complicated. And it is not surprising that modernist theories of imperialism and dependency have largely passed into history.

New attempts at describing the politics of empire have their own problems. The present chapter parts company on many points with the recent attempt by Hardt and Negri to bring back the concept of 'empire'.[39] Nevertheless, *Globalism, Nationalism, Tribalism* continues to work from a premise close to the hearts of those writers: structure is the patterned instantiation of people doing things. In these terms, although globalization and global subjection should be treated as socially-contingent, historically-specific and analytically-limited processes, they can be usefully interlinked within a framework which continues to take seriously the Marxist notion that people make history but not under conditions of their own choosing. Global capitalism is the dominant condition of our time. In that context, *global subjection* is a relational process, defined as a condition of subjection (used in both senses of that word) within a dominant pattern of social practices or institutional framework(s). It is one of the arguments of this chapter that across the second half of the twentieth century and into the present, we have seen an increasing dependency of locales, regions and states upon processes of global capitalism. Ironically, delinking a community/polity from the global economy and culture has become less possible at the very time (and partly for the very reason) that most people, including policy-makers in the Third World, have no way of thinking outside the terms of the global condition. The structures of globalism involve both constantly-reproduced material constraints and actively-lived sensibilities. In this sense, as has been a consistent theme of *Globalism, Nationalism, Tribalism*, the term 'structure' is used to indicate a pattern of lived practices and ideologies, not to refer to a thing out there. This argument can be presented as a series of interconnected propositions about globalism and subjection that extend upon the earlier propositions. For example, as an extension upon Proposition 4 on the nature of power at a distance we can talk about the nature of domination across different degrees of extension:

> *Proposition 7.* Domination and subjection operate differently across various degrees of geographical extension – local, regional, nation-state and global relations – and across various levels of social integration – from the embodied to the disembodied. In the past couple of decades, a framework of globalizing connections has emerged as the dominant form of geographical extension through which power is exercised.

To say that we have seen the emerging dominance and increasing penetration of various modes of practice including production and communication conducted across a global reach is not to imply that the immediacy and efficacy of other levels of extension from the local to the regional are simply subordinated within what some theorists have ontologically flattened out as 'the global flow'. This simple proposition has not been handled well in the literature. Dependency theory, for example, became self-contradictory by statistically documenting dependency and subjection in terms of state-bounded development, and simultaneously treating the world-system as the primary object of enquiry. World-system theory countered this problem by designating 'the region' as the primary sub-unit of the world-economy,⁴⁰ however, this overly restricts the analysis while at the same time problematically leaving the category 'world-economy' as a definitional totality characterized by a single mode of production.

In response, it is worth repeating the point that the geo-political designations – locale, region, nation-state and global relations – can usefully be deployed as descriptive of various overlaying levels of spatial extension so long as the approach goes beyond a proposition about spatial reach. This kind of argument allows us to show how cultural contradictions and tensions of interest emerge in the overlaying of levels.⁴¹ The corporate and communications culture of globalism is the most obvious area where we can see the levels of extension being ideologically collapsed into each other while continuing in practice to raise questions of power. On the one hand, transnational corporations increasingly present themselves as bridging the local and the global. Recall the patronizing Toyota advertisement run in the *Cambodian Daily* (discussed in Chapter 1) which plays across the shifting reference points of place: *'This is our town. It's the global village. We live here. You do too. We're neighbours. And since we're neighbours, we should be friends ...'* Similarly, in his introduction to the *News Corporation Annual Report, 2002,* Rupert Murdoch writes:

> Our efforts have always been driven by a fierce egalitarian spirit, by a deep belief in fair play and the rights of individuals. This is the spirit that guided our diverse operations as we've catered for audiences from Britain to Bangalore; as our newspapers have earned one loyal reader at a time from New York to New Guinea. ⁴²

On the other hand, this kind of presentation allows the anti-corporate globalization movement to point up the hypocrisy of such a claim given that the corporations are so obviously oriented to globalizing their profit. 'Therefore, I am pleased to report', Rupert Murdoch continues, 'revenues rose 10 per cent to US$15.2 billion.'

> *Proposition 8.* As the contradictions of globalism and localism have increased, the critical responses to globalization have taken an increasingly-intense form, bringing symbolic and embodied responses onto the street. As the effects of globalized modes of practice have become more penetrating and targeted, rather than counter-targeting the narrow instrumentalization of abstract processes of global interchange, the focus of action has been to counter the immediately-visible agents of the spirit of capitalist globalization – from Starbuck's shopfronts to high-profile conferences such as the World Trade Organization and World Economic Forum meetings. In summary, the predominant activist response has been understandably enacted in

embodied terms and directed at the manifestations of systemic abstraction rather than against the perversion of those processes themselves.[43]

The response to the McDonald's fast-food chain provides a good example. In Chapter 2 it was mentioned that McDonald's began during the 1990s to locate themselves more self-consciously within the local communities that bought their hamburgers. This continued into the new century with advertisements in Great Britain depicting working-class boys playing soccer under the refrain, 'We're as dedicated to grass-roots football as you are.' This high-profile advertising was a direct response to, and a spiralling cause of, the growing political targeting of that company as a pre-eminently-global corporation. The golden arches had become an ambiguous symbol. On the one hand, it was longingly recognized as marking the well-remembered well-lit place of childhood parties. On the other hand, it stood as an icon under which all global corporations were linked to the problem of homogenizing capitalism – McDonaldization. In 1985, London Greenpeace organized an International Day of Action against McDonald's. Leaflets were distributed, which over the next few years became the basis for a libel trial that was to take two-and-a-half years, concluding in June 1997. The action taken against two community activists in London became known as the McLibel Trial. In the years that followed we saw the destruction in 1999 of one outlet in the French town of Millau, another in 2000 during the May Day anti-capitalist riots in London and a bomb explosion in Dinan, north-western France, killing an employee. A week later in mid-April 2000, the company carried the spiral further by running an advertisement demanding an end to attacks on its restaurants. In June, Jose Bové, the French farmer who had led the 1999 crusade against McDonald's was sentenced to prison. He arrived at the prison after a seven-hour tractor procession to Montpellier that gathered a cortege of other vehicles as it progressed. In other words, while McDonald's took to the courts and media (systems of agency and disembodied extension), the counter-responses tended to either take to the streets or react in the mainstream media. Building alternative practices of production and exchange had become a politics of an earlier generation.

*Proposition 9.* The changing structures of capitalism, a racing globalization and an enhanced sense of comparative place and comparative identity have both subjectively and objectively reframed (though not necessarily replaced) the old imperial connections. Subjection is no longer predominantly based upon the old lines of imperial exploitation and domination. Globalizing disembodied capitalism, not classical imperialism, I suggest, now frames the various forms of dependency and exploitation. However, in making this argument the concept of 'framing' is intended to emphasize the reconstitutive and delimiting processes of social reproduction, not to suggest that historically long-term institutions such as colonialism or imperialism are magically irrelevant to the picture of the present. It is certainly not to agree with the post-structuralist Gianni Vattimo that we have seen 'the end of colonialism and imperialism'.[44]

Within this emerging global (postmodern) setting at the turn of the twenty-first century, acts of imperially-driven (modernizing) activity continue to occur with unfortunate regularity. When the French resumed nuclear testing at Mururoa Atoll in the mid-1990s it indicated that a European power could still treat its old colonies as part of its sovereign territory. When the 'Coalition of the Willing' invaded the territory of Iraq in 2002 it was clear that they were not doing so only to liberate the Iraqi people from Saddam Hussein. Just as in the case of the United States' precipitous involvement in the first Gulf War of 1991 – with a heavier bombing of Iraq in 43 days than in Vietnam in eight years – one of the concerns was imperial geopolitical: the anticipated destabilizing of the world's oil production. Nevertheless, despite the regularity of such acts in which imperial power still plays a part, state-based imperialism no longer constitutes a way of life. Despite the comprehensiveness of the War on Terror, it no longer completely dominates the structures of world politics. Acts of domination for extending national interest claims now have to be socially legitimated, politically rationalized and ethically defended against ever-more acerbic scrutiny. Increasingly, they have become ethically-ambiguous and half-thought-through reactionary attempts to ameliorate problems exacerbated by earlier activities of imperialism. Compare the following examples. The British establishment defended their involvement in the Falklands/Malvinas War of 1982 as necessary to uphold old imperial obligations. No sense of irony was involved and no moral ambiguity could be admitted. However, by the middle of the 1980s it was no longer upheld as simple commonsense that such intervention would always be a good thing to do. The US invasion of Panama, the defensively named 'Operation Just Cause' involving the fatal bombing of an estimated 2000 civilians in 1989, was justified as delivering the people from an evil drug-lord general. However, it was a more than a quaint embarrassment that General Manuel Noriega had previously been supported by the United States as a client dictator to aid their covert war against the Nicaraguan Sandinistas. And in the new century we have witnessed the complicated rationalizations of Western intervention in Iraq to oust an 'evil dictator' once afforded support as a secularizing force in the Middle East.

Despite the carry-overs, much has changed. Classical imperialism, from the ancient and traditional empires to early twentieth-century colonialism and mid-century neo-colonialism was based largely upon a control of territory (however uneven that might have been) and the relatively-direct exploitation of the production and trading of material commodities. It entailed forms of agency extension, that is, the presence on the ground of agents of the empire. With the development of electronic trading, computerized storage of information, and an exponentially-increasing movement of capital, there has been an abstraction of the possibilities of control and exploitation, an abstraction of the relationship between territory and power, and an abstraction of the dominant level of integration. The term 'casino capitalism' (Susan Strange's term) partly captures this process, but together with terms such as 'fictitious capital formation' (that is, capital produced without a growth in production of material objects) it gives the misleading impression that this abstraction is less real than gunboat diplomacy, more ethereal than factory production. To the contrary, when, for example, global electronic markets sell futures options on agricultural goods not yet produced and transnational corporations speculate on the basis of satellite weather-forecasting, both the relations and the power-effects are very real. Interests other than the importance of feeding people are framing production choices. When economically-viable agricultural production in the post-Green Revolution stage is increasingly bound up with a mode of enquiry that accentuates genetically-engineered plant hybrids, farmers are seemingly caught between two choices – independent but marginal productivity or enhanced but ecologically-vulnerable production with increasing dependence on Western bio-tech corporations.[44]

> *Proposition 10.* Despite the usual assumption about the process of subjection, it is not a passive process. There was a tendency in much international relations theory to treat subjection as a one-sided activity – as something done to the Third World by the West and supported by local compradors. The alternative concept of 'subjection' is used here with an imbrication of meanings, analytically separable, but in practice bound up with each other: first, it is used in the old-fashioned political sense of being subordinate rather than independent, 'a subject of the realm', whatever that realm might be – state, corporation, peace-keeping force, the world-economy. It is important that we do not lose sight of this crude sense of 'the power of the realm'. People living in Rwanda, Eritrea, Tahiti and Burma, as well as in Europe and North America are regularly confronted by it in their everyday lives. Second, it is used in the current theoretical sense of the 'subject as agent', with a nod to the way in which Homi Bhabha

uses the concept as emphasizing the contingency of outside inscription and the temporary closure involved in self-active enunciation, but much closer to writers such as Raymond Williams and Aijaz Ahmad who talk of persons being self-active in their own constitution as subjects with the self-activity itself being framed by intersubjective structures.[46] To paraphrase the classic Marxist premise to which I referred earlier: people make themselves but not as monads and not under conditions of their own choosing.

Subjection within global capitalism is a thoroughly double-sided and self-active process. In Nigeria, the November 1995 execution by General Sani Abacha's military regime of the novelist Ken Saro-Wiwa and eight other Ogoni environmental activists is evidence of the point but with a couple of moral twists. The Anglo-Dutch oil company, Royal Dutch Shell, which has operated in Nigeria for almost 40 years and owns about 30 per cent of the state oil company, has been involved in a public-relations attempt to distance itself from the 'judicial killings' as international accusations of moral complicity circulate the global media. Ken Saro-Wiwa was a leader of the Movement for the Survival of the Ogoni People (MOSOP), a group who more than a decade ago began campaigning against Shell's role in environmentally degrading their region. In 1990 the Etche people demonstrated peaceably against Shell. The company responded by asking for military protection. The Mobile Police Force was sent in: it massacred 80 people and destroyed 495 homes. Against its critics, Shell can claim that it halted its operations in Ogoniland three years later in 1993 (though it continued as the largest oil producer in Nigeria). Similarly, the Commonwealth countries, which responded ineffectively to the oil fields killings through the early 1990s, can claim to have symbolically censured Abacha, finally suspending Nigeria from the Commonwealth forum. Be that as it may, through all of this the ruling junta clearly want Shell to continue operations. They did not understand that the executives of Shell have to leave a decent amount of time before they return to the task of making profits. On the world-stage, killing novelists (or women and children) gets a very bad reception: much worse than executing 'dissidents' or precision-targeting 'terrorists'.

How does global subjection work? In this case, and many others, it is through Third World regimes binding themselves to the global market nexus both economically and culturally, thus confirming a historical condition which makes the nexus tighter. Through most of Nigeria's four decades of independence the country has been under repressive military rule with the bulk of its income coming from oil-export revenue. Such regimes need the corporations, just as the corporations are constantly searching out new markets and sites of production, but it is not so clear that the state-corporate interdependence is benignly balanced.

*Proposition 11.* The various forms of subjection are structured by the dominant modes of practice operating across various levels of spatial extension. In over-accentuating the capitalist mode of production or exchange as the basic determinant of contemporary international relations, dependency theory, world-system theory and some of their recent variants present us with a thoroughly-reductive account of social practice.[47] One problem, as I began to discuss earlier, is that capitalism is treated as a system of economics that reconfigures and replaces everything that came before it. Dependency theory gave market-capitalism the upper hand centuries before it came to be the predominant formation of practice, but even in the present period it is important not to turn late capitalism into a one-dimensional system. Fredric Jameson is a brilliant exponent of this ultimately problematic position. With late or consumer capitalism of the post-war period, he says, has come,

> the purest form of capitalism yet to have emerged, a prodigious expansion of capital into hitherto uncommodified areas. This purer capitalism of our own time thus eliminates the enclaves of precapitalist organization it had hitherto tolerated and exploited in a tributary way. One is tempted to speak in this connection of a new and original penetration of Nature and the Unconscious: that is, the destruction of precapitalist Third World agriculture by the Green Revolution, and the rise of the media and the advertising industry.[48]

It seems churlish to take issue with Jameson on methodological grounds when I so thoroughly agree with him about the expansion and changing nature of capital over the last couple of decades, but the points of contention have important political consequences. If we accept that late capitalism has completely replaced prior modes of production then we have no way of understanding why the penetration of capitalism, as extensive and intensive as it is, has not produced a homogenization of cultures and economies. Practices of resistance keep occurring in the Third World and the First, but even that is not the answer. In the same way that *Proposition 8* put forward an alternative analytic scheme based on the metaphor of overlaying (or imbricating) levels of extension, here I am suggesting that modes of production, indeed all modes of practice, should be treated in the same way – that is as overlaying modes with the dominant mode of practice setting the framing conditions for subordinate modes.

*Proposition 12.* Subjection, defined as a dominant pattern of social practices and institutions, has an ontological dimension. This dimension is usually badly handled by contemporary theory, so in making this point let me repeat the central methodological claim of this book.

The most complex and politically-useful accounts of social life are conducted across the full range of theoretical abstraction from the most 'concrete' kinds of analysis involving empirical generalization to the most 'abstract' explorations of categories of existence such as time, space, embodiment, desire, ambivalence and so on. Marxist scholars have tended to concentrate on two levels of analysis – conjunctural studies of particular developments, and social formational studies of systemic structures. However, as Theda Skocpol writes of one important theorist in this tradition,

> Wallerstein creates an opposition between a formalistic theoretical model of universal reference, on the one hand, and the particularities and 'accidents' of history on the other hand – an opposition that uncannily resembles the relationship between theory and history in the ideal type method of the modernization approach.[49]

The problem here lies not in making an analytic distinction between empirical description and social formational analysis, or between theory and history, but in setting them up as two sides of a great divide. Attempting to get around this problem, post-structuralists writing from the standpoints of postcolonialism or subaltern studies problematically head off in the opposite direction, tending to collapse theory and practice into each other. As I argued in Chapter 4, they start from the most abstract level of analysis, deconstructing categories of ontology such as identity and difference, and draw back to the particularities of history without the use of any middle-order structural concepts such as 'social formation' or 'mode of practice'. Moreover, as Phillip Darby argues, the most excessively abstract postcolonial tracts reduce social life to a textual landscape of ambivalences and hybridities – that is, to ontologies without a living subject. The practices of actual people become allegories of this and that.[50]

The concept of 'ontology' is intended to refer to the most basic framing categories of existence, but we have to careful to distinguish the use of the concept from the psychologistic tendency to attribute dependent personalities to the dispossessed of the world. It is found in the most unlikely places from the travelogues of the post-structuralist Jean Baudrillard to occasional moments in the revolutionary writings of Frantz Fanon. Baudrillard writes that the weak are imbued with 'contempt for themselves by a sort of capillary action from the superior race'; and on Africa we are told that 'the West will be hard-pressed to rid itself of this generation of simiesque and prosaic despots born of the monstrous crossing of the jungle with the shining values of ideology.'[51] Fanon writes that: 'The colonized man is an envious man ... It is true, for there is no native who does not dream at least once of setting himself up in the settler's place.'[52] I am neither objecting here to Fanon's use of psychoanalysis nor to Baudrillard's implicit point about the intersection of the values of tradition and modernity (that is, leaving aside Baudrillard's appalling expressions of racism). Rather, I am questioning the way in which, as subjectivity is totalized and the layers of categorical meaning are read off in terms of the dominant level, the ontological complexity of peoples and individuals is reduced to a psychology of common personality traits.

Wary of such tendencies some writers have shied away from delving into the depths of social existence. However, questions about how people live their bodies, how they understand the nature of identity, how they exist in overlaying senses of place and space – are crucial to understanding the settings across which the so-designated major actors of international relations strut their stuff. This brings us to the final section in this chapter. How is it, despite the reams of material on globalization and its discontents, that writers such as Anthony Giddens can end with bland having-it-every-which-way comments such as the following?

> In making these points I do not wish to say that the worries of the anti-globalisers are without foundation. On the contrary, they are real and justified. A retreat from globalisation, however, even if it were possible, would not resolve them. We need to advance globalisation further rather than retard it, but globalisation has to be managed more effectively and equitably than has happened over the past few decades, and the ideological agenda of economic development shifted.[53]

## Conclusion

Contemporary globalization is a remarkable creature. She is an agile blousy Hollywood-style genie who rarely lives up to her promises yet all too often slips relatively unscathed between the legs of her fiercest critics.[54] The evasion of critique occurs through many manoeuvres, but two key ways in which the critics themselves inadvertently contribute to capitalist globalization becoming seen either as inevitable or as a (contested) cultural commonsense are worth singling out. First, as I have been concerned to argue, to the extent that globalization is treated as a process of spatial extension pertaining only to the last two or three decades, we tend to overlook the long-term development of practices and ideas that underpin its contemporary power. Second, as to the extent that globalism is reduced to an ideology of capitalist economic expansion, we tend to miss out on the way in which it is now carried by a matrix of ideological assumptions across the whole range of contemporary modes of practice from globalizing capitalism to disembodying techno-science. A number of scholars such as John Tomlinson, Arjun Appadurai, Manfred Steger, Roland Robertson and James Mittelman have recognized the broader dynamics of globalization, but when it comes to discussing globalism as an ideology-subjectivity most commentators critically focus on deconstructing ideologies and practices that directly defend the globalizing market. In an elaboration of Proposition 4 above, I suggest that both of these critical moves contribute to reducing globalism to one of its expressions – neo-liberal globalism. To be sure, neo-liberalism is one of the dominant philosophies of our time, but strangely part of the power of neo-liberalism is that it is at one level so contested. Its glaring prominence blinds us to the breadth and depth of a matrix of associated ideologies and practices that are left relatively uninterrogated.

As the theoretical moves and questions of method compound, it is worth returning to the underlying political concern of the chapter. One of its key premises has been that major discrepancies of power operate across the supposedly-free and open flows of global exchange and interdependence. Contemporary globalization has also brought with it heightening inequalities and increasing political violence. It is this very ambiguity that the proponents of globalization find so hard to admit. One year after September 11, and just before the Allied invasion of Afghanistan, *The Economist* ran a major lift-out survey called 'Globalisation and its Critics'. As I quoted earlier, the stand-first for the opening article read thus: 'globalisation is a great force for good'. It continued: 'But neither governments nor businesses, Clive Crook argues, can be trusted to make the case.'[55] Savage globalization thus defends itself in tortuously tenuous ways.

By contrast, in the argument being presented here, global capitalism may have brought varying degrees of 'development' to Third World countries such as Brazil and Thailand, but it has brought a certain kind of perverted one-dimensional development with enormous social costs. This is another of the faces of global savagery. Sixty per cent of the people of Brazil now live below a harsh poverty line, but without the old means of agricultural subsistence, they face a difficult future that its new government will not be able to solve in the short term. Over the last couple of decades the tourist mecca of Rio has been through a stage of poverty cleansing – including the murder and clearing out of its street-children – but over a million people still cling to its outskirts, living in shanty towns with nowhere else to go. Thailand's capital, Bangkok, is one of the most polluted cities in the world with people commuting hours each day along the congested freeways. One of its major industries is tourism. The Tourism Authority of Thailand advertises itself in the West as 'An exotic mixture of floating markets, street stalls and designer boutiques ... Have a stopover in Thailand and you'll soon see why they call it the land of smiles.' No mention is made of the largest component of Thai tourism, the sex industry, including the burgeoning use of an estimated 200,000 young teenage and child prostitutes brought in because they have not yet contracted AIDS. Global capitalism in conjunction with the expansion of consumerism and travel has revived the body as a form of traded commodity in ways, which, unlike eighteenth-century slavery, has subverted local village and family life. As the rural north-east becomes more impoverished, families sell their children into sex slavery for lonely Western *fahrangs*. Thus a country that remained relatively independent during the colonial era is now thoroughly bound into the global economy from its growing development-based debt to the increasing incidence of child-indenture. In short, even in the 'economic miracles' of the Third World, development is associated with costs: being bound within the fluctuations of global capital, going through an uprooting of rural populations, and living with metropolitan overcrowding, ecological degradation, and an increased domestic division between rich and poor. We can thus enunciate a final proposition that will become the focus of the next and final chapter:

> *Proposition 13.* Globalization, like state or nation formation, is always ethically ambiguous. That is, it is always potentially and actually both good and bad. The task that we face is not just to understand its glorious projections and horrific realities, but also to develop sustainable principles and practices for doing something about completely remaking it.

In the next and final chapter, *Globalism, Nationalism, Tribalism* takes some of the ideologies of the present and attempts to retrieve the positive side of them in the context of an alternative matrix of ethical considerations.

## Notes

1 Earlier examples of the commodification of pictures of planet earth can be found, particularly from travel companies. For example, advertisements from Thomas Cook, Shaw Savill Lines, and Nippon Yusen Kaisya at the beginning of *The Geographical Magazine Atlas* (George Philip, ed., published by the *Geographical Magazine* and George Philip & Son, London, no date but *c.* 1938) use images of the globe. However, they are quite limited.
2 Malcolm Waters, *Globalization*, Routledge, London, 2nd edn, 2001, p. 5 (his emphasis). I chose this book because it is so widely used on university courses.
3 Waters, *Globalization*, p. 7.
4 *Ibid.*, p. 19. All the following quotes are from pp. 19–20.

5 Christian Jacob, 'Mapping in the Mind: The Earth from Ancient Alexandria', in Denis Cosgrove, *Mappings*, Reaktion Books, London, 1999; William Arthur Heidal, *The Frame of the Ancient Greek Maps*, Arno Press, New York, 1976.

6 Asa Briggs and Peter Burke, *A Social History of the Media: From Gutenberg to the Internet*, Polity Press, Cambridge, 2002.

7 See for example, Ulrich Beck's presumptive and therefore unhelpful definition of globalization as denoting 'the processes through which sovereign national states are criss-crossed and undermined' (*What is Globalization?* Polity Press, Cambridge, 2000, p. 11).

8 Michael Freeman, 'Theories of Ethnicity, Tribalism and Nationalism' in Kenneth Christie (ed.), *Ethnic Conflict, Tribal Politics: A Global Perspective*, Curzon Press, Richmond, 1998, p. 27.

9 Arjun Appadurai, *Modernity at Large: Cultural Dimensions of Globalization*, University of Minnesota Press, Minneapolis, 1996.

10 See Geoff Sharp, 'An Overview for the Next Millennium', *Arena Journal*, new series no. 9, 1997, pp. 1–8.

11 The classic early statement on the fragmentations of postmodernity by a structuralist is Fredric Jameson's 'Postmodernism, or the Cultural Logic of Late Capitalism' republished as chapter 1 of *Postmodernism or, the Cultural Logic of Late Capitalism*, Verso, London, 1991. Similarly, David Harvey's *The Condition of Postmodernity*, Basil Blackwell, Oxford, 1989, is a brilliant attempt to theorize the structures of the changing world, but he still falls back upon the postmodernist language of fragmentation without providing us with an account of the levels at which fragmentation actually occurs.

12 Scott Lash and John Urry, *The End of Organized Capitalism*, Polity Press, Cambridge, 1987; Claus Offe, *Disorganized Capitalism*, Polity Press, Cambridge, 1985.

13 *The Australian*, 12 July 2002.

14 Manfred Steger, *Globalism: The New Market Ideology*, Rowman and Littlefield, Lanham, MD, 2002, p. 17.

15 Paul Hirst and Grahame Thompson, *Globalization in Question*, Polity Press, Cambridge, 2nd edn, 1999.

16 Waters, *Globalization*; Martin Albrow, *The Global Age: State and Society Beyond Modernity*, Polity Press, Cambridge, 1996.

17 Harold James, *The End of Globalisation: Lessons from the Great Depression*, Harvard University Press, Cambridge, MA, 2001.

18 John Gray, London School of Economics, cited in *The Economist*, 29 September 2001.

19 Richard Langhorne, *The Coming of Globalization: Its Evolutionary and Contemporary Consequences*, Palgrave, Basingstoke, 2001, p. 2.

20 *Ibid.*, pp. xi–xii.

21 Anthony Giddens, *Runaway World: How Globalisation is Reshaping Our Lives*, Profile Books, London, 2nd edn, 2002, p. 10 and pp. 12–13. This descent into methodological incoherence does not compare well with his overall position presented in the two volumes of *A Critique of Historical Materialism*. There he posited a gently modified mode-of-production argument in intersection with an emphasis on the mode of organization: the extension of allocative resources under conditions of capitalism/industrialism.

22 Susan Strange, *The Retreat of the State: The Diffusion of Power in the World Economy*, Cambridge University Press, Cambridge, 1996, Chapters 1–2.

23 Figures from cyberatlas.com and neilsen-netratings.com See also Armand Mattelart, *Networking the World: 1794–2000*, University of Minnesota Press, Minneapolis, 2000; and David Held, Anthony McGrew, David Goldblatt and Jonathan Perraton, *Global Transformations*, Polity Press, Cambridge, 1999, Chapter 7.

24 Robin Cohen, *The New Helots: Migrants in the International Division of Labour*, Gower, Aldershot, 1987; Stephen Castles, *Ethnicity and Globalization*, Sage Publications, London, 2000.

25 Hirst and Thompson, *Globalization in Question*, Chapter 2; Held, *et al.*, *Global Transformations* (1999), Chapter 6.

26 *Wantok* is Papua New Guinean Pidgin for one who speaks the same language.

27 Justin Rosenberg, *The Follies of Globalisation Theory*, Verso, London, 2000, p. 63.

28 Saskia Sassen, 'Digital Networks and the State', *Theory, Culture & Society*, vol. 17, no. 4, 2000, pp. 19-33.

29 Hirst and Thompson, *Globalization in Question*, p. 29.

30 From the opening article of the special lift-out on globalization by The *Economist*, 29 September 2001.

31 Department of Foreign Affairs and Trade, *Globalisation: Keeping the Gains*, Commonwealth of Australia, Canberra, 2003, p. 1.

32 The following section recontextualizes research that I first did for a chapter in Phillip Darby (ed.), *At the Edge of International Relations: Postcolonialism, Gender and Dependency*, Pinter, London, 1997.

33 UN annual development report figures reported in *The Guardian*, 9 July 2003.

34 Going back to the early period of writings on globalization, see, for example, Robert Keohane's highly regarded text, *After Hegemony: Co-operation and Discord in the World Economy*, Princeton University Press, Princeton, NJ, 1984. Despite the title of his book, he devotes a grand total of two paragraphs to what he calls 'negative reciprocity', that is, 'attempts to maximize utility at the expense of others' (*ibid.*, p. 128). There were of course exceptions. See for example, Samir Amin, *Maldevelopment: Anatomy of a Global Failure*, Zed Books, London, 1990.

35 Reading Aijaz Ahmad's essay, 'Three Worlds Theory', is instructive on the contradictory political layers of meaning in the term 'the Third World' – from *In Theory: Classes, Nations, Literatures*, Verso, London, 1992 – but I use it here nevertheless as a collective noun naming the very diverse regions and nation-states that were historically not included in the industrial capitalist and industrial (post)communist 'worlds'. Its use here presumes no homogeneity, no hierarchy of centrality, and no sense of a continuing political bloc.

36 During the 1990s, when Benetton had 6,500 shops in 100 countries, a turnover of $US2.3 billion, and an advertising budget of $US80 million, it used images of South American toddlers working as slave labourers in a brick yard to promote Luciano Benetton's concept 'of a world without borders'. The aid agency World Vision continues to advertise its project by using images of poverty-stricken Third World children asking Westerners to sponsor individual cases.

37 The title of Chapter 4 in P.T. Bauer, *Equality, the Third World and Economic Delusion*, Weidenfeld and Nicolson, London, 1981.

38 *Trust*, Hamish Hamilton, London, 1995, p. 27 (his emphasis). See also Fukuyama's *The End of History and the Last Man*, Free Press, New York, 1992.

39 Michael Hardt and Antonio Negri, *Empire*, Harvard University Press, Cambridge, MA, 2000.

40 Christopher Chase-Dunn, *Global Formation: Structures of World Economy*, Blackwell, Oxford, pp. 207-10.

41 For a discussion of levels of extension in relation to the changing form of the economy, see John Hinkson, 'Postmodern Economy: Value, Self-Formation and Intellectual Practice', *Arena Journal*, new series no. 1, 1993, pp. 23-44.

42 *News Corporation Annual Report, 2002*, p. 6.

43 James Goodman (ed.), *Protest and Globalisation: Prospects for Transnational Solidarity*, Pluto Press, Sydney, 2002. For example, while Damian Grenfell's chapter in that volume, 'Environmentalism, State Power and "National Interests"', argues that there is a strong need for social movements to develop a global 'public sphere', it recognizes that an alternative politics requires much more.

44 Gianni Vattimo, *The Transparent Society*, Polity Press, Cambridge, 1992, p. 4. Cf. the writings of Walter D. Mignolo who rightly continues to emphasize the continuing relevance of colonialism: *Local Histories/Global Designs: Coloniality, Subaltern Knowledges and Border Thinking*, Princeton University Press, Princeton, NJ, 2000.

45 Gyorgy Scrinis, *Colonizing the Seed: Genetic Engineering and Techno-Industrial Agriculture*, Friends of the Earth, Melbourne, 1995; and Jeremy Seabrook, *Victims of Development*, Verso, London, 1993, Chapter 7, 'Replacing the Biosphere'.

46 Homi Bhabha, *The Location of Culture*, Routledge, London, 1994, ch. 9; Raymond Williams, *Marxism and Literature*, Oxford University Press, Oxford, 1977; Ahmad, *In Theory*, pp. 128-9.

47 For a useful discussion of the relevance of a non-reductive 'modes of production' approach to the study of international relations see Robert Cox, *Production, Power and World Order: Social Forces in the Making of History*, Columbia University Press, New York, 1987.

48 Jameson, *Postmodernism or, the Cultural Logic*, p. 36.

49 Theda Skocpol, 'Wallerstein's World Capitalist System: A Theoretical and Historical Critique,' in Mitchell Seligson and John Passé-Smith (eds), *Development and Underdevelopment: The Political Economy of Inequality*, Lynne Reinner Publishers, Boulder, CO, 1993, p. 236.

50 Phillip Darby, 'Postcolonialism', in his edited collection, *At the Edge of International Politics*, Continuum, London, 1997.

51 From *Cool Memories*, cited in David Slater, 'Exploring other Zones of the Postmodern', in Ali Rattansi and Sallie Westwood, eds, *Racism, Modernity and Identity on the Western Front*, Polity Press, Cambridge, 1994, p. 95.

52 Frantz Fanon *The Wretched of the Earth*, Penguin, Harmondsworth, 1977, p. 30. See also Albert Memmi, *The Colonizer and the Colonized*, Souvenir Press, London, 1974; and Octave Mannoni, *Prospero and Caliban*, Frederick Praeger, New York, 1964.

53 Giddens, *Runaway World*, p. xxix.

54 The metaphor of the genie is not really any different from the metaphor of the juggernaut used by Anthony Giddens (*The Consequences of Modernity*, Polity Press, Cambridge, 1990) or the Hindu god Shiva used by Manfred Steger (*Globalism: The New Market Ideology*, Rowman and Littlefield, Lanham, MD, 2002. It is used here because, it highlights historical tensions of meaning that are relevant to globalization: in this instance between the evil genie of the darker Arabian tales and the rock-and-roll cowboy-style genie of Hollywood's *Aladdin*.

55 *The Economist*, 29 September 2001.

# TWELVE Conclusion

## Principles for a Postnational World

In this changing world, with increasing tensions between globalism, nationalism and localism, the search has intensified for an alternative to the current emphasis on militarized security, state-projected order and consumer-oriented freedom. Some people, for example, are beginning to put their faith in the new possibilities of postnationalism. From one perspective, those who live far from the madding crowd, present this subjectivity as a postmodern politics of retrieval. In effect, they want to retrieve colour and vitality from a past that has been subjected to the limitations of rational modernity and the dominating nation-state. This parallels the kind of nostalgia for the future with which I began this book. However, it is not just a postmodern gloss. It has deeper foundations in the upheavals of contemporary globalization. As a lived subjectivity, postnationalism can be described as a discursive 'attachment' to others like oneself who have been lifted out of the modern boundaries of national identification but still look back with emotion on 'prior' forms of identity.[1] In this definition, postnationalism is a subjectivity that has been abstracted from and therefore only residually beholden to imagined past forms of national identification such as ethnicity, felt common history or bounded territory.[2] It is the late-modern, and sometimes postmodern, subjectivity of the mobile person in a world of traversed spaces.

Some theorists go so far as to suggest that it is possible to discern the beginnings of a 'postnational imaginary'. These writers find it in the messy configurations of modern migrant consciousness, transnational religious revivals of tradition and movements of postmodern hybridity. It is treated as an incipient development: both good and bad in the short term, but with positive, almost utopian, possibilities. These possibilities, they say, will become apparent as the nation-state ceases to enthral and enrage. For example, Arjun Appadurai writes, 'These elements for those who wish to hasten the demise of the nation-state, for all their contradictions, require both nurture and critique. In this way, transnational social forms may generate not only postnational yearnings but also actually existing postnational movements, organizations, and spaces.'[3]

For all the sympathy we may have with such a view,[4] this chapter argues that without a thorough-going exploration of the principles of solidarity and community, advocating postnationalism mounts to little more than a postmodern passion for mobile openness, on the one hand, or an ideologically-insensitive support for 'banal' official nationalism and global capitalism, on the other.[5] As Chris Scanlon argues, this is a trend in contemporary Third Way politics and Compassionate Conservativism, a trend that is emptying out community while calling for its revival.[6] Supporting this line of argument is another confusing development – the nation-states at the centre of the international order, including the United States and Britain, are becoming increasingly nationalistic while their politicians simultaneously present their countries as postnational carriers of a global freedom. Different politicians emphasize alternative sides of this dialectic. Bill Clinton tended towards postnational globalism while George W. Bush's second term has confirmed a renewed comfort with asserting the national interest. Nevertheless, even as the American-Century nationalists maintain a modern defence of the national projection of globalizing power, these leading proponents of global capitalism no longer comfortably proclaim 'my country, right or wrong'.[7] Instead, they invoke variants on the postnational language of 'my country as exemplary of the new openness to global mobility and freedom'; 'we make mistakes, but we are essentially good.' In doing so, they mask the iniquitous nature of the structural conditions that frame such words. The postcolonial advocates of postnational globalization fail to see that they walk in the shadow of these quite differently-motivated advocates of global mobility. Here Craig Calhoun's careful critique of cosmopolitanism accords with the point that I am making:

> as practical projects in the world (and sometimes even as theory) cosmopolitanism and democracy have both been intertwined with capitalism and Western hegemony. If cosmopolitan democracy is to flourish and be fully open to human beings of diverse circumstances and identities then it needs to disentangle itself from neo-liberalism. It needs to approach both cross-cultural relations and the construction of social solidarities with deeper recognition of the significance of diverse starting points and potential outcomes.[8]

My argument is expressed more bluntly, but it should not be taken to mean that I think postnationalism is damnable. It does offer positive possibilities. What I will be criticizing is the tendency to look uncritically to postnationalism or postmodern cosmopolitanism – much as some nineteenth-century philosophers looked to nationalism – as the way out of the problems of an earlier social formation. In this case, we face problems that we have created through the excesses of modernity. However, it does not mean that a postmodern politics of either the Left or the Right provides the answer. One such excess is the increasingly intensified and contradictory use of modern rationalized violence, projected in the name of either abstract peace or 'traditional' integrity. From above, it comes in the form of NATO bombers over Iraq or Kosovo. From below, it is clothed in the language of re-traditionalization: from the violent nationalism of the UCK (better known by their English acronym the KLA, the Kosovo Liberation Army) to the modernist millenarianism of Saddam Hussein and the neo-traditionalism of Osama bin Laden.

It is clear that we need to develop new institutionalized forms of polity and community that go beyond the modern national state, but designating the way of the future as postnationalism does little to achieve that purpose. Nor does emphasizing the virtues of deterritorialized mobility. The chapter takes as its central task the need for a critical exploration of some of the contemporary alternative ideologies of our time: communitarianism, postnationalism and cosmopolitanism. It concludes the book by arguing that we need to put ethics back into the centre of politics – that is, deliberations over the *principles* that frame how we are to live with each other. Unless this is given priority, the current debates over postnationalism and cosmopolitanism, globalism and localism, are bound to end up repeating, in late-modern or postmodern terms, the dead-end modernist arguments over the relative merits of nationalism and internationalism.

## Liberation movements and the politics of modern nationalism

Nationalist-inspired movements have inspired the best and worst of outcomes. At their best, national liberation movements have involved sustained and glorious passions of solidarity and commitment. However, without principles that go beyond 'liberation from oppression', as worthy as that aim is, they have all too often involved desperate violence of the kind that rarely translates into sustainable, ethically-driven polity-communities. In many cases, the best that we can hope for is the restoration of legitimate authority.[9] Whether we take our lead from Fretilin and the East Timorese struggling against Indonesian imperialism, the KLA in Kosovo or the Irish Republican Army in Britain, the prospects for current movements only look a little brighter if you believe like George W. Bush and Condoleezza Rice that instituting the procedures of liberal democracy is a laudable end in itself.

Even considered more narrowly, there have been a few exceptions to the counterproductive retaliatory violence of liberatory nationalism. Examples such as Gandhi's salt march soon got lost in the excesses of modern national*ism*. The most recent positive instance is the Zapatista movement whose moment of express violence was confined to a battle with the Mexican Army in early 1994. Relevant to our argument that positive (and non-violent) forms of postnationalism do not necessarily derive from de-territorialization and mobility, the uprising in Chiapas was initiated on 1 January 1994, the first day of the North American Free Trade Zone Agreement (NAFTA). The people of Chiapas were fighting to stabilize their relationship to *place* against a national government that had just signed a treaty to transnationalize their borders in the context of the intensified mobility of global capitalism. For all of the postmodern romanticism of the Zapatistas, the underlying strength of the movement is not its connections across cyberspace, but its attempt to bring together an on-the-ground commitment to place and embodied ways of life with a web-based means of communicating its politics to the outside world.[10]

In this sense, the counter-position to postnationalism is not an argument for an uncritical political defence of territorial place or integral community. One example of counterproductive attachment to territorialized place will suffice: the Kosovo Liberation Army, a group that for a time the Western media lionized as freedom fighters. From the moment that a group of masked men carrying Kalashnikovs first proclaimed the need for an armed response to Slobodan Milošević, the possibility of Rugova's non-violent alternative was closed off. The KLA's response may have been understandable. Their proclamation came in 1997 as 20,000 Albanians met at the funeral of a school teacher who had been killed by Serbian police.[11] However, the form of the response counterproductively hardened the actions of the ruling national government. Arjun Appadurai gets to the heart of the matter when he writes:

> This incapacity of many deterritorialized groups to think their way out of the imaginary of the nation-state is itself the cause of much global violence because many movements of emancipation and identity are forced, in their struggles against existing nation-states, to embrace the very imaginary they seek to escape. Postnational or non-national movements are forced by the very logic of actually existing nation-states to become antinational or antistate and thus to inspire the very state power that forces them to respond in the language of counternationalism.[12]

This is the last time in this chapter that I will agree with Appadurai, at least politically. If we read the sentence that follows this insightful passage the limitations of his proposed alternative become clear: 'This vicious circle', he says, 'can only be escaped when a language is found to capture complex, nonterritorial, postnational forms of allegiance.'[13] In my view, escaping the vicious circle of reactionary re-embedding of liberatory hopes in the proceduralism of the modern rationalizing state has very little to do with finding a *language* with which to express postnational forms of allegiance, nor with simply becoming postnational. It certainly need not fetishize mobility or the end of strong attachments to place. For Appadurai, postnationalism involves a kind of post-territorial sensibility of multiple belonging. What the analysis misses out are the structures and subjectivities of change and the necessity to re-embed different levels of belonging. Polities and communities alike are being swept up in the race to leave behind the *modern* nation-state and to accommodate what has been described as the processes of 'deterritorialization'.[14] If reactionary violence is often the outcome of the sudden disjunctive loss of community, then effectively advocating the end of sustained community will not lead us to a post-violent world.

The disturbing irony of this aporia of understanding is that some postcolonial writers thus advocate a process of liberation from a form of polity-community – the modern nation-state – that is already being reconstituted by processes that are bigger than both the nation-state and the transnational groupings that appear to be going beyond it. One aspect of this is the contradiction that in the context of *postmodern* pressures to 'deterritorialization', modern politicians are reflexively and instrumentally invoking *tradition* to consolidate both their personal power and the sovereignty of the *modern* nation-state while that kind of sovereignty is no longer the assumed basis of international politics.

In the particular case of Kosovo, Milošević needs to be understood as a modern politician with an ambiguous relation to the southern lands. On the one hand, he worked in the shadow of the philosopher Clausewitz who treated war as politics by other means to consolidate control of territory – in this case he was able to efficiently effect the 'ethnic cleansing' in the space opened to him by the KLA on the ground and the NATO war-machine in the air. On the other hand, he had come to believe in and understand the depth of attachment of 'his people' to the territory. This modernist approach, self-consciously drawing upon tradition, is brought to our attention by Noel Malcolm in his book, *Kosovo*[15]. Milošević's impassioned April 1987 speech, spurred on by the crowd at Kosovo Polje, marked a turning point for a politician who had not previously shown any interest in Kosovo. Two months later in June 1987, Milošević made a speech to the Central Committee of the Serbia Communist Party warning of the dangers of 'darkest nationalism'.¹⁶ With this as background, any critical commentator who knew anything about the region could have foretold that strategic bombing by NATO planes would at best 'win' the war only by shattering the country. And this is what happened. Deterritorializing Yugoslavia became as much part of the problem as it might be relevant to the solution. To state the almost obvious, a positive politics depends how a territory is lived and governed. For all the technological abstraction of time and space there is no escaping it: questions of territory will always be with us as long as we live in embodied relations with others.

## The misplaced faith in postnationalism and cosmopolitanism

Whereas modern nationalism was, and continues to be, expressed at the political-institutional level through social movements of compatriots acting in concert to achieve a *singular* nation-state, one form of postnationalism is expressed as the subjectivity of mobile diasporas of individuals. If these individuals in mutual exile seek 'communal' connection it is not on the basis of an underlying attachment to territorial foundations. It is as a loosely configured imagined community that may or may not have continuing embodied ties.¹⁷ Avant-garde cosmopolitanism has gone through a parallel shift from the modern to the postmodern. Whereas modern cosmopolitanism was problematically projected as a universalistic and *singular* world community, the advocates of postmodern cosmopolitanism rightly acknowledge the diverse historical and spatial contexts that they say still residually frame it. However, they go on to defend multiple attachments or displaced attachments without any obvious exploration of what is a good way of living.¹⁸ In either of these moves – either to advocate postnationalism or postmodern cosmopolitanism – past forms of solidarity such as the modern nation tend to be reduced to clichés of horror. For example, in Appadurai's words, 'As the ideological alibi of the territorial state, [the nation] is the last refuge of totalitarianism.'¹⁹ Similarly, David Campbell in a gross over-generalization presents the territorial nation as *the* source of the problem. 'This is because inscribing the boundaries that make the installation of the nationalist imaginary possible requires expulsion from the resultant "domestic" space of all that comes to be regarded as alien, foreign, and dangerous. The nationalist imaginary thus demands a violent relationship with the other.'²⁰ Emergent trends are presented as a *fait accompli*: 'the nation-state has become obsolete.'²¹ And solidaristic attachment and relatively-bounded and embodied placement, both principles that I will be arguing for later in the chapter, come to be described as part of the problem. Appadurai writes: 'As I oscillate between the detachment of a postcolonial, diasporic, academic identity (taking advantage of the mood of exile and the space of displacement) and the ugly realities of being racialized, minoritized, and tribalized in my everyday encounters, theory encounters practice.'[22] I may be reading this incorrectly, but it appears to treat displacement and exile as a simple opportunity to detach (at least for the privileged), rather than as a vexed dialectic of abstracted insight and more concrete loss.

One can get a sense of the intellectual fear of boundedness, closure and attributed attachment from Iris Marion Young's claim that racism and ethnic chauvinism derive in part from the desire for community. Appeals to community in settings of xenophobia, she says, 'can validate the impulses that reproduce racist and ethnically chauvinist identification'.[23] Of course, in the narrow sense, she is right. It helps to make sense of Radovan Karadzic's Bosnia, Slobodan Milošević's Serbia-Kosovo and the whole horrorhouse of official national-ethnic violence going back into the nineteenth century. Similarly, Julia Kristeva is half-right when she describes the cult of origins as 'a hate reaction' – a reaction of defensive hatred: 'so they withdraw into a sullen, warm private world, unnameable and biological, the impregnable "aloofness" of a weird primal paradise – family, ethnicity, nation, race'.[24] It has some limited application to the defensive ethnocentrisms of Pauline Hanson's One Nation in Australia when she presents the tightly bounded nation-state as a haven in a heartless world, and it has considerable relevance to Jean-Marie Le Pen's National Front when he talks of expelling all immigrants from France.

However, it is only part of the story, and it certainly does not mean that the ideals of community and its various expressions – tribe, locale, nation, world – should be dismissed forthwith in favour of cosmopolitan cities of contiguous strangers.[25] Here I am not being critical of city-life *per se* with its rich possibilities of overlapping and multicultural life-settings. I am railing against the one-sidedness of arguments such as expressed by Young when she says, 'politics must be conceived as a relationship of strangers who do not understand each other in a subjective and immediate sense, relating across time and space.' Her ideal becomes the metropolitan world of *Manhattan* situation-comedies with Jerry *Seinfeld* and *Friends*: 'Our political ideal is the unoppressive city ... City life is the "being-together" of strangers. Strangers encounter one another, either face to face or through the media, often remaining strangers and yet acknowledging their contiguity in living and the contributions each makes to the other.'

Bruce Robbins' introduction to *Cosmopolitics* reveals a parallel discomfort with bounded community and place, arguing instead for a located cosmopolitanism characterized by 'multiple attachment and attachment at a distance':

> To embrace this style of residence on earth (Pablo Neruda's phrase) means repudiating the romantic localism of a certain portion of the left, which feels it must counter capitalist globalization with a strongly rooted and exclusivist sort of belonging ... The devastation covered over by the complacent talk of globalization is of course very real. But precisely *because* it is real, we cannot be content to set against it only the *childish reassurance* of belonging to 'a' place.[26]

If attachment to place were actually being conceived as exclusivist by sections of the Left, then there would be something to criticize, but such examples are so rare or so irrelevant to core debates that it suggests that something else is driving the critique. What Robbins does, despite his sophistication about 'actually existing cosmopolitanism', is engage in misplaced derision. He so concentrates on the definite article 'a', 'a place', that he first of all misses out on the actuality that 'place' is most often lived in practice as a layering of more and less extended relations of interchange and more and less abstract forms of association. It is how we tie those layers together that is the crucial political-ontological question. Second, he turns place into an empty form of spatial connection: 'We are connected to all sorts of places, causally if not always consciously, including many that we have never travelled to, that we have perhaps only seen on television.'[27] As he later implicitly acknowledges, 'place' is not the same as specified geographical locale.[28]

It is not the romance of place *per se* which is deeply problematic, but the uncritical appropriation of it as it enters politics. The writers of books such as *Rooted in the Land* or *People, Land and Community*[29] are struggling to counter, even minimally, their mainstream counterparts in the 'community relations' bureaus of Nescafé, McDonald's, Coca-Cola and IBM. Transnational corporate advertising is now dominated by the global-village motif, whether it is Buddhist monks in mountain settings using computers or rural farmers in Tuscany taking flexible delivery of commodified global education. Television series depicting rural idylls – *Ballykissangel* (Ireland), *Heartbeat* (Yorkshire), *Northern Exposure* (Alaska) or *Seachange* (coastal Victoria) – are indicative of a longing for simple stability that is thoroughly exploited by the global-local style advertising campaigns of the world's largest corporations. Their image-campaigns link the global and the local by simultaneously romanticizing and emptying out the meaning of place. In short, much more than a few souls positing romantic alternatives to the metropolitan polity, it is instrumental management of a continuing and heart-felt desire for placement that has to be challenged, particularly when it is orchestrated by modernist barbarians such as Milošević, or by postmodernist ones such as Bill Clinton.

There are many issues to take up, but there is only the space to mention three:

> *Proposition 1.* Advocates of postnationalism and cosmopolitanism tend to miss out on the social and ethical ambiguity of national community by treating national attachment as either simply a bad thing or begrudgingly accepting this form of attachment as a necessary limitation that will wither away as it is deconstructed by a maturing cosmopolitanism.

In a sense, the advocates of postnationalism repeat the mistake of the theorists of nationalism when the latter make the common moral distinction between ethnic nationalism (bad) and civic nationalism (good). There is certainly an analytic distinction to be made here, but not an ethical one. In some hands it becomes the basis for extolling the virtues of the kind of nationalism that the writer happens to hold. For example, Liah Greenfeld reveals her blind belief in Anglo-American versions of the ideology when she advocates 'individualistic-libertarian' nationalism (her term). By contrast, she says, 'Collectivist ideologies are inherently authoritarian.'[30] I would not bother to refer to this claim except that it is positively taken up by an articulate advocate of postnationalism, Richard Kearney.[31] By contrast, writing years ago Tom Nairn sagely drew our attention to the ambiguity in all nationalisms: 'the substance of national*ism* as such is always morally, politically, humanly ambiguous. This is why moralizing perspectives on the phenomenon always fail, whether they praise or berate it.[32]

In short, even the most positive forms of nationalism are *potentially* problematic, but they are not essentially so. They are potentially problematic in the same way that personal expressions of embodied human interconnection such as romantic love have the potential for the tragic consequences. Most murders are committed by significant others, but it does not mean that we blame 'love' itself. Good and evil cannot so easily be attributed. If this is right, the follow-up question needs to be 'Where do we go from here?' Presently there is an ethical hierarchy that follows a line from particularism to universalism, from ethnic to civic nationalism and onto postnational and cosmopolitanism. Should we conclude by dismissing nationalism out of hand and putting postnationalism in its place? Or should we instead focus our attention on principles for underpinning and maintaining complex ethical social relations. I am arguing for the latter and suggesting that the naming of the relationship is much less important than the form that relationship takes.

> *Proposition 2.* Postnationalism is wrongly presented as a novel development of the turn of the millennium leaving behind modern nationalism. Such a presentation shows insufficient attention both to the continuities of the past and the precedents of the present. In some quite specific ways (although I will qualify the claim in a moment), we can agree that postnationalism does *at one level* represent a new development. However, it has to be recognized that modern nationalism continues to be expressed through social movements of compatriots acting in concert to achieve a *singular* nation-state. Moreover, these continuing modern nationalisms are ironically often a response to the same disruptions of globalism that produce postnationalisms. By the same argument, modern nation-states continue to be relevant to contemporary social relations, despite the modern and postmodern crossings of their borders.
>
> *Proposition 3.* Postnational advocates do not adequately incorporate into their positions an understanding of the paradox that postnationalism is now also the refuge of the instrumental nation-state as it also attempts to find its place in a globalizing world.[33]

The kind of postnationalism being described by postcolonial writers such as Arjun Appadurai is, I suggest, only one form of a number of different kinds of postnationalism. In fact I will go further and argue that the diasporic postnation highlighted by postmodern writers does not represent the most novel form of postnationalism at all. The postcolonial identity of the person who has moved along the tracks of globalism in fact has stronger continuities with past forms of hybrid assertions of identity than the new postnationalisms expressed by the academics and politicians of the capitalist West. When modern states such as the United States of America present themselves as postnational, it suggests that the sensibility of postnationalism needs to be understood in much broader terms than those of hybridity. Hybridity has always been with us, even if the postmodern defences of it are quite new.

Moreover, it is salutary for the direct advocates of postnationalism such as such as Arjun Appadurai, and less explicit postnationalists such as Anthony Appiah[34] and Richard Rorty,[35] to remember that it is that very nation-state that they present as a post-melting-pot, postnational experiment – the United States of America – that has over the last decade been involved in more systematic violence projected outside its borders than any state since Hitler's Third Reich. In the 1991 war against Iraq, filmed as a war without significant casualties, thousands of anonymous soldiers were drowned in sand as NATO tanks with bulldozer-fronted shields filled in Iraqi-held trenches. In the 1999 war against Serbia, the aerial bombing, intended to limit the ethnic cleansing of Kosovo, first of all exacerbated the possibility for the Yugoslav militia effecting the mass exodus of hundreds of thousands of Albanian Kosovars, and, second, stabilized the situation around a reverse ethnic homogeneity. Some 1200 civilians were killed by the bombs, members of the very community supposedly being protected. At present, we do not know how many civilians have been killed in the current wars in Afghanistan and Iraq.

Although not intended as a totalizing denunciation, these facts sit uncomfortably alongside Arjun Appadurai's extolling of the 'sheer cultural vitality of this free-trade zone' called America. True, it *is* possible to have a pluralistic cultural vitality that celebrates difference at the time that the world is made safe for a homogenizing system of economic exchange. True, Appadurai does call for the further pursuit of liberty and cultural difference through legal protections. However, the full force of his call to America takes the form of going with the flow of postmodern global capitalism:

> For the United States, to play a major role in the cultural politics of a postnational world has very complex domestic entailments ... It may mean a painful break from a fundamentally Fordist, manufacture-centred conception of the American economy, as we learn to be global information brokers, service providers, style doctors. It may mean embracing as part of our livelihood what we have so far confined to the world of Broadway, Hollywood, and Disneyland: the import of experiments, the production of fantasies, the export of styles, the hammering out of pluralities. It may mean distinguishing our attachment to America from our willingness to die for the United States ... America may yet construct another narrative of enduring existence, as narrative about the uses of loyalty after the end of the nation-state.[36]

While many good things have come out of America, Appadurai's argument here is bizarre. For too long American cultural exporters has been constructing narratives for others. This passage recalls his argument, discussed in Chapter 5, about the commodity as a source of liberation from social control and freedom. Three glaring problems with the passage deserve critical noting. First, as many other writers have argued, it is misguided to think that the movement from Fordism to what David Harvey calls 'flexible accumulation'[37] brings about a brave new world of equality-in-difference. One has only to look to the plight of the diasporic Chicano community of the eastern seaboard to see how immigrant cultures can be super-exploited in the information age. Second, although separating attachment to America (presumably good) from willingness to die for it (supposedly bad) may be laudable depending upon what it means in practice, it no longer takes us very far into a developing a positive form of postnationalism. In the presentation of the technologically-sophisticated wars conducted by US-led forces over the First Gulf War, Kosovo and Afghanistan much was made of the fact that very few of 'our boys' died. The developments in Iraq in the Second Gulf War notwithstanding, willingness to kill from a distance has largely surpassed the old-fashioned willingness to die for one's nation as basis of the call to arms. It has become connected to a soft-totalizing surveillance state.[38]

The third problem with the passage cited above concerns its embrace of Hollywood and the style-doctors. For a long time now Hollywood has joined in the postmodern game of presenting America as if it were already postnational and therefore able to stand in for the world at moments of crisis. Postnationalist films such as *Independence Day* (1996), *Armageddon* (1997) and *The Day after Tomorrow* (2004) have largely replaced the kind of Cold War nationalism that had Rocky Bilboa wearing stars-and-stripes boxing shorts and stepping into the ring to defeat Ivan Drago, the best that Soviet science could create.[39] Hollywood's America now only fights wars over the thin red line of national territory as re-runs of old conflicts. With some notable exceptions such as *Wag the Dog* (1997), the American warmachine is uncritically portrayed as projected globally rather than nationally self-serving in orientation.[40] However, if you read between the lines, the thrust of the set speeches in these films still assume that the United States – as, on the one hand, postnational representative of a set of universalistic values and, on the other, as exemplary open-textured nation-state – sits at the helm of world politics. It is the kind of postnationalism that makes 'humanitarian' interventions into Iraq and Kosovo as easily thinkable as leaving to others the peacekeeping mission into East Timor. In *Independence Day*, Bill Pullman, President of the United States, speaks of the fourth of July becoming the rallying point for all mankind:

> Good morning. In less than an hour, aircraft from here will join with others from around the world. And you will be launching the largest aerial battle in the history of mankind. 'Mankind' – that word should have new meaning for all of us. We can't be consumed by petty differences any more. We will be united in our common interest. Perhaps it's faith. Today is the fourth of July, and you will once more fight for our freedom. Not from tyranny, oppression or persecution, but from alienation. We're fighting for our right to live, to exist. And should we win the day, the Fourth of July will no longer be known as an American holiday, but as the day when the whole world declared in one voice: 'we will not go quietly into the night, we will not vanish without a fight, we are going to survive'. Today we celebrate *our* independence day! (emphasis added).

It is striking how comfortably Hollywood translates fighting for transnational peace back into the heritage of one nation: *pax Americana*. The Fourth of July is not just another American holiday. It signifies the formation of the *modern* American nation. When we get to the last line,

'Today we celebrate *our* independence day', the ambiguous appellation 'our' has linked modern nationalism and postmodern cosmopolitanism in a comfortable pastiche that challenges nothing. The latest line in this idea of *Pax Americana* is George W. Bush's War on Terror. As he said on 9 November 2002 in relation to invading Iraq, 'If action becomes necessary, we will act in the interest of the world.'

Hollywood even makes it sound as if it is hard work. In *The American President*, the President of the United States, Andrew Shepherd, talks about the need to acknowledge the struggle:

> America isn't easy. America is advanced citizenship. You've got to want it bad, 'cause it's going to put up a fight. It's going to say 'You want free speech? Let's see you acknowledge a man who makes your blood boil, who's standing centre-stage and advocating at the top of his lungs that which you would spend a life-time opposing at the top of yours. You want to claim this land as the land of the free? Then the symbol of your country cannot just be the flag. The symbol has also to be one of its citizens exercising his right to burn that flag in protest.'

In one very particular way, the transnational nation *is* hard work.[41] It is different work from that of the modern imperial nation such as nineteenth-century England. Rudyard Kipling's England projected itself as engaged in the 'white man's burden' to spread its civilization territorially and globally. The new global nations[42] are not really interested in extending global territoriality or painting the map the latest version of 'empire red'. The denizens of such countries, including those of Tony Blair's new England and Bill Clinton and George W. Bush's USA, have too many competing and contradictory issues to consider: modern ideas of old-fashioned national interest; late-modern concerns about universalistic human rights; and postmodern aversions to the 'ultimate sacrifice' such as dying for a cause, or watching the body-bags return from a place of foreign military intervention. They are caught up in postnational hopes, which under pressure quickly slip back into mis-remembered national ideals. Rather than get caught up in these complexities – although I do think that it would be possible to tease out the various strands through a 'constitutive levels' argument – I want to now turn to exploring the beginnings of an alternative.

## An alternative approach to solidarity and community

The chapter opened with the argument that without a thorough-going exploration of the principles of solidarity and community, postnationalism and uncritical cosmopolitanism amounts to little more than a postmodern yearning for openness on the one hand, and an ideological compatriot of globalism on the other. The postmodernist critics do have assumed set of articles of provisional belief expressed in their politics, but it is my argument here that these 'implicit principles' are grotesquely one-dimensional. These implicit principles (it is not possible simply to call them principles) can be summarized as based upon the *aesthetic* virtue of the following inter-related ways of acting-in-the-world:

1. *Radicalized choosing.* This involves emphasizing the ethic of autonomy, where the individual chooses and rechooses the constituents of life from amongst the pastiche of possibilities, past, present and future. It is usually associated with a critique of the search for roots or a place to belong. This is where postmodernism repeats, at a more radical and abstracted level, the politics of modern liberalism.

2. *Boundary crossing.* This involves an emphasis on 'the transnational [domestic] dimension of cultural translation – migration, diaspora, displacement, relocation'.[43] It is as if being on the margin is *always* better than stabilizing one's place, as if being related to territory is *always* a root cause of conflict. It is certainly not the fault of the postmodernists that global capitalists extol the same virtue of the borderless world, but it should give them pause for reflection.

3. *Fragmented subjectification.* This involves emphasis on identity-as-hybridity, and a particular process of hybridity at that – hybridity-always-in-process.

4. *Ambivalence* of identity, authority, power, etc.

5. *Difference and alterity* (at its most radical it is anti-communitarian).

6. *Cosmopolitanism*, or at least post-nationalism/multiculturalism.

7. *Deconstruction* as a method of viewing the world. This is relevant to the themes of this chapter. The postmodern form of 'deconstruction' involves an ongoing deconstructing of the 'totalization' of national culture, always deferring the possibility of putting anything structural in place that might become a common culture.

I do not want to dismiss these articles of provisional belief entirely but to question them as one-sided. The following discussion only goes a couple of faltering steps beyond earlier discussions in *Arena Journal*,[44] but it is intended nevertheless to contribute to what might be called a reflexive politics of *ontological socialism*.[45] Rather than arguing for nationalism or cosmopolitanism, transnationalism or internationalism, postnationalism or postmodern hybridity, it suggests that social relations should be based ethically and practically on positive principles of interrelationship. As will become apparent I want to treat these principles as positively contradictory. As principles-in-tension they can only be worked out thoroughly in reflexive practice, rather than left exclusively in the hands of philosophers and critics to be passed down for occasional trials. Nevertheless, there is a place for discussion in the abstract. In this spirit, the principles will be presented here schematically with no great claims being made for the terms of the schema, only for the indicative nature of the approach. The principles and their lived meaning, it is suggested, need to be argued about, negotiated, and worked through over various modes of practice, and over varying levels of space-time extension and social integration. It is dangerous to begin by listing a possible set principles and leaving them loosely defined, but that is part of the point. The following discussion can only be contingent and introductory. It faces the dilemma that ethics is dependent upon lived enactment and dialogue, of which writing can only be one small part.

The discussion begins by setting up four basic kinds of principles, presented in terms of levels of increasing ontological depth: an ethic of agonism, an ethic of rights, an ethic of care, and an ethic of foundations (Figure 12.1). Presenting ethics in this layered way is not intended to privilege depth, but it is an argument against those who in fear of a foundational ethic turn to liberal pragmatics. I am thinking here of Richard Rorty when he says that ideally a new ethics should 'culminate in our no longer being able to see any use for the notion that finite, mortal, contingently existing human beings might derive the meanings of their lives from anything except other finite, mortal, contingently existing human beings'.[46] My response is 'maybe, however, ...' The 'however' says that if we care to look at the ontological meaning of finitude and mortality in human inter-relationship (however historically contingent and variable this has been in practice), we are already in the realm of a foundational ethics. This realm takes us far deeper than any liberal pragmatics. The move follows writers such as Bryan Turner and Chris Rojek in arguing for a foundational basis to discussions of human rights.[47] Principles such as the importance of reciprocity in co-operation or an emphasis upon equality are thus treated not as discrete liberal rights but as interwoven into a tapestry of contingent rights founded in relation to deeper 'ways of being'. Agonizing over relativized fragments of what is right and good (the level of an ethics of agonism) even if it is institutionalized in an ethic of rights is not sufficient.

I begin with the level of an ethic of rights not only because it is the most familiar to us, but also because, despite my qualms about its one-dimensional predominance in contemporary social relations and discourse, it is important for any alternative politics.

### An ethic of rights

These are principles conceived at the level of disembodied rights and procedures including democracy, rule of law, civility and justice. This list is

- an ethic of agonism
- an ethic of rights
- an ethic of care
- an ethic of foundations

increasing ontological depth

Figure 12.1　Levels of ethics

not exhaustive. It is used as a short-hand for a clustering of *procedural* principles commonly referred in the literature as *rights*, and draws across the traditions of liberal-participatory and socialist democracy.[48] This is the level at which modern law works. Even when black letter law refers to such apparently particularistic entities as 'the person in the street', it sets up that person as the abstract indicative person, not as the actual person-in-the-flesh. Commentators invoking the universalistic language of human rights may refer to more ontologically-basic issues as the right to food and shelter, but the framing of such rights-based discussion is usually conducted at the level of either prosaic taken-for-granted needs or through vague conceptions of fairness. We need this level – it is crucial to enacting a politics – but an ethic of rights usually draws upon the next level without making that connection explicit. For example, implicitly, and in theory, the ideal of democracy draws upon notions of equality and participation where authority is invested in the demos, but in practice the grounding assumptions of democracy are too embarrassingly unfulfilled for them to be part of everyday public debate. In practice, we tend to retreat back to the thin idea that regularized voting doth a democracy make.

### An ethic of care

The ethics of care is an ontologically-deeper form of ethics than the ethic of rights. It includes the following principles: reciprocity-co-operation, freedom-autonomy, equality-empathy, solidarity-authority, and identity-difference. Grouping these couplets together under the nomination *ethic of care* is perhaps too restrictive, but it gets closer to providing a general description than any other I can think of among the terms in current use. The present discussion is intended to give more structural specificity to the work done by feminist and other writers including Carol Gilligan and Joan Tronto.[49] The dual concepts presented here, alongside the others that could also be added to the list, put *social relational* concepts together – as opposed to universalistic procedural concepts – with the definitions of each concept drawing broadly from existing traditions of ethics from socialism to liberalism, and from Confucianism to Christianity. Why have I chosen these particular concepts? They are chosen precisely because they are embedded in existing debates and derive from social forms across human history. However, rather than being a pastiche of all that has been, historically and humanly, they are chosen as most simply expressing the ethical range of human interrelations in practice. The principles are in tension with each other, but more than that the dual concepts used to describe each principle are intended to resonate against each other. For example, reciprocity and co-operation are not synonyms: the concept of 'co-operation' qualifies the form of reciprocity, particularly the modality that is referred to in the anthropological literature as antagonistic reciprocity. This qualifying of reciprocity by co-operation, identity by difference, and so on, is intended to mitigate the tendency to drag such concepts back to the level of procedures without ongoing reflection on their meaning. Modern reciprocity can very easily become an exercise in counting the cost-benefit. This is not to suggest that this manifold of principles should not be operationalized, but it is to stop accounting methods being used to measure the 'implementation' of each principle as a disembodied singularity.

## An ethic of foundations

This level refers to ethics conceived at the level of categorical relations: ecology-ontology. It is a short-hand way of referring to a clustering of principles relevant to our relationship to nature and place and to others similarly bound up in finitude and embodied life-mortality.[50] This is the level at which questions of the sacred are often raised, deontological questions about the meaning of life itself. While this dimension is pressing for some, I want to remain agnostic about the questions of theology and simply suggest that it is at this level it is possible to argue that social relations should be conditionally founded upon and therefore qualified by our cultural embedding within nature and the categorical limitations of us having social bodies.

This level is 'foundational' in the sense that our various ethical houses cannot stand up in the long-term without such a basis; not in the sense that foundations determine more than a couple of dimensions of the shape of the house let alone how it is made or what its aesthetics might be. It is *conditionally* foundational in the sense that categorical imperatives are always cultural rather than based on human nature as immutable essence. Related to Max Weber's injunction that 'we must create our ideals from within our chests in the very age of subjectivist culture', it suggests that ethics must be reflexively negotiated rather than treated as delivered from on high as absolutist edict. Thus, two ideals are emphasized here: first, the importance of treating nature as ecologically limited and therefore economically limiting;[51] and, second, the importance of treating nature-culture as ontologically foundational and therefore potentially culturally limiting. Importantly, this last principle has the effect of decentring the primacy of 'the cultural' in the so-called culture/nature divide or 'the intellect' in the so-called mind/body divide. This way of conceiving of an ethic of foundations differs from Teresa Brennan's concern to enunciate a 'prime directive': *'we shall not use up nature and humankind at a rate faster than they can replenish themselves and be replenished'.*[52] The present concern by comparison is not to find a directive that can be measured and weighed, but rather a foundation for negotiating the meaning and practice of categorical ideals.

## Elaborating ethical complications

Individual principles in this four-level matrix have a long history of being embedded within various traditions, Western and Eastern, recent and old, tribal, traditional and modern. However, these principles are usually set negatively against each other within discursive formations such as socialism and liberalism as they battle it out for the ascendant moral ground. In short, what is being argued here is that social practices should be set within the social context of negotiated principles-in-tension, given some procedural meaning, and conducted across intersecting levels of social relations qualified by ecological-cultural limits.

In setting up this approach to ethics, a number of complications need to be noted. The first major complication, already hinted at, is that each of these principles contradicts or is at least in productive tension with each of the others. The second complication, to be discussed in a moment, is that each principle needs not only to be discussed in relation to other principles but across the range of human interrelations from embodied relations of face-to-face community through to thoroughly-mediated relations of abstracted sociality.

Beginning with the first point – namely, the importance of maintaining a productive tension between principles – it is imperative for example that the principle of equality goes significantly deeper than the liberal notion of equality of opportunity. For too long that notion has been used as an excuse for increasing divisions of wealth: the current UN *Annual*

*Human Development Report* records that the wealth of the three richest people in the world is greater than the combined GNP of 48 of the world's poorest countries. It is clear that in the contemporary world, projecting the social-democratic ideal of distribution of wealth as it might be expressed at the level of procedural rights does not take us much beyond the nationally-framed welfare liberalism. On the other hand, giving depth to 'equality' should not mean turning that principle into an ontological absolute. Proclaiming equality for indigenous tribal peoples in settings where they are dominated by integrative modernisms should not, for example, involve over-riding the identity-difference principle. This unfortunately is what is happening in countries as diverse as Australia, the United States and Indonesia. When Australia's One Nation argues that Aboriginal people should be treated no differently from other Australians, the in-effect thrust of that position is to argue against land rights. Those rights are based upon a different cultural relationship to place. They are utterly defensible rights if we acknowledge that ethical questions can also be conceived at the level of ontological foundations. It is through the identity-difference principle at the level of an ethic of care in conjunction with claims about difference at the level of an ethic of ontological foundation, that we can defend the possibility of different forms of living and therefore of layered forms of governance and law being constituted into all postcolonial settings (and thus, instituted as an ethic of rights). For example, the Inuit have been granted relatively-autonomous governmental status in one of the Canadian territories without this involving completely separate nation-statehood. Terry Eagleton expresses this complication, with an elegant swipe at the postmodern position on the way:

> Equality, then, is a deeply paradoxical notion. It means that everyone must non-particularly have their particularity attended to – 'non-particularity' here meaning without privilege or exception or exclusion ... A genuine concept of equality thus deconstructs the notions of identity and non-identity, sameness and difference, the individual and the universal, in contrast to the more rigidly binary theorists of postmodernism who would line up difference on one side of the ontological fence and abstract universality on the other.[53]

The principle of equality has to work across the philosophical tensions between particularity and universality. Moreover, the tensions have to be worked out in practice between people across the various levels of association – local community, region, nation, world – rather than through setting up *a priori* formulations which tend to privilege the particularized local or the global-universal. In advocating an alternative politics of layered community, including national community, we need not aim to annul these tensions, but instead aim productively to open them up to transparent and self-reflexive regimes of negotiation. Instead, for example, of arguing for the abstract market as a means of limiting the obligatory implications of reciprocal community,[54] and thus supposedly enhancing autonomy,[55] the principles of reciprocity and autonomy (expressed superficially in liberal terms as contractual obligation and liberty) are considered here to pertain to all realms of social life including the market and the state. In this, the market and the state are not treated as spheres of autonomous activity. The nature of the abstract market and the abstract state themselves need to be fundamentally qualified by practical and more embodied expressions of reciprocity across the various levels of extension from the local to the global.

This brings us to the second complication: the need to consider how principles are lived across various levels of abstraction. 'Reciprocity' as one of the principles-in-tension to be negotiated in the broad canvas of human relations readily lends itself to the discussion.[56] However, without some sense of the levels of abstraction across which reciprocity can be lived (and given the contemporary pressures of globalization), we too easily find ourselves taking the more comfortable path of institutionally-abstracted forms of reciprocity and solidarity. Just as tribal peoples give us principles through which to think through identity-difference dialectic – for example, the Yolngu extend the child–mother relation to the Yothu Yindi relation of all nature and culture – the practice of reciprocity has a much longer history than the modern of concept of contract relations. We allow institutionalized exchange relations conducted by nation-states, corporations, aid agencies and the like to mediate our relations to others, all in the name of contractual fairness. It thus reduces the layered possibilities of public reciprocity to national tax redistribution regimes, regional balance-of-trade agreements and global aid programs. There is nothing wrong with these kinds of abstract reciprocity as such: quite the opposite. Nevertheless, we do need to keep in mind the proviso that the way in which abstract reciprocity is handled is often instrumental, self-serving and oriented to the extension of institutional power. This is not to dismiss it as such. Abstract and universalizing reciprocity, especially if based upon a modified version of the old Marxist maxim, 'between each according to their means' would be integral to a manifold of levels of reciprocity. The problem comes when we are relying exclusively on the institutions of the nation-state or quasi-governmental instrumentalities to manage this exchange.

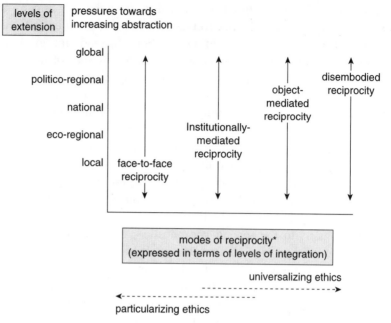

Figure 12.2  Lines of reciprocity
*The solid arrows represent the increasing and decreasing salience of particular modes of reciprocity over changed levels of integration.

The possibilities of abstract reciprocity range across the various levels of time–space extension from local exchanges between acquaintances and strangers to global regimes of exchange, co-operation and support (Figure 12.2). The overriding issue is that in contemporary market-driven cultures, abstract rather than embodied reciprocity dominates the public sphere, while more concrete, embodied and particularized forms of reciprocity have retreated to the private realm of family and immediate friends. In the context of communications, the problem is that disembodied communication through the media and internet are more likely to be the source of sentimental solidarity with far-flung liberation movements than the much more demanding kinds of communication entailed in a relationship of embodied reciprocity.

The contrast being made here is not simply between instances of mediated and face-to-face communication, that is, communication as mere interaction. We are talking about the nature of the relationship in terms of how it is bound by deeper levels of integration. By contrast with abstract reciprocity, embodied reciprocity or reciprocity at the level of the face-to-face involves producing, exchanging and communicating with, and for, known others. It is where the act of co-operation is part of a long-term, relatively-unmediated relationship of mutuality and interdependence. For obvious reasons, embodied reciprocity is more easily conducted the closer one gets to home, but in theory (and practice) it is possible across the reaches of social extension from the immediate locale to the other side of the globe. In the case of the continuing struggle in independent East Timor, for example, it means being more than part of a solidarity group that writes notes of support or puts pressure on politicians. Here it would ideally involve working with particular East Timorese people both in Australia and in East Timor across a range of activities – political, cultural and economic.

Expressed more generally, enriching the depth and range of such a co-operative's relations of reciprocity would, on the one hand, entail the individuals who participate, *choosing* to make the activities of the interconnected activities of the interconnected face-to-face groups more central to their rounds of everyday life (under the qualified and qualifying principle of autonomy-freedom). On the other, it would involve setting up specific solidaristic relations for the interchange of goods and visitors with groups from other places, particular places in which people can be supported in working projects of participatory mutual support. This kind of reciprocity, drawing lines of connection within the region or across the globe, all too obviously involves confronting the obscenity that the abstract state-system does little to alleviate the deaths by malnutrition and bad water of approximately one-tenth of the children born on this planet. By contrast, billions of dollars can too easily be spent on wars over Kosovo, Afghanistan or Iraq, especially when one's principles are based on the abstract notions of transnational sovereignty and 'humanitarian' intervention. The optimal aim would be develop lines of co-operation based upon ongoing negotiation, reflexively conducted in awareness of the tensions between the principles of reciprocity, equality, solidarity and autonomy. Rather than facilitating autonomous hybrid individuals keeping in touch with others in moments of superficial reciprocity and solidarity, the kind of politics being advocated here embraces long-term solidarity with particular others, conducted as a way of life.

The last century, more than any before it, has been marked by the horrors of mass wars over territory and cultural integrity. It is understandable then that the postmodern and cosmopolitan response is to put the burden of blame upon attempts to stabilize relations to place and community. It is just as understandable that in the new century the avant-garde late-modernist response is to call for new forms of universalism based on non-exclusionary cosmopolitan citizenship. These approaches are nevertheless part of the problem. By comparison, advocating a discussion of the principles of social life – reciprocity, freedom, equality, solidarity, and ecology – and critically assessing how they are lived across extensions of space from the local to the global, is intended to take us beyond those responses, linking the particularities and differences of place and identity to the generalities and universalities of ethical debate. We need a new series of manifestos for sustainable sociality that go beyond the current tendency to either treat everything as too hard and complex or as only achievable through millenarian force of will. Such an alternative involves a slow revolution. It will begin, this book has argued, in different places with different peoples, all sensitive to the necessity of grounding politics and community in lived and never-ending negotiations over contradictory principles and relations.

## Notes

1 The concept 'lifted out' is used here to indicate that transcending the modernist meaning of exclusive territorial attachment can take other forms than just physically crossing national borders. It means that the definition incorporates quite different forms of postnationalism including those that derive, on the one hand, from postcolonial diaspora cultures and, on the other, from dominant nation-state cultures as they redefine themselves in terms of (postmodern) multiculturalism and the imperative to globalize.

2 The emphasis here on 'subjectification' should not be taken to imply that postnationalism is other than constituted through quite material processes.

3 Arjun Appadurai, *Modernity at Large: Cultural Dimensions of Globalization*, University of Minnesota Press, Minneapolis, 1996, p. 177. For a variety of different takes on the same question, see Martin Albrow, *The Global Age: Society and State Beyond Modernity*, Polity Press, Cambridge, 1996; Homi K. Bhabha, *The Location of Culture*, Routledge, London, 1994; Frederick Buell, *National Culture and the New Global System*, Johns Hopkins University Press, Baltimore, MD, 1994; Peter Cochrane and David Goodman, 'The Great Australian Journey: Cultural Logic and Nationalism in the Postmodern Era', in Tony Bennett, Pat Buckridge, David Carter and Colin Mercer (eds), *Celebrating the Nation: A Critical Study of Australia's Bicentenary*, Allen & Unwin, St Leonards, NSW, 1992; Mike Featherstone, *Undoing Culture: Globalization, Postmodernism and Identity*, Sage Publications, London, 1995; Richard Kearney, *Postnationalist Ireland: Politics, Culture, Philosophy*, Routledge, London, 1997.

4 The 'we' here refers to the 'intellectually trained'. This is a grouping that partly through being trained in the art and technique of analytical dismemberment becomes 'instinctively' ambivalent about the classically-conceived closures of modern national community. Notwithstanding examples to the contrary, in the late-twentieth century this ambivalence has often moved to acute discomfort. We have to be careful that our framing mode of enquiry does not lead us to treat ideologies of openness, freedom and autonomy as naturally good things.

5 The term 'banal nationalism', coined by Michael Billig (*Banal Nationalism*, Sage Publications, London, 1995), or what I would call the 'new civic nationalism', describes a kind of nationalism that cannot see itself as such. It is the flagged patriotism of those who naturalize their attachments to constitution and country as civic loyalty rather than as intense 'primordial' passion.

6 Chris Scanlon, 'The Network of Moral Sentiments: The Third Way and Community', *Arena Journal*, New Series no. 15, 2000, pp. 57–79.

7 This point qualifies the argument of Anatol Lieven, *America Right or Wrong: An Anatomy of American Nationalism*, HarperCollins, London, 2004. I acknowledge his point about the two nationalisms – the 'American creed' of extending civic democratic virtue and the 'American antithesis' of bellicose chauvinism – but also I want to suggest that these ideologies are cross-cut by subjectivities of globalism.

8 Craig Calhoun, 'The Class Consciousness of Frequent Travellers: Towards a Critique of Actually Existing Cosmopolitanism', in Daniel Archibugi (ed.), *Debating Cosmopolitics*, Verso, London, 2003, p. 211.

9 I. William Zartman (ed.), *Collapsed States: The Disintegration and Restoration of Legitimate Authority*, Lynne Reinner, Boulder, CO, 1995.

10 See Leanne Reinke's chapter in James Goodman (ed.), *Protest and Globalisation: Prospects for Transnational Solidarity*, Pluto Press, Sydney, 2002, and Walter D. Mignolo, 'The Zapatistas's Theoretical Revolution: Its Historical, Ethical, and Political Consequences', *Review*, vol. 25, no. 3, 2002, pp. 245–75.

11 Geoff Kitney and David Lague, 'The Seeds of War', *The Age*, 17 April 1999.

12 Appadurai, *Modernity at Large*, p. 166.

13 *Ibid.*

14 Gilles Deleuze and Félix Guattari, *A Thousand Plateaus: Capitalism and Schizophrenia*, University of Minnesota Press, Minneapolis, 1987. The term is in fact not very satisfactory but it points to processes of the abstraction of space, part of the more general trend towards the abstraction of categories of social being including space, time and embodiment. This does not mean that the nation-state is about to disappear: it means that its 'classical' *modern* variant is under challenge.

15 Noel Malcolm, *Kosovo: A Short History*, Macmillan Publishers, London, 1998.

16 Tim Judah, 'Kosovo's Road to War', *Survival*, vol. 41, no. 2, 1999, pp. 5–18.

17 Appadurai, *Modernity at Large*, Chapter 8, 'Patriotism and Its Futures'.

18 Bruce Robbins ('Actually Existing Cosmopolitanism', in Pheng Cheah and Bruce Robbins, eds, *Cosmopolitics: Thinking and Feeling Beyond the Nation*, University of Minnesota Press, Minneapolis, 1998, p. 3) represents a critical cosmopolitanism that largely avoids the valorization of mobility and detachment endemic in postmodern cosmopolitanisms, but in criticizing its critics he occasionally falls off the balancing beam. Pheng Cheah's introductory chapter 'The Cosmopolitical – Today' in the same volume turns the critique back on the postnationalists, convincingly arguing that cosmopolitanism need not be postnational.

19 Appadurai, *Modernity at Large*, p. 159.

20 David Campbell, *National Deconstruction: Violence, Identity and Justice in Bosnia*, University of Minnesota Press, Minneapolis, 1998, p. 13.

21 The quote comes from Appadurai (*Modernity at Large*, p. 169) but the sentiment ranges widely from postmodernists to radical liberals: for examples of the latter group, see from the Left, Jean-Marie Guéhenno, *The End of the Nation-State*, University of Minnesota Press, Minneapolis, 1995; and from the Right, Kenichi Ohmae, *The End of the Nation State: The Rise of Regional Economies*, HarperCollins, London, 1996.

22 Appadurai, *Modernity at Large*, p. 170.

23 Iris Marion Young, 'The Ideal of Community and the Politics of Difference', in Linda J. Nicholson (ed.), *Feminism/Postmodernism*, Routledge, New York, 1990.

24 Julia Kristeva, *Nations without Nationalism*, Columbia University Press, New York, 1993, p. 3.

25 Young, 'Ideal of Community', pp. 317 and 318. By contrast, see Robyn Eckersley's reconciliation of communitarianism and cosmopolitanism: 'Communitarianism', in Andrew Dobson and Robyn Eckersley (eds), *Political Theory and the Ecological Challenge*, Cambridge University Press, Cambridge, 2005.

26 Robbins, 'Actually Existing Cosmopolitanism', p. 3 (emphasis added).

27 *Ibid.*

28 And even then as Robbins writes in another essay in *Cosmopolitics* ('Comparative Cosmopolitanism', p. 253), 'Hidden away in the miniaturizing precision of "locality" with its associations of presence and uniqueness, empirical concreteness, complex experience, and accessible subjectivity, has been the nostalgia for a collective subject-in-action that is no longer so easy to localize.' It should be said that in many ways I like the approach taken by Robbins. In pointing to the (minor) slips and slides in his position I am more concerned

about them as indicative of more general problems beyond the text than on the philosophical complexities of 'place', see Edward S. Casey, *The Fate of Place: A Philosophical History*, University of California Press, Berkeley, CA, 1998. On the levels of theoretical abstraction from which one can examine a particular local place, see Elspeth Probyn, 'Travels in the Postmodern: Making Sense of the Local', in Linda J. Nicholson (ed.), *Feminism/Postmodernism*, Routledge, New York, 1990.

29 Hildegarde Hannum (ed.), *People, Land, and Community*, Yale University Press, New Haven, CT, 1997; William Vitek and Wes Jackson (eds), *Rooted in the Land: Essays on Community and Place*, Yale University Press, New Haven, CT, 1996.

30 Liah Greenfeld, *Nationalism: Five Roads to Modernity*, Harvard University Press, Cambridge, MA, 1992, p. 11.

31 Kearney, *Postnationalist Ireland*, p. 23.

32 Tom Nairn, *The Break-Up of Britain: Crisis and Neo-Nationalism*, Verso, London (1973), 2nd edn, 1981, pp. 348–9.

33 There is no hyphen here in 'nation state' to signify the contemporary reconstitution of the classical modern assumption of the hyphenated unity one-nation-for-one-state.

34 Appiah's argument for 'rooted cosmopolitanism' is based on the defence of the liberal freedom to have elective affinities. It is, in his words, a 'distinctively American tradition'. He writes: 'Those of us who are American not by birth but by election, ... love this country precisely for that freedom of self-invention' (Kwame Anthony Appiah, 'Cosmopolitan Patriots', in Pheng Cheah and Bruce Robbins (eds), *Cosmopolitics: Thinking and Feeling Beyond the Nation*, University of Minnesota Press, Minneapolis, 1998, p. 106.)

35 For Rorty's postmodern patriotism, a kind of postnationalism that at once allows him to romanticize and be utterly critical of the politics of his nation state, America, see his *Achieving Our Country*, Harvard University Press, Cambridge, MA, 1998. As Michael Billig notes: 'Rorty directly associates himself with Dewey's vision of America: "I see America pretty much as Whitman and Dewey did, as opening up a prospect of illimitable democratic vistas"' (*Banal Nationalism*, Sage Publications, London, 1995, p. 170). Billig continues: 'In such writings it is possible to identify a tone suited to the new *Pax Americana*. The philosophy distances itself from the rhetoric of the Cold War is ... [At the same time, the] American way – the way of non-ideological pragmatism – is recommended for all' (p. 172). I'm afraid, for all Rorty's ironical distance from that thing called 'America', I agree with Billig.

36 Appadurai, *Modernity at Large*, pp. 175–6.

37 See David Harvey, *The Condition of Postmodernity: An Enquiry into the Origins of Cultural Change*, Basil Blackwell, Oxford, 1989; and also Manuel Castells, *The Information Age: Economy, Society and Culture:* Vol. 1, *The Rise of the Network Society*, Blackwell Publishers, Cambridge, MA, 1996.

38 Simon Cooper, 'Perpetual War within the State of Exception', *Arena Journal*, New Series, no. 21, 2003/04, pp. 99–125; Lyon, David, *Surveillance after September 11*, Polity Press, Cambridge, 2003.

39 *Rocky IV*, 1985, a United Artists film, written and directed by Sylvester Stallone.

40 Criticism is reserved for those unethical individuals perverting the system who fail to live up to the abstract ideals of life, liberty and the American way. Usually these individuals and their cronies are exposed by the Harrison Ford or Denzel Washington hero.

41 The term 'postnational nation' may sound oxymoronic, but it is explicable in terms of a levels argument that treats modernism (which frames the experience of bounded national community) and postmodernism (which frames the experience of heterogeneous multicultural society) as contradictory formations overlaying each other and coexisting in the same world-time.

42 The term 'global nation' comes from John Wiseman's book of the same name: *Global Nation?* Cambridge University Press, Cambridge, 1998.

43 Bhabha, *Location of Culture*, p. 172.

44 The editors of *Arena Journal* including Geoff Sharp, John Hinkson and Simon Cooper work with a framework of understanding, the constitutive abstraction approach, which puts the emphasis on the lived process of intersecting levels of abstraction. As one way of giving this approach more specificity I have attempted here to

distinguish different levels of epistemological abstraction (from empirical generalization through integrational analysis to categorical analysis) and different levels of ontological abstraction (from the face-to-face to the disembodied). It is not necessarily a way of working though the constitutive abstraction approach with which all the editors are comfortable. What I am attempting to do here is connected to my previous work, with the levels of ethical abstraction cross-cutting with levels of epistemological and ontological abstraction. See Table 4.5 above.

45 Ontological socialism is defined as a form of social interrelations that negotiates its practical expressions – cultural, political and economic – across the full range of what it has historically meant to be human from the level of procedural rights to the much more basic questions of co-existence as mortal embodied beings born of both nature and culture. See Chapter 4.

46 Richard Rorty, *Contingency, Irony and Solidarity*, Cambridge University Press, Cambridge, 1989.

47 Bryan S. Turner and Chris Rojek, *Society and Culture: Principles of Scarcity and Solidarity*, Sage Publications, London, 2001.

48 See Micheline Ishay, *The History of Human Rights: From Ancient Times to the Globalization Era*, University of California Press, Berkeley, CA, 2004.

49 Joan C. Tronto, *Moral Boundaries: A Political Argument for an Ethic of Care*, Routledge, New York, 1993. There are lots of departures from such writings in the present Chapter.

50 See, for example, Gerry Gill, 'Landscape as Symbolic Form: Remembering Thick Place in Deep Time', *Critical Horizons*, vol. 3, no. 2, 2002, pp. 177–99; and William M. Adams and Martin Mulligan, *Decolonizing Nature: Strategies for Conservation in a Post-Colonial Era*, Earthscan, London, 2003.

51 See, for example, Robyn Eckersley (*The Green State: Rethinking Democracy and Sovereignty*, MIT Press, Cambridge MA, 2004) for a brilliant exposition of how this foundational principle should make a difference at the level of institutional politics.

52 Teresa Brennan, *Globalization and its Terrors: Daily Life in the West*, Routledge, London, 2003, p. 164 (her emphasis).

53 Terry Eagleton, 'Five Types of Identity and Difference', in David Bennett (ed.), *Multicultural States: Rethinking Difference and Identity*, Routledge, London, p. 50.

54 Claus Offe and Rolfe G. Heinze, *Beyond Employment: Time, Work and the Informal Economy*, Polity Press, Cambridge, 1992.

55 Geoff Sharp, 'Constitutive Abstraction and Social Practice', *Arena*, 70, 1985, pp. 48–82. The irony here is that under the rubric of the 'ideology of autonomy', market relations in fact set up unacknowledged structures of authority (power) which limit the *de facto* freedoms of people in ways that close-knit communities could not sustain.

56 Within the *Arena* circle of writers, it is Nonie Sharp who has done most to elaborate the concept of reciprocity – mostly in relation to tribal society. See her book *The Stars of Tagai*, Aboriginal Studies Press, Canberra, 1993. This paragraph and part of the next are a rewriting of an earlier article of mine: 'Reconstituting Work', in *Arena Journal*, no. 10, 1998, pp. 85–111.

# Glossary

Items in bold refer to concepts defined elsewhere in the Glossary. Italics are used either for emphasis or when the reference is to the concept rather than the thing.

**Abstract community**  While all manifestations of **community** from the kinship associations of tribe to the virtual communities of the internet are formed through the **abstraction** and **extension** of social relations, the concept has a more specific sense. It is used to refer to those associations of people whose relationship to each other is characterized by the dominance of a mode of integration that can be called *disembodied*. The dominant form of abstract community since the beginning of the twentieth century has been the **nation-state**, but this is increasingly being reconstituted through processes of **globalization**, including the mobility enabled through space-altering and time-altering technologies. In their computer-mediated forms, abstract assemblies, sometimes called virtual communities, enable increased disembodied interactivity between individuals while at the same time increasing the embodied anonymity of each member of that community.

**Abstraction**  Abstraction is the process of drawing away from the embodied or particular while maintaining a generalizing connection between those particularities and embodied relations. Abstraction is not, however, the same as dematerialization although in the literature they are often used as synonyms. In the present argument, abstraction is understood as occurring both through ideas and concepts *and* through material practices and relations. For example, the current concept of the **state** is an abstraction from the much more concrete early-modern use as the *standing* or *status* of the prince, his visible *estates*. Similarly, the practice of statehood is now constitutively and materially more abstract than at the time when princes ruled as the embodiment of extended power. To take another example, a commodity is more abstract than a gift. This especially so when the gift is given under conditions of reciprocity: first, commodification involves an abstraction of value which allows unrelated objects to be assessed in terms of a medium of equivalence – namely, money; second, a commodity can be exchanged between persons whose embodied relationship to each other is irrelevant for the purposes of the exchange.

**Agency-extended integration**   With the dominance of this level, the form of social integration is abstracted beyond being based predominantly on the directly embodied and/or particularized mutuality of persons in social contact. It is at this level that persons act in the capacity of being the representatives, the agents, or the mediators of institutions – including church and state, guild and corporation – and their various constituencies. It is only at this level that it makes sense to use abstract terms such as *constituency* or *citizenry*.

**Community**   The concept of *community* was established in the English language with an open definition of social connectedness that derived from the Latin for relations or feelings in common. By the nineteenth century, *community* came to refer to more immediate relationship of commonality as compared to the more abstract concepts of *society,* **polity** and *state*. However, the concept still retained its defining condition as being a category of people with relations in common.

| | |
|---|---|
| **Constitutive abstraction** | This term is used to suggest that process of **abstraction** is constitutive of social relations and social being rather than just an activity that occurs in people's heads. |
| **Constitutive abstraction thesis** | The 'constitutive abstraction thesis' is the general name given to an approach or set of approaches associated with the Melbourne-based journal of social criticism, *Arena*. It is the basis of the methodology employed in the present book. |
| **Disembodied integration** | Disembodied integration is the level at which the constraints of embodiment, for example, being in one place at one time, can be overcome by means of technological extension, for example, by broadcasting, computer networking or telephoning. As described, this level is more abstract than the 'prior' levels of institutional integration or face-to-face integration. Each level of integration is implicated quite differently in the ways we live the relationship between nature and culture, and the ways we live our bodies and the 'presence' of others. |
| **Extension** | The concept of *social extension* provides a way of drawing attention to the different ways in which social interrelations can cross time and space. Radical social extension, for example, through technologies such as electronic communication devices, involves the projection of the possibilities of human interchange far beyond the immediacy of face-to-face interaction. Technologies and techniques from writing letters to setting up digitalized computer banks involve the storage of information extended far beyond the embodied time of a person's memory. |
| **Face-to-face integration** | This primary form of integration is defined as the level where the modalities of being in the presence of others constitute the dominant ontological meaning of the relationship between people even when they are apart. The modalities of face-to-face integration include reciprocity, interdependence, long-term continuity of |

association, embodied mutuality, and concrete otherness. Under such forms of interrelation, the absence of a significant other, even through death, does not annul his/her presence to us. Hence, it is important to emphasize here that integration is not used as a synonym for interaction. Just as it is possible for persons to be bound to each other at the level of face-to-face integration even when the self and the other are not engaged in immediate and embodied interaction, instances of interaction do not in themselves necessarily indicate anything about the dominant level of integration.

**Globalism** *Globalism* is used primarily to refer to the ideology and subjectivity of **globalization**. It is possible to have objective processes of globalization occur without either any subjective awareness of the process or any ideological presumptions about its meaning. However, the present condition of self-conscious relative **globality** is marked by the generalization of an unprecedented **reflexivity**. *Globalism* is also used as the generic term that bundles together other concepts such as *globalization* and *globality*.

**Globality** Although there is a tendency in the literature to use the concept of *globality* in an absolute way to suggest that any event, however local, now has global consequences, the concept here is defined relatively. It is used to emphasize, first, the generalized **subjectivity** of living in a world-space that is taken in a relatively-undisputed way to be globally connected; and, second, the relative immediacy, by comparison to the past, of objective global interconnections and the globalizing effects of actions or decisions taken in networked nodes upon other locales.

**Globalization** *Globalization* is defined as the uneven and structured manifold of social connections drawn across world-space, taking that space in the historically-variable terms that it has been socially understood through changing **world-time**, and understanding the matrix of connections as materially enacted through one or more of the various dominant modes of practice: exchange, production, communication, organization and enquiry.

**Historicalism** If **globalism** refers to the subjectivity and ideology associated with the generalizing of connections across **world-space**, then historicalism is a parallel temporal process referring to the generalizing connection across **world-time** – the consciousness of history as linking past, present and future in themselves rather than as teleologically or messianically-connected dimensions. Historicalism is related to the more familiar term, *historicism,* meaning the increasing **reflexivity** about the process of being in history.

**Institutional integration** See **agency-extended integration**.

**Modernism** *Modernism* can be characterized in terms of its dominant ontological forms – that is, by the overlaying of empty, relative and/or bio-technological space-time, corporeality, and epistemology. *Modernism*, like *tribalism, traditionalism* and *postmodernism,* is used in a double sense as an **ontological formation** and as a form of **subjectivity**. Modernism as an artistic aesthetic is a subcategory of the subjectivity of modernism.

**Nation** A *nation* is an abstract community of strangers – objectively abstract in that it draws together people who never need to meet – but experienced subjectively as a community with a distinct form of perceived foundational connection in time, space and/or embodiment.

**Nationalism** *Nationalism* is an ideology and, more deeply, a subjectivity associated with being part of a **nation**. One of the dominant forms of nationalism is the political assertion of state sovereignty for one's nation, but there are many other forms of nationalism that do not depend upon being part of, or wanting to institute, a **nation-state**. The concept of *nationalism*, most obviously when used as part of the phrase 'nationalism studies', also denotes the general field of scholarly work in the area.

| | |
|---|---|
| Nation-state | The nation-state is a very peculiar community-polity that involves the intersection of **state** and **nation**. This intersection involves the historical coming together of a particular form of the state – as objectively an increasingly rationalized, modern bureaucratic apparatus – and a particular form of the nation – as an increasingly-abstracted community of strangers, experienced subjectively as a **community** with some form of perceived foundational connection. Across the world, nation-states were constituted in the uneven intersection of globalizing changes in the dominant modes of practice that included a combination of the following: modern state formation as the outcome of a changing mode of organization bringing with it new ways of organizing authoritative power, including the means of violence; print as the emerging dominant mode of communication; capitalism as an intersection of changing modes of production and exchange; and secular and scientific rationalism as expressive of a changing mode of enquiry that brought with it new forms of education and cultural standardization. |
| Nature/culture contradiction | This contradiction arises in the tension between being culturally reflexive about what it is *to relate* to nature as a human being, and being *part of* nature as a embodied being. It is one of the foundational **ontological contradictions** of being human. When the hyphenated form of the concept is used, namely, *nature-culture*, it is to refer to settings where the contradiction in the relationship between culture and nature is so condensed as to be barely relevant. |
| Ontological contradiction | Such contradictions arise in the intersection of different levels of integration, and in the intersection of the cultural practices conducted at those different levels with the world-as-given, 'the natural'. (See for example the **nature/culture contradiction**.) They occur as persons negotiate their lives across different **ontological formations**. |
| Ontological formation | To use the concept of *ontological formation* is to describe a set of social relations in terms of its dominant categories |

of temporality, spatiality, corporeality and epistemology. The present version of the **constitutive abstraction** approach refers to the following kinds of formation: **tribalism, traditionalism, modernism** and **postmodernism**.

**Ontological security**  To feel such basic security is to live a settled life within the framework of a particular ontological formation without being assailed by ontological contradictions.

**Ontological socialism**  *Ontological socialism* is defined as a form of social interrelation that negotiates its practical expressions – cultural, political and economic – across the full range of what it has meant historically to be human, from the level of procedural rights to the much more basic questions of co-existence as mortal embodied beings born of both nature and culture. It other words, it refers to a social practice that provides the possibilities for systematically negotiating questions of how we are to live well.

**Ontology**  The concept of *ontology* refers to the most basic framing categories of social existence: temporality, spatiality, corporeality, epistemology, and so on. These are modes of being-in-the-world, historically constituted in the structures of human interrelations. It does not imply a human essence, nor is it confined to the sphere of selfhood.

**Polity**  A polity is an organizational form of governance that a **community** either brings into being or is instituted from above to manage persons and territory. The **nation-state** is the dominant form of polity at present.

**Postmodernism**  *Postmodernism* is defined in terms of its dominant ontological forms: that is, by the intersection of virtual and/or relativized space-time, corporeality, and epistemology. *Postmodernism* is used in a double sense as an **ontological formation** and as a **subjectivity**. *Postmodernism* as an aesthetic is a subcategory of postmodernism as a **subjectivity**.

| | |
|---|---|
| Reflexivity | Reflexive consciousness is a form of consciousness that reflects on the particularities and patterns on ideas and reflections. It extends beyond *practical consciousness* in reflecting on the 'why' question while ceasing to take it own framing conditions for granted. |
| Social formation | The concept of *social formation* is used to displace the concept of *society* and put the emphasis on the process of always coming into being. |
| State | The *state* is a very particular form of corporate institution. It is both an abstract administrative body and a complex of abstractly-interconnected bodies – both an association of persons and the name for an apparatus of governance. It is a body that exerts legitimized and/or enacted power over a people or peoples within a designated territory. Crucial to the definition, each of those notions – legitimation, people, and territory – are taken to vary in meaning according to the cultural definitions of their **world-time**, and relative to the **community** or communities in question. |
| Structure | The concept of *structure* is used here as an analytical shorthand for the always-changing patterns of instantiated practice and **subjectivity**. It is not treated as a fixed or reified thing. |
| Subjectivity | *Subjectivity* refers to one's way of being-in-the-world and how that being is experienced. |
| Traditionalism | *Traditionalism* is used in a double sense as an **ontological formation** and as a **subjectivity**. *Traditionalism* is defined by the overlaying of cosmologically and metaphorically-framed forms of temporality, spatiality, corporeality and epistemology. |
| Tribalism | Like the concept of *traditionalism*, *tribalism* is used in a double sense as an **ontological formation** and as a **subjectivity** and ideology. As a level of ontological formation, *tribalism* is defined as a social frame in which communities are bound socially beyond immediate |

birth ties by the dominance of various modalities of face-to-face and object integration, for example, genealogical placement, embodied reciprocity and mythological enquiry. As a subjectivity and ideology, *tribalism* refers to the accumulation of practices and meanings of identity, practically assumed or self-consciously effected, that either take the social frame as given (as subjectivity) or as politicized in some commonsensical way (as ideology). Tribalism, the pre-historical phenomenon available to us through archaeological research, can only be theorized by inference and circumstantial evidence. It is thus easier to examine tribes-in-history, through oral, material or written evidence. It is this historical tribalism that we can characterize as most often ontologically framed as variously customary tribalism, traditional tribalism, modern tribalism and postmodern tribalism.

**World-time** *World-time*, akin to the better-known concept of *world-view*, refers to the broadest framing conditions of the objective or subjective relations under consideration.

# Select Bibliography

Achebe, Chinua, *Arrow of God*, Heinemann, London, 1964.
Adam, Barbara, 'Social Versus Natural Time, A Traditional Distinction Re-examined', in Michael Young and Tom Schuller, *The Rhythms of Society*, Routledge, London, 1988.
Adams, William M., and Martin Mulligan, *Decolonizing Nature: Strategies for Conservation in a Post-Colonial Era*, Earthscan, London, 2003.
Ahmad, Aijaz, *In Theory: Classes, Nations, Literatures*, Verso, London, 1992.
Ahmed, Ali Jimale (ed.), *The Invention of Somalia*, Red Sea Press, Lawrenceville, 1995.
Al-Azmeh, Aziz, *Islam and Modernities*, Verso, London, 2nd edn, 1996.
Albrow, Martin, *The Global Age: Society and State Beyond Modernity*, Polity Press, Cambridge, 1996.
Alder, Ken, *The Measure of All Things: The Seven-Year Odyssey that Transformed the World*, Little, Brown, London, 2002.
Allen, Judith, 'Does Feminism Need a Theory of "the State"?', in Sophie Watson (ed.), *Playing the State*, Verso, London, 1990.
Amin, Samir, *Maldevelopment: Anatomy of a Global Failure*, Zed Books, London, 1990.
Anderson, Benedict, *Imagined Communities: Reflections on the Origins and Spread of Nationalism*, Verso, London (1983), 2nd edn, 1991.
Anderson, Benedict, 'Eastern and Western Nationalism', *Arena Journal*, New Series no. 16, 2000/1, pp. 121–131.
Anderson, Hans Christian, *The Silver Shilling*, Fabbri Publishing, Milan, 1990.
Appadurai, Arjun, *Modernity at Large: Cultural Dimensions of Globalization*, University of Minnesota Press, Minneapolis, 1996.
Appadurai, Arjun, 'Dead Certainty: Ethnic Violence in the Era of Globalization', in Birgit Meyer and Peter Geschiere (eds), *Globalization and Identity: Dialectics of Flow and Closure*, Blackwell Publishers, Oxford, 1999.
Appadurai, Arjun, 'Introduction: Commodities and the Politics of Value' in Appadurai, ed., *The Social Life of Things*, 1986a.
Appadurai, Arjun (ed.), *The Social Life of Things: Commodities in Cultural Perspective*, Cambridge University Press, Cambridge, 1986b.
Appiah, Anthony, 'Cosmopolitan Patriots', in Pheng Cheah and Bruce Robbins, eds, *Cosmopolitics: Thinking and Feeling Beyond the Nation*, University of Minnesota Press, Minneapolis, 1998.
Armstrong, Karen, *Remembering Karelia: A Family's Story of Displacement during and after the Finnish Wars*, Berghahn Books, New York, 2004.
Aveni, Anthony, *Empires of Time: Calendars, Clocks and Cultures*, Basic Books, New York, 1989.

## SELECT BIBLIOGRAPHY

Baecque, Antoine de, *The Body Politic: Corporeal Metaphor in Revolutionary France, 1770-1800*, Stanford University Press, Stanford, 1997.

Balsamo, Anne, *Technologies of the Gendered Body: Reading Cyborg Women*, Durham, CA, Duke University Press, 1996.

Balz, Dan, and Bob Woodward, 'The First Twenty-Four Hours', *Washington Post*, syndicated to *The Sunday Age*, 3 February 2002.

Barber, Benjamin R., *Jihad vs. McWorld: How Globalism and Tribalism are Reshaping the World*, Ballantine Books, New York, 1996.

Barrow, Clyde, *Critical Theories of the State*, University of Wisconsin Press, Madison, WI, 1993.

Barrow, Harold T., *Guarding the Crown Jewels*, Uplift Books, Croydon, 1947.

Bauer, P.T., *Equality, the Third World and Economic Delusion*, Weidenfeld and Nicolson, London, 1981.

Baumann, Gerd, *Contesting Culture: Discourses of Identity in Multi-Ethnic London*, Cambridge University Press, Cambridge, 1996.

Beck, Ulrich, *The Risk Society: Towards a New Modernity*, Sage, London, 1992.

Beck, Ulrich, *What is Globalization?* Polity Press, Cambridge, 2000.

Bendix, Reinhard, *Kings or People: Power and the Mandate to Rule*, University of California Press, Berkeley, 1978.

Bentley, Jerry H., 'Hemispheric Integration, 500-1,500 C.E.', *Journal of World History*, vol. 9, no. 2, pp. 237-54.

Bhabha, Homi, *The Location of Culture*, Routledge, London, 1994.

Billig, Michael, *Banal Nationalism*, Sage Publications, London, 1995.

Black, Jeremy, *Maps and History: Constructing Images of the Past*, Yale University Press, New Haven, CT, 1997.

Blaise, Clark, *Time Lord: Sir Sandford Fleming and the Creation of Standard Time*, Vintage Books, New York, 2000.

Bloch, Marc, *Feudal Society*, University of Chicago Press, Chicago, 1961.

Borst, Arno, *The Ordering of Time: From Ancient Computus to the Modern Computer*, Polity Press, Cambridge, 1993.

Bouman, C.A., *Sacring and Crowning: The Development of the Latin Ritual for Anointing Kings and the Coronation of an Emperor before the Eleventh Century*, J.B. Wolters, Groningen, 1957.

Bourdieu, Pierre, *Outline of a Theory of Practice*, Cambridge University Press, Cambridge, 1977.

Bourdieu, Pierre, *Algeria, 1960: The Disenchantment of the World*, Cambridge University Press, Cambridge, 1979.

Bourdieu, Pierre, *Distinction: A Social Critique of the Judgement of Taste*, Cambridge University Press, Harvard, 1984.

Bourdieu, Pierre, *Homo Academicus*, Polity Press, Cambridge, 1988.

Bourdieu, Pierre, *In Other Words: Essays Towards a Reflexive Sociology*, Polity Press, Oxford, 1990a.

Bourdieu, Pierre, *The Logic of Practice*, Polity Press, Cambridge, 1990b.

Bourdieu, Pierre, *Language and Symbolic Power*, Polity Press, Cambridge, 1991.

Braudel, Fernand, *Civilization and Capitalism 15th-18th Century: Vol. III, The Perspective of the World*, Collins, London, 1984.

Breeze, David, and Graeme Munro, *The Stone of Destiny: Symbol of Nationhood*, Historic Scotland, Edinburgh, 1997.

Brennan, Teresa, *Globalization and its Terrors: Daily Life in the West*, Routledge, London, 2003.

Breuilly, John, *Nationalism and the State*, University of Chicago Press, Chicago, 2nd edn, 1994.

Briggs, Asa, and Peter Burke, *A Social History of the Media: From Gutenberg to the Internet*, Polity Press, Cambridge, 2002.

Bringa, Tone, *Being Muslim the Bosnian Way: Identity and Community in a Central Bosnian Village*, Princeton University Press, Princeton, NJ, 1995.

Buell, Frederick, *National Culture and the New Global System*, Johns Hopkins University Press, Baltimore, MD, 1994.
Burchell, Graham, Colin Gordon, and Peter Miller (eds), *The Foucault Effect: Studies in Governmentality*, University of Chicago Press, Chicago, 1991.
Burke, Jason, *Al-Qaeda: Casting a Shadow of Terror*, I.B. Tauris, London, 2003.
Burke, Kenneth, *The Philosophy of Literary Form: Studies in Symbolic Action*, Vintage Books, New York, 1957.
Burke, Peter, *A Social History of Knowledge: From Gutenberg to Diderot*, Polity Press, Cambridge, 2000.
Caddick, Alison, 'Feminism and the Body', *Arena*, no. 74, 1986, pp. 60–88.
Calhoun, Craig, 'The Class Consciousness of Frequent Travellers: Towards a Critique of Actually Existing Cosmopolitanism', in Daniel Archibugi (ed.), *Debating Cosmopolitics*, Verso, London, 2003.
Campbell, David, *National Deconstruction: Violence, Identity and Justice in Bosnia*, University of Minnesota Press, Minneapolis, 1998.
Casey, Edward S., *The Fate of Place: A Philosophical History*, University of California Press, Berkeley, CA, 1998.
Cassidy-Welch, Megan, *Monastic Spaces and Their Meanings: Thirteenth-Century English Cistercian Monasteries*, Brepols, Turnhout, 2001.
Castells, Manuel, *The Information Age: Economy, Society and Culture:* Vol. 1: *The Rise of the Network Society*, Blackwell Publishers, Cambridge, MA, 1996.
Castles, Stephen, *Ethnicity and Globalization*, Sage Publications, London, 2000.
Chase-Dunn, Christopher, *Global Formation: Structures of World Economy*, Blackwell, New York, 1989.
Chatterjee, Partha, *Nationalist Thought and the Colonial World*, Zed Books, London, 1986.
Chatterjee, Partha, *The Nation and its Fragments*, Princeton University Press, Princeton, NJ, 1993.
Chatterjee, Partha, 'Whose Imagined Community?' in Gopal Balakrishnan (ed.), *Mapping the Nation*, Verso, London, 1996.
Cheal, David, *The Gift Economy*, Routledge, London, 1988.
Chown, John F., *A History of Money: From AD 800*, Routledge, London, 1994.
Clarke, Grahame, *Symbols of Excellence: Precious Metals as Expressions of Status*, Cambridge University Press, Cambridge, 1986.
Coates, Ken S., *A Global History of Indigenous Peoples: Struggle and Survival*, Palgrave Macmillan, Basingstoke, 2004.
Cochrane, Peter, and David Goodman, 'The Great Australian Journey: Cultural Logic and Nationalism in the Postmodern Era', in Tony Bennett, Pat Buckridge, David Carter and Colin Mercer (eds), *Celebrating the Nation: A Critical Study of Australia's Bicentenary*, Allen & Unwin, St Leonards, 1992.
Cohen, Abner, *Two-Dimensional Man: An Essay on the Anthropology of Power and Symbolism in Complex Society*, Routledge & Kegan Paul, London, 1974.
Cohen, Jean, and Andrew Arato, *Civil Society and Political Theory*, MIT Press, Cambridge, MA, 1992.
Cohen, Robin, *The New Helots: Migrants in the International Division of Labour*, Gower, Aldershot, 1987.
Connah, Graham (ed.), *Transformations in Africa: Essays on Africa's Later Past*, Leicester University Press, London, 1998.
Cooper, Simon, *Technoculture and Critical Theory: In the Service of the Machine*, Routledge, London, 2002.
Cooper, Simon, 'Perpetual War within the State of Exception', *Arena Journal*, New Series, no. 21, 2003/04, pp. 99–125.
Cooper, Simon, John Hinkson and Geoff Sharp (eds), *Scholars and Entrepreneurs: The Universities in Crisis*, Arena Publications, Melbourne, 2002.
Cope, Bill, and Mary Kalantzis, *Text-Made Text*, Common Ground Publishing, Altona, 2003.
Coulmas, Florian, *The Writing Systems of the World*, Blackwell, Oxford, 1989.
Coward, Rosalind, *Female Desire: Women's Sexuality Today*, Paladin Books, London, 1984.
Cox, Robert, *Production, Power and World Order: Social Forces in the Making of History*, Columbia University Press, New York, 1987.

Cregan, Kate, '[S]he was Convicted and Condemned', *Social Semiotics*, vol. 11, no. 2, pp. 125–37.
Crook, Stephen, Jan Pakulski and Malcolm Waters, *Postmodernization: Change in Advanced Society*, Sage, London, 1992.
Crump, Thomas, *The Phenomenon of Money*, Routledge & Kegan Paul, London, 1981.
Darby, Phillip (ed.), *At the Edge of International Relations: Postcolonialism, Gender and Dependency*, Pinter, London, 1997.
Darby, Phillip, *The Fiction of Imperialism: Reading Between International Relations and Postcolonialism*, Cassell, London, 1998.
Deleuze, Gilles, and Félix Guattari, *A Thousand Plateaus: Capitalism and Schizophrenia*, University of Minnesota Press, Minneapolis (1987) 1991.
Department of Foreign Affairs and Trade, *Globalisation: Keeping the Gains*, Commonwealth of Australia, Canberra, 2003.
Derrida, Jacques, *'Europe': The Other Heading*, Indiana University Press, Bloomington, IN, 1992.
Diamond, Jared, *Guns, Germs and Steel: A Short History of Everybody for the Last 13,000 Years*, Vintage, London, 1998.
Dodge, Martin, and Rob Kitchin, *Mapping Cyberspace*, Routledge, London, 2001.
Dodgshon, Robert A., *From Chiefs to Landlords: Social and Economic Change in the Western Highlands and Islands, c. 1493–1820*, Edinburgh University Press, Edinburgh, 1998.
Douglas, Mary, *Natural Symbols, Explorations in Cosmology*, The Cresset Press, London, 1970.
Dreyfus, Hubert L., and Paul Rabinow, *Michel Foucault: Beyond Structuralism and Hermeneutics*, University of Chicago Press, Chicago, 1982.
Dumont, Louis, *Essays on Individualism: Modern Ideology in Anthropological Perspective*, University of Chicago Press, Chicago, 1986.
Duncan, David Ewing, *The Calendar: The 5,000-Year Struggle to Align the Clock and the Heavens*, Fourth Estate, London, 1999.
Durham, M.E., *Some Tribal Origins, Laws and Customs of the Balkans*, George Allen & Unwin, London, 1928.
Eagleton, Terry, 'Five Types of Identity and Difference', in David Bennett (ed.), *Multicultural States: Rethinking Difference and Identity*, Routledge, London, 1998.
Easton, David, *The Political System: An Inquiry into the State of Political Science*, Alfred Knopf, New York, 1953.
Eberhard, Wolfram, *Conquerors and Rulers*, E.J. Brill, Leiden, revised edition 1965.
Eckersley, Robyn, *The Green State: Rethinking Democracy and Sovereignty*, MIT Press, Cambridge, MA, 2004.
Eckersley, Robyn, 'Communitarianism', in Andrew Dobson and Robyn Eckersley (eds), *Political Theory and the Ecological Challenge*, Cambridge University Press, Cambridge, 2005.
Eco, Umberto, and Constantino Marmo (eds), *On the Medieval Theory of Signs*, John Benjamins, Amsterdam, 1989.
Eisenstein, Elizabeth, *The Printing Revolution in Early Modern Europe*, Cambridge University Press, Cambridge, 1983.
Elias, Norbert, *Time: An Essay*, Blackwell Publishers, Oxford, 1992.
Esposito, John L., *Unholy War: Terror in the Name of Islam*, Oxford University Press, Oxford, 2002.
Evans, Joan, *Magical Jewels of the Middle Ages and Renaissance, Particularly in England*, Oxford University Press, London, 1922.
Evans, Peter, Dietrich Reuschemeyer and Theda Skocpol (eds), *Bringing the State Back In*, Cambridge University Press, Cambridge, 1985.
Fallers, Lloyd A., *The Social Anthropology of the Nation-State*, Aldine Publishing, Chicago, 1974.
Fanon, Frantz, *The Wretched of the Earth*, Penguin, Harmondsworth, 1977.
Featherstone, Mike, *Undoing Culture: Globalization, Postmodernism and Identity*, Sage Publications, London, 1995.

Feist, Raymond E., *Shards of a Broken Crown*, BCA HarperCollins, London, 1998.
Ferguson, William, *The Identity of the Scottish Nation: An Historic Quest*, Edinburgh University Press, Edinburgh, 1998.
Forset, Edward, *A Comparative Discourse of the Bodies Natvral and Politiqve*, Theatrum Orbis Terrarum, Amsterdam (1606), 1973.
Foster, Gaines M., 'A Christian Nation: Signs of a Covenant', in John Bodnar (ed.), *Bonds of Affection: Americans Define their Patriotism*, Princeton University Press, Princeton, NJ, 1996.
Foucault, Michel, *The Order of Things: An Archaeology of the Human Sciences*, Tavistock Publications, London (1966), 1970.
Foucault, Michel, *The Archaeology of Knowledge*, Routledge, London (1969), 1989.
Foucault, Michel, *Discipline and Punish: The Birth of the Prison*, Penguin, Harmondsworth (1975), 1977.
Foucault, Michel, 'Politics and the Study of Discourse', and 'Governmentality', in Graham Burchell, Colin Gordon, and Peter Miller (eds), *The Foucault Effect: Studies in Governmentality*, University of Chicago Press, Chicago, 1991.
Frazer, Elizabeth, and Nicola Lacey, *The Politics of Community*, Harvester Wheatsheaf, New York, 1993.
Freeman, Michael, 'Theories of Ethnicity, Tribalism and Nationalism' in Kenneth Christie (ed.), *Ethnic Conflict, Tribal Politics: A Global Perspective*, Curzon Press, Richmond, 1998.
Friedman, Jonathan, *Cultural Identity and Global Process*, Sage Publications, London, 1994.
Friedman, Jonathan (ed.), *Globalization, the State and Violence*, Alta Mira Press, Walnut Creek, CA, 2003.
Fukuyama, Francis, *The End of History and the Last Man*, Free Press, New York, 1992.
Gabirol, Solomon Ibn, *A Crown for a King*, Oxford University Press, Oxford, 1998.
Gellner, Ernest, *Saints of the Atlas*, Weidenfeld and Nicolson, London, 1969.
Gellner, Ernest, *Nations and Nationalism*, Basil Blackwell, Cambridge, 1983.
Gellner, Ernest, *Culture, Identity and Politics*, Cambridge University Press, Cambridge, 1987.
Gellner, Ernest, *Plough, Sword and Book: The Structure of Human History*, Collins Harvill, London, 1988.
Gellner, Ernest, *Encounters with Nationalism*, Blackwell Publishers, Oxford, 1994.
Gellner, Ernest, 'Do Nations Have Navels?' *Nations and Nationalism*, vol. 2, no. 3, 1996a, pp. 366–70.
Gellner, Ernest, 'The Coming of Nationalism and its Interpretation', in Gopal Balakrishnan (ed.), *Mapping the Nation*, Verso, London, 1996b.
Gellner, Ernest, *Conditions of Liberty: Civil Society and its Rivals*, Penguin, Harmondsworth, 1996c.
Gellner, Ernest, *Nationalism*, Orion Books, London, 1998.
Gerber, Pat, *Stone of Destiny*, Canongate Books, Edinburgh, 1997.
Gibson, William, *Virtual Light*, Bantam Books, New York, 1993.
Giddens, Anthony, *A Contemporary Critique of Historical Materialism, Vol. 1. Power, Property and the State*, Macmillan, London, 1981.
Giddens, Anthony, *The Constitution of Society: Outline of the Theory of Structuration*, Polity Press, Cambridge, 1984.
Giddens, Anthony, *The Nation-State and Violence: Volume Two of a Contemporary Critique of Historical Materialism*, Polity Press, Cambridge, 1985.
Giddens, Anthony, *The Consequences of Modernity*, Polity Press, Cambridge, 1990.
Giddens, Anthony, *Modernity and Self-Identity: Self and Society in the Late Modern Age*, Polity Press, Cambridge, 1991.
Giddens, Anthony, *The Transformation of Intimacy: Sexuality, Love and Eroticism in Modern Societies*, Polity Press, Cambridge, 1992.
Giddens, Anthony, *Runaway World: How Globalisation is Reshaping Our Lives*, Profile Books, London, 2nd edn, 2002.
Gierke, Otto von, *Political Theories of the Middle Age*, Cambridge University Press, Cambridge, 1900.

## SELECT BIBLIOGRAPHY

Gilbert, Trond, 'Ethnic Conflict in the Balkans: Comparing Ex-Yugoslavia, Romania and Albania', in Kenneth Christie (ed.), *Ethnic Conflict, Tribal Politics: A Global Perspective*, Curzon Press, Richmond, 1998.

Gill, Gerry, 'Post-Structuralism as Ideology', *Arena*, no. 69, 1984, pp. 60-96.

Gill, Gerry, 'Landscape as Symbolic Form: Remembering Thick Place in Deep Time', *Critical Horizons*, vol. 3, no. 2, 2002, pp. 177-99.

Gilson, Etienne, *History of Christian Philosophy in the Middle Ages*, Sheed and Ward, London (1955), 1980.

Godelier, Maurice, *The Making of Great Men: Male Domination and Power Among the New Guinea Baruya*, Cambridge University Press, Cambridge, 1986.

Godelier, Maurice, *The Mental and the Material: Thought, Economy and Society*, Verso, London, 1988.

Godelier, Maurice, *The Enigma of the Gift*, Polity Press, Cambridge, 1999.

Golan, Daphna, *Inventing Shaka: Using History in the Construction of Zulu Nationalism*, Lynne Rienner Publishers, Boulder, CO, 1994.

Goodman, James (ed.), *Protest and Globalisation: Prospects for Transnational Solidarity*, Pluto Press, Sydney, 2002.

Goody, Jack, *The Domestication of the Savage Mind*, Cambridge University Press, Cambridge, 1977.

Goody, Jack, *The Logic of Writing and the Organization of Society*, Cambridge University Press, Cambridge, 1986.

Goody, Jack, *The Interface Between the Written and the Oral*, Cambridge University Press, Cambridge, 1987.

Gouldner, Alvin, *Enter Plato: Classical Greece and the Origins of Social Theory*, Routledge and Kegan Paul, London, 1965.

Greenfeld, Liah, *Nationalism: Five Roads to Modernity*, Harvard University Press, Cambridge, MA, 1992.

Greenfeld, Liah, *The Spirit of Capitalism: Nationalism and Economic Growth*, Harvard University Press, Cambridge, MA, 2003.

Gregory, C.A., *Gifts and Commodities*, Academic Press, London, 1982.

Gregory, C.A., *Savage Money: The Anthropology and Politics of Commodity Exchange*, Harwood Academic Publishers, Amsterdam, 1997.

Gregory, Derek, 'Presences and Absences: Time-Space Relations and Structuration Theory', in David Held and John B. Thompson (eds), *Social Theory of Modern Societies: Anthony Giddens and his Critics*, Cambridge University Press, Cambridge, 1989.

Gregory, Derek, and John Urry (eds), *Social Relations and Spatial Structures*, London, Macmillan, 1985.

Grenfell, Damian, 'Environmentalism, State Power and "National Interests"', in James Goodman (ed.), *Protest and Globalisation: Prospects for Transnational Solidarity*, Pluto Press, Sydney, 2002.

Grosby, Steven, 'The Nation of the United States and the Vision of Israel', in Roger Michener (ed.), *Nationality, Patriotism and Nationalism in Liberal Democratic Societies*, Professors of World Peace Academy, St. Paul, MN, 1993.

Gross, Feliks, *The Civic and Tribal State: the State, Ethnicity and the Multiethnic State*, Greenwood Press, Westport, CT, 1998.

Guéhenno, Jean-Marie, *The End of the Nation-State*, University of Minnesota Press, Minneapolis, 1995.

Habermas, Jürgen, *Communication and the Evolution of Society*, Beacon, Boston, 1979.

Hall, John A., 'Conditions of Our Existence: Ernest Gellner (1925-1995)', *New Left Review*, no. 215, 1995, pp. 156-60.

Hall, John A., and G. John Ikenberry, *The State*, Open University Press, Milton Keynes, 1989.

Hammond, Basil Edward, *Bodies Politic and their Governments*, Cambridge University Press, Cambridge, 1915.

Hannerz, Ulf, *Cultural Complexity: Cultural Complexity in the Social Organization of Meaning*, Columbia University Press, New York, 1992.

Hannum, Hildegarde (ed.), *People, Land, and Community*, Yale University Press, New Haven, CT, 1997.

Haraway, Donna J., *Modest_Witness@Second_Millennium. FemaleMan©_Meets_OncoMouse™: Feminism and Technoscience*, Routledge, New York, 1997.
Hardt, Michael, and Antonio Negri, *Empire*, Harvard University Press, Cambridge, MA, 2000.
Harvey, David, *The Condition of Postmodernity*, Basil Blackwell, Oxford, 1989.
Hastings, Adrian, *The Construction of Nationhood: Ethnicity, Religion and Nationalism*, Cambridge University Press, Cambridge, 1997.
Hay, Ian, *Their Name Liveth: The Book of the Scottish National War Memorial*, Trustees of the Scottish National War Memorial, Edinburgh (1931), 1985.
Heidal, William Arthur, *The Frame of the Ancient Greek Maps*, Arno Press, New York, 1976.
Heidegger, Martin, *The Question Concerning Technology and Other Essays*, Harper & Row (1954–5), 1977.
Heller, Agnes, *Renaissance Man*, Schocken Books, New York, 1978.
Held, David, Anthony McGrew, David Goldblatt and Jonathan Perraton, *Global Transformations*, Polity Press, Cambridge, 1999.
Herzfeld, Michael, *The Social Production of Indifference: Exploring the Symbolic Roots of Western Bureaucracy*, University of Chicago Press, Chicago, 1992.
Hinkson, John, 'Postmodern Economy: Value, Self-Formation and Intellectual Practice', *Arena Journal*, New Series, no. 1, 1993, pp. 23–44.
Hinkson, John, 'The Postmodern State' in P. James (ed.), *The State in Question*, Allen & Unwin, Sydney, 1996.
Hirst, Paul, and Grahame Thompson, *Globalization in Question*, Polity Press, Cambridge, 2nd edn, 1999.
Hobsbawm, Eric, and Terence Ranger (eds), *The Invention of Tradition*, Cambridge University Press, Cambridge, 1983.
Hoëm, Ingjerd, 'Processes of Identification and the Incipient National Level: A Tokelau Case', *Social Anthropology*, vol. 7, no. 3, 1999.
Hopkins, A.G. (ed.), *Globalization in World History*, Pimlico, London, 2002.
Humphrey, Michael, *The Politics of Atrocity and Reconciliation: From Terror to Trauma*, Routledge, London, 2002.
Huntington, Samuel P., *The Clash of Civilizations and the Remaking of World Order*, Simon & Schuster, London, 1998.
Isaacs, Harold R., *Idols of the Tribe: Group Identity and Political Change*, Harper & Row, New York, 1975.
Ishay, Micheline, *The History of Human Rights: From Ancient Times to the Globalization Era*, University of California Press, Berkeley, CA, 2004.
Jacob, Christian, 'Mapping in the Mind: The Earth from Ancient Alexandria', in Denis Cosgrove, *Mappings*, Reaktion Books, London, 1999.
James, Harold, *The End of Globalisation: Lessons from the Great Depression*, Harvard University Press, Cambridge, MA, 2001.
James, Paul, *Nation Formation: Towards a Theory of Abstract Community*, Sage, London, 1996a.
James, Paul (ed.), *The State in Question*, Allen & Unwin, Sydney, 1996b.
Jameson, Fredric, *Postmodernism, or, the Cultural Logic of Late Capitalism*, Verso, London, 1991.
Jessop, Bob, *State Theory*, Polity Press, Cambridge, 1990.
Johnston, Alexander, 'Ethnic Conflict in Post Cold War Africa: Four Case Studies', in Kenneth Christie (ed.), *Ethnic Conflict, Tribal Politics: A Global Perspective*, Curzon Press, Richmond, 1998.
Judah, Tim, 'Kosovo's Road to War', *Survival*, vol. 41, no. 2, 1999, pp. 5–18.
Kaku, Michio, *Hyperspace: A Scientific Odyssey Through Parallel Universes, Time Warps, and the Tenth Dimension*, Oxford University Press, New York, 1994.
Kearney, Richard, *Postnationalist Ireland: Politics, Culture, Philosophy*, Routledge, London, 1997.
Keating, Michael, 'Minority Nationalism or Tribal Sentiments', in Christie Kenneth (ed.), *Ethnic Conflict, Tribal Politics: A Global Perspective*, Curzon, Richmond, 1998.

## SELECT BIBLIOGRAPHY

Keohane, Robert, *After Hegemony: Co-operation and Discord in the World Economy*, Princeton University Press, Princeton, NJ, 1984.
Kern, Stephen, *The Culture of Time and Space, 1880–1918*, Harvard University Press, Cambridge, MA, 1983.
Kitney, Geoff, and David Lague, 'The Seeds of War', *The Age*, 17 April 1999.
Klein, Naomi, *Fences and Windows: Dispatches from the Front Lines of the Globalization Debate*, Flamingo, London, 2002.
Knapman, Gareth, 'Regionalism, a Form of Proto-Nationalism in Acehnese Politics', Honours Thesis, Department of Politics, Monash University, 2001.
Kopytoff, Igor, 'The Cultural Biography of Things: Commoditization as a Process', in Arjun Appadurai (ed.), *The Social Life of Things: Commodities in Cultural Perspective*, Cambridge University Press, Cambridge, 1986.
Kristeva, Julia, *Strangers to Ourselves*, Harvester Wheatsheaf, New York, 1991.
Kristeva, Julia, *Nations without Nationalism*, Columbia University Press, New York, 1993.
Kumar, Krishan, *The Making of English National Identity*, Cambridge University Press, Cambridge, 2003.
Kuper, Adam, *The Invention of Primitive Society: The Transformation of an Illusion*, Routledge, London, 1988.
Kurke, Leslie, *Coins, Bodies, Games and Gold: The Politics of Meaning in Archaic Greece*, Princeton University Press, Princeton, NJ, 1999.
Kurth, James, 'The Post-Modern State', *The National Interest*, no. 28, 1992, pp. 26–35.
Landes, David S., *Revolution in Time: Clocks and the Making of the Modern World*, Belknap Press, Cambridge, 1983.
Langhorne, Richard, *The Coming of Globalization: Its Evolutionary and Contemporary Consequences*, Palgrave, Basingstoke, 2001.
Lash, Scott, *Another Modernity: A Different Rationality*, Blackwell Publishers, Oxford, 1999.
Lash, Scott, and John Urry, *The End of Organized Capitalism*, Polity Press, Cambridge, 1987.
Lefebvre, Henri, *The Production of Space*, Oxford, Blackwell, 1991.
LeMarchand, René, *Rwanda and Burundi*, Pall Mall Press, London, 1970.
Lestringant, Frank, *Mapping the Renaissance World*, University of California Press, Berkeley, CA, 1994.
Lévi-Strauss, Claude, *The Savage Mind*, Weidenfeld and Nicolson, London, 1966.
Lévi-Strauss, Claude, *The Elementary Structures of Kinship*, Beacon Press, Boston (1949), 1969.
Lieven, Anatol, *America Right or Wrong: An Anatomy of American Nationalism*, HarperCollins Publishers, London, 2004.
Linklater, Andro, *Measuring America: How the United States was Shaped by the Greatest Land Sale in History*, HarperCollins Publishers, London, 2002.
Louis, Roger, *Ruanda-Urundi: 1884–1914*, Clarendon Press, Oxford, 1963.
Lourandos, Harry, *Continent of Hunter Gatherers: New Perspectives on Australian Prehistory*, Cambridge University Press, Cambridge, 1997.
Lufrano, Richard John, *Honorable Merchants: Commerce and Self-Cultivation in Late Imperial China*, University of Hawai'i Press, Honolulu, 1997.
Lyon, David, *The Electronic Eye: The Rise of the Surveillance Society*, University of Minnesota Press, Minneapolis, 1994.
Lyon, David, *Surveillance after September 11*, Polity Press, Cambridge, 2003.
Lyotard, Jean-François, *The Postmodern Condition: A Report on Knowledge*, Manchester University Press, Manchester, 1984.
Maffesoli, Michel, *The Time of the Tribes: The Decline of Individualism in Mass Society*, Sage Publications, London, 1996.
Malcolm, Noel, *Kosovo: A Short History*, Macmillan Publishers, London, 1998.
Malinowski, Bronislaw, *Argonauts of the Western Pacific*, London, Routledge & Kegan Paul (1922), 1972.

Malkki, Liisa, 'Context and Consciousness: Local Conditions for the Production of Historical Thought and National Among Hutu Refugees in Tanzania', in Richard G. Fox, (ed.), *Nationalist Ideologies and the Production of National Cultures*, American Ethnography Society, Washington, DC, 1990.
Mamdani, Mahmood, 'From Conquest to Consent as the Basis of State Formation: Reflections on Rwanda', *New Left Review*, no. 216, 1996, pp. 3–36.
Mandel, Lewis, *The Credit Card Industry*, Twayne Publishers, Boston, 1990.
Mann, Michael, *The Sources of Social Power*, Vol. 1: *A History of Power From the Beginning to A.D. 1760*, Cambridge University Press, Cambridge, 1986a.
Mann, Michael, 'The Autonomous Power of the State: Its Origins, Mechanisms and Results', in John A. Hall, (ed.), *States in History*, Basil Blackwell, Oxford, 1986b.
Mann, Michael, *States, War and Capitalism: Studies in Political Sociology*, Basil Blackwell, Oxford, 1988.
Mann, Michael (ed.), *The Rise and Decline of the Nation State*, Basil Blackwell, Oxford, 1990.
Mann, Michael, *The Sources of Social Power*, Vol. 2: *The Rise of Classes and Nation-States, 1760–1914*, Cambridge University Press, Cambridge, 1993.
Mannoni, Octave, *Prospero and Caliban*, Frederick Praeger, New York, 1964.
Mansur, Abdalla Omar, 'The Nature of the Somali Clan System', in Ali Jimale Ahmed, (ed.), *The Invention of Somalia*, Red Sea Press, Lawrenceville, 1995.
Maquet, Jacques J., *The Premise of Inequality in Ruanda*, Oxford University Press, London, 1961.
Marvin, Carolyn, and David W. Ingle, *Blood Sacrifice and the Nation*, Cambridge University Press, Cambridge, 1999.
Marx, Karl, *Capital: Vol. 1*, Progress Publishers, Moscow (1887), 1977.
Marx, Karl, and Friedrich Engels, *Selected Works*, Foreign Languages Publishing House, Moscow, 1962.
Mattelart, Armand, *Networking the World: 1794–2000*, University of Minnesota Press, Minneapolis, 2000.
Mauss, Marcel, *The Gift: Forms and Functions of Exchange in Archaic Societies*, Routledge & Kegan Paul, London (1925), 1974.
McNeill, Daniel, *The Face*, Hamish Hamilton, London, 1998.
Meillassoux, Claude, *Maidens, Meal and Money*, Cambridge University Press, Cambridge, 1981.
Memmi, Albert, *The Colonizer and the Colonized*, Souvenir Press, London, 1974.
Meyer, Birgit, and Peter Geschiere (eds), *Globalization and Identity: Dialectics of Flow and Closure*, Blackwell Publishers, Oxford, 1999.
Mignolo, Walter D., 'The Zapatistas's Theoretical Revolution: Its Historical, Ethical, and Political Consequences', *Review*, vol. 25, no. 3, 2002, pp. 245–75.
Mignolo, Walter D., *Local Histories/Global Designs: Coloniality, Subaltern Knowledges and Border Thinking*, Princeton University Press, Princeton, NJ, 2000.
Miller, Perry, *Nature's Nation*, Harvard University Press, Cambridge, MA, 1967.
Mittleman, James H., *The Globalization Syndrome: Transformation and Resistance*, Princeton University Press, Princeton, NJ, 2000.
Mohamad, Goenawan, 'Australia by Name, Postmodernist by Nature', *Sunday Age*, 12 July 1992.
Moore, Mike, *A World Without Walls: Freedom, Development, Free Trade and Global Governance*, University of Cambridge Press, Cambridge, 2003.
Mullan, Bob, *The Mating Trade*, Routledge & Kegan Paul, London, 1984.
Mutoro, Henry W., 'Pre-colonial Trading Systems of the East African Interior', in Graham Connah (ed.), *Transformations in Africa: Essays on Africa's Later Past*, Leicester University Press, London, 1998.
Myers, Fred R., *Pintupi Country, Pintupi Self: Sentiment, Place and Politics among Western Desert Aborigines*, University of California Press, Berkeley, CA, 1991.
Nairn, Tom, *The Break-Up of Britain: Crisis and Neo-Nationalism*, Verso, London (1973), 2nd edn, 1981.

Nairn, Tom, and Paul James, *Global Matrix: Nationalism, Globalism and State-Terror*, Pluto Press, London, 2005.
Nancy, Jean-Luc, *The Inoperative Community*, University of Minnesota Press, Minneapolis, 1991.
Nandy, Ashis, *Time Warps: The Insistent Politics of Silent and Evasive Pasts*, Permanent Black, Delhi, 2001.
Newbury, David, *Kings and Clans*, University of Wisconsin Press, Madison, WI, 1991.
Newton, Stella, *Fashion in the Age of the Black Prince: A Study of the Years 1340-1365*, Boydell Press, London, 1980.
Offe, Claus, *Disorganized Capitalism*, Polity Press, Cambridge, 1985.
Offe, Claus, and Rolfe G. Heinze, *Beyond Employment: Time, Work and the Informal Economy*, Polity Press, Cambridge, 1992.
Ohmae, Kenichi, *The End of the Nation State: The Rise of Regional Economies*, HarperCollins, London, 1996.
Olson, David R., *The World on Paper: The Conceptual and Cognitive Implications of Writing and Reading*, Cambridge University Press, Cambridge, 1994.
Ong, Walter, *Orality and Literacy: The Technologizing of the Word*, Methuen, London, 1982.
Orizio, Riccardo, *Lost White Tribes: Journeys among the Forgotten*, Vintage, London, 2001.
Ovid, *Metamorphoses*, Penguin, Harmondsworth, 1955.
Pahl, Jan, *Invisible Money: Family Finances in the Electronic Economy*, Policy Press, Bristol, 1999.
Perkins, Jocelyn, *The Crowning of the Sovereign of Great Britain and the Dominions Overseas*, Methuen, London, 1937.
Peterson, Anna L., *Being Human: Ethics, Environment and Our Place in the World*, California University Press, Berkeley, CA, 2001.
Poster, Mark, *The Mode of Information*, Polity, Cambridge, 1990.
Poulantzas, Nicos, *State, Power, Socialism*, Verso, London, 1980.
Probyn, Elspeth, 'Travels in the Postmodern: Making Sense of the Local', in Linda J. Nicholson, ed., *Feminism/Postmodernism*, Routledge, New York, 1990.
Prost, Antoine, 'Public and Private Space in France', in Antoine Prost and Gerard Vincent (eds), *A History of Private Life*, vol. 5, Harvard University Press, Cambridge, MA, 1991.
Prunier, Gérard, *The Rwandan Crisis: History of a Genocide*, Columbia University Press, New York, 1997.
Rae, Heather, *State Identities and the Homogenisation of Peoples*, Cambridge University Press, Cambridge, 2002.
Reinke, Leanne, 'Utopia in Chiapas? Questioning Disembodied Politics', in James Goodman (ed.), *Protest and Globalisation: Prospects for Transnational Solidarity*, Pluto Press, Sydney, 2002.
Reus-Smit, Christian, *The Moral Purpose of the State: Culture, Social Identity, and Institutional Rationality in International Relations*, Princeton University Press, Princeton, NJ, 1999.
Rigby, Peter, 'Time and Historical Consciousness: The Case of the Ilparakuyo Maasai', in Diane Owen Hughes and Thomas R. Trautmann (eds), *Time: Histories and Ethnologies*, University of Michigan Press, Ann Arbor, MI, 1995.
Robbins, Bruce, 'Actually Existing Cosmopolitanism', in Pheng Cheah and Bruce Robbins (eds), *Cosmopolitics: Thinking and Feeling Beyond the Nation*, University of Minnesota Press, Minneapolis, 1998.
Robbins, Derek, *The Work of Pierre Bourdieu*, Open University Press, Milton Keynes, 1991.
Robertson, Robbie, *The Three Waves of Globalization: A History of a Developing Global Consciousness*, Zed Books, London, 2003.
Robertson, Roland, 'Glocalization: Time-Space and Homogeneity-Heterogeneity', in Mike Featherstone, Scott Lash and Roland Robertson (eds), *Global Modernities*, Sage, London, 1995.
Robertson, Roland, *Globalization: Social Theory and Global Culture*, Sage, London, 1992.
Rorty, Richard, *Contingency, Irony and Solidarity*, Cambridge University Press, Cambridge, 1989.
Rorty, Richard, *Achieving Our Country: Leftist Thought in Twentieth-Century America*, Harvard University Press, Cambridge, MA, 1998.

Rosenberg, Justin, *The Follies of Globalisation Theory: Polemical Essays,* Verso, London, 2000.
Rossum, Gerhard Dohrn-van, *The History of the Hour: Clocks and Modern Temporal Orders,* Chicago University Press, Chicago, 1996.
Royal Commission, *Kilmartin: Prehistoric and Early Historic Monuments* (An Inventory of the Monuments Extracted from Argyll), Volume 6, Royal Commission on the Ancient and Historical Monuments of Scotland, Edinburgh, 1999.
Runciman, W.G., *A Treatise on Social Theory:* Vol. 2: *Substantive Social Theory,* Cambridge University Press, Cambridge, 1989.
Sahlins, Marshall, *Stone Age Economics,* Tavistock Publications, London, 1974.
Sahlins, Marshall, 'Two or Three Things that I Know About Culture', *Journal of the Royal Anthropological Institute,* vol. 5, no. 3, 1999, pp. 399–421.
Sassen, Saskia, 'Digital Networks and the State', *Theory, Culture & Society,* vol. 17, no. 4, 2000, pp. 19–33.
Sather, Clifford, *The Bajau Laut: Adaption, History, and Fate in a Maritime Fishing Society of South-Eastern Sabah,* Oxford University Press, Kuala Lumpur, 1997.
Scafi, Alessandro, 'Mapping Eden: Cartographies of the Earthly Paradise', in Denis Cosgrove, *Mappings,* Reaktion Books, London, 1999.
Scanlon, Chris, 'The Network of Moral Sentiments: The Third Way and Community', *Arena Journal,* New Series no. 15, 2000, pp. 57-79.
Scholte, Jan Aart, *Globalization: A Critical Introduction,* Palgrave, Basingstoke, 2000.
Scrinis, Gyorgy, *Colonizing the Seed: Genetic Engineering and Techno-Industrial Agriculture,* Friends of the Earth, Melbourne, 1995.
Seabrook, Jeremy, *Victims of Development,* Verso, London, 1993.
Sebesta, Edward H., 'The Confederate Memorial Tartan', *Scottish Affairs,* no. 31, 2000, pp. 55–84.
Sennett, Richard, *Flesh and Stone: The Body and the City in Western Civilization,* Faber and Faber, London, 1994.
Sharp, Geoff, 'Constitutive Abstraction and Social Practice', *Arena,* 70, 1985, pp. 48–82.
Sharp, Geoff, 'An Overview for the Next Millennium', *Arena Journal,* New Series no. 9, 1997, pp. 1–8.
Sharp, Geoff, 'The Idea of the Intellectual and After', *Arena Journal,* New Series no. 17-18, 2002, pp. 269–316.
Sharp, Nonie, *Stars of Tagai: The Torres Strait Islanders,* Aboriginal Studies Press, Canberra, 1993.
Siikala, Jukka (ed.), *Departures: How Societies Distribute their People,* The Finnish Anthropological Society, Helsinki, 2001.
Silberman, Steve, 'Just Say Nokia', *Wired Magazine,* vol. 7, no. 9, 1999 (downloaded from www.wired.com/wired/archive).
Simmel, Georg, *The Philosophy of Money,* Routledge, London (1900), 1990.
Skocpol, Theda, 'Wallerstein's World Capitalist System: A Theoretical and Historical Critique', in Mitchell Seligson and John Passé-Smith (eds), *Development and Underdevelopment: The Political Economy of Inequality,* Lynne Rienner Publishers, Boulder, CO, 1993.
Slater, David, 'Exploring Other Zones of the Postmodern', in Ali Rattansi and Sallie Westwood (eds), *Racism, Modernity and Identity on the Western Front,* Polity Press, Cambridge, 1994.
Slouka, Mark, 'A Year Later: Notes on America's Intimations of Mortality', *Harper's Magazine,* September 2002, pp. 35–43.
Smith, Alfred P., *Warlords and Holy Men: Scotland A.D. 80–1000,* Edinburgh Press, Edinburgh, 1984.
Smith, Anthony D., *The Ethnic Origins of Nations,* Blackwell, London, 1986.
Smith, Anthony D., 'Memory and Modernity: Reflections on Ernest Gellner's Theory of Nationalism', *Nations and Nationalism,* vol. 2, no. 3, 1996, pp. 371–88.
Smith, Dennis, *The Rise of Historical Sociology,* Polity Press, Cambridge, 1991.
Smith, Edwin W., *The Golden Stool: Some Aspects of the Conflict of Cultures in Modern Africa,* Holborn Publishing, London, 1926.

Springborg, Patricia, *Royal Persons: Patriarchal Monarchy and the Feminine Principle*, Unwin Hyman, London, 1990.
Steger, Manfred, *Globalization: A Very Short Introduction*, Oxford University Press, Oxford, 2003.
Steger, Manfred, *Globalism: The New Market Ideology*, Rowman and Littlefield, Lanham, MD, 2002.
Stephenson, Neal, *Snow Crash*, Penguin, Harmondsworth, 1992.
Stevens, Jacqueline, *Reproducing the State*, Princeton University Press, Princeton, NJ, 1999.
Strange, Susan, *The Retreat of the State: The Diffusion of Power in the World Economy*, Cambridge University Press, Cambridge, 1996.
Strange, Susan, *Casino Capitalism*, Manchester University Press, Manchester (1986) 1997.
Strange, Susan, *Mad Money*, Manchester University Press, Manchester, 1998.
Sutton, David E., *Memories Cast in Stone: The Relevance of the Past in Everyday Life*, Berg, Oxford, 1998.
Swain, Tony, *A Place for Strangers: Towards a History of Australian Aboriginal Being*, Cambridge University Press, Cambridge, 1993.
Swantz, Marja-Liisa, Salome Mjema and Zenya Wild, *Blood, Milk and Death: Bodily Symbols and the Power of Regeneration among the Zaramo of Tanzania*, Bergin & Garvey, Westport, CT, 1995.
Taylor, Arthur, *The Glory of Regality: An Historical Treatise on the Anointing and Crowning of the Kings and Queens of England*, Taylor, London, 1820, book 1.
Thomas, Nicholas C., *Entangled Objects: Exchange, Material Culture, and Colonialism in the Pacific*, Harvard University Press, Cambridge, MA, 1991.
Thrower, Norman J.W., *Maps and Man: An Examination of Cartography in Relation to Culture and Civilization*, Prentice-Hall, Englewood Cliffs, NJ, 1972.
Traube, Elizabeth, *Cosmology and Social Life: Ritual Exchange among the Mambai of East Timor*, University of Chicago Press, Chicago, 1986.
Tronto, Joan C., *Moral Boundaries: A Political Argument for an Ethic of Care*, Routledge, New York, 1993.
Turner, Bryan S., *The Body and Society: Explorations in Social Theory*, Basil Blackwell, Oxford, 1984.
Turner, Bryan S., and Chris Rojek, *Society and Culture: Principles of Scarcity and Solidarity*, Sage Publications, London, 2001.
Vattimo, Gianni, *The Transparent Society*, Polity Press, Cambridge, 1992.
Verran, Helen, 'A Story about Doing "The Dreaming"', *Postcolonial Studies*, vol. 7, no. 2, pp. 149–64.
(Verran) Watson, Helen, *Singing the Land, Signing the Land*, Deakin University, Geelong, 1989.
Vilar, Pierre, *A History of Gold and Money: 1450–1920*, Verso, London (1960), 1976.
Vincent, Andrew, *Theories of the State*, Basil Blackwell, Oxford, 1987.
Vitek, William, and Wes Jackson (eds), *Rooted in the Land: Essays on Community and Place*, Yale University Press, New Haven, CT, 1996.
Walker Bynum, Caroline, *Holy Feast and Holy Fast*, University of California Press, Berkeley, CA, 1987.
Walzer, Michael, 'The New Tribalism: Notes on a Difficult Problem' in Ronald Beiner (ed.), *Theorising Nationalism*, State University of New York Press, Albany, NY, 1999.
Waters, Malcolm, *Globalization*, Routledge, London, 2nd edn, 2001.
Watson, Don, 'Birth of a Post-Modern Nation', The *Australian*, 24 July 1993.
Watters, Ethan, *Urban Tribes: A Generation Redefines Friendship, Family and Commitment*, Bloomsbury, New York, 2003.
Weiner, Annette B., *Inalienable Possessions: The Paradox of Keeping-While-Giving*, University of California Press, Berkeley, CA, 1992.
Wells, Peter, S., *The Barbarians Speak: How the Conquered Peoples Shaped the Roman Empire*, Princeton University Press, Princeton, NJ, 1999.
Wertheim, Margaret, *The Pearly Gates of Cyberspace: A History of Space from Dante to the Internet*, Doubleday, Sydney, 1999.

Williams, Jonathan (ed.), *Money: A History*, British Museum Press, London, 1998.
Williams, Raymond, *Marxism and Literature*, Oxford University Press, Oxford, 1977.
Wills, Gary, *Inventing America: Jefferson's Declaration of Independence*, Vintage Books, New York, 1979.
Winichakul, Thongchai, *Siam Mapped: A History of the Geo-Body of the Nation*, University of Hawaii Press, Honolulu, 1994.
Wiseman, John, *Global Nation?* Cambridge University Press, Cambridge, 1998.
Wood, Ellen Meiksins, *The Pristine Culture of Capitalism: A Historical Essay on the Old Regimes and Modern States*, Verso, London, 1991.
Young, Iris Marion, 'The Ideal of Community and the Politics of Difference', in Linda J. Nicholson (ed.), *Feminism/Postmodernism*, Routledge, New York, 1990.
Zartman, William (ed.), *Collapsed States: The Disintegration and Restoration of Legitimate Authority*, Lynne Rienner, Boulder, CO, 1995.
Ziguras, Christopher, *Self-Care: Embodiment, Personal Autonomy and the Shaping of Health Consciousness*, Routledge, London, 2004.

# Index

Abacha, General Sani 283
Abbé Sieyès 189
Aborigines of Australia 164, 310;
 Aboriginality 167; Ancestral
 Beings 167-8; 'Dreamtime' or 'The
 Dreaming' 166-7; initiation
 ceremonies 196; Pintupi people
 167; Yolgnu people 93, 172, 311;
 Yothu Yindi 311
absolutism 114-15
abstract community 4, 17-18, 21, 26,
 28-30, 34-5, 86, 179, 196, 222,
 228, 231-59 passim
abstract society 8, 26
abstraction 53, 71, 73, 94, 106, 112, 121,
 124-5, 127, 134, 166, 182, 184, 188,
 190, 198, 209, 217, 274-5, 282, 311;
 analogical abstraction 92;
 cosmological abstraction 92; degree
 of 184; deontological abstraction
 95; and embeddedness 16; of
 embodiment 8, 15, 18;
 epistemological abstraction 25, 70,
 72, 80, 94-5, 121; ethical abstraction
 92; of exchange 118, 161; figures of
 69-73 passim; across history 135;
 ideational abstraction 120, 134; of
 individuals 275; integrative
 abstraction 136; of language 3; of
 law 25, 59; material abstraction 8,
 120, 134, 147-8, 213; metaphorical
 abstraction 73; methodological
 abstraction 74; monetary abstraction
 134; objective abstraction 232;
 ontological abstraction 95; perceptual
 abstraction 92; postmodern
 abstraction 67; processes of 141;
 reflexive ethical abstraction 95;
 representational abstraction 183; of
 social formations 7; of social life 67;
 of sociality 8; of space and spatiality
 15, 25, 172-6 passim, 181, 297, 312;
 systematic abstraction 89, 280;
 tableaux of 72; technical abstraction
 92; time-space abstraction 60;
 of time and temporality 8, 17-18, 25,
 137, 161-72 passim, 181, 297, 312;
 theoretical abstraction 94, 110, 213,
 285; see also analytical abstraction,
 constitutive abstraction,
 contradictions and contradictory
 relations, practices and processes,
 modes of practice, money,
 state, value
Abu-Graib 45, 198
Aceh and Acehnese 170, 234; Acehnese
 Declaration of Independence 234;
 *atjehtimes.com* website 234; and
 nationalistic Islam 234
advertising 1-3, 14-15, 68, 133,
 262-3, 279-80, 299
Afghanistan and Afghani 37-8;
 see also war and wars
Africa and African 1, 3, 28, 31, 115,
 155-6, 237, 240, 242, 244, 247, 263,
 277, 285; Afrikaner *see* Pretoria;
 East Africa 23; Northern Africa 30,
 219; West Africa 139; *see also*
 empires, kingdoms
agency and agents 22-3, 25, 47, 50, 55,
 59, 162, 212, 228, 282; commercial
 agents 116; reciprocal agency 87;

# INDEX

as self-reflexive 58-9; *see also* kinship, methodological dichotomies, structures, subjectivity and subjects
agency-extended or institutional integration 81, 87-8, 90, 139, 169, 184, 282; *see also* globalism
Aglietta, Michel 75
agrarian society 48-50, 159 *see also* economy, history
Ahmad, Aijaz 283
Ahmed, Ali Jimale 31
AIDS 31, 67, 288
Al Azmeh, Aziz 93
Al-Jazeera news network 272
al-Khwarizmi, Mohammed Ibn Musa 170
al-Qaeda/al-Qaida/al-Qa'ida 66, 89
Alaska 299
Albania and Albanian 36, 295, 302
Albrow, Martin 24
Alexander III, *see* kings
Algeria and Algerian 57, 109; Association pour la Recherche Démographique 57; Berber 57; Kabyle people 57, 190
Alice-in-Wonderland 113
Allen, Judith 212
Allen, Peter 197
alphabets 16-17; *see also* writing
'The Ambassadors' 192
ambivalence 285; *see also* postmodern principles
*America: A Tribute to Heroes* 27
America and American, *see* United States of America; *see also* the Americas
American Express 147
American Revolution 145, 175, 250; and the Declaration of Independence 250-2
American Political Science Association 210
*The American President* 304
Americas 240, 243-4, 250; North America 242, 250, 282; Spanish America 242-3; *see also* United States of America
Amish people 78
Amsterdam 143
analogy 7, 123, 172, 189-90, 192; *see also* abstraction, body, modes of enquiry, power, reciprocity, science, time
analytical abstraction, the levels of 21, 25, 73-83 *passim*, 111, 124, 134, 138, 222, 269-76 *passim*; categorical analysis 21, 76-7, 79, 82, 109, 128, 171, 274-6 *passim*; conjunctural analysis 6, 73-4, 79, 81, 104, 171, 223-4, 270-3 *passim*; empirical analysis 21, 73, 79, 81-2, 222-3, 269-70 *passim*, 272; integrational analysis 76, 81, 83, 104, 128, 171, 273-4 *passim*
*ancien regime* 242
Anderson, Benedict 18, 44, 153-4, 168, 175, 179, 224, 226-7, 233-4, 241-6
Anderson, Hans Christian 144, 146, 218
Anderson, Perry 220
Andorra 18, 238
Anglia 23
Anglo-Saxon 165
*Annual Human Development Report* 308-9
anthropology, the discipline of 4-5, 19, 28, 31, 48, 55, 58, 73, 85, 103-4, 107, 120, 126, 150, 166, 210-11, 308; *see also* Marxism
anthropomorphism 135, 144, 212
anti-globalization movement, *see* globalization
Anzac Day, *see* Australia and Australian
Apollo 11 262
Appadurai, Arjun 7, 44, 104, 107, 109-11, 113, 149, 164, 184-5, 268, 287, 293, 295-8, 301-2
Appiah, Anthony 301
Aquinas, Thomas 91
Arab and Arabic 31, 170; Arabic language 16
archaeology 104, 114, 139; of knowledge 17; *see also* methodology
*The Archaeology of Knowledge* 61
*Arena Journal* 305
Argentina 272
*Argonauts of the Western Pacific* 108, 113
Aristotle 94, 136
*Arlington Road* 68
Armageddon 159; *Armageddon*, the film 303
Armstrong, Karen 126
*Art of Rhetoric* 136
Aruba 272-3
Aryabhata 170
ascetism 183
Ashanti 115
Asia and Asian 226, 237, 240, 244, 256; East Asia 243, 275; Eurasia 263; Southeast Asia 242
Assenisipia 175
Association pour la Recherche Démographique, *see* Algeria and Algerian

# INDEX

astronomy 170
atavism 13
Atlantic ocean 158
atlases, *see* maps and mapping
Attenborough, David 262
Aum Shinrikyo, *see* Japan and Japanese
Australia and Australian 2, 14, 32, 86, 120, 146, 164, 167, 175, 182, 187, 196–7, 228, 236, 255, 257, 270, 272–3, 275, 298, 310, 313; Anzac Day 228; Australian-American Leadership dialogue 269; Australian Broadcasting Corporation (ABC) 144; Australian Constitutional Bill 119; Australian war shrine 119; Bicentenary 196; One Nation party 298, 310; Order of Australia 196; *see also* Aborigines of Australia
Austria and Austrian 272; *see also* empires
authenticism and authenticity 30, 32, 183, 221
autonomy 13, 179, 231, 238, 268, 305, 307, 310, 313

Bacon, Roger 170
Baecque, Antoine de 188
Baiturrahman Grand Mosque 170
Balkans 28, 36–7 *see also* Bosnia
*Ballykissangel* 299
banal nationalism, *see* nationalism
Bandoran, *see* Ireland and Irish
banking industry 143; Bank of England 144; Barclays Global Investors corporation 262; Lloyds bank 148
Baptist 257
barbarianism 3
Barber, Benjamin 46, 73
Barrow, Claude 213
Barrow, Harold 117–18
Basque people, *see* France and French
Baudrillard, Jean 75, 82, 285–6
Bauer, Peter 277
Bauman, Zygmunt 44, 105
Baumann, Gerd 33
Bangalore 279
Beck, Ulrich 67
Bedhouin people 185
being 74, 94, 269; categories of 164; being-in-time 167; being-in-the-world 159, 180, modes of 77–8, 258; *see also* maps and mapping
Belgium and Belgian 247, 248
belonging 296, 305; *see also* nation-state

Benetton corporation 277
Bengal and Bengali 244–5
Benjamin, Walter 168, 226
Bentley, Jerry 23
Berber, *see* Algeria and Algerian
Berkeley, Bishop 264
*bezants* 141
Bhabha, Homi 282
Bible 152, 154–6, 193, 251–3; Abraham and Jacob 115, 117–18, 250, 251; Bible Commonwealth 250; *Genesis* 117, 250; Isaac 251; Jehovah 250; *John* 117, 154; New Testament 117; Old Testament 85, 117, 152; *see also* Torah
Biel 160
Bilboa, Rocky 303
Billig, Michael 254
bin Laden, Osama 93, 294
Binyamin tribe 31
birth 84, 127, 166, 173, 186, 196, 252; *see also* blood
Blair, Tony 14, 37, 116–17, 119, 136, 158, 304
Blaise, Clarke 171
Blancs Matignon 29
blood 34, 84, 105, 128, 179–202 *passim*, 218; and bile, semen and milk 179, 188, 191–2; blood-by-birth 236; blood ties 13, 28, 30, 85, 127, 190, 237; bloodlines 127, 193, 219, 235–6; of Christ 118; and flesh 183, 185, 218; and kin, or 'consanguinal ties' 13, 28–30, 84–5, 127–8, 190–1, 193, 237; menstrual blood 186, 188; and place 76; and sacrifice 30, 118, 196, 228, 253–4, 258; and soil 77, 236, 254; and violence 34, 185, 249
*Blood Sacrifice and the Nation* 253–4
*Blue Velvet* 68
Boadicea 197
Body Shop corporation 277
body, the ontological category of, and embodiment 6, 8, 15–16, 18–19, 28, 34–5, 45, 60, 78, 80, 83–4, 87–9, 91, 106, 115, 117, 123, 129, 134–5, 159, 165–7, 172–3, 176, 179–202 *passim*, 227, 231, 237, 239, 255, 258, 262–88 *passim*; administrative body 207; analogical embodiment 186–7, 196, 200; analogous embodiment 194; bio-technological embodiment 187, 189, 200; body fashions and modifications (including cosmetic

surgery and tattooing) 32, 186, 197–9; body parts 199; body-policing 183; corporate body 82, 207; cosmological embodiment 187–8, 200; cross-gender body 198; cyborg body 198; cyborg-technological embodiment 150, 187, 189, 200; and difference and commonality 183–6; and disembodiment 45, 88, 106; embodied extension 267; embodied iconography 146; embodied interchange 111; embodied perfection 183; embodied relations 144, 169, 183, 228, 297, 309; embodied self 87; embodied speech 135; embodied ties and loyalty 87, 297; embodiment as individualized postmodern project 197–201 *passim*; ethically-reflexive embodiment 202; ethnic embodiment 236; familial bodies 68; as flesh; gendered bodies 190, 217; genealogical embodiment 186–187, 200; metaphorical embodiment 117, 187–9, 200; modern bodies and embodiment 195–198 *passim*; and money 133, 146; mythological embodiment 187, 200; national bodies 68; orifices 184; personal bodies 68; and the post-gendered face 162; postmodern bodies and embodiment 198; sexual bodies 197; social bodies and embodiment 186–9 *passim*, 308; subjectively embodied 255; and statues 2; traditional bodies and embodiment 192–6 *passim*; transcendence of embodiment 180, 183; tribal bodies and embodiment 189–92 *passim*, 196; *see also* bones, embodied connection, flesh, face-to-face, kingship, maps and mapping, money, testicles
body politic 17–18, 83, 87–8, 92, 115, 172, 181, 188, 195, 199, 215, 250
body as symbol 91, 179, 182, 185, 187; body as natural symbol 179, 182, 185, 191, 196
Bohemian 48
bones 112, 120
books 5, 94, 150, 154, 259; as novels 14; *Books of Chilan Balan* 163; Books of Honour 119
borders, *see* boundaries and borders
Borges, Jorge 16–17, 71

Bosnia and Bosnian 13, 33–8 *passim*, 187, 298; Catholics 187; Muslims 35, 37; Orthodox Christians 187; *see also* war and wars
Bouman, C.A. 219
boundaries and borders 52, 274, 292, 295; borderless world 267, 276, 305; boundaries-as-given 184; boundaries of identification 247; boundary-crossing 180, 196 (*see also* postmodern principles, strangers); boundary formation 268; cultural (embodied) boundaries 202; deterritorialized borders 266; social boundaries 51; spatial boundaries 265; temporal boundaries 265; territorial boundaries 51, 54; transcending borders 266; *see also* security and insecurity
Bourdieu, Pierre 7, 19, 43–4, 54–8 *passim*, 70–2, 75, 104, 108–11, 127, 137, 166, 171, 185–6, 190
Bové, Jose 280
Braudel, Fernand 143
*Braveheart* 2, 117
Brazil and Brazilian 287, Rio de Janeiro 287
Brennan, Teresa 309
Breton people, *see* France and French
Breuilly, John 222–3
*bricolage* 91, 121
Bringa, Tony 36
*Bringing the State Back In* 210
Britain, *see* United Kingdom and British
British Broadcasting Corporation (BBC) 144
Broadway 302
Browning, Richard 85
Brutus of Troy 194
Buddhism *see* religion
bureaucracy 35, 208, 220; bureaucratization 134; legal-rational 215; traditional-bureaucratic 87; *see also* modes of organization, rationality, state
Burghers, Dutch 23, 29
Burgundian people, *see* France and French
Burridge, Louise 3
Burundi 32, 34, 248–9
Burma and Burmese 175, 282
Bush, George W. 37–8, 45, 73, 136, 179, 182, 228, 293–5, 304
Bynum, Caroline Walker 93
Byzantine 141

# INDEX

Caledonia 23
calendars 16, 72, 158–76 *passim*;
    calendrical systems 161; Chinese
    159; of the French revolution 159;
    Muslim 159, 165; *see also* time
Calhoun, Craig 293
Calvin, John 170; Calvinism 250
Cambodia and Cambodian 15
*Cambodian Daily* 279
Cambridge University 48
Campbell, David 297
Canada and Canadian 175, 236, 310;
    Canadian Pacific Railway 171;
    Inuit people 310
capital 138, 214, 231, 273, 275, 282;
    accumulation of 60; fiduciary 78;
    finance 21, 266; globalization of 13,
    25; social 277; symbolic 55; *see also*
    capitalism, imperialism, modes
    of exchange
capitalism 22, 32, 59–60, 79, 89, 111, 114,
    134, 136, 153, 171, 175, 179, 182,
    197, 199, 224, 241, 243, 251, 267,
    269, 280, 284, 286, 301; anti-
    capitalism 280; casino 79, 282;
    commodity 116; disembodied 280;
    disorganized 269; industrial 75;
    information 75; late-modern
    capitalist societies 32, 137; organized
    269; postmodern 180, 302; time-
    measured 169; *see also* economy,
    global capitalism, globalization,
    market, print-capitalism
care, embodied relations of 86; *see also*
    ethics and principles
cartography, *see* maps and mapping
Castells, Manuel 268
Castles, Stephen 274
Castro, Fidel 182
Catalan people and language, *see* France
    and French
categorization, *see* modes of categorization
Celestial Kingdom, *see* kingdoms, historical
Celtic and Celt 2
cenotaphs and tombs 3, 173, 197; of the
    Unknown Soldier 120, 197; *see also*
    death and mortality
censuses 226, 235
Central European University 48
Ceylon 29
change 46, 61–2, 80, 122, 134, 224, 232,
    234, 296; global and globalizing 104,
    224; ontological 95; patterns of 65,
    172, 247; *see also* epochs

Chapel of St Mary 119
Charlemagne 142
Charles I and II, *see* kings, historical
Chatterjee, Partha 243–5
Chechnya and Chechen 13
Chiapas, *see* Mexico and Mexican
Chicano community 302
China and Chinese 201, 218, 238, 276;
    Chinese encyclopedia 71; Chinese
    language; *Guanxi* family 143; Qing
    dynasty 143; Shang dynasty 218;
    Tiananmen Square 201; *see also*
    calendars, empires, universalism
    and universalization
Chou Empire, *see* empires, historical
Christendom 54, 170, 219, 273
Christian God, *see* god, gods and
    goddesses
Christianity, *see* religion, *see also* Bosnia
    and Bosnian, religious institutions,
    the West and Western
Christmas 107, 137, 159, 182
*Chronica de Sex Aetatibus* 194
church, the institution of 87, 114, 127,
    151, 161, 181, 250; *see also* East
    Timor and East Timorese, Latin
    language, Rome and Roman,
    Scotland, Scottish and Scot, World
    Church of the Creator
citizens, citizenry and citizenship 181,
    188–9, 196, 215, 227, 250, 304;
    cosmopolitan 314; global 28;
    national 28, 83, 240; *see also* identity
    and identification
cities and metropolitan areas 298, 300;
    cyber-cities 14
City of God 91; City of Man 91
civic identity 26; *see also* nationalism
civil society 50
civilizations 51, 304; clash of 65
clans 58, 104, 127, 188
class and class society 59, 72, 210
Clausewitz, Otto von 296
Cleopatra's Needle and the Ram in the
    Thicket from Ur 273
clerics 23, 49, 68, 241, 243
Clinton, Bill 37, 293, 300, 304
clocks and watches 5, 160, 169–70;
    *see also* time, United States Time
    Corporation
Clooney, George 89
CNN broadcasting network 147, 272
Coalition of the Willing 45, 262, 281
Coates, Ken 103

Coca-Cola 270, 299
codification 60, 152, 186; abstract 185; agencies of 139; electronic 147; Morse code 158; systems of 136; *see also* ethics and principles, meaning, modes of communication
coercion *see* human activity
cognition *see* human activity
Cohen, Robin 274
coinage, *see* money
collateral damage 67
colonialism 126, 167, 245, 247, 281–2; *see also* neo-colonialism, nationalism, polity, state
colonization 163, 167, 174, 225–6; decolonization 242, 249; traditional 24; commercial 88
commonality 26–7; *see also* body
commodities and commodification 60, 86, 105–20 *passim*, 134, 179, 181, 199, 215, 241, 262, 275, 277, 283, 288, 302; commodity-futures 137, 149; commodity situations 113; fetishized 86; postmodern 116; tribal 86; *see also* capitalism, culture and cultures, economy, modernity, modes of exchange, objects, space, value
Common Era Time, *see* time and temporality
Commonwealth 283
communal identity 247
communes 87
communication, *see* modes of communication
communications theory 135
communism and communist 48
communitarianism 294
community 13, 15, 24, 51, 68, 76, 82, 109, 112, 114, 139, 151, 180–1, 183, 185, 189, 207, 224, 226, 231–2, 278, 292–314 *passim*; computer-based 14; embodied 27; ethics of 19; ethnic 182, 235; global 21, 182; globalizing 96; horizontal 243; local 182, 262; localized 86; and nation 4, 50, 231; national 182, 197, 226, 251, 300; political 96; and polity 4–5, 7, 9, 15, 17–20 *passim*, 45, 59, 96, 192, 218, 220, 223–4, 232, 258–9; post-kin-related 34; postmodernizing 96; sense of 182; traditional-tribal-modern 161; *see also* abstract community, customary, face-to-face community, nation, nation-state, traditional community, tribal community-polity
Compassionate Conservatism 293
computers 5, 19; *see also* community
Comte, August 124
Concerned Christians 159
Condorcet, Cariat de 175
Confederate States of America, *see* League of the South
*Confessions of a Dangerous Mind* 89
Congo 32, 65
Conrad, Joseph 171
consanguinal relations 84, 86, 190; *see also* blood
constitutive abstraction 215, 304; *see also* levels approach
consumerism 32, 198–9, 292
consumption 69, 75, 198, 269
contingency/determination dichotomy, *see* methodological dichotomies
continuity and discontinuity 232, 234, 240, 243, 247–9 *passim*, 258
contract of purchase 106
contradictions and contradictory relations, practices and processes 3, 34, 44, 61, 66, 79, 183, 198, 231–2, 234, 236, 242, 279, 296, 305, 314; abstraction-embeddedness 16; cultural contradictions 183; globalism-localism 16; homogenization-fragmention 16; layers in contradiction 80; universalism-particularism 16, 310; *see also* globalization, nation, ontological contradictions
Convention of the Metre conference 175
convivial relations 84–6
Cooper, James Fenimore 103
co-operation, *see* reciprocity, mutuality and co-operation
Co-ordinated Universal Time, *see* time, the ontological category of, and temporality
Cope, Bill 152
Copernican revolution 264
corporate body, *see* body
corporate icon, *see* iconography 262
corporations 14, 68, 87, 139, 158, 215, 271, 280, 282–3, 299, 311; communications-connected 263; corporatization 216; globalizing 116; *see also particular corporations such as* IBM, McDonald's, News Corporation, Nike, Starbucks

corporeality 16, 198, 227; corporeal metaphor 133
Corsican people, *see* France and French
cosmetic surgery, *see* body
*Cosmetic Surgery: A Consumer Guide* 198
cosmography 174
cosmology 124, 154, 174, 185, 192, 194, 228, 248; *see also* abstraction, body, knowledge, modes of enquiry, space, subjectivity and subjects, time
cosmopolitanism 14, 256, 267, 293-4, 297-304; *passim,* 313; *see also* citizens, citizenry and citizenship, postmodern principles
*Cosmopolitics* 299
Coulmas, Florian 20
Coward, Rosalind 199
credit notes, *see* money
creole 242-6; *see also* nationalism
Croatia, Croatian and Croat 36
criminology, the discipline of 211
crisis 65, 80, 236, 276-88 *passim;* cultural 66; economic 66; environmental 65; *krisis* 66; of meaning 65; of explanation 69; military 66; of the nation and nation-state 231; of international organization 65; of structural adjustment 65; political 66
Critical Theory, the discipline of 38
Cromwell, Oliver 155 195
Crook, Clive 216, 287
crowns 113-20 *passim,* 140; Crown Jewellers 116; crown jewels 113, 116; state crown 116; *see also* United Kingdom and British, kingship
Crusoe, Robinson 31
Cuba and Cuban 182, 255; Bay of Pigs 255; Cuban Missile back-down 255
'cultural biography of things' 114
cultural dominant 78
cultural studies and theory, the discipline of 16, 19
culture and cultures 20, 46, 53, 67, 82, 91, 104, 111, 165, 217-20 *passim,* 231, 264-5, 309; cinematic 3, 14, 303; civic 27; commercialized 13; commodified globalized 134; contemporary 182; cross-cultural relations 23; electronic broadcast 21; enduring 118; integrative 5; global 278; literate 103; mobile 50; oral 103; political 36; popular 1; and structure 19; *see also* boundaries and borders, contradictions and contradictory relations, difference and differentiation, practices and processes
customary relations 204, 247; and community 103-29 *passim,* 186; rights 78; *see also* modes of exchange, tribal community-polity, tribalism
customary tribalism 24, 29-31, 103, 126, 180, 189-91
cyberspace 14, 295
cyborg 14; cyborg-machine 133; *see also* body, modes of communication
Czechoslovakia and Czech 48; Jewish-Czech 48

Daarood clan, *see* Somalia and Somali
*dabbawalas* 152
*Daedalus* 210
*Daily Telegraph* 31, 146
Darby, Phillip 285
Darwinism 4
David I, *see* kings, historical
Davis, Jefferson 2
*The Day after Tomorrow* 303
De Beers corporation 116
death and mortality 3, 84, 158, 166, 173, 180, 186, 188, 190, 192, 194, 201, 236, 246, 304, 306, 308; and embodiment 3; and tombs 3; *see also* nation
Declaration of Southern Independence, *see* League of the South
decolonization, *see* colonization
Deleuze, Gilles 214
democracy 240, 293, 307; *see also* market
Denmark and Danish 144; *see also* Queen Anne of Denmark and son Henry
deontology and deontological systems 92, 308; *see also* abstraction
dependency theory 278, 284
deregulation 216; *see also* regulation
Derrida, Jacques 82; Derridean deconstruction 211
desire 197, 285
determination and determinism 48, 50-1, 53, 55-6, 244; *see also* methodological dichotomies
deterritorialization 292-7 *passim; see also* boundaries and borders
Diamond, Neil 133
diasporas 297-298, 301-302, 305; *see also* nation
difference and differentiation 1, 46, 76, 120, 126, 150, 185-6, 202, 285, 302,

307–8, 310–11; of age 183; cultural 238; embodied 26, 185; equality-in-difference 302; essential 247; as ethnic 183; of family 183; as flat pluralism 46; gendered 183; ideologies of 13; and images of integration 191; and indifference to difference 34; ontological 90; processes of 190; tribal 247; xenophobic intolerance to 105; *see also* body, embeddedness, globalism, integration, postmodern principles
digitalization 152–3
Dion, Celine 27
DirecTV 272
discourse 61; discursive attachment 292; discursive formations 17, 20, 61, 181, 213–14; discursive patterning of social life 61; fields of discourse 78; *see also* ethnicity, modes of practice
disembodied integration (and extension) 21, 76, 81, 88–96 *passim*, 180, 183–4, 197, 199, 227–8, 232, 267, 278
disembodiment 197, 262–88 *passim*; abstract disembodied 255; disembodied inter-relation 265; techno-disembodiment 198
Disneyland 14, 302
disorganization complex 215–16
distance, and attachment 299; bridging distances 60; as spatial metaphor 1, 60, 84; as temporal metaphor 84; *see also* power, reflexivity
division of labour 50–2, 58–9, 225
*dochakuka* 15
Document Type Definitions 153
*The Domestication of the Savage Mind* 121
dominance 57; ontological 89
domination 75, 278, 281; *see also* structure
Doric language 117
Douglas, Mary 44, 91, 182, 185–6, 190
Drago, Ivan 303
'Dreamtime' or 'The Dreaming', *see* Aborigines of Australia
dualism 58
Dumont, Louis 67
Durkheim, Emile 254; Durkheimian theory 43
Dyck, Anthony van 195

Eagleton, Terry 310
East Africa, *see* Africa and African
East Asia, *see* Asia and Asian
East Timor and East Timorese 118, 123, 150, 165, 228, 246, 294, 303, 313; and the Catholic Church 5; Fretilin 294; Maubisse 3; *see also* Portugal and Portuguese
East and Eastern 239, 246, 309
Easter Friday agreement, *see* Ireland and Irish
Easton, David 209–10
Eastwood, Clint 27
ecclesial relations 88
ecology 51, 314; ecology-ontology 308–309
*The Economist* 287
e-commerce 13, 159
economics, the discipline of 18, 111
economic rationalism 108, 215
economy 135, 264–5; agrarian 109; capitalist 109; commodification of 161; free-market 111; global 278, 288; knowledge-based 14; national 143; world 279, 282; *see also* crisis, globalism, globalization, sources of social power
Edinburgh 2, 114, 118; Edinburgh Castle 113, 116, 119; Edinburgh Memorial 119
Edward I, *see* kings
EFTPOS (electronic funds transfer system) 148
Egypt and Egyptian 91, 139, 148, 155, 193–4, 219, 248; dynasties and kingdoms 218; Hatshepsut 217; Luz 114; Pharaoh and Pharaonic 194, 217–18
Eid al-Adha holy day 170
Eisenstein, Elizabeth 20, 150
Einstein, Albert 164
Einsteinian relativity 160
electronic financial revolution 148
embeddedness 15; and difference 35; and disembeddedness 66; of objects 113; *see also* abstraction, contradictions and contradictory relations, ontological categories, practices and processes, local embodied connection 119, 126, 181–2, 197, 300; *see also* grounding and grounding categories, nostalgia
embodiment *see* body
Emperor Jimmu, *see* Japan and Japanese
empire 5, 23–4, 46, 65, 146, 155–6, 186, 207–28 *passim*, 240, 243–6 *passim*, 276–86 *passim*; empire red 304;

modern 207; modern empire-nations 237; traditional 207
*Empire* magazine 25
empires, historical 29, 237; African 116; Ancient Near East 54; Austro-Hungarian 48; British 155, 223; Chinese 23; Chou 218; Roman 22-3, 216, 273; Russian 241
empirical generalization 108, 171, 222, 225, 238, 273, 285
empiricism 69, 83, 213; *see also* analytical abstraction
*Encarta Encyclopedia* 234
*Encyclopedia Britannica* 234
End-of-History ideology 4
Energex corporation 262
engagement 94-5
England and English 2, 86, 116-17, 141, 144, 155, 171, 192, 194, 196, 220, 226, 238-9, 304; Act of Parliament 144; English Channel 263; English language 162, 165, 219; English Revolution 155; *see also* Bank of England, King of Great Brittaine France and England
England, Lyndie 198
*Enigma of the Gift* 107, 111
Enlightenment 155
environmentalism 65; *see also* crisis
enquiry *see* modes of enquiry
Epicurean 168
epistemology *see* knowledge
epochs 50, 159; conflicting 16; epochalism 51, 270; epochal nature of social change 48, 153, 234, 236; of order 48-50 *passim*
equality 307, 310, 313-14; and empathy 307; liberal notions of equality-equals-sameness and equality of opportunity 46, 309; *see also* difference and differentiation
Eritrea and Eritrean 282
essentialism 53, 62; *see also* difference and differentiation
ethics and principles 78, 92, 180, 292-314 *passim*; codified 92-4; ethic of agonism 306; ethic of care 306-8; ethic of foundations 306, 308-9; ethic of rights 306-7, 310; exemplary-sacred ethics 93; exemplary-universal ethics 92-4; reflexive ethics 92, 94; relational ethics 92; relational-particularistic ethics 92;

procedural ethics 307-8, 310; *see also* abstraction, community
ethnic nations and nationalism, *see* nation, nationalism
ethnicity 20, 26, 29, 36, 76, 184, 235-8, 242, 246, 292, 298; as a discursive fiction 26; ethnic chauvinism 298; ethnic cleansing 36-7, 296, 302; ethnic homogeneity 302; ethnic revival 238; ethnicity studies 28; nationally-bounded 76; *see also* body, community, difference and differentiation, genealogy, groupings, kinship, subjectivity and subjects, tribalism, violence
*ethnie* 222, 235, 237-9
ethnocentrism 36, 128, 168, 298
ethnography 24, 106
ethno-symbolism 223, 225, 233
eucharist 93
Euclidean theory 223
Eurasia, *see* Asia and Asian
Eurocentrism 241
Europe and European 1-2, 23, 28, 30, 32, 84, 115-16, 137, 141-3, 150, 152, 158, 168, 210, 216, 219, 225-6, 237, 239-45, 247, 277, 281-2; Eastern 36, 237, 242; Eurotrash 199; Iron Age 54; Western 141, 241; *see also* kingdoms, Middle Ages
Euskadi government 238
Evans-Pritchard, E.E. 163
*Evening Standard* 144
evolutionism 31
exceptionalism 256
exchange, *see* modes of exchange
exogamy 254
Extensible Markup Language (XML) 153
extension 60, 134, 278-9, 284; abstracted 267; objective 266; *see also* body, disembodied integration (and extension), global, imperialism, object extension, social extension, social relations, space
*Extreme Make-Over* 45

face-to-face community 5, 29, 33, 36, 124, 241, 309
face-to-face integration or embodied extension 29, 75-6, 81, 83-6, 90, 105, 129, 137, 161, 166, 180, 183-4, 265, 278
face-to-face interaction and relations 34-5, 83-4, 92, 136, 143, 152, 185-6, 239

face-to-face, the level of 47, 126, 182, 190, 228, 231, 257, 263, 269, 311-14; and attachment 192; and communion68; and confrontation 35; and contractual connection 181; and embodiment 190; and gangs 32; and interchange 265; and killing 185; and metaphors 87; *see also* modes of communication
*fahrangs* 288
Falklands/Malvinas War, *see* war and wars
Fallers, Lloyd 28
Fanon, Frantz 285-6
Farrari, Lolo 199
fecundity and fertility 16
*fei ch'ien* (flying money) 143
feminist theory, the discipline of 75, 212, 307
Fenius the Scythian 193
Fergus mor mac Erc 193
Ferguson, William 194
Fertile Crescent 263
fetishism 45, 61-2, 135, 198, 296; fetishized symbols 108; meta-fetishization 149; *see also* commodities and commodification
Finland and Finnish 15, 126
First World 246, 284
flags 27, 154, 253-4, 272, 303-4
Flaubert, Gustave 73
Fleming, Sandford 171
flesh 112, 117, 183, 192, 218-19, 307; *see also* blood, body, stone and rock
Florence 142-143
*The Follies of Globalisation Theory* 22
Ford cars 270
Fordism 302
formalism 91
Forset, Edvvard 195
Fort Dunadd 114
Foucault, Michel 7, 16-17, 20, 38, 44, 52, 61-2, 70-1, 74, 82, 189, 212, 214-15, 264, Foucauldian theory 227
Fox Entertainment and News Channel 270, 272
fragmentation 13, 96, 199, 201, 231, 268-9; *see also* contradictions and contradictory relations, practices and processes, methodological dichotomies, postmodern principles
France and French 35, 55, 57, 73, 75, 86, 106, 114, 120, 141, 195, 219, 223, 226, 237-9, 241, 246, 257, 281, 298; Basque people 238; Breton people 238; Burgundian people 238; Catalan people and language 238; Corsican people 238; Francification 238; French language 219; French Revolution 188, 197, 202, 242; Millau 280; Montpellier 280; National Front party 298; Provençal people 238; Villers-Bretonneux 120; *see also* calendars, King of Great Brittaine France and England
freedom 45, 111, 292-3, 302, 306, 313-14
Freeman, Cathy 182
Freeman, Michael 268
Freud, Sigmund 58, 85, 92
Freudian theory 72
Friedman, Jonathan 32
*Friends* 32, 298
Fukuyama, Francis 277
fundamentalism, Islamic 93; neo-traditional 78, 93

Gabirol, Solomon Ibn 124
Gaedel Glas 193
Gaelic language 117, 193
Galileo 91
Gallipoli 228
Gandhi, Mahatma 295
*ga*n*ma* 172
Garden of Eden 174
Gaza Strip 67
Geertz, Clifford 73
Gellner, Ernest 5, 7, 19, 43-4, 48-50 *passim*, 53, 58-9, 103-4, 153, 222-4, 227, 233, 235, 241-2, 244, 246; *see also* history, human activity
*Gemeinschaft* and *Gesellschaft* 18, 46
George IV, *see* kings
gender 82, 190-1, 216-17; *see also* body, difference and differentiation
genealogical connection 152, 155, 237, 239, 241
genealogical placement 29-30, 33, 193, 209, 235-6
genealogy 76, 82, 87, 92, 125-129 *passim*, 139, 149, 173, 189-190, 192-4, 217, 219, 235-8, 243, 274; and ethnicity 27; of kinship 30, 126; genealogical hierarchy 191; national 236; relations of 55; *see also* body, mode of organization, space, time
genocide 33, 35, 65, 184, 247; globalized 103; modern 184
Geoffrey of Monmouth 194

## INDEX

geography, the discipline of 4, 19; geography-theology 174
Germany and German 84, 145, 226, 236-7, 244, 247, 256; *see also* Hitler, Nazism and Nazi
Gerner, John 133
Gettysburg address 252
Gibson, Mel 2, 117
Giddens, Anthony 7, 19, 24, 38, 44, 47, 56, 58-61, 66-7, 82, 103-4, 110, 163, 190, 210, 220, 224, 233, 242, 271, 286; *see also* layers of consciousness, structure
*The Gift* 107-108
gifts and gift exchange 5-6, 84, 86, 105-20 *passim*, 134, 137, 164, 217-18; enduring gifts 118; gift-return 137; postmodern gifts 116; top-rank gifts 140; *see also* reciprocity, mutuality and co-operation
Gilbert, Tron 36
Gillen, F. 167
Gilligan, Carol 307
Glenorchy, *see* Scotland, Scottish and Scots
global capital 32, 110, 156, 214, 273, 276, 278, 280, 283, 287-8, 293, 295, 302; globalizing capital 67, 75-6, 257, 287
Global Distribution Systems 274
global formation 232, 263-88 *passim*
global, the level of 262, 265, 299; global connection 22, 278; global extension 247, 267; global flow 278; global subjection 277-8, 283
Global Positioning System (GPS) 273
globalism 2-3, 7, 14-15, 21-5 *passim*, 33-4, 37, 79, 96, 104, 144, 146, 153-6 *passim*, 171, 273, 276-86 *passim*, 292-314 *passim*; agency-extended 273; anti-globalism 8, 286; disembodied 6, 15, 136, 175, 273; economic 267; embodied 273; globalism studies, the discipline of 4; mercantile 24; modern 23-24, 175; neo-liberal 287; object-extended 273; open 13; as social formation 4; structures of 5; subjectivities of 5, 266; traditional 23-4; as transcending difference; *see also* contradictions and contradictory relations, practices and processes, nationalism, social theory
globality 24, 2066

globalization 1, 4-5, 13, 21-3, 44, 60, 65, 96, 155-6, 176, 200, 215-16, 224, 262-88 *passim*, 292, 299, 311; abstract 67; anti-globalization movement 65; capitalist 279, 286, 299; of cinematic culture 3, 25, 89; and contradiction 1-2; as a descriptive category 22; disembodied 4; economic 268; of metric measure 175; objective 263; postmodern 105, 267; postnational 293; practice of 263; processes of 24, 30, 74, 207, 264, 266, 268; savage 276, 287; structures of 269-76 *passim*; subjective 264; technological 268; totalizing layer of 37; traditional 22, 267; *see also* capital, modern globalization
globe 65, 171, 174-5, 189, 226, 258, 262-88 *passim*
glocalization 15, 79
god, gods and goddesses 23, 79, 95, 111, 118, 124, 137, 165, 168, 174, 217-20 *passim*; Christian God 2-3, 27, 93, 119, 154, 186, 197, 250-251; Gaia 158; Greek gods 158, 165, 168; god of time 158; Iphigeneia 168; Islamic Prophet 93; Jesus Christ 93, 186, 188, 196-197 (*see also* blood); and Joshua 168; Kronos 158, 166; and Lazarus 168; Mambai Father and Mother Heaven 5-6, 123, 150-151; Rhea; transcendent 94; Uranus 158; Zeus 158, 165; *see also* Nike, Greek goddess and corporation
Godelier, Maurice 19, 44, 55-6, 87, 107, 111-13, 118, 137-8, 145, 190
Golan, Daphna 31
gold 115, 138, 140, 145, 171, 275
Gold Coast 115
Golden Age of humanity 158
*Good Morning America* 32
goods 105-20 *passim*, 168; sacred 112, 137; valuable 113 *see also* commodities
Goody, Jack 20, 44, 121-2, 139, 150, 152
Gore, Al 272
*gotong-royong* 14
Goux, Joseph 138
governance 211, 213, 215, 227, 296, 310; governmentality 214-15
Gramsci, Antonio 57
grand narratives and theory 7, 18, 43-44, 69, 165, 173; *see also* methodology

*350*

Granges, David des 192
Great Chain of Being, see kingship
Great Depression 270
Great Divide 31, 46, 104, 108, 122, 147, 150-1, 165, 173, 200, 208, 285
Greece and Greek 22, 94, 158, 168, 170, 181, 257, 266; agora 136; see also god, gods and goddesses, Nike
Green Revolution 282, 284
Greenfeld, Liah 155, 251, 300
Greenpeace 280
Greenwich 171; Greenwich Electronic Time (GeT); Greenwich Mean Time; Greenwich Observatory 171
Gregory, Christopher 87, 107, 139, 169
Gregory, Derek 60
ground zero 27
grounding and grounding categories 232-3, 267; and places of enduring nature 233
groupings 109, 127; ethnic 26, 30; racial 26; sub-cultural 32
Guadeloupe 29
*Guanxi* family, see China and Chinese
*guaffres* 141
Guattari, Félix 214
Guinness Book of Records 199
Gulf Wars, see war and wars
Gusmão, Xanana 228
Gutenberg, Johann 153-4

Habermas, Jürgen 19, 44, 75, 82, 210
*habitus* 16, 55-8 *passim*, 171
Haggard, Rider H. 1, 248
Hammond, Basil 17
Hanks, Tom 27
Hanson, Pauline 298
Hanukkah 107
Haraway, Donna 44, 198
Hardt, Michael 78, 277
Hartman, Heidi 75
Harvey, David 268, 302
Hastings, Adrian 155
Hatshepsut, see Egypt and Egyptian
*hau* of the gift 107-9, 218
*Heartbeat* 299
Hegel, Georg 124
hegemony 37, 57, 293
Heideggerian theory 58
Helsinki 14
Henry III and VIII, see kings
hermeneutics 105
Hermes Paris corporation 277
Hesiod 165-6

*hieros gamos* 252
High Atlas, see Morocco and Moroccan
*Highlander IV* 160
Hilferding, Rudolf 269
Hill of Tara, see Ireland and Irish
Hinduism, see religion
Hinkson, John 79, 215
Hip Hop Nation 231
Hiroshima 38, 67, 69
Hirst, Paul 275
historical materialism, see social theory
historicalism 21-5 *passim*, 170-1; modern 25; postmodern 25
*Historia Brittonum* 194
*Historia Regum Brittaniae* 194
historicism 25
historicity 116, 163, 168, 245
history 26-7, 50, 60, 73, 76-7, 91, 104, 154, 160, 168, 172, 181, 219, 221, 231-2, 266-7, 292; Ernest Gellner's classification of 48-9, 224; History, the discipline of 25, 150, 211; see also abstraction, End-of-History ideology, time, tribalism
Hitler, Adolf 84, 236, 301
Ho Chi Minh 228
Hoëm, Ingjerd 161-2
Hodgson, Governor Sir Frank 115
Holbein, Hans, the Younger 192
Hollywood 2, 25, 27, 302-3; Planet Hollywood 13
*holos* 23
Holy Writ 194
Homeland Security, United States office of, see United States of America
homogenization 268, 302; see also contradictions and contradictory relations, practices and processes, rationalization
Hondius, Jodocus 174
*hora* 170
hospital, the institution of 161
host 86; *hôte* and *hoste* 86
house and household 36, 126-7, 190-1, 196
HTML, see Hypertext Markup Language
humanitarian bombing 37
humanitarian intervention and peacekeeping, see intervention
human activity, Ernest Gellner's classification of 49, 59; coercion 49, 54, 59; cognition 49, 59; persuasion 49 production 49, 59 W.G. Runciman's classification of 49

human rights 8, 304, 306-7
hunting-gathering 159; *see also* history
Hussein, Saddam 84, 188, 273, 294
Hutu people 35, 126, 184, 191-2, 247-9
hybridity 285, 292, 301, 305, 313
Hypertext Markup Language (HTML) 153

Iber Scot 193
IBM (International Business Machines) corporation 14, 148, 277, 299
iconography, abstracted icons 197; corporate icons 262; *see also* body
identity and identification 1, 33, 104, 120, 126-7, 150-1, 184-5, 196, 198, 215, 242, 249, 280, 285-6, 298, 301, 305, 307-8, 310-11, 314; ascribed 25; chosen 26; fixing of 247-9; group identification 182; identity formation 179, 245; identity transformation 196; lifting out of 151; prior forms of 292; *see also* boundaries and borders, neo-colonialism, *and the particular examples of identity:* civic identity, communal identity, national identity and identification, personal identity, social identity, traditional identity, tribal identity
ideology 47-8, 53-4, 103, 213, 215, 228, 240, 257, 267, 270, 278, 285-8, 294, 300, 304; ideological legitimization 30; nationalist 117; *see also* difference and differentiation, End-of-History ideology, nationalism, sources of social power, United States of America and American
*Idols of the Tribe* 253
*Imagined Communities* 17, 227
imperialism 25, 50, 276-7, 281-2, 294; of globalizing capital 30; imperial centres 24; imperial extension 24; imperial states 242; neo-imperial states 14
*Impuzamugambi* and *Interahamwe* militias, *see* Rwanda and Rwandan
*In the Line of Fire* 27
*Inalienable Possessions* 107
*Independence Day* 303
India and Indian 116, 152, 185, 245-6; Indian National Congress 244; Indian Ocean 170; India-Pakistan border 231; modern, public-political nationalism 244; Mumbai 152; Scheduled Castes 185; Untouchables 185

indigenous peoples and cultures 24, 46, 103, 167, 242, 245, 310
individualism 179; *see also* methodology, nationalism
individualization 179, 182; *see also* body
Indonesia and Indonesian 170, 201, 226, 228, 236-7, 246, 255-6, 294, 310
industrial society 159; industrialism 233
industrialization 50;time-industrialization 169
Ingle, David 254-5
Inkatha people, *see* Zulu people
insecurity, *see* security and insecurity
institutional integration, *see* agency-extended or institutional integration
institutional projection 185
instrumentalism 228
integration 65, 182-3, 306; abstract in form 91, 96; and differentiation 76; images of 191; objectified relations of 145; processes of 189; *see also* abstraction, analytical abstraction, difference and differentiation, micro-biological integration, modes and levels of integration, social relations, structures
intellectuals and the intellectually trained 30, 49, 92, 239, 241, 245-6, 267; interpreters 152; *see also* clerics, knowledge
Interactive Media in Retail Group (IMRG) 158
interchange 299;   forms of 149-53 *passim*; global 279; symbolic 111; *see also* body, face-to-face
*The Interface between the Written and the Oral* 20
International Day of Action 280
international relations, the system of 37, 265, 284, 286
internationalism 294, 305
intervention 36, 281; humanitarian intervention and peacekeeping 3, 79, 303
Inuit people, *see* Canada and Canadian
*Inventing America* 252
*Inventing Shaka* 31
invention 31; *see also* nation, tribe
*The Invention of Primitive Society* 31
*The Invention of Somalia* 31
Iphigeneia, *see* god, gods and goddesses
iPods 200

Iraq and Iraqi 33, 37, 45, 118; Iraq National Museum 273; see also war and wars
Ireland and Irish 2, 114, 171, 193, 259, 299; Bandoran 171; Catholics and Protestants 259; Easter Friday agreement 259; Hill of Tara 115; Irish Republican Army 294
Isaacs, Harold 253
*Isendingabók (Book of the Islanders)* 194
Isidore of Seville 194
Islam, see religion
Islamic Dome of the Rock, see Jerusalem
Islamic prophet, see god, gods and goddesses
Islamic world 144-5
Israel, Israeli and Israelite 29, 31, 65, 118, 152, 155, 185, 194, 236, 251, 259
Italy and Italian 226, 278

Jakarta 234
James I, see kings, historical
Jameson, Fredric 44, 78, 268, 284
Japan and Japanese 15, 200, 218, 239, 244, 256; Aum Shinrikyo 159; Emperor Jimmu 218; Tokugawa modernizing revolution 239; Tokyo 159, 200
Java 234; Java Minor 23
Jefferson, Thomas 175, 251
Jerusalem 118, 159; Islamic Dome of the Rock 118, 258
Jessop, Bob 210, 212
Jesus Christ, see god, gods and goddesses
jewels 115-16; see also crowns
Jewish and Jew 29-31, 33, 185; Iberian Jewish 124; Jewish Wailing Wall 258; see also Czechoslovakia and Czech, Middle Ages, mythology
Jihad verus McWorld 46, 65, 73
Joan of Arc 197
John of Fordoun 114
Judaism see religion
*jus ad bellum* (right to make war) 78

Kabyle people, see Algeria and Algerian
Kaiser Wilhelm's Land 108
Kalantzis, Mary 152
*kännykkä* 15
Kant, Immanuel 168
Karadzic, Radovan 298
Karelian region 126
*kata* 23
*katholikos* 23

*kdain* 123
Kearney, Richard 300
Keating, Paul 120
Kennedy, John F. 254-5
Kigali 34-5
Kigwa 191
Kilmartin Valley 114, 193
King of Great Brittaine France and England, portrait 195
*King Solomon's Mines* 248
kingdom, the concept of 5, 46, 125, 207-28 passim, 240, 258; traditional 30; traditional-tribal 207
kingdoms, historical, Celestial 23; East African 248; European 248; Kingdom of God 252; Tutsi 29, 247; see also Egypt and Egyptian
kings, historical, Alexander III 114, 193-4; Charles I 195; Charles II 195; Dalriadic 193; David I 119; Edward I 116, 141, 194; George IV 116; Henry III 194; Henry VIII 141; James I 154, 192; Malcolm III 193; Mswati 31; Prempeh 115; Rujugira 248; of Siam 248
kingship 113, 115, 127, 141, 155, 161, 188, 193-4, 209, 216-20 passim, 236; abstract body of the king 115; charisma of the king 219; Great Chain of Being 218; Mandate theory of 218; traditional 114; tribal 114; see also kingship
kinship 30, 56, 68, 76, 83, 86, 93, 105-29 passim, 135, 152, 166, 180, 186, 190-1, 193-4, 207-9, 216, 236, 254; agents of mercantile kinship 87; and ethnicity 26; fictive 85, 127; kinship group 21, 104; kinship networks 36, 182; official 127; post-tribal 193; practical 127; pseudo-kinship 33; relations of 28-9, 84-5, 125-6, 161; tribal 190, 193; and trust 143; see also blood, community, genealogy, modes of organization, reciprocity, mutuality and co-operation, tribe
Kipling, Rudyard 119, 304
*kitoum* 87
Knoll, Max
knowledge, the ontological category of, and epistemology 6, 16, 46, 50, 53, 57, 61, 69, 72, 77-8, 80, 82, 84, 91-2, 94, 121-4, 129, 167-8, 172-3, 211,

213, 226, 235, 271, 274; content of knowledge 125; cosmological-gnoseological knowledge (sacred, spiritual and universal) 91; epistemes 17; epistemological fields 17; knowledge production 125; modes of knowledge 56, 58; sacred; traditional 235; tribal 123, 235; Western scientific 61; *see also* abstraction, archaeology, economy, philosophy, space, trees
Kohn, Hans 237
*kokutai* 239
Kopytoff, Igor 114
*Kosovo* 296
Kosovo, Kosovan and Kosovar 13, 33–8 *passim,* 294, 296-8, 302; Kosovo Liberation Army (KLA or UCK) 36, 294-6; Kosovo Polje 296; Llaushe village 36; *see also* war and wars
Kristeva, Julia 44, 201, 298
Kronos, *see* god, gods and goddesses
Kuala Lumpur 33
Kubrick, Stanley 128
Kuper, Adam 31
Kurke, Leslie 140
*kwaimatnie* 110
*kwihutura* 247

labour, exchange of 264; mobility of 50; *see also* division of labour
Langhorne, Richard 271
language 26–7, 296; *see also* abstraction, *particular languages such as* Arabic, Chinese, Doric, Gaelic, Latin, Occitan
Lash, Scott 16
*The Last of the Mohicans* 103
Latin language 28, 154, 193; Church Latin 154
Laurence, Janet 257
law 189, 220, 307, 310; codes of 93; natural 94; of nature 92; transcendent Law 94; *see also* abstraction, bureaucracy, modes of organization
Lawrence of Arabia 73
layers of consciousness, Anthony Giddens's concept of 58; practical consciousness 58; reflexive consciousness 58; the unconscious 58; *see also* national consciousness, subjective consciousness
Le Pen, Jean-Marie 298

League of the South 2; and the American Civil War 2 (*see also* war and wars); and the Confederate States of America 2; and the Declaration of Southern Independence 2
Lee Kuan Yew 14
Leeds 3, 32; Leeds University 155
legitimation 208, 221; *see also* structure
Lessing, Doris 1
Lestringant, Frank 174
levels of integration, *see* modes and levels of integration
levels, metaphor of and approach 85, 234, 244–5, 264; *see also* analytical abstraction, face-to-face, global, international, modes and levels of integration,
Lévi-Bruhl, Lucien 121
Lévi-Strauss, Claude 74, 91, 108–9, 111, 121, 186
liberalism 308–10; liberal pragmatics 306; *see also* equality, neo-liberalism, social theory
liberation 96, 183, 294, 296, 302
liberation movements, *see* nationalist and liberation movements
Liberia and Liberian 175
Liberty 197, 201
*Life on Earth* 262
life, forms and ways of, and life-worlds 45, 56–7, 173, 236, 269; embodied 295; modern 164, 231; postmodern 68, 231; traditional 66, 164, 231; tribal 84; tribal-traditional 84, 126; *see also* abstraction, discourse, phenomena, tableaux
liminality 188
Lincoln, Abraham 252
Linnaeus, Carolus 125
Lipietz, Alain 75
literacy 152; *see also* writing
local, the level of 44, 200, 265, 299; and embeddedness 44
localism 13–15, 279, 292, 294, 299; *see also* contradictions and contradictory relations, practices and processes
locality, *see* place, locality and locale
localization 79, 271; *see also* community, glocalization
Lockheed Martin corporation 262
Lombert, Peter 195
London 14, 33, 143, 145, 280; Islington 14; London School of Economics 48;

Parliament 145; Tower of London 116; Westminster Cathedral 119
Looksmart internet search engine 270
*Lord of the Rings* 89
Louis XIV 219, 242
Luhmann, Niklas 44
*lukolo* 188
Luther, Martin 154, 170
Lyotard, Jean-François 78

MacDonald, Lord of the Isles 114
McDonald's corporation 14, 280, 299; McDonaldization 280
MacKinnon, Catherine 75
McKinsey and Company 144
Maffesoli, Michael 33
magic 121, 190
*Malaia* 150-151
Malaysia, Malaysian and Malay 14
Malcolm, Noel 296
Malcolm III, *see* kings, historical
Malinowski, Bronislow 107-8, 113-14
Malkki, Liisa 184
Mambai people and culture 5, 72, 123, 150-1, 154, 165; *see also* god, gods and goddesses
Mamdani, Mahmood 247
*mana* 107, 114, 218
*Manhattan* 298
*Manu* 163
Mann, Michael 7, 19, 38, 44, 50-5, 58-9, 103-4, 210, 216, 264; *see also* sources of social power
Manuel, Don Juan 218
Mansur, Abdalla Omar 235
maps and mapping 83, 94, 105, 158-76 *passim*, 226, 235; atlases 23; of being in the world 94; bio-cartography 105; body 184-5; cartography 248; common global 159; of the human genome 125; necrographic 185; of reflecting upon acting in the world 94; of seeing and enquiring about the world 94; social 70-96 *passim*
Marconi, Guglielmo 158
Marianne 197
market 49, 82, 311; abstract market 87, 311; capitalist 141; electronic 134, 282; financial 89; free 149; futures 158, 179; global 143, 159, 282-3, 287; market-democracy 50; monetary 141; *see also* economy, society
marriage 84, 111; inter-marriage 29
Marvin, Carolyn 30, 254-5

Marx, Karl 58-9, 70, 75, 92, 94, 134, 147, 149, 275; Marxian theory 72; *see also* social theory
Marxism 311; base-superstructure 56, 75; Marxist anthropology 55; neo-Marxism 20; orthodox 56; *see also* social theory
mass media 35, 89, 179, 267, 272, 280, 295; and embodied content 89; globalizing 89; *see also* Murdoch
massacres 35, 184, 191
Mastercard 147
materialism/idealism dichotomy, *see* methodological dichotomies
mathematics 170
Mauritius 14
Mauss, Marcel 107-8, 110
Maussian theory 108
May Day demonstrations 280
Mead, George 199
meaning 69, 117, 153, 181-2, 185, 224, 258, 305-6, 308; categorical 233; codified 152; contextualized 120; embodied 137; layers of 113; matrix of 186; networks of 182; patterns of 61-2 *passim*, 160; subjective 114; techniques and media for abstractly encoding 88; *see also* crisis, modes of exchange
media 91, 138; abstract 135; disembodying 88; media-projection 68; of storage 60; *see also* mass media
mediation 60, 68, 91, 134, 198, 202, 265, 268; processes of 45; technological 174; *see also* modes of communication
mediatism 136, 171, 175, 267
medieval 231-59 *passim*; medieval period 114, 141, 143, 219, 239; neo-medieval burbclaves 14
memory 186, 193, 226; and commemoration 190; embodied 166; and remembrance 179; *see also* grounding and grounding categories
Mendaki, the Muslim organization 14
*Memories Cast in Stone* 123
Mercator projection 174
Mesopotamia and Mesopotamian 139
meta-human 143
*Metamorphoses* 23
metaphysical dialectics 44
methodological dichotomies, contingency/determination 47-8; materialism/idealism 47;

## INDEX

structure/agency 47;
structures/fragmentation 47, 79;
subject/object 47
methodology 65–96 *passim*, 127, 222–23, 236; analytical methods 44; archaeological method 61; contingent nature of 91; and content 222, 233; deconstruction 305; and form 222; generalizing method 5, 62; grand method 7, 50, 62; interpretative method 69; methodological individualism 18; methodological nationalism 17; *see also* abstraction
Metropotamia 175
Mexico and Mexican 163, 175, 223, 226; Chiapas 295; Maya Indians 163; Mexican Army 296; Yucatan 163; Zapatista movement 295
micro-biological integration 23
Microsoft corporation 1–2, 14, 148
Middles Ages, Christian, Moslem and Jewish 91; European 141
Middle East 237, 281
migration 274, *see also* people movement
military and militarism 36–7, 48, 60, 66–7, 238–9, 272, 292 *see also* crisis, power, sources of social power, United States of America, surveillance, violence
milk 93, 158, 179–202 *passim*; *see also* blood
millenarianism, modernist 294; neo-traditional forms of 159
Miller, Perry 250
Miloŝoviæ, Slobodan 37, 295–8, 300
Mittelman, James 287
*mkole* and *mkolo* 188
mobility 292–4, 296–7; *see also* culture and cultures, labour, space
modern formations 60, 129
modern globalization 23–4, 104, 232, 242, 267–8
modern society 104, 182, 195, 199
modernism 21, 24, 33, 50, 57, 71, 77–8, 80, 82, 91, 124–5, 147, 151, 153, 159, 165, 168, 172–3, 184, 188, 200, 220, 228, 232–58 *passim*, 309–10; reflexive 109; sacred and secular counter-modernism 78; structures of 104; *see also* body, modes of enquiry, nostalgia,
modernity 24, 60, 66, 147, 151, 165, 173, 200, 214, 258, 268, 286, 294; late-modernity 47, 70, 258; rational 13, 16, 292; secular commodified 108

modernization 79, 248–9
modes of categorization 80, 82, 231; *see also* analytical abstraction, the levels of, meaning
modes of information 75
modes and levels of integration 69, 80, 82–96, 106, 165, 184, 258, 269, 282, 312; *see also the particular modes of integration*: agency-extended or institutional integration, disembodied integration, face-to-face integration, object-extended integration
modes (and means) of communication 4–6, 16, 19, 25, 27, 75–6, 81, 122, 133–56 *passim*, 161, 181, 224–5, 231, 243, 246, 265, 267, 269, 271–2; as digital transmission 88; cyborg 150; disembodied 6, 150; electronic 6, 25, 135, 150, 159, 269, 272–3; encoded broadcasting 150; encoded transmission 150; face-to-face communication 312; generalized dissemination 88; global communications 271; globalizing tele-communications 136; image-messages 136; mass communications 5, 88; mediated 312; modality of 162; oral 135, 150, 193–4, 227, 265; oral-symbolic 128, 150; post-oral 137; print 19, 88, 150, 153, 156, 224; script 150, 154, 227; relations 133–56 *passim*; techniques of 20, 88; technologies of 20, 88; writing 8, 88, 122, 124, 133–56 *passim*, 194; *see also* corporations
modes (and means) of enquiry 6, 16, 25, 75–6, 81, 92, 94, 105–29 *passim*, 135, 224–5, 231, 246, 267, 271, 282; analytical 90, 92 (*see also* analytical abstraction); analogy 7, 105–29 *passim*, 186; early modern rational 250; forms of 95; modernist 234; mythological 29; perceptual 91; perceptual-analogical 91, 123; rationalism and rationalized 224, 234; scientific 160; systems of 150; technical 91 ;technical-analytical 266; techno-scientific 6, 271; traditional 124, 235; traditional-cosmological 250; tribal 122, 124, 135; *see also* mapping
modes (and means) of exchange 16, 74–7, 81, 87, 105–29 *passim*, 133–56 *passim*, 223, 225, 246, 271, 284;

*356*

abstracted 6; as barter system 6, 106, 110; capital trading 271; of commodities 25, 106, 267, 271; computerized 273; customary reciprocal 137; disembodied 143; fiduciary 5; financial 25, 267; global 287; institutionalization, rationalization and codification of 143; meaning of 140; materials of exchange 140; postmodern 231-59 *passim*; postmodern exchange systems 78; postmodern global information exchange 79; post-reciprocal 137-8, 149; process of 137; and reciprocity 7-8, 68, 105-29 *passim*, 137, 218; relations of 105-29 *passim*, 133-56 *passim*, 311; systems of 142, 149; tribal exchange systems 87; *see also* abstraction, gifts and gift exchange, money, network, objects of exchange, reciprocity, mutuality and co-operation, types of exchange, value

modes (and means) of organization 16, 20, 28, 53, 75-7, 81, 105-29 *passim*, 147, 189, 208-9, 224-5, 238, 267, 271; bureaucratic rational 75, 271; genealogically-placed 128; institutions of organization 114; and kinship 7, 105-29 *passim*; legal-rational 215; rationalizing 243; political 33, 208; *see also* power, structures

modes (and means) of production 5-6, 16, 21, 28, 52, 55, 75-7, 81, 89, 122-3, 128, 147, 152, 223-5, 246, 267, 271, 279, 284; computer-based 5, 24, 271; electronic 267; of food 159; manual 6, 128; post-industrial 6; relations of 56, 149; robotic 6; techniques of 5; *see also* human activity, reciprocity, mutuality and co-operation

modes of practice 6, 16, 23, 45, 49, 59, 74-7, 81-2, 105-29 *passim*, 134-6, 152, 161, 215, 224-6, 228, 231, 246, 257-8, 267, 269, 271, 284-5; abstracted 96, 232; disembodied 25; embodied 136; fields of practice 78; formations of 67, 75, 78, 114; globalized 96, 279; increasing abstraction of 77; intersection of 75; *see also* globalization, patterns of practice, tribalism, *and particular*

*modes of practice such as* modes of communication, modes of enquiry, modes of exchange, modes of organization, modes of production; patterns of practice

monarchy 114-16, 154-5, 192, 232; monarchical ascension 115, 219; monarchical hierarchy 218; monarchical states 207; postmodern 217; *see also* kingship

money 5, 8, 19, 86, 88, 133-56 *passim*, 161, 169, 171, 273; abstract 6, 138; Carolingian system of pence 142; coinage 139-47 *passim*; credit notes 141-7 *passim*; currency 146; the Euro 146; and exchange 6; the fiscal reorganization of 60; metaphor of 133; paper 138, 141-49 *passim*; Royal Mint of Britain 146; systemization of 139; tokens 140-1; *see also* abstraction, body, *fei ch'ien* (flying money), market, value

'Money Talks', song 133

monuments, *see* stone, Scotland, Scottish and Scot

Morocco and Moroccan 103; High Atlas 103

mortality, *see* death and mortality

Moses 94, 193, 195, 235

Mountain, Gerrit 192

Movement for the Survival of the Ogoni People (MOSOP) *see* Nigeria and Nigerian

MSNBC news network 272

MTV 27

Münster, Sebastian 174

Muranano, Quirizio da 93

Murdoch, Rupert 196, 270, 272, 279; Murdoch media empire 272

Mururoa Atoll 281

Muslim, *see* calendars, religion

mutuality, *see* reciprocity

Myers, Fred 167

myth complexes 150-1, 154, 225

mythical thought 121

mythology 167, 189-92, 194, 228, 235-7, 246; Jewish and Christian 118; universalistic 167-8; *see also* body, modes of enquiry, space, time

*mythomoteur* 245

Nairn, Tom 224, 227, 246, 300

Nandy, Ashis 245

Napoleonic wars, *see* war and wars

*narod* 35
*natio* 151, 154, 239
nation 4, 20-1, 26-8 *passim*, 29, 30, 59, 86, 136, 146, 153, 175-6, 182, 197, 215, 231-59 *passim*, 298; civil 235; as community of strangers 34, 196, 222, 232; as contradictory objective-subjective form 26; diaspora 29; ethnic 233-43 *passim*; global 394; grand-nation exceptionalism 44; immortality of 120; as invented formation 26; modern (contradictory) 120, 196, 236-7, 239, 253; nation-building 29, 33, 248; sacred 252; territorial 233-43 *passim*, 297; traditional 152, 239-40; tribal 253-59 *passim*; without nationalism 120; *see also* community, crisis, empire, the concept of, Hip Hop Nation, nationalism, nation-state, society
nation formation 5, 30-1, 127, 155-6, 225, 231-59 *passim*, 268, 288
*Nation Formation* 19, 83, 242
National Front party, *see* France and French
national identity and identification 85, 221, 231, 235, 292; national heroes 179
National Wallace Monument, *see* Scotland, *see also* stone
nationalism 3, 7-8, 26-28 *passim*, 34, 36, 104, 118, 153-6 *passim*, 222-3, 225, 228, 231-59 *passim*, 292-314 *passim*; anti-colonial 244-5; banal 293; civic 30, 36, 300; Cold War 303; creole 244; darkest 297; Eastern 36; ethnic 2, 36, 300; and globalism 4; as ideology 38, 228; individualistic-libertarian 300; liberatory 295 (*see also* nationalistic and liberation movements); linguistic/popular 244; modern 118, 240-1, 256, 294-7 *passim*, 301, 303; modular 237-45 *passim*; national attachment 300; national consciousness 153; nationalist imaginary 297; postmodern 196, 240; official 243, 293; as social formation 4; studies 28; subjectivity of 240; territorial 240; violent 294; as Western 36; *see also* India and Indian, methodology, nation, patriotism, social theory
nationalist and liberation movements 50, 240, 294-297 *passim*, 312
*Nations and Nationalism* 48, 233

nation-state 5, 26, 45, 58-59, 74, 76, 79, 128, 136, 148, 151, 163, 175, 179, 207-228 *passim*, 231-259 *passim*, 265-266, 268, 272, 292-293, 295, 297-298, 301, 303, 311; and belonging 228; civil 241; classical modern 240, 258; as disembodied community of abstracted strangers 76, 179; late-modern 78; modern 79, 96, 175, 207, 221, 227, 257, 268, 296; nation-state formation 50, 221, 225; postcolonial 247-9 *passim*; post-modern 30; primordial 221; and social theory 4, 18; welcoming 86; *see also* crisis, nation, state
*The Nation-State and Violence* 59
NATO 34, 37, 294, 296-7, 302
naturalization 196
nature/culture contradiction, *see* ontological contradictions
nature and the natural 56, 72, 82, 91, 95, 124-5, 160, 165, 168, 170, 172, 183, 199, 217-20 *passim*, 271, 308-9; embodied 124; enduring 118, 152 (*see also* grounding and grounding categories); nature-culture 83, 309, 113, 311; traditional-modern cataloguing of 125; transcendent Nature 94; *see also* body as symbol, law, symbols and signs, time
*natus* 154
Navajo 78, 93
Nazism and Nazi 48; Nazi Germany 185; Nazi Holocaust 33, 69; *see also* Hitler
Ndembu people, *see* Zambia and Zambian
NEC corporation 263
Neeson, Liam 2
Negri, Antonio 78, 277
Neilsen/NetRatings 272
Nennius of Bangor 194
neo-colonialism 282; neo-colonial identity 276
neo-liberalism 8, 44, 136, 215, 267, 287, 293; *see also* globalism
Neolithic revolution 49
Neruda, Pablo 299
Nescafé coffee 68, 89, 299
Netherlands and Dutch 86, 148, 239, 246, 283
Netscape 2, 148
networks 32, 46, 82; of association 232; of exchange relations 105; global 182; of networks 66, 89; of power 51-52; network society 268; of social

interaction 51–2; of stone-age economics 108; *see also* kinship, meaning, mediation, trade
New Age 32, 200
New England and New Englanders 155, 250
New World 175, 243
New York 196, 279 *see also* World Trade Center
New York Mercantile Exchange 149
*The New York Times* 36
New Zealand 14
News Corporation 272; *News Corporation Annual Report* 279
Newton, Isaac 164, 168; Newtonian treatment of time, *see* time
*ngurra* 167
Nicaraguan Sandinistas 281
*Nichomachean Ethics* 94
Nigeria and Nigerian 283; Etche people 283; Mobile Police Force 283; Movement for the Survival of the Ogoni People 283; Ogoni people and Ogoniland 283
Nike, Greek goddess and corporation 273
Noble Savage 1, 103; *see also* tribalism
Nokia corporation 15
Noriega, General Manuel 281
Nortel corporation 262
North American Free Trade Zone Agreement (NAFTA) 295
North Waziristan 86
*Northern Exposure* 299
nostalgia, for embodied connection 68; for the future 292; for home 68; modernist 68; Western 68
Nuer people 163

*ob sanguinis continuationem* 193
object-extended integration 29, 81, 86–87, 90, 139, 169, 184; *see also* globalism
object extension 84; commercial forms of 86
object-subject relation 56, 58
objects 110–11, 113, 147, 215, 218, 255; basic 112; commodified 112; currency 112; inalienable 116; movement 273; object-of-value 142; sacred 87, 112, 123; valuable 112–13; *see also* embeddedness
objects of exchange 133, 138, 143, 159, 169, 266, 273
objectification (reification) 46, 57, 60, 106, 134, 179, 181; *see also* integration, other and Otherness

objective 108, 222; objective reality 109, 135; objective relations 172; *see also* abstraction, extension, globalization, integration, nation, subjective, tracks of social power
objectivism 57, 168
Occitan language or *langue d'oc* 238
*Oecumene* 262–88 *passim*
Offe, Claus 210
Ogoni people and Ogoniland, *see* Nigeria and Nigerian
Old Corruption 220
Old Glory Condom Company 255
*One Minute Bedtime Stories* 158
Ong, Walter 20, 150
ontological, ontological constraints 96; ontological depth 304–9 *passim*; ontological disjuncture 107; ontological modes 57; ontological security 33–4, 182, 195; ontological socialism 305; ontological truth 154; *see also* abstraction, difference and differentiation, domination, value
ontological categories 77, 160, 237; embedded 233; *see also the specific categories of* body, the ontological category of, and embodiment, knowledge, the ontological category of, and epistemology, space, the ontological category of, and spatiality, time, the ontological category of, and temporality
ontological contradictions 69, 79, 183, 255; nature/culture 183–4, 186, 188, 191, 309
ontological formations 21, 29, 33, 69, 78, 80, 82, 92, 114, 129, 138, 151, 153, 158, 162–4, 208, 220, 236, 241, 245, 249 *see also the particular formations of* modernism, postmodernism, traditionalism, tribalism
ontology 6, 82–3, 94, 285–6; clash of ontologies 163; post-tribal 185; turn-over 49; *see also* abstraction, ecology, space, time
Operation Freedom for Iraq 272
orality 136, 226; *see also* modes of communication
Order of Matins 160
*The Order of Things* 16, 61
O'Reilly, Bill 272; *The O'Reilly Factor* 272
organization, *see* modes of organization
origin 228, 233, 248, 298
Orizio, Riccardo 29

## INDEX

Ortelius 23
Orthodox Serbs, see Serbia, Serbian and Serb
other and Otherness 107, 181, 185, 200, 202, 228, 249, 256, 276, 297, 313; dehumanization and objectification of the other 185
Ovid 23

pain 201
Paine, Thomas 94
Pakistan and Pakistani 68; India-Pakistan border 231
Pakulski, Jan 216
Palestine and Palestinian 65, 185, 236, 259
Papua New Guinea and Papuan 123, 148, 279; Baruya people 190-1, 195; Binandere people 123
Paris 32, 145, 169
Parsonian theory, see also society
particularism 118, 183, 300; see also contradictions and contradictory relations, practices and processes, ethics and principles
Pashtun tribes 68, 86
Passe, William de 155, 192
patriarchy 192-3, 216
patrimony 87
patriotism 27, 253-254 see also nationalism
patterns of practice 54-58 passim, 82, 160, 213
pax Americana 303-304
pedagogy 162
Pentagon 27, 66, 89
people and the population 208, 213, 215, 217, 225, 227, 265, 274, 296
People, Land and Community 299
people movement (of refugees, migrants, travellers) 22, 29, 86, 266-267, 273-274, 292; see also refugees, migration
perceptual relations 84-85; see also abstraction, modes of enquiry
Periodic Table of Elements, see tables
periphery 241
Persian Gulf 23
personal identity 17, 34
Peru and Peruvian 148
phenomena 74; phenomenal expressions of forms of life 77-8
phenomenology 57, 73
Phillips corporation 148

philosophy, the discipline of 19, 48, 94, 106, 170, 266, 294, 296; as epistemology 90; metaphysical 91
Phuc, Kim 182
Pintupi people. see Aborigines of Australia
place, locality and locale 1, 13, 15-16, 30, 60, 68, 73, 123, 162, 167, 171-2, 174, 190, 196, 228, 237, 241, 243, 258, 265, 271, 280, 286, 295-6, 298-298, 305, 308, 310, 313-14; see also blood, grounding and grounding categories
plane, metaphor of 24
planetary exploitation 262-88 passim
Plato 91, 164
*Pleasantville* 14
*Plough, Sword and Book* 5, 48
Poggi, Gianfranco 213
*polis* 140, 143
political science, the discipline of 19
political system 209
political theory, the discipline of 4, 44, 207, 211
politics 264-5, 281, 294-7 passim, 303, 305; alternative 304-14 passim; of the Left and Right 294
polity 24, 29, 51, 76, 82, 109, 114, 127, 139, 151-2, 180, 193, 202-28 passim, 232, 240, 252, 278, 292-314 passim; colonial 247; modern 217; national 239; as state 4; structures of 207; subjectivities of 207; as traditional 193; see also community, state, tribal community-polity and society
Polynesia and Polynesian 107, 161; Tokelau Islands and people 161-2, 175
Pope Gregory VIII 170
Popper, Karl 25
popular imaginary 13-14
Portugal and Portuguese 246; see also East Timor and East Timorese
postcolonial settings 310; see also nation-state, social theory
Poster, Mark 75
postmodern, aesthetics 32, 228, 305; ambivalence 305; boundary crossing 305; cosmopolitanism 305; deconstruction 305; difference and alterity 305; film 2; formations 129; fragmented subjectivity 305; layer 79; principles 305; society 7, 182, 195, 199; radicalized choosing 305; relativism 29

postmodernism 2, 21, 33, 77-80, 82, 104, 109, 114, 120, 122, 134, 147, 151, 159, 165, 173, 184, 200, 220, 234, 249-58 *passim*, 292-314 *passim*; see also abstraction, body, globalization, social theory, subjectivity
postmodernity 79, 160, 269
postmodernization 79, 215-16
*Postmodernization* 215-16
postnationalism 292-314 *passim*; principles for 292-314 *passim*; postnational imaginary 292
post-structuralism 16, 19; see also social theory
Poulantzas, Nicos 210
power 46, 52-3, 55, 78, 123-4, 136, 151, 181, 211, 214, 217, 223, 264, 268, 273, 278, 282, 287, 293, 296; administrative 60; analogical 195; authoritative 224; bio-power 189, 215; boundedness of 54; at a distance 176; formation of 126; hierarchy of 87, 249; as ideal types 51; institutional 311; micro-power 212; military 54, 78; organization of 59, 224; political 53-54, 207-208; relations of 267; social 89; surveillance 78; techniques and technologies of 136; see also networks, sources of social power, state, tracks of social power, types of exchange
practical consciousness 236; see also layers of consciousness, national consciousness, reflexive consciousness, subjective consciousness, types of exchange
practice 231, 258, 287, 309; see also contradictions and contradictory relations, practices and processes, globalization, modes of practice, patterns of practice, state, tribalism,
Prague 48
Pretoria 3; and Afrikaners and Zulus 3; Battle of Blood River 3
prime directive 309
Prime Meridian Conference 171, 175
'primitive societies' 163
primitivism 103, 126
primordialism 1-3, 13, 28, 30, 126, 190, 221, 234, 245; see also nation-state
Prince of Wales 217
Princess Anne and daughter Zara 32

print 6, 19, 153; printing industry 143; see also modes of communication
print-capitalism 154, 224, 226-7; see also *capitalism*
private property 51, 174
privatization 216
problems of understanding 46-8 *passim*
production, see human activity, modes of production
'The progenie of the most renouned Prince James King', painting 192
Provençal people, see France and French
Prunier, Gérard 35, 248
Ptolemaeus, Claudius 23
Ptolemy 170
public service, institution of 161-2
Pullman, Bill 303
Puritan 155, 250
Putin, Vladimir 136
*Pygmalion* 199
Pythagorean theory 23

Qantas Airlines 274; e-Travel Planitgo website 274
Qing dynasty, see China and Chinese
Queen Anne of Denmark and son Henry 155, 192
Queen Elizabeth I 217
Queen Elizabeth II 146-7, 149
Queen Victoria 73, 115
Qur'an 194, 235

race 20, 26, 298; see also groupings
racism 185, 286, 298
Ramallah 31
rational-choice approach, see social theory
rationality, bureaucratic 6; technical 6; see also bureaucracy, economic rationalism, modernity, modes of enquiry, modes of organization, time
rationalization 60, 106, 134, 159, 166, 170, 181; rationalized Christianity 30; rationalizing homogenization 13; see also modes of enquiry, modes of exchange, state, violence
reciprocity, mutuality and co-operation 8, 15, 105-29 *passim*, 137, 180, 182, 306-8, 310-14; abstract reciprocity 311-13; and analogy 7; antagonistic reciprocity 308; embodied 29, 312-13; face-to-face reciprocity 312; and gift exchange 5; and kinship 7; modern 308; object-mediated reciprocity 312; and production 5;

tribal 5, 202; *see also* agents and agency, modes of exchange, modes of production
Reden, Sitta von 140
reflexive consciousness 236 *see also* layers of consciousness, national consciousness, practical consciousness, subjective consciousness, types of exchange
reflexivity 94, 180, 198, 305, 309; modern national 234; reflexive distance 61; *see also* abstraction, agency and agents, body, ethics and principles, modernism, social theory, sociology, subjectivity and subjects
Reformation and Counter-Reformation 154
refugees 33, 86, 266, 274; *see also* people movement
regulation, agencies of 139; mode of 75; state 143; *see also* deregulation
regulationist theory 75
reification, *see* objectification
religion 29, 35, 91, 93, 122, 124, 152, 208, 234; Buddhism 270, 277; Christianity 44, 91, 93, 113, 117–18, 122, 152, 169, 181, 188, 192, 194, 196–7, 258, 308); Confucianism 122, 152, 243, 308; Hinduism 44, 163, 170; Islam 14, 44, 68, 93, 122, 152, 169, 234–5, 259 (*see also* Wahhabite Islam); Judaism 122, 152, 169; universalistic 152
religious rituals, *see* rituals
Renan, Ernest 26
Renaissance 87, 168, 174
reproduction 75
republics and republicanism 232, 251, 257; postmodern 255
resources 59; allocative 59; authoritative 59
*ressentiment* 249
Rhea, *see* god, gods and goddesses
Rice, Condoleezza 295
Ricoeur, Paul 164
*The Rights of Man* 94
risk society 67
rituals and ritualization 35, 53, 123, 166, 173, 186, 188, 190, 196–7, 208, 218–19, 257; of intimacy 36; and recognition 105; of religion 36; ritual relations 84–5, 190–1
Robbins, Bruce 299
Robbins, Derek 57
Robert the Bruce 195
Robertson, Roland 23, 287

*Rob Roy* 2
Rojek, Chris 75, 306
Rome and Roman 28; Roman Catholic Church 23; Roman Peutinger Table 23; Roman world-view 23; *see also* empires
romanticism 13, 295, 299
Roosevelt, Franklin D. 254–5
*Rooted in the Land* 299
Rorty, Richard 301, 306
Rosenberg, Justin 22, 274
Ross, Betsy 255
routine and routinization 45, 66; *see also* security and insecurity
Royal Armouries Museum, *see* Zulu people
Royal Dutch Shell 283
Royal Mint of Britain, *see* money
Rumsfeld, Donald 179
Runciman, W.G. 44, 49; *see also* human activity
rupture 61–62, 268
Rushdie, Salman 277
Ruska, Ernst 91
Russia and Russian 126, 171, 239; *see also* empires, historical
Rwanda and Rwandan 13, 29, 33–6, 126, 184, 191–2, 219, 226, 237, 246–9, 253, 282; *Impuzamugambi* and *Interahamwe* militias 35; Presidential Guards 35; Rwandan Patriotic Front 249
Ryangombe 248

*sacré* and *sacré et couronnement* 219
sacred 112, 118, 125, 217–19, 241; liturgy 117; postmodern destabilizing of 79; *see also* ethics and principles, goods, grounding and grounding categories, knowledge, modernism, nation, objects, time, universalism and universalization
Saltonstall Family 192
San Martino 18
Saro-Wiwa, Ken 283
Sassen, Saskia 275
satellites 159, 282; Okonos 159; satellite phone 273; satellite TV network 272
*The Savage Mind* 121
*Savage Money* 107, 169
*Saving Private Ryan* 27
*The Saviour* 93
*sayyid* 218
Scandinavia and Scandinavian 238

Scanlon, Chris 84, 293
Scheduled Castes, *see* India and Indian
Scholte, Jan Aart 24
school, institution of 161
science 49, 121, 124; and analogical certainty 175; modern 121; technical 125; tribal science of the concrete 121; *see also* modes of enquiry, state, techno-science
Scota 193 *Scoti* 115
*Scotland the Brave* 2
Scotland, Scottish and Scot 1-2, 114, 116-18, 193, 217; Argyleshire 115; and the Campbells 29-30; and the Church 117; Glenorchy 29; Highland soil 2; identity 117; Kirk, patron saint and Simon Peter 117-118; and the National Wallace Monument 2; nationhood 117; Scottish National War Memorial 119; Stirling 2; tartan 2; *see also* kings
*The Scotsman* 144, 217
*Scottish Nation* 235
scribes 152, 219; *see also* clerics
script, *see* modes of communication
scripture 93
*Seachange* 299
Second World 246
*The Secret Agent* 171
secular and secularization 134; *see also* grounding and grounding categories, modernism, modernity, state, traditionalism, universalism and universalization
security and insecurity 45, 148, 214, 246, 249, 271, 292; and borders 86; of late-modern expert systems 66; routinization of 79; *see also* ontological
Seirios 165
*Seinfeld* 32, 298
Seinfeld, Jerry 298
self 179-80
Sennett, Richard 169, 201
September 11 (2001) 27, 65-7, 84, 235, 253, 287
sequestration 220
Serbia, Serbian and Serb 36, 295, 298; Central Committee of the Serbia Communist Party 296; Orthodox Serbs 36; *see also* war and wars
*The Sex Lives of Savages* 108
Shakespeare, William 219
Shang dynasty, *see* China and Chinese

Shanghai 143
Sharon, Ariel 31
Sharp, Geoff 60-1, 70-2, 74, 109, 246
Sharp, Nonie 123
Shaw, George Bernard 199
Sheridan, Richard Brinsley 144
Siam, *see* kings, Thailand
Sicily 115
signification 69, 144, 182, 211, 252 *also* structure
silver 142, 145
*The Silver Shilling* 144
Simmel, Georg 60, 70, 134
simulacrum 68
Singapore and Singaporean 14, 236; Singapore 21 14; Tanjong Pagar Development Council 14
*sirawa* 123
*Sittlichkeit* 16
Skocpol, Theda 210, 213, 285
Slouka, Mark 253
Smith, Anthony 222-4, 226, 233-4, 236-7, 244-6
Smith, Edward W. 115
Smyrna 140
*Snow Crash* 14
social formation, the concept of 20-1, 31, 34, 43, 55, 57-8, 62, 65-96 *passim*, 103, 134, 160, 165, 173, 180, 185-6, 200, 208, 218, 232, 285; *see also* abstraction, globalism, state
social framing/enframing 58, 192, 281
sociality, concept of 58, 90, 135, 309, 314; *see also* abstraction
social caging 51, 58, 104
social extension 49; *see also* agency-extended integration, disembodied integration, face-to-face integration, object-extended integration
social identity 34, 182, 186
*The Social Life of Things* 110
social power, *see* power
social relations (*passim*) 80, 106, 114, 180, 224, 263, 269, 300; abstract 231; extension of 266, 274; layers of 66; modern 67; reconfiguration of 13; spatial integration of 264; traditional 67; *see also* body, face-to-face interaction and relations, kinship
social relational concepts 307
social theory, the discipline of 4, 6, 8, 43-62 *passim*, 65-96 *passim*, 103, 120, 147, 150, 209, 236; classical 43, 76, 212; classical post-structuralism 47;

classical structuralism 47; engaged 45-6; historical materialist 43, 47, 55, 73-4, 81; liberal 212-13, 305; Marxist 81, 212, 278, 285; modern 212; neo-classical 43; neo-Marxist 43, 74, 81, 210, 212; post-classical 43, 76; postcolonial 43, 48, 285, 293, 296, 301; postmodern 69, 292-304 *passim*; post-structuralist 6, 43, 48, 73, 82-3, 92, 181, 198, 212, 214, 276, 281, 285; psychoanalytic 198, 286; rational-choice approach 6; reflexive 57, 135; structuralist 55, 73, 198; *see also* nation-state
social welfare, the discipline of 211
socialism 308-9; *see also* ontological
Société des Ambianceurs et Personnes Elégantes (*sapeurs*) 32
society 51-2, 82, 109, 126, 136, 182, 191, 214; and nation 18; Parsonian systems-model of 52; society-as-market 143; *see also particular examples of society such as* abstract society, agrarian society, agricultural society, civil society, risk society, postmodern society, traditional community and society, tribal community-polity and society
sociology, the discipline of 4-5, 19, 55, 58, 92, 211; historical 51, 55, 73, 210; reflexive 16
sodalities 5, 259 *see also* religion
soil, *see* blood, Scotland, Scottish and Scot
solidarity 293-294, 296-297, 304-309 *passim*; and authority 307
Somalia and Somali 31, 235; Ajuuran clan 235; Daarood clan 235
Sopho-net WAN global funds-transfer system 148
*Sources of Social Power* 51, 54
sources of social power, Michael Mann's schema of 51-54; IEMP (ideological, economic, military and political) relationships 51-54
South Africa 175
Southall 33
Southeast Asia, *see* Asia and Asian
Southland 2
sovereignty 210, 220, 239, 240, 242, 268, 296; *see also* state, subjectivity and subjects
space, the ontological category of, and spatiality 6, 8, 16, 19, 22, 28, 60, 77-8, 80, 82, 84-5, 88, 129, 153, 158-76 *passim*, 189-90, 195, 227, 231, 237, 239, 241, 243, 263, 274-6, 285-6, 292, 298; anological 172; beyond space-time 176; commodified 174; cosmological 173; empty 173, 176; epistemological 224; genealogical 173; homogeneous empty 173; hyperspace 176; institutionalized 174; mobility across space 263; modern 159; mythological 173; ontologies of 173; postmodern 159; relative space-time 173, 175; space-as-territory 175; space-time extension 306; virtual space-time 173; world-space 21-22, 170-1, 181, 263, 266, 274; *see also* abstraction, boundaries and borders, cyberspace, social relations, spatial extension, time-space abstraction, time-space distantiation, time-space edges, time
Spain and Spanish 218, 238-239; Compostella 115; *see also* the Americas
spatial extension 4, 21-2, 172, 182, 190, 279, 274
Spencer, Baldwin 167
Spielberg, Steven 27
spirit 107, 144; of the age 61; extension of 87-8
Spivak, Gayatri Chakravorty 44
Springborg, Anna 217
spontaneous sociability 277
Sri Lanka and Sri Lankan 201
St Andrews, Bishop of 114; St Andrew's day 117
St Giles Cathedral 117
Stalinist gulags 69
Stanner, W.E.H. 167
Starbucks coffee and corporation 32, 279
state 18, 50-1, 87, 112, 114, 116, 127, 136, 139, 151, 175, 195, 207-28 *passim*, 231-59 *passim*, 266, 271, 282-3, 292, 294, 311; absolutist 220, 238, 240, 258; abstract 116, 240, 242, 251, 311; abstraction of 18; as abstraction 212-13; as administrative system 191; anti-state 295; bureaucratic 152, 222; colonial 247; first retreat 209-11; formation 122, 126, 193, 207-28 *passim*; 288 modern 94, 215, 220, 296; postmodern 215-16; rationalized and rationalizing 222, 296; scientific 225; second retreat 211-16; secular 252; as social form

209-16 *passim*; state-as-polity 208, 216; state power 53-4; state practices 214; state sovereignty 175; surveillance state 60, 211, 303; territorial 237; welfare 211; *see also* crowns, imperialism, monarchy, nation-state, polity, power, regulation, territory and territoriality, violence
statues, *see* body, stone and rock
Steger, Manfred 24, 270, 287
Stirling, *see* Scotland, Scottish and Scot
Stoics 168
stone and rock 5, 110, 113-20 *passim*, 123, 150, 154, 158, 164, 173, 218; and flesh 3; monuments 3, 16; statues 2 (*see also* body); Stone of Destiny 116-17, 258; Stone of Scone 115, 118, 193-4; and the Ten Commandments 94; and wood 3
Stone, Gillian 3, 68, 89
story-telling 135, 167
Strange, Susan 271, 282
strangers 86, 136, 169, 182, 235, 239, 277, 298, 312; abstracted 67, 106; boundary-crossing 107; needs of 182; to ourselves 201; *see also* nation, nation-state
string and superstring theory 92, 172
structuralism, *see* social theory, the discipline of
structuration 59-60, 96; patterns of 105; processes 195; theory of 56; *see also* Giddens
structure/agency dichotomy, *see* methodological dichotomies
structure, Anthony Giddens's schema of 59; domination 59; legitimation 59; signification 59
structures 46, 59, 61, 79, 96, 224, 231, 277, 296; of agency 58-61 *passim*; of integration 47; organizational 217; social 104; of the social whole 268; structural patterns 17; and the subject-object divide 47; *see also* crisis, culture and cultures, globalism, globalization, methodological dichotomies, modernism, polity, subjective, tribalism
structures/fragmentation dichotomy, *see* methodological dichotomies
*Studio Bambini* 277
subjective 108, 144, 162, 179, 222; subjective imaginary 89; subjective-objective structuring 114; subjective reality 109; subjective relations 172; *see also* body, globalism, globalization, meaning, nation
subjective consciousness 109
subjectivism 57
subjectivity and subjects 20, 32, 45, 56, 80, 85, 96, 189, 208, 221, 224, 234, 240-1, 255, 257, 276, 286-7, 292, 296, 298, 309; cosmological 173; cultural 228; embodied subjectivities of nationality/ethnicity 86, 235; postmodern 66, 292; reflexive 25; sovereign 87-8; subject as agent 282; traditional 234; tribal 110; *see also* globalism, nationalism, object-subject relation, polity, postmodern principles
subject-object dichotomy, *see* methodological dichotomies *see also* object-subject relation
subjection 278, 282-4; *see also* global, the level of
Sumatra 234
surveillance 274; administrative 174; juridical 174; military 174; *see also* power, state
*Survivor* 32
sustainability 45
Sutton, David 123
Swain, Tony 164
Swantz, Marja-Liisa 188
Swatch corporation 160
Swaziland 31
Switzerland and Swiss 160
symbolic capital, *see* capital
symbols and signs 179-202 *passim*, 209, 237, 304; natural symbols 181-189 *passim*; symbolic imagery 183; symbolic representation 140, 182; symbolic taxes 109; *symbolon* 181; *see also* fetishism
*Systema Naturae* 125
systems 124

tableaux, of global human activity 263; of life 69-73 *passim*, 236; *see also* abstraction
tables 70-96 *passim*; Periodic Table of Elements 72
Tahiti and Tahitian 282
Taliban 68, 86
Tampa crisis 86
Tanzania and Tanzanian 187-8; Zaramo people 187-8

tattooing, *see* body
taxonomy 71, 125; tribal 121
techno-machines 181-9 *passim*
techno-science and techno-scientism 24, 44, 67, 89, 125, 171, 175, 183, 199, 267, 287; *see also* modes of enquiry
technology, *see* modes of technology
temporality, *see* time
teleology 59, 110, 135
Ten Commandments, *see* stone
*terra cognita* 266
territory and territoriality 23, 26, 28, 60, 196, 213, 237, 241-2, 264, 275, 282, 292, 295-7, 304, 305, 313; state-organized 174, 208; *see also* boundaries and borders, deterritorialization, nation, space, state
terrorism and terrorists 27, 65-8 *passim*, 262, 283; anti-terrorist bombing 37
testicles 113, 117-18; Castle of Manhood 118
Thailand and Thai 201, 226, 287-8; Bangkok 287; Tourist Authority of Thailand 287
Thatcher, Margaret 197
theology 124, 188, 250, 308, 155; *see also* geography, the discipline of
things 73, 110, 123; *see also* cultural biography of things; gifts; goods
Third Reich 301 *see also* Nazism
Third Way 37, 293
Third World 45, 226, 240-1, 244, 246, 276-8, 282-4, 287-8
Thompson, Grahame 275
Thorgilsson, Ari 194
thrones 115, 218
Tiananmen Square, *see* China and Chinese
Tilly, Charles 210
time, the ontological category of, and temporality 6, 8, 16, 19, 25, 28, 45, 77-8, 80, 82, 84, 88, 109, 129, 137, 153, 158-76 *passim*, 188-90, 195, 231, 237, 239, 241, 243, 258, 274-5, 285, 298; abstracted 226; analogical 164-5, 170, 172; analogous 168; analogue 160; calendrical 166; circular 163; Common Era 158; Co-ordinated Universal 158; cosmological 158, 164-5, 167-70, 226; cyclical 163; embodied 161; empty, rationally calculable and disembodied 137, 158, 164-5, 168-75; genealogical 164-6; global

internet 160; historical 168, 226; homogeneous empty 166, 170, 226, 245; linear 163-4; messianic 25, 168, 241; metaphors of 164; modality of 172; modern 159; mythological 164-7, 245; natural 161, 168; Newtonian treatment of 160; office 161; ontologies of 165; pendulum-like 163; postmodern 159, 172; relative space-time 164-5, 172; reversible 163; rhythmic 163-4; sacred 152, 170, 245; sacring 219; simultaneous 85; temporal extension 170, 182; temporal modalities 159; temporal projection 110; temporal risk 159; *tid* 165; time-as-history 175; time-measure 170; tribal 172; tribal-traditional 161; virtual space-time 164-5, 172; World Standard 145, 171; world-time 22, 25, 167, 170-1, 180, 208, 242, 266; *see also* Aborigines of Australia, abstraction, being, boundaries and borders, capitalism, god, gods and goddesses, Greenwich, industrialization, space, time-space distantiation, time-space edges, time-space pathways
*Time* magazine 84, 188, 198
*Times* newspaper 145
time-space distantiation 60
time-space edges 60, 103
time-space pathways 106
Tito 36
Tokelau Islands and people, *see* Polynesia and Polynesian
Tokugawa modernizing revolution, *see* Japan and Japanese
Tokyo, *see* Japan and Japanese
tombs, *see* cenotaphs and tombs
Tomlinson, John 287
Tönnies, Ferdinand 18, 46
Torah and Torah Bible 168, 194
Torres Strait 123
totalization 67, 286, 305; *see also* globalization
totems 253-5
Tower of Babel 193
Tower of London, *see* London
Toyota corporation 15, 279
tracks of social power 50-4 *passim*; objective 45; *see also* power
trade 23, 140, 264, 275, 302; electronic trading 282; traded derivatives 148; trading networks 107, 144

*366*

tradition 296 *see* traditionalism
traditional community and society 7, 78, 182, 186, 235, 239-40
traditional identity 234
traditional-modern divide 233-43 *passim*
traditionalism 21, 23, 33, 50, 57, 67, 77-8, 80, 82, 120, 122, 124-5, 147, 151, 153, 159, 165, 168, 173, 184, 193, 200, 217, 220, 227, 233-243 *passim*, 245, 247-58 *passim*, 309; neo-traditionalism 2, 35, 37, 68, 240; sacred 168; secular 168; tribal 208;
traditionalization, re-traditionalization 294
transactions, patterns of 139 *see* mode of exchange
transnationalism 292-3, 295, 304-5
Traube, Elizabeth 5, 123, 150
trees 150, 154, 165-6, 173, 188, 235-6; of knowledge 72, 124-5
tribal bodies and embodiment, *see* body
tribal community-polity and society 7, 54, 56, 59, 78, 87, 91-2, 103-29 *passim*, 166, 182, 186, 189-90; customary tribal cultures 163, 166; post-tribal societies 124-5, 164; tribal divisions 36; tribal formations 60; tribal identity 248; tribalization 79
*The Tribal Eye* 262
tribalism 1-4, 7, 8, 21, 28-33 *passim*, 34, 36, 57, 67, 77-8, 80, 82, 96, 104, 114, 121, 125, 134, 147, 151, 153-6 *passim*, 159, 162-5, 173, 184, 200, 202, 227, 234, 247-49 *passim*, 268, 309; as ethnic divisiveness 28; hunter-gatherer 104; as modern 30-3, 240; as neo-national 13; as neo-tribal 33; new tribalism 105, 268; as postmodern 30-3; reciprocal 179; and relationship to global violence 3; as resurgent 3; and savagery 103; as social formation 4; structures and practices of 105; as traditional 24, 30, 32, 103-4, 127; tribal history 31; *see also* customary tribalism, kinship, reciprocity, mutuality and co-operation, social theory, subjectivity and subjects
tribe, the concept of, and tribal peoples 1, 20, 28-33 *passim*, 46, 58, 68, 110, 127, 162, 208, 236, 239, 298, 311; as kinship-based society 126; modern 34, 126, 246; as modern invention 28; traditional 194; *tribus* 29; urban 32
Triumphus Jacobi Regus 154, 192

Trobriand Islands 108, 113; and kula shells 113, 149
Tronto, Joan 307
trouble spots 65
*The Truman Show* 14
*Trust: The Social Virtues and the Creation of Prosperity* 277
truth 168, 236; *see also* ontological truth, words
Tua people 147, 191-2
Turner, Bryan 44, 199, 306
Turner, Victor 191
Tuscany 299
Tutsi people 29, 33-5, 126, 184-5, 191-2, 247-9; *see also* kingdoms, historical
*2001* 128
types of exchange, Malcolm Waters's schema 264; material exchanges 264-265; power exchanges 264-265; symbolic exchanges 264-265

UCK (Kosovo Liberation Army), *see* Kosovo, Kosovan and Kosovar
Uganda and Ugandan 249
United Kingdom and British 31, 33, 36, 45, 86, 115, 117, 119, 142, 145, 148, 155, 197, 223, 228, 246, 249, 279-1, 293-4; British Crown 251; British Royal Family 32, 146, 217; Heath government 197; Rule Britannia 171; *see also* empires, historical
United Nations (UN) 248-9, 309
United States of America and American 2, 28, 30, 32-3, 36, 45, 66, 78, 119, 144, 158, 175, 182, 196, 210, 223, 235-7, 242, 246, 249-58 *passim*, 269-70, 272, 281, 293, 301-4, 310; American-Century Nationalism 293; Americanization 270; Anglo-American ideology 300; Bureau of Statistics 27; Constitution 251; military 68, 78; Fourth of July 303-4; God Bless America 27; Homeland Security, US office of 68; United States Congress 175, 252; *see also* American Revolution, the Americas, war and wars
United States Time Corporation 170; Timex watch 170
universalism and universalization 44, 91, 118, 183, 188, 199, 245, 297, 300, 303, 307; abstract 154; Chinese form of 23; sacred 23, 44; secular 44; *see also* contradictions and contradictory

relations, practices and processes, ethics and principles, knowledge, epistemology, mythology, religion.
Unknown Soldier 179, 197, 257; Arlington Unknown Soldier 197; see also cenotaphs and tombs
Untouchables, see India and Indian upheaval 65, 234, 246, 258, 292
Uranus, see god, gods and goddesses
*usance* 169
*usury* 169

value 45, 88, 115, 135, 145; abstraction of 143; commodity 142; cost-value 137; disembodied system of 145; of exchange 71, 106; forms of 137–49 *passim*; ghosted 142; globalized abstract 145; monetary 116; ontological framing of 113; systems of 140–1; *specie* or tale 142; transcendent 116; see also goods, objects
Vattimo, Gianni 75, 281
Venerable Bede 170
Venezuela 223
Vodafone corporation 1
Victoria 299
Victorian 196
Vietnam and Vietnamese 67, 187
village 36, 46, 191, 239, 299; global 14–15, 279; virtual 14
Villers-Bretonneux, see France and French
violence 33–5, 184, 246, 249, 294–297; ethnic 298; ethnocidal 184; global 295; means of 224; military 38, 54; national conflict 298; political 287; rationalized 294; state 228; systematic 35–6; see also blood, nationalism, rationalization, tribalism
Virgin Mary 93
*Virtual Light* 14
Visa 147
Visigoth 219

*Wag the Dog* 303
Wahhabite Islam 93
Wakefield, Edward Gibbon 175
Walkman radios 200
Wallace, William 2
Wallerstein, Immanel 285
*walytja* 167
Wamba 219
*wantok* 274

war and wars 67, 79, 120, 210, 242, 262, 296, 302–3, 313; in Afghanistan 37–8, 67, 89, 262, 273, 287, 302–303, 313; American Civil War 2 (see also League of the South); of attrition 31; Bosnian War 35–8; electronic warfare 21; Holy War 68; invasion of Panama, Operation Just Cause 281; Falklands/Malvinas War 197, 281; First Gulf War 38, 79, 281, 301–3; Kosovo war 34, 37–8, 65, 294, 296–7, 303, 313; meta-war 37; modern 37; Napoleonic wars 145; postmodern 37–8; abstract, modern, postmodern and post-national war-machines 33, 67, 69, 89, 296, 303; Second Gulf War/war in Iraq 37–8, 67, 79, 179, 262, 272, 281, 293, 302–3, 313; in Serbia 302; in Vietnam 255, 262, 281; War on Terror 3, 66, 79, 89, 281, 304; World War I 48, 138, 145, 228, 257; World War II 38, 276; see also *jus ad bellum* (the right to make war)
Washington, D.C. 171, 269
watches, see clocks and watches
Waters, Malcolm 216, 263–5; see also types of exchange
Watson, Don 255–6
Watters, Ethan 32
*wauri* shells 123
wealth 136; distribution and redistribution of 139, 310
weaponry 34, 36; AK-47 rifles 34; bamboo sticks 184–5; bombs 67, 302; daisy-cutters 67; grenades 34; guns 3; Kalashnikovs 295; machetes 34; missiles 45; *panga* 34; Patriot missiles 179; spears 1; swords 49; weapons of mass destruction 38
Weber, Max 17, 54, 58, 75, 134, 308–9; Weberian theory 43, 72, 212, 219; neo-Weberian theory 48
well-being 45
Weiner, Annette 44, 107, 111, 116
West and Western 13, 31, 37, 68, 127, 133, 226, 237–9, 244–6, 263, 276, 282, 285, 287–8, 293, 295, 301, 309; Christian 119; revolutions 225–6; scholarship 128, 167; society 179–80; see also nostaglia
West Papua 246
Westminster Cathedral, see London
Williams, Raymond 283
Wills, Gary 252

Winfrey, Oprah 133
Wittgenstein, Ludwig 58
Womad 32
wood, *see* stone
Wood, Ellen Meiksins 220
words 123-4, 152; Abstract Word 155; Word 188, 253; Word of Communication 154; Word of Truth 152
work 35
*Works and Days* 165
World Church of the Creator 78
World Cup 33
World Economic Forum 279
world of flows 268
world-space, *see* space
World Standard Time, *see* time
world-system theory 278-9, 284
world-time, *see* time
World Trade Center 27, 38, 66, 84, 235, 262, 270
World Trade Organization (WTO) 65, 262, 279
World Vision 277
World Wide Web 153, 158
wretchedness 45
writing 133-56 *passim*, 219; pens 150, 154 *see also* modes of communication

xenophobia 298

Yolgnu people, *see* Aborigines of Australia
Yorkshire 299
Yothu Yindi, *see* Aborigines of Australia
Young, Iris Marion 298
Y2K 158
Yucatan, *see* Mexico and Mexican
Yugoslavia and Yugoslav 33-7, 240; militia 302

Zaramo people, *see* Tanzania and Tanzanian
Zambia and Zambian 191; Ndembu people 191
Zapatista movement, *see* Mexico and Mexican
Zeus, *see* god, gods and goddesses
Zionism 31
Zoellick, Robert 269
Zulu people 3, 31; Anglo-Historical Zulu Society 3; and the Inkatha people 31; the Mighty Zulu Nation, exhibition at the Royal Armouries Museum 3; *see also* Pretoria
*Zulu* 1-3